Contents

KT-226-689

The Author

Damien Simonis
With a degree in languages and several years' reporting and sub-editing on Australian newspapers (including the *Australian* and the *Age*), Sydney-born Damien left Australia in 1989. He has since lived, worked and travelled extensively throughout Europe, the Middle East and North Africa. Since 1992, Lonely Planet has kept him busy writing *Jordan & Syria, Egypt & the Sudan, Morocco, North Africa, Italy, Spain, The Canary Islands, Barcelona, Tuscany* and *Venice*. Damien is now back in Spain working on several titles, including a new one on Madrid. He has also written and snapped for other publications in Australia, the UK and North America. When not on the road, Damien resides in splendid Stoke Newington, deep in the heart of north London.

FROM THE AUTHOR

Turning up in a city where you don't know a soul from Adam can be an interesting exercise. I owe a debt of thanks to several people for welcoming me in Florence and helping me get a feel for the place. Ottobrina Voccoli in particular gets many *grazie* and a great big *bacio*. Otto and her band of pals (Silvia, Ruggero, Claudia, Michela, Anna et al) helped make my time on the Arno more than just an assignment. Thanks also to Monica Fontani.

The crowd at No 62, led by fearless Julie, were a good crew to live with and often had ideas on potential venues – for work and play. Thanks in no particular order to Tiarna, Andrew, Georgina and, above all, the New York Boyz (Camille and Laura).

Thanks to DB, GB and the Villa gang for the timely fashion hints.

Increasingly the creation and maintenance of LP's books is a collective effort. I owe a lot to my colleagues in Italy, Helen Gillman, Stefano Cavedoni and Sally Webb, for information pooled and traded. Thanks also to Katharine Leck and the guys in the London office for their input, editorial and otherwise.

This Book

This 1st edition of *Florence* was researched and written by Damien Simonis and is based on the relevant chapter of Lonely Planet's *Italy* guide.

From the Publisher

This edition of *Florence* was edited in Lonely Planet's London office by Amanda Canning with invaluable assistance from Tim Ryder. Anna Jacomb-Hood cast an eagle eye over the text at proof stage. Gadi Farfour drew the maps and designed the book, colour pages and cover, assisted by Adam McCrow. The illustrations were drawn by Jane Smith and the photographs were provided by Lonely Planet Images, with additional images for the 'Painting & Sculpture in Florence' section from Scala Picture Library. Jim Miller drew the back cover map. Thanks to Quentin Frayne, who put his expert knowledge on the Tuscan dialect to good use in checking the Language chapter. Thanks also to Marcel Gaston for last-minute design checks, and Paul Bloomfield for the nuggets of wisdom and hands-on help during the whole process.

Foreword

ABOUT LONELY PLANET GUIDEBOOKS

The story begins with a classic travel adventure: Tony and Maureen Wheeler's 1972 journey across Europe and Asia to Australia. Useful information about the overland trail did not exist at that time, so Tony and Maureen published the first Lonely Planet guidebook to meet a growing need.

From a kitchen table, then from a tiny office in Melbourne (Australia), Lonely Planet has become the largest independent travel publisher in the world, an international company with offices in Melbourne, Oakland (USA), London (UK) and Paris (France).

Today Lonely Planet guidebooks cover the globe. There is an ever-growing list of books and there's information in a variety of forms and media. Some things haven't changed. The main aim is still to help make it possible for adventurous travellers to get out there – to explore and better understand the world.

At Lonely Planet we believe travellers can make a positive contribution to the countries they visit – if they respect their host communities and spend their money wisely. Since 1986 a percentage of the income from each book has been donated to aid projects and human rights campaigns.

Updates Lonely Planet thoroughly updates each guidebook as often as possible. This usually means there are around two years between editions, although for more unusual or more stable destinations the gap can be longer. Check the imprint page (following the colour map at the beginning of the book) for publication dates.

Between editions up-to-date information is available in two free newsletters – the paper *Planet Talk* and email *Comet* (to subscribe, contact any Lonely Planet office) – and on our Web site at www.lonelyplanet.com. The *Upgrades* section of the Web site covers a number of important and volatile destinations and is regularly updated by Lonely Planet authors. *Scoop* covers news and current affairs relevant to travellers. And, lastly, the *Thorn Tree* bulletin board and *Postcards* section of the site carry unverified, but fascinating, reports from travellers.

Correspondence The process of creating new editions begins with the letters, postcards and emails received from travellers. This correspondence often includes suggestions, criticisms and comments about the current editions. Interesting excerpts are immediately passed on via newsletters and the Web site, and everything goes to our authors to be verified when they're researching on the road. We're keen to get more feedback from organisations or individuals who represent communities visited by travellers.

Lonely Planet gathers information for everyone who's curious about the planet – and especially for those who explore it first-hand. Through guidebooks, phrasebooks, activity guides, maps, literature, newsletters, image library, TV series and Web site we act as an information exchange for a worldwide community of travellers.

Research Authors aim to gather sufficient practical information to enable travellers to make informed choices and to make the mechanics of a journey run smoothly. They also research historical and cultural background to help enrich the travel experience and allow travellers to understand and respond appropriately to cultural and environmental issues.

Authors don't stay in every hotel because that would mean spending a couple of months in each medium-sized city and, no, they don't eat at every restaurant because that would mean stretching belts beyond capacity. They do visit hotels and restaurants to check standards and prices, but feedback based on readers' direct experiences can be very helpful.

Many of our authors work undercover, others aren't so secretive. None of them accept freebies in exchange for positive write-ups. And none of our guidebooks contain any advertising.

Production Authors submit their raw manuscripts and maps to offices in Australia, USA, UK or France. Editors and cartographers – all experienced travellers themselves – then begin the process of assembling the pieces. When the book finally hits the shops some things are already out of date, we start getting feedback from readers, and the process begins again ...

WARNING & REQUEST

Things change – prices go up, schedules change, good places go bad and bad places go bankrupt – nothing stays the same. So, if you find things better or worse, recently opened or long since closed, please tell us and help make the next edition even more accurate and useful. We genuinely value all the feedback we receive. Julie Young coordinates a well-travelled team that reads and acknowledges every letter, postcard and email and ensures that every morsel of information finds its way to the appropriate authors, editors and cartographers for verification.

Everyone who writes to us will find their name in the next edition of the appropriate guidebook. They will also receive the latest issue of *Planet Talk*, our quarterly printed newsletter, or *Comet*, our monthly email newsletter. Subscriptions to both newsletters are free. The very best contributions will be rewarded with a free guidebook.

Excerpts from your correspondence may appear in new editions of Lonely Planet guidebooks, the Lonely Planet Web site, *Planet Talk* or *Comet*, so please let us know if you *don't* want your letter published or your name acknowledged.

Send all correspondence to the Lonely Planet office closest to you:

Australia: PO Box 617, Hawthorn, Victoria 3122
UK: 10A Spring Place, London NW5 3BH
USA: 150 Linden St, Oakland CA 94607
France: 1 rue du Dahomey, Paris 75011

Or email us at: talk2us@lonelyplanet.com.au

For news, views and updates see our Web site: www.lonelyplanet.com

HOW TO USE A LONELY PLANET GUIDEBOOK

The best way to use a Lonely Planet guidebook is any way you choose. At Lonely Planet we believe the most memorable travel experiences are often those that are unexpected, and the finest discoveries are those you make yourself. Guidebooks are not intended to be used as if they provide a detailed set of infallible instructions!

Contents All Lonely Planet guidebooks follow roughly the same format. The Facts about the Destination chapter or section gives background information ranging from history to weather. Facts for the Visitor gives practical information on issues like visas and health. Getting There & Away gives a brief starting point for researching travel to and from the destination. Getting Around gives an overview of the transport options when you arrive.

The peculiar demands of each destination determine how subsequent chapters are broken up, but some things remain constant. We always start with background, then proceed to sights, places to stay, places to eat, entertainment, getting there and away, and getting around information – in that order.

Heading Hierarchy Lonely Planet headings are used in a strict hierarchical structure that can be visualised as a set of Russian dolls. Each heading (and its following text) is encompassed by any preceding heading that is higher on the hierarchical ladder.

Entry Points We do not assume guidebooks will be read from beginning to end, but that people will dip into them. The traditional entry points are the list of contents and the index. In addition, however, some books have a complete list of maps and an index map illustrating map coverage.

There may also be a colour map that shows highlights. These highlights are dealt with in greater detail in the Facts for the Visitor chapter, along with planning questions and suggested itineraries. Each chapter covering a geographical region usually begins with a locator map and another list of highlights. Once you find something of interest in a list of highlights, turn to the index.

Maps Maps play a crucial role in Lonely Planet guidebooks and include a huge amount of information. A legend is printed on the back page. We seek to have complete consistency between maps and text, and to have every important place in the text captured on a map. Map key numbers usually start in the top left corner.

Although inclusion in a guidebook usually implies a recommendation we cannot list every good place. Exclusion does not necessarily imply criticism. In fact there are a number of reasons why we might exclude a place – sometimes it is simply inappropriate to encourage an influx of travellers.

Introduction

The fortunate few get their first view of Florence from the south. The road from Siena, centuries-old arch rival and ultimately loser in the struggle for Tuscan domination, leads you to the heights backing the southern bank of the Fiume Arno (River Arno). Suddenly, glimpsed through the trees, the glories of Florence burst into view – Giotto's Campanile (bell tower), Brunelleschi's dome, the Santa Croce. Only the hardest of hearts remains indifferent to this first sight of the valley town. You could even be forgiven a little self-indulgent romanticism as you wonder whether or not you will get *A Room with a View*.

The glory of Florence is firmly rooted in its past. Love 'em or hate 'em, the memory of the Medicis, who for centuries commanded the city's fortunes and were in great measure instrumental in unleashing the artistic revolution that was the Renaissance, still lives on. To this day the family crest of six balls adorns many public buildings, although the city's official emblem (the medi-

eval Guelph faction's red lily on a white background) is older still. Florence lives off its past.

So it might be said with some justice that the city seems at first to be one big museum. But what a museum! Florence is a dizzying cornucopia of artistic wealth. The French writer Stendhal found himself swooning before it all, thus giving a name to the condition ('stendhalismo') that some visitors still 'contract' today – a kind of nervous exhaustion brought on by too intense an exposure to art.

In its great buildings, from the Romanesque Baptistry (Battistero) through to the Gothic Duomo and Renaissance basilicas and palaces, Florence is a showplace of architectural prowess.

The city's artists and sculptors, who found such rich patronage in the Medicis and other powerful families, regaled the city with the finest of their creations. Michelangelo, Leonardo, Donatello, Giotto, the Lippis, Masaccio, Botticelli, Pontormo

Florence's skyline viewed from afar offers an awe-inspiring introduction to the city.

and hosts of others left their mark. Formidable galleries such as the Uffizi, Pitti and Accademia house many of their works. The central square, Piazza della Signoria, seems itself to be an outdoor sculpture gallery. But they are only the beginning. The more you look the more you realise is hidden away here.

The Florence of the late Middle Ages and Renaissance was a financial powerhouse with a Europe-wide reputation. But it was never a romantic place. Its great families built fine mansions to live in and lavished money on the raising of churches and public buildings and their ornamentation. But while some, such as the greatest of the Medici rulers, had a genuinely passionate interest in and knowledge of the arts, there was an element of hard-headed showiness in it all. To *display* greatness was to be great. Florence, even long after it had been eclipsed and was little more than a provincial backwater, remained stubbornly determined to excel in appearance (not always with happy results).

To this day other Italians will tell you that Florentines are a vain lot, heaping money on fine clothes and flashy cars even if doing so means debt. And yet, surprisingly, they seem to have retained something of their banking forbears' financial common sense. The Florentines, at least in the average Italian's mind, are to Italy in money matters what the Scots are to Britain.

The truth probably lies in the middle, and when it comes to dressing well, not a few visitors to Florence succumb to the desire to join the Florentines rather than beat them.

Tired of art and architecture they frequently seek relief in the gratifying business of spending money. Home to Gucci and Ferragamo, Florence for some means only one thing – clothes. And for decades people have flocked here for the leather goods. Prices are not as breathtakingly low as they once were, but deals can still be found.

When the shops close it's time to eat. Although Tuscan cuisine may take simplicity to extremes, with little effort you can keep your tastebuds tingling for weeks. With a little judicious sidestepping of tourist traps you will find some delightful food...and not for thought.

And the wine! Florence lies at the heart of one of the world's great centres of quality wine production. The many top-grade wines of the Chianti region are the best known globally, but you can try other exquisite Tuscan drops here too – from Montalcino's Brunello to the Vino Nobile di Montepulciano.

Aside from the grape, Tuscany has a little of everything. Using Florence as a base you can easily enjoy the medieval splendours of Siena, Pisa, Lucca and San Gimignano and wander the splendid countryside of the Chianti. It is even possible to flee the bulk of tourists by exploring such little-touched areas as Il Mugello and Vallombrosa.

Florence is a multiple assault on the senses that leaves many rubbing their eyes and smacking their lips. And, while it may have been on travellers' itineraries since the days of the Grand Tour, it never ceases to astound.

Facts about Florence

HISTORY
Setting the Scene

As long ago as the Neolithic age, tribes of Liguri from northern Italy are thought to have inhabited the valley where Florence would later be founded by the Roman empire. Other tribes also moved in to the area between the 10th and 5th centuries BC and there remains little doubt that the point on the Arno where the city would much later grow had already long been busy with trade and traffic. Here the Arno is at its narrowest, but still navigable.

Of all the tribes to pass through the area, it was the Etruscans who gained the upper hand. They preferred the heights to the valley and established a settlement at Fiesole (Faesulae to the Romans) in the hills above the as-yet uninhabited site of Florence, possibly as early as the 9th century BC, although some date foundation of the city as late as the 5th century BC.

Although not formally allied, the dozen or so Etruscan towns together had formed the most powerful group in Italy by the 6th century BC. The origins of the Etruscans remain unknown, although the Greek historian Herodotus maintained they had arrived from Asia Minor (modern Turkey) after the Trojan wars. They now dominated an area stretching from Rome to the Apennines (Appennini). Able warriors and mariners, they embarked on a series of conquests south through Latium (Lazio) and into Campania, and north into the Po valley. They also took Corsica.

Emergence of Rome

Etruscan domination expressed itself in Rome by the election of three Etruscan kings during the 6th century BC. They had a profound influence on the social, artistic and military life of the Latin city. By the time they were toppled in 509 BC the Etruscans could to some degree be said to have laid the foundations of a power that in the following centuries would in turn be used to reduce Etruria to the status of subservient province in a new empire.

It didn't happen overnight. The southern Etruscan stronghold of Veio fell in 392 BC and other southern towns, such as Arrezo (Arretium), later passed under Roman control. At the same time the Etruscans lost their Po valley possessions to invading Gauls.

Repeated attempts by the Etruscans to recover their lost territory failed and in 351 BC they signed the first of a series of peace treaties. Rebellion was repaid with conquest and the reimposition of peace, and finally the enforced acceptance of the status of ally. Fiesole fell in this way in 283 BC. By 265 all of Etruria was firmly locked into Rome's system of conquest and alliance. At that point the entire peninsula, stretching south from modern Tuscany and Umbria, was united under Rome.

Florentia

By the time Gaius Julius Caesar was made a consul in Rome in 59 BC much had changed. By force of arms and diplomacy, Rome had passed from being the head of a federation of two-thirds of the Italian peninsula to master of the greatest empire ever seen, stretching from Spain in the west to the Middle East.

In 88 BC, civil war had induced the empire to grant full Roman citizenship and hence substantial equality of rights to all its federated Italian allies, including the Etruscan cities. The flip side was that henceforth Roman public and private law, along with the Latin language, came to dominate the peninsula. Indigenous cultures, already heavily downtrodden, were eased out of existence.

In the year he became consul, Caesar decided to establish a garrison town for army veterans on the Arno, naming it Florentia ('the flourishing one'). The project was part of his *lex Iulia* (which allotted farm plots to veterans) and construction only began around 30 BC.

Controversy is growing over whether or not Caesar's settlement was the first of its kind, or merely the latest incarnation of a long-standing village. Archaeological evidence suggests the existence of a settlement here prior to the arrival of the Romans. At the very least, it seems possible a Roman town had been established here under the Republic and then destroyed by Sulla (a consul and later dictator of Rome) around 80 BC.

The town lay on a strategic river crossing and was laid out in classic Roman form, with the main east–west street, the *decumanus*, intersected from north to south by the *cardo*. The first corresponds to Via del Corso and Via degli Strozzi, while the latter follows Via Roma and Via Calimala. Piazza della Repubblica marks the site of the forum. The town walls followed Via del Proconsolo, Via de' Cerretani, Via de' Tornabuoni and, to the south, roughly a line from Piazza Santa Trinita to the Palazzo Vecchio.

The first significant urban revolution came in the 2nd century AD under Hadrian, who graced the city with a generous building programme. The area around what is now the Palazzo Vecchio was a particularly busy construction site, where baths and an amphitheatre (which occupied most of the site of the Palazzo Vecchio, Via de' Gondi and part of Palazzo Gondi) went up. Florentia had prospered on the back of brisk maritime trade along the Arno.

Under Diocletian in the late 3rd century, Florentia became the capital of the Regio Tuscia et Umbria (the name Etruria was banned), which it remained until the end of the empire. Although the first Christian churches were raised in the following century, Greco-Syriac merchants had brought the religion to pagan Florentia as early as AD 250, when St Minias (San Miniato) was martyred here.

By now Italy and the western Roman empire were in deep trouble. Barbarian invasions came in swift succession in the 5th century and culminated in Theodoric the Ostrogoth's coronation as king in 493. The peace that ensued ended when Justinian, the eastern emperor in Constantinople, decided to recover Italy and so restore the heartland of the Roman empire. The 20-year campaign and subsequent 20 years of Byzantine rule brought devastation and ruin to large tracts of Italy, and Florentia suffered with the rest.

Early Middle Ages

In 570 Florentia and the rest of Tuscany fell to the Lombards. Comparatively little is known about the fate of the city in the following three centuries.

The Lombards may have been Christianised, but these uncouth warrior folk appealed little to local sensibilities. What better way to get rid of one lot than to invite another to boot them out. When the pope asked Charlemagne, king of the Franks, to deal with the Lombards, he jumped at the opportunity. His campaign began in 774. By 800 he had been crowned head of the Holy Roman Empire.

The temporal leader of this empire required papal sanction for legitimacy in the eyes of Christian lords and princes – so the papacy hoped to achieve hegemony by proxy over the Christian world. Instead, empire and papacy would clash repeatedly in the following centuries and help tear apart the political life of many Italian cities, not least among them Florence.

The duchy of Tuscia, which encompassed Tuscany, Umbria, much of Lazio and Corsica, passed under the control of the empire. By the end of the 11th century, particularly under the administration of Countess Matilda Canossa, the duchy had achieved considerable independence. Florence, with a population of 20,000, was a robust and flourishing regional capital.

The death of Matilda spelled the end of Tuscia as a political unit. In a confusing free-for-all, the untangling of which would (and has) filled tomes, each of the Tuscan cities sought independence. From this point on the cities would act as city-states, and the musical chairs of alliance and counter-alliance would remain a constant for centuries to come.

Florence and its rivals sought to impose their rule on their immediate neighbours,

A Woman's Touch

Boniface Canossa's tendency to disregard imperial wishes did his daughter little good. On his death Matilda was packed off to Germany as a prisoner of Emperor Henry III. She clearly was not taken with her Teutonic interlude and when released returned to Florence ill-disposed to cooperate with her imperial masters. From 1069 until 1115 she ruled Florence serenely, proving to be one of the great women rulers of the Middle Ages.

When hostilities broke out between Emperor Henry IV and Pope Gregory VII, Matilda allied herself with the pope, setting a precedent that would long resonate through Florentine history. Henry tried to have the pope deposed in 1076 but instead found himself at Countess Matilda's castle at Canossa, in Emilia, imploring him to lift an order of excommunication.

This was little more than a truce, and this round of the papal-imperial struggle only ended when Henry was deposed by his son, Henry V, in 1105. Matilda meanwhile managed to keep control of Florence and the duchy of Tuscia for another 10 years.

Her decision to build a new set of walls (the fourth since the city's foundation) was a defensive measure, but also served to stimulate greater growth within the new town perimeter. Her rule appears to have been one of unusual peace and wisdom.

and the first skirmishes took place between them. Florence reduced Fiesole to submission in 1123. In 1173 a new set of defensive walls was built and, the following year, Florentine troops were battling Sienese soldiers in the Chianti area over boundary disputes between their respective counties.

By now a system of communal government was emerging, a kind of oligarchy in which the top families (increasingly a mix of landed nobility and the burgeoning merchant class) shared out the leading positions in the government, or *signoria*. Powerful guilds, or *arti*, had also by now emerged. They would long play a key role in the distribution of power in Florence.

Emperor Frederick Barbarossa waltzed into the Italian labyrinth, determined to re-establish imperial control. In Florence in 1173 he decreed the city's jurisdiction limited to the city *intra muros* and installed governors in most Tuscan cities. The latter, however, took little notice and pursued their own interests.

Guelphs & Ghibellines

Factional fighting between Florence's leading families was so intense that it was agreed to invite a foreign *podestà*, an external martial, to act as chief magistrate and head of police and to assure the running of the city, which by the late 12th century numbered some 30,000 inhabitants.

The family feuding crystallised to some extent as the city divided into two factions, the pro-imperial Ghibellines (Ghibellini) and the pro-papal Guelphs (Guelfi). Traditionally the spark that set off this powder keg is identified as the murder of Buondelmonte dei Buondelmonti in 1216. The story goes that he had earlier wounded a certain Oddo Arrighi at a riotous banquet and so started a feud that had only been quelled when Buondelmonte agreed to marry Arrighi's rich but ugly niece, of the Amidei family. He backed out and two months later married a prettier wench more to his liking. On his wedding day the Amidei family, who had not forgotten the affront and had gathered other families around them as allies, cut him to pieces on the southern side of the Ponte Vecchio, beneath the statue of Mars that had become something of a symbol of the city. After that it was all on for young and old.

The Guelphs, generally wealthy merchants, sought greater independence than the Holy Roman Emperor wished to countenance. The Ghibellines tended to be noble families of the feudal school whose sense of power rested to some extent on the notion of being part of the imperial order.

The Guelphs took their name from Welf, the family name of Emperor Otto IV, while Ghibelline is the rendering of the name of a castle, Weiblingen, that belonged to Otto's foes, the Hohenstaufen. How the names came to be used in Italy is unclear and by the early 13th century, as the two factions came to dominate Florentine politics, they had certainly lost any original meaning.

During this period the town bristled with towers, each belonging to one family or another and some allied in so-called tower associations. Every time one faction gained the upper hand they would tear down the towers of opposing families.

Today it is hard to picture central Florence with around 150 brick and stone towers, some close to 80m high. They were, in a sense, a hangover from the countryside. Nobles, who in the district *(contado)* surrounding Florence had owned hilltop castles with defensive towers, were slowly drifting to the towns as the latter's economic power and attraction grew. They brought the habit of building towers and entertaining blood feuds with them.

Until 1250 the Ghibellines were in the driver's seat. On the death of Emperor Frederick II, exiled Guelphs returned to Florence, turfed out the Ghibellines and created a new government. A militia chief, or *capitano del popolo,* was installed in the Palazzo del Podestà (later known as the Bargello). A council of elders was created and the red lily on a white background was chosen as the city's emblem. The Ghibellines took the same emblem but reversed the colour scheme. This first attempt at Florentine democracy came to be known as the Primo Popolo. In an apparent attempt to blunt the bloody one-upmanship of Florence's rival families (noble and otherwise) the government ordered the reduction to an equal height of all towers in the city.

The Guelphs were no shrinking violets. They set about attempting to subdue surrounding towns and in 1260 marched on Ghibelline Siena, Florence's arch rival. The Battle of Montaperti was a stinging defeat for Florence, but only a temporary setback.

By 1270 the Ghibellines were on the run, with Siena, Pisa and other Tuscan cities accepting the appointment of a Guelph podestà in their respective communes.

Nothing Is Ever Black & White

Although the terms would long continue to be bandied about, the conflict between Guelphs and Ghibellines sputtered away to nothing as the Guelphs (known as the Parte Guelfa) affirmed their control over the political life of the city. But hostilities soon flared up again as the arti came to the fore at the end of the century.

Of the arti, seven Arti Maggiori (Senior Guilds) represented the economic force of Florence. The Arte di Calimala (named after the street in which its headquarters stood) represented the senior textile merchants of the city and was the most powerful.

Fourteen Arti Minori (Lesser Guilds) represented the artisans, but they held no political power. The working classes, mostly wage slaves grinding away at the worst jobs in the wool industry (such as dyeing) and totalling a mere three-quarters of the city's population, had no representation (and at times became understandably a little hot under the collar about the situation).

By 1282 the Arti Maggiori had become pivotal in government. It was from their ranks alone that the city's governors, or *priori*, were elected on a two-monthly rotational basis. From the ranks of the governors the *gonfaloniere* (or standard-bearer) was selected as a kind of president. Together they became the signoria and had to reside in the Palazzo della Signoria (today known as the Palazzo Vecchio) for the duration of their mandate. The signoria was frequently obliged to refer to other special councils on specific issues such as finance, war and so on.

In times of crisis, the mournful bell (known as *la vacca,* or 'the cow') of the Palazzo Vecchio was tolled to call the menfolk of the city to Piazza della Signoria for a people's plebiscite, or *parlamento*. The plebiscite would be asked to approve the creation of an emergency committee, or *balia,* to deal with the situation.

The Florentines extolled the virtues of their apparently democratic system, but in truth there was little democracy at all. Even before the two-monthly elections were held, potential candidates were screened by their peers and anyone thought likely to buck the system was kept out of the running. The leading merchant families made sure that only they would guide political decisions, which of course were made to suit their own interests.

This didn't please everyone. The old noble families saw their position eroded by the merchants and began to protest. The arti raised a citizens' militia from the members of the Arti Minori and rammed through the Ordinamenti di Giustizia (Justice Ordinances) in 1293. Effectively a new constitution, they excluded from official positions any of the so-called *magnati*, members of blue-blooded families.

Again Florence's leading families descended into bitter and futile quarrelling as those for and against the Ordinamenti took their row to the streets. Even among the older families there were those who did not see the Ordinamenti as an insuperable obstacle to power – they simply required more wheeling and dealing to ensure favourable candidates were made priori.

At the core of the conflict were the Cerchi and Donati families, who came to be known as the Bianchi (Whites) and the Neri (Blacks). The conservative Neri, who wanted the abrogation of the Ordinamenti, appealed to Pope Boniface VIII, who saw the conflict as a great chance to submerge Tuscany into the Papal States. At his behest, the French Charles de Valois sent in a peace-keeping force in 1301 and by the following year the Neri were in control. The Bianchi, among them Dante Alighieri, were forced into exile.

A Lucky Star

The first 30 years of the 14th century could have spelled the end of Florence on several occasions, but its patron saint, St John the Baptist (San Giovanni Battista), must have been working overtime to protect it.

First the Holy Roman Emperor, Henry VII, decided to reclaim control of Italy. In 1311, Florence, other Tuscan towns and Bologna formed a league to defeat him. In fact, Henry called off an unpromising looking siege against Florence and died shortly thereafter. No sooner had this threat disappeared than another surfaced, with Ghibelline forces set to march from Pisa and Lucca on Florence.

Internal squabbling put the mockers on such plans, but out of the melee emerged another adventurer, Lucca's Castruccio Castracani, bent on breaking Florence. He smashed a Florentine army in 1326 and the priori appealed for help to the duke of Calabria. He agreed to garrison Florence with his own knights for five years in exchange for almost complete power over the city.

Two years later Castruccio died and the duke of Calabria was obliged to race south to take care of more pressing problems at home. Florence could breath again.

A Plague on Florence & the People Are Revolting

St John couldn't do much about natural disasters, however. In 1333 Giovanni Villani, the city's medieval chronicler, reports that a devastating flood ripped through the city, killing many and washing away the Ponte Vecchio.

Then the plague of 1348 decimated Florence's population. As much as half the populace perished. Recovery should have kept Florence and the other cities of Europe occupied for a long time, but it seems the Europeans had an unlimited capacity for absorbing punishment in those dark times. In 1350 Florence was again on the warpath, reasserting control over San Gimignano and other towns. Further wars in the next 15 years brought Volterra, Pistoia, Prato and Pisa under Florentine control. And there was time for wars against and then alongside the Visconti rulers of Milan.

Quiet times were rare and fleeting. In 1375 a rather nasty band of unemployed mercenaries, led by Essex man Sir John Hawkwood, descended on Florentine territory from the Papal States demanding a huge payoff in return for not devastating the whole area. Florence was convinced the pope had actually sent Hawkwood and so declared war. The pope placed an interdict on the city but the Florentines remained defiant. In the end, Hawkwood, or Giovanni Acuto as he became known to the locals, entered the pay of Florence and remained one of its more capable soldiers.

All the blood-letting and instability had a price. Grumblings of discontent were growing louder among the lower classes, increasingly squeezed by taxes and food shortages, and members of the Arti Minori were clearly aiming at securing some power for themselves. The oligarchy instituted a witch-hunt, naming anyone they considered a threat a Ghibelline (by now an almost meaningless term) and declaring them ineligible for election as priori.

The atmosphere was unbearably tense and it was the mob that finally cut loose, unleashing revolution in 1378. The Ciompi, as the working class *(popolo minuto)* had come to be known, demanded the right to create their own guilds and accede to power. On 21 July the Ciompi took the Palazzo della Signoria, installed their own gonfaloniere and created three new guilds – the dyers *(tintori)*, doublet makers *(farsettai)* and a general wool labourers' guild, that of the Ciompi.

The upper classes soon hit back, the Ciompi were brutally suppressed and their guild was dissolved. Four years later, the other two new guilds disappeared too.

All the while, the warring went on. If Florence managed to expand its control of Tuscany by peacefully acquiring Arezzo, Livorno (or Leghorn) and Cortona, the priori watched aghast as Pisa slipped out of their hold under the Milanese Visconti clan's attempts to expand east and south. The wars between Milan and a league formed to oppose the Lombard city proved costly but, by 1430, Florence was in control of most of Tuscany. An attempt that year to take Lucca by storm failed miserably and Siena remained Florence's implacable enemy. To meet the costs of war, the Florentines at this time introduced the *catasto*, the world's first graduated income tax system. Tax was assessed in proportion to

wealth as measured in fixed goods and income-producing potential. Of course tax avoidance and evasion in the modern sense were born with the catasto!

The Rise of the Medici

In these first decades of the 15th century, the Albizi family called most of the shots in Florence. It was by now a given that the real power lay with people behind the scenes, not directly in the hands of any one gonfaloniere.

Another family was growing in influence, however. Giovanni di Bicci de' Medici had steered his bank to becoming one of the most successful investment houses in Europe. His eldest son Cosimo became paterfamilias in 1429, by which time the increasing wealth and influence of his family so upset the Albizi that they contrived to have Cosimo arrested in the hope of trumping up some serious enough charges to warrant his execution.

The Albizi, however, had miscalculated. Not only were several powerful families allied to Cosimo, he had enormous international support through his banking network. Money talks. At the other end of the scales, the Medici also enjoyed wide popular support since they had shown themselves sympathetic to the plight of the lower classes during the Ciompi revolt.

The Albizi forced Cosimo into exile in 1433 after subjecting him to a short stint behind bars, but his absence lasted little more than a year. When Cosimo returned, the Albizi and many of their associates were forced to flee.

The Medici family crest was made up of six balls *(palle)*, which must have been cause for some mirth through the years as Medici supporters would clatter down the street on horseback crying out: 'Balls! Balls! Balls!' The word has the same less than decorous meaning in Italian that it does in English.

Now that Cosimo was back he had a fine, though given the family's wealth relatively modest, mansion *(palazzo)* built on the corner of Via Larga (now Via Cavour) and Via de' Gori. It still stands.

VIVET·DVX·ALEXANDER
MED·SECVLAPEROMNIA·

JANE SMITH

The Medici family crest of six balls can still be seen on public buildings in Florence today.

Father of the Country

For 30 years Cosimo de' Medici steered Florence on a course that, for the most part, only served to increase the power and prosperity of the city and, incidentally, that of his family and supporters.

Cosimo tended to remain in the background, believing discretion to be the better part of valour. By the 1450s, Pope Pius II was saying that Cosimo was 'master of all Italy'. The Medici party kept the government stacked with its own people and when dissenting voices were raised indirect means were found to silence them, such as special taxes and other rulings to ruin their opponents financially. The Medicis were not beyond tinkering with the constitution to head off potential opposition.

Foreign policy could have been Cosimo's undoing. His unswerving allegiance to the Milanese usurper, Francesco Sforza, brought on Florence the enmity of Venice and the kingdom of Naples. Opposition to the ensuing war in Florence was strong and

things were looking a trifle dodgy when Neapolitan forces breached the Tuscan frontier in 1450. Cosimo remained unperturbed and the doubters were proved wrong. Venice was too concerned with threats from Turkey, and the other Italian states worried lest a French army march into Italy to aid Florence. As so often in the peninsula, the boys put away their toys and signed a pact in 1454 aimed at creating unity in the face of potential outside aggression.

The following 10 years were a period of rare and much appreciated peace, in which the city flourished. The population reached about 70,000, taxes fell, trade blossomed and the city's leading families all felt in a position to enhance their home town and personal reputations with grand new buildings.

The ever prudent Cosimo, who protested regularly that he was no more than a private citizen (except on those rare occasions when elected gonfaloniere), was not just a shrewd statesman and consummate businessman. He also had an eye for the finer things in life. Under his patronage, the artistic and intellectual life of the city exploded into a kaleidoscope of magnificent activity.

Even before his rise to power, the artistic world had been in ferment. Indeed, by the time Cosimo returned to Florence from exile in 1434, the Renaissance style had definitively dislodged the Gothic. The old-fashioned artists, sculptors and architects simply couldn't get the commissions in Florence any more.

In 1436 Brunelleschi completed his extraordinary dome on the Duomo cathedral and from this time on Cosimo employed artists such as Donatello, Fra Angelico and Fra Filippo Lippi to work on various projects. He often put up money to promote the construction or embellishment of new public buildings and churches and encouraged the work of the Platonic Academy, which translated all the Greek thinker's works into Latin, making the philosophy of the ancients accessible to an emerging generation of inquiring minds.

Cosimo moved on to the next world in 1464 and he was one of the few Florentine chiefs to be genuinely mourned by his people. The signoria even went so far as to award Cosimo the posthumous title of Pater Patriae – Father of the Country.

Piero de' Medici & Lorenzo the Magnificent

Within two years of succeeding his father as head of the family, Piero de' Medici found himself faced by a revolt; however, his swift response and appeal to Milan for help soon had his opponents on the run. That sorted out, he arranged for the right candidates to be put in control of the signoria. A people's plebiscite was called to confirm a regulation effectively putting control of the elections of priori and gonfalonieri in the hands of selected people. The illusion of democracy was thus maintained (elections would continue as before) but few were in any doubt that Piero had done little else than consolidate his dynasty.

Piero, if anything, maintained a still more abiding interest in the arts than his father. In addition to the likes of Donatello, he fostered the work of Michelozzo, Paolo Uccello, Domenico Veneziano, Luca della Robbia, Benozzo Gozzoli, Il Pollaiuolo, Filippino Lippi and Botticelli.

On Piero's death in 1469, his son Lorenzo was 20 years old. It fell to him to take on the mantle as head of the family and of the state. Lorenzo, like his predecessors, attached great importance to Florence's appearance as a democratic republic, but soon no one was in doubt as to who was in charge.

His was a case of 'when the going gets tough…'. The rival Pazzi family cooked up a plot, not to overthrow Lorenzo but simply to murder him and invest the city of Florence with mercenaries already hired for the purpose. The pope and several other figures were also involved in the plan, which went into effect on 26 April 1478. Lorenzo was wounded and his brother Giuliano ferociously torn to shreds in the assassination attempt during Mass in the Duomo.

Lorenzo escaped and Medici supporters gave the Pazzi troops short shrift in the Palazzo della Signoria. It was all over in no time at all and punishment meted out to the

conspirators (whose family name, which literally means 'insane', must have had some of them wondering whether they really hadn't been entirely potty).

The fun wasn't over yet. The pope, allied with the kingdom of Naples, sent in an army to crush Florence. Things were not going particularly well for Florence when, in 1479, Lorenzo decided to go personally to Naples to negotiate a settlement. This he managed to pull off, and on returning to Florence he set about putting his own house in order. The constitution was again altered. Lorenzo had a Consiglio dei Settanta (Council of Seventy) created, which had powers overriding those of the signoria. Two departments were created to look after home and foreign affairs and Lorenzo il Magnifico (the Magnificent), as he was by now dubbed, had the reins of power solidly in his hands. Like his forbears, however, he continued to insist that he was no more than a private citizen.

Lorenzo continued the promotion of the arts (the young Michelangelo came to live in the Medici household for a time) but there were some worrying signs on the horizon. Since the days of Cosimo, the Medici bank had declined significantly. Branches across Europe continued to close through mismanagement and the family fortunes dwindled accordingly. Lorenzo was often skint, although other branches of the family were still doing comparatively well.

It was in the momentous year of 1492 that Lorenzo expired, aged 43, to be succeeded by his nasty and incompetent son Piero. The era of the great Medici rulers was over.

A Whiff of Hellfire

Within two years Piero was out on his ear and the Medici family in disgrace after his abject submission to the invading French army of Charles VIII. The republic was restored and the constitution again remodelled. The flavour this time was altogether novel. A city of commercial families and luxury-lovers seemed to have temporarily lost its collective sanity as it meekly submitted to the fiery theocracy of Girolamo Savonarola. When Piero de' Medici was

America, America

No one would claim that Florence has a proud naval history – located some 85km inland from the nearest sea, that would have been a tall order. And yet to one of the city's sons fell the honour of having a whole new world named after him – America.

Amerigo Vespucci had been sent to Seville, in Spain, in 1491 to join a business associate of the Medici family, one Giannotto Berardi. Vespucci had been in the employ of Lorenzo and Giovanni di Pierfrancesco de' Medici in Florence and his prospects looked good.

Little could he know that he would spend the rest of his days in the shipping business in Spain and Portugal. These were exciting times in Spain. The last of the Muslims were thrown out of Granada in 1492 and that same year Columbus made his first voyage to what he was convinced was Asia, but was in fact the Caribbean. Vespucci helped fit out the next two of Columbus' voyages and in 1496 became head of the Medici Seville agency.

Between 1497 and 1504 Vespucci set out himself to explore what everyone still remained convinced was Asia or India. There is some dispute about how many trips he made, but at least two seem certain and well documented. On the second of these, in which he sailed down the south American coast into Patagonia and was the first European to lay eyes on the Río de la Plata (River Plate, between Uruguay and Argentina), Vespucci became convinced that this wasn't Asia or India, but a hitherto utterly unheard of world. In 1507 a humanist philosopher, Martin Waldseemüller, printed a treatise in which he described Amerigo as the 'inventor' of a new place called America. The name stuck, at first only to the southern continent, but later to all of what are to this day known as the Americas.

Vespucci had proved himself a capable navigator, so much so that Spain awarded him citizenship and appointed him Pilota Mayor (Master Navigator) in 1508, with the task of organising further expeditions and coordinating the survey of the newly discovered (and conquered) territories. He remained in the post until his death in 1512.

tossed out, a republic on the lines of the Venetian model was called and a Consiglio dei Cinquecento (Council of 500) set up as a parliament.

Savonarola, the Dominican friar with the staring eyes, big nose and fat lips, had arrived in Florence in 1481 to preach repentance in the Chiesa di San Marco. He found a susceptible audience that, over the years, filled the church and church square to bursting to hear his bloodcurdling warnings of horrors to come if Florentines did not repent of their ways and return to the basics.

Announcing himself the instrument through which God spoke, he appears to have had an enormous impact on Florentines. He hailed the French invasion as an army of liberators sent to help cleanse Florence and the rest of Italy. Charles VIII had a more prosaic agenda, wanting to press home French claims to the kingdom of Naples, but this strangely intense monk

must have seemed to him a useful instrument for keeping Florence busy while he headed south.

Savonarola urged the people to renounce their evil ways and called on the government to proceed on the basis of his divine inspiration. Drinking, whoring, partying, gambling, wearing flashy clothes and other signs of wrongdoing were pushed well underground. Books, clothes, jewellery, fancy furnishings and art burned on 'bonfires of the vanities'. Bands of children marched around the city ferreting out adults still seemingly attached to their old habits and possessions.

Opposition by what came to be known as the *arrabiati* ('angry ones') was vociferous but splintered.

The licentious Pope Alexander VI and various Italian states now banded together in an ultimately abortive attempt to turf the French out of Italy. Florence refused to join the alliance because the French were good business and the Florentines had no desire to attract Charles VIII's wrath. Savonarola provided the propaganda by maintaining that the presence of the French would be the salvation of true Christians.

No doubt feeling the sting of Savonarola's accusations of corruption and debauchery in the Church, the pope was losing his cool. He demanded Savonarola be sent to Rome, and the signoria started to worry. Bad harvests were hurting the people and Savonarola seemed increasingly outlandish with his claims of being God's special emissary.

The rival Franciscans, especially, had had enough. As 1498 wore on, street violence between the friar's supporters and opponents rose. The Franciscans challenged Savonarola to an ordeal by fire, an invitation he declined to take up, although he had no problem with sending a deputy in his stead. The trial was washed out by rain but in the ensuing riots the signoria finally decided to arrest Savonarola. After weeks at the hands of the city rack-master he was finally hanged and burned at the stake as a heretic, along with two supporters, in Piazza della Signoria on 22 May.

The Medici Strike Back

It took some time and a good deal of bloodshed, but Giovanni de' Medici returned home in 1512 backed by a Spanish-led army. He set about restoring the position of his family in Florence, which should have been further strengthened when Giovanni was elected Pope Leo X one year later.

But the Medici line seemed to have lost much of its lustre. Florence in any case was not the same city as that of Cosimo's day. Most of its banks had failed and business was not so good. A series of Medici lads, culminating in the utterly useless bastards Ippolito and Alessandro, managed to so alienate Florentines that when Pope Clement VII (another Medici) was cornered in Rome by an uncompromising imperial army, the people rejoiced and threw the Medici out.

Of course, deals were done and the im-perial forces subsequently promised to reinstate the Medici in Florence if the pope recognised imperial suzerainty of all Italy. Florence, which had enjoyed a few short Medici-free years, was reduced by siege in 1530. Alessandro and Ippolito returned. Alessandro was made duke, bringing to an end even the pretence at a republic, and assassinated by a jealous cousin, Lorenzino, in 1537.

Grand Duke Cosimo I

The Medici party activists decided on Cosimo (a descendant of the first Cosimo's brother Lorenzo) as successor, hoping he would be easily manipulated. They got that wrong. Cosimo, who in 1569 would be officially declared grand duke of Tuscany after the definitive fall of Siena to Florence, was a tough leader who brooked no opposition. In his long reign from 1537 to 1574 he

JANE SMITH

Cellini's bronze cast of Cosimo I shows the duke in elaborate warrior garb.

was no doubt a despot, but a comparatively enlightened one. He sorted out the city's finances, built a fleet (which participated in the crushing defeat of the Turkish navy in the Battle of Lepanto in 1571) and promoted economic growth across Tuscany, with irrigation programmes for agriculture and mining.

Cosimo I was a patron of the arts and sciences and he also reformed the civil service, building the Uffizi to house all government departments in one, more easily controlled building. He and his family also acquired and moved into the Palazzo Pitti, which they proceeded to expand.

The Medicis' Grand Duchy

From the death of Cosimo I until that of the dissolute lout Gian Gastone de' Medici in 1737, the once glorious family continued to rule over Tuscany with uneven results.

Cosimo's immediate successors, Francesco and Ferdinando I, between them managed to keep Tuscany out of trouble and go some way to stimulating the local economy and promoting agriculture, building hospitals and bringing some relief to the poor. Cosimo II invited Galileo Galilei to Florence, where the scientist could continue his research under Tuscan protection and undisturbed by the bellyaching of the Church.

Ferdinando II was ineffectual if well meaning – during the three terrible years of plague that scourged Florence from 1630, he stayed behind when anyone else that could was hotfooting it to the countryside.

Next in line was Cosimo III, a dour, depressing man if ever there was one. Perhaps he had read his Savonarola. In any event he embarked on a puritan crusade. Not exactly a fun-loving guy, Cosimo was also an ill-educated bigot. Persecution of the Jews was one of his contributions to Florentine society and he also backed the Inquisition in its opposition to virtually any kind of scientific learning. Inevitably, sex was one of his biggest bugbears. A little stretch on the rack was the prescribed tonic for sex outside marriage, while buggery was punished with decapitation.

Busy as Cosimo III was overseeing the mores of his subjects, they were either dying or going hungry. The population not only of Florence but of all Tuscany was in decline; the economy was a mess and taxes were skyrocketing.

Before the drunkard Gian Gastone had kicked the bucket, the European powers had decided the issue of the 'Tuscan succession' and appointed Francis, duke of Lorraine and husband of the Austrian empress Maria Theresa, as grand duke of Tuscany. The last significant act of the Medicis came six years after the death of Gian Gastone. His sister, Anna Maria, who died in 1743, bequeathed all the Medici property and art collections to the grand duchy of Tuscany, on condition that they never leave Florence.

Austrians in Charge

The imperial Austrian couple popped down for a three-month sojourn in Florence and liked it well enough, but from then until 1765 the city and grand duchy were to be ruled by regents (whose rule was known as the Reggenza).

They brought a feeling of (mostly) quiet discontent to their subjects. It is true that much-needed reforms swept away glaring inequities in taxation, somewhat streamlined civil administration and curbed the powers of the Inquisition. At the same time, the regents' main task seemed to be little more than the systematic plunder of Tuscany's resources in the service of the Austrian empire. The grand duchy of Tuscany was supposedly an independent entity, but you'd have hardly thought so.

Things looked up a little in 1765, when Pietro Leopoldo became grand duke and moved down from Vienna. He threw himself into his task with considerable vim and vigour.

The list of reforms and initiatives is impressive, though some of them ultimately proved less than satisfactory. The grand duke abolished torture and the death penalty, suppressed the Inquisition, embarked on a schools building programme for the poor, busied himself with matters of agriculture and prodded Florence's administrative council *(comune)* to clean up the city, improve lighting and introduce street names. He also saw to it that at least some of the art and furnishings that had been removed to Austria under Grand Duke Francis were returned.

Pietro Leopoldo, as heir to the Austrian throne, had to pack up and leave Tuscany in 1790 upon the death of his brother, Emperor Josef II. Until Grand Duke Ferdinando III arrived the following year, Tuscany was governed by a regents' council that within weeks found itself struggling to put down food riots across the city of Florence.

Napoleonic Shenanigans

The events that had so profoundly rocked France in the meantime could not fail to have an impact, sooner or later, on the rest of Europe.

When Napoleon Bonaparte marched into Italy at the head of his ill-equipped but highly motivated republican army in 1796, he shocked everyone by the speed of his advance. Grand Duke Ferdinando III declared Tuscany neutral, not surprisingly given that his father had disbanded the Tuscan army and navy years before.

Then Neapolitan troops sailed into Livorno to launch an attack on Napoleon's forces in Rome, giving the French a pretext to march on Florence on 24 March 1799. Within a couple of days, Grand Duke Ferdinando III had been obliged to leave and the French tricolour flew over Palazzo Pitti.

This first round of French occupation of the northern half of Italy was as fleeting as it was spectacular. By the end of July, Ferdinando III was again grand duke (although he was hedging his bets back in Vienna).

The following year Napoleon was back, not as a republican general but as consul and virtual ruler of France. He retook Florence and made it capital of the kingdom of Etruria, which for the following nine years was run by Louis, son of the Bourbon duke of Parma, and his wife, the Infanta Maria Luisa of Spain.

In 1809, Napoleon, by now emperor, handed Tuscany over to his sister Elisa,

who remained grand duchess for the five years left to Napoleon as warrior emperor. Before the year 1814 was out, Grand Duke Ferdinando III was back in town.

Towards Italian Unity

Grand Duke Ferdinando III proved to be one of the more popular of the Tuscan overlords. He pushed through a raft of reforms at every level of city and grand ducal administration and by all accounts was an all-round good fellow. He eschewed many of the trappings of his position and mingled freely with his subjects.

His death in 1824 was greeted with dismay, not least because no one knew what to expect from his gloomy son Leopoldo.

Grand Duke Leopoldo II actually proved more up to the task than many had thought. As the years wore on, however, the task grew steadily more onerous. The independence of the grand duchy was menaced not only by more direct interference from Vienna, but also by the growing calls for a united Italian state.

Leopoldo took a fairly lenient line in Florence, allowing dissent and so attracting to the city intellectuals from all over the country, including writers such as Ugo Foscolo and Giacomo Leopardi.

Indeed, Florence was something of a magnet for writers, activists and a fair sprinkling of dilettantes from all over the place. Since the middle of the previous century, Florence had been a favourite choice of self-imposed exile for a considerable number of Brits. Now it attracted the likes of Byron and Shelley, and non-Anglos like Chateaubriand.

Leopoldo also encouraged urban development and a series of improvements, including the introduction of gas street-lighting, the widening of roads and housing programmes for the poor.

The 1840s, a time of ferment across all of Europe, were no less trying in Florence. In 1844 the most disastrous floods in living memory struck the city. And although Florence itself did not rise in 1848, it did become an overnight recruitment centre for volunteers keen to join a Piedmontese army in the fight against Austrian troops that ensued after the Cinque Giornate (Five Days) rising of Milan.

Leopoldo was sufficiently worried about his own position to leave Florence in 1849. Into the breach stepped a radical government among whose leaders was the key pro-unity figure of Giuseppe Mazzini. Their rule was short-lived and Leopoldo was asked back after only three months. He acquiesced, but from then on adopted a distinctly conservative, pro-Austrian approach. In doing so he hardly won new friends in Florence, but by now it was perhaps immaterial anyway. The fate of Florence, and of all Italy, was to be decided elsewhere. A whirlwind of plotting and a few turns of the wheel of fortune brought events to a head in 1859, when a combined French and Piedmontese army marched against the Austrians and defeated them in two bloody battles at Magenta and Solferino in June.

Already in April that year, Leopoldo had been convinced it would be better to leave after mass demonstrations against him and in favour of a united Italy.

On 15 March 1860, the provisional government in Florence announced the adhesion of the grand duchy to the kingdom of Piedmont. As other parts of Italy also joined, so in 1861 a united Italy under a constitutional monarch was born.

In February 1865, King Vittorio Emanuele and the national government arrived in Florence to take up residence. Turin had been the first seat of the national parliament, but was deemed too far north to remain capital. The natural choice would have been Rome, but Rome was yet to be wrenched from papal hands. And so an 'army' of 30,000, including bureaucrats and their families, descended on Florence, a city of around 115,000. A year later, the military hero of the Italian Risorgimento ('Resurrection'), Giuseppe Garibaldi, was given a thunderous welcome in Florence. His 'Red Shirts' had become famous throughout the world, although their victories had been balanced by a fair share of disasters.

The incorporation of Rome into the kingdom and the end of fighting throughout the peninsula finally came in 1870, and the government shifted there the following year.

In those five brief years of 'occupation' the city was given much of its present appearance. A good deal of the public works programme, including the demolition of the city walls, went to the Anglo-Italian Florence Land and Public Works Ltd. Ring roads (the broad *viali*) that follow the line of the former city walls were paved. Large new squares appeared, including Piazzale Michelangelo. The growth of whole new suburbs to the north and north-west of the centre got under way. In short, a modern middle-class Florence was born out of the torpor that had left it, in spite of some improvements under the grand dukes, largely locked in a medieval time warp. The work continued after 1871. By 1888, for instance, the first electric street-lighting was going up.

Some of the works were a disaster. Central Florence was brutally wounded by the creation of Piazza della Repubblica, to which were sacrificed countless buildings of historic value. Not to mention the almost 6000 inhabitants forcibly removed from the area to make way for this vast empty space.

The inhabitants of Florence continued in large measure to live poorly. Local accounts suggest that in the 1860s and 70s delinquency was rife, poverty and begging widespread. The trinket-selling and touting of cab drivers for rides in their horse-driven coaches was not unlike what you might see in some touristed cities of Egypt today.

When one remembers that the last of the Medici rulers had left behind them a city in penury a century and a half before, it is not surprising that for many Florentines life was still far from ideal. The wars and crises since, the tendency towards heavy taxation that in turn discouraged local investment in any kind of production – all this had helped keep the city in check. Indeed, one of the things that made Florence so attractive to its large foreign community was that it was so cheap.

Although there were some signs that the quality of life was slowly improving after unity, problems were never far away. Another major flood struck in 1864. The economic crisis of the late 1890s pushed up the price of staples and led to bread riots. An 1892 report suggested that, of a total population of 180,000, 72,000 were officially considered poor.

By the turn of the century, however, mortality rates had sunk spectacularly, and the phenomenon of leaving town for seaside holidays in summer was growing. Entertainment in the form of popular theatre, *cafés chantants* and the like added a pleasurable dimension to the lives of even the lowest classes.

In the 10 years prior to the outbreak of WWI, Florence became something of a cultural capital in Italy. Numerous literary, political and often free-thinking newspapers and reviews came into existence at this time.

Florentine politics was radicalising too. By 1914 the Socialist Party had almost 3000 party members in Florence, and the previous year, when universal male suffrage was granted, almost 30% of Tuscan votes went to them. Florence was also becoming a fulcrum of anarchist activity.

The Two World Wars

Italy's decision to enter WWI on 24 May 1915 had little initial impact on Florence, tucked far away from the front lines in the north. By the end of the struggle some 11,000 young men from Florence and its province had died in the field. By 1917 the situation on the home front had become grim too. All basic products were strictly rationed and that winter, a harsh one, brought intense hardship as heating fuel was virtually unavailable.

Italy, like the rest of Europe, emerged from the war in a state of collective shock. The fighting had cost the fledgling country dear in lives and resources and the political turmoil that ensued was inevitable.

In Florence, postwar urban plans included creating a factory zone, to include the gasworks and the Pignone smelters, in the Rifredi area north-west of the centre. This in turn aided the growth of workers'

groups and support for left-wing parties and action, creating the scene for clashes between right and left.

By 1920 Benito Mussolini's Fascists had established branches in Florence. Virtually ignored at first, they soon began to attract membership in spite of the rise in political street violence that year.

In less than two years Florence would become one of the Fascists' biggest strongholds. By the end of 1922 the region of Tuscany as a whole was one of the single biggest sources of card-carrying Fascist members.

On 28 October 1922, Mussolini rolled the dice and marched on Rome. Had the king been truly opposed to the Fascists, it is likely they would have failed in this endeavour, but in the event Mussolini emerged the victor. In Florence, 2000 Fascists took control of strategic buildings, the railway and telecommunications posts. The police stayed pretty much out of the way.

The Florentine version of Fascism was particularly violent. In 1924, after the assassination in Rome of the Socialist Giacomo Matteotti had particularly aroused anti-Fascist sentiment, the black-shirted squads *(squadre)* set about terrorising anyone suspected of antipathy towards their glorious movement. The violence became so alarming that Mussolini sent people in to shake out local organisations and put a brake on the bloodshed.

In the following years, the opposition gradually went further underground or was suppressed altogether. For its loyalty the city got a new stadium at Campo di Marte (1932) and the train station at Santa Maria Novella (1933–35). Then in 1938 the Florentines received another gift, a joint visit in all possible pomp and circumstance by Mussolini and his new buddy with the toothbrush moustache, Adolf Hitler. The multitude duly cheered and waved Florentine lilies with Nazi swastikas. They had no idea what they were heading for.

For Italy, the tragedy began in June 1940 when Mussolini decided to take the plunge and join Hitler's European tour. Things went Germany's way for a while, but for the

Italians the difficulties began almost from the outset. Florence's war clothes included asbestos blocks and sandbags, placed to protect the city's monuments.

By 8 September 1943, when Italy surrendered to the Allies, the latter's troops were about to land at Salerno, south of Naples – a long way from Florence.

Italy surrendered but not the Germans. They established their local military HQ in Piazza San Marco, while the SS (the Schutzstaffel, Hitler's paramilitary forces) found a nice quiet place to carry out torture on Via Bolognese in the north of the city. More zealous than the SS in the search for enemies to torture, however, were those Fascists who remained and threw in their lot with the Germans. From here on, Florence, which Mussolini had once proudly declared *Fascistissima* (*very*, *very* Fascist), was an occupied city.

Allied air raids on Florence were infrequent but anyhow many of its artworks had been removed to safer locations beyond the city. When Allied forces approached the German lines near Florence in July 1944, the German high command decided to blow up the city's bridges. The Germans were not completely insensitive to the situation and spared the Ponte Vecchio, blocking it at either end and mining its shops instead. Early in the morning of 4 August, the other bridges went up in smoke.

While Italian Resistance fighters continued to battle Fascist snipers in the city over the following days, the Allies chose to envelop the city in a pincer movement before pursuing the fight north of the city. Apart from wanting to avoid further unnecessary destruction to the city, the Allies no doubt found it easier to swing around the city through open country than yomp through the middle of it.

The first Allied scouts entered from the south the day the bridges were blown up but it was almost two weeks before they attacked the German forces concentrated north of the city. The Germans retreated, as planned by the Allies, to stronger defensive lines further north, finally leaving Fiesole on 7 September.

By May the following year, the war in Europe was over.

Aftermath & the Floods of 1966

Within three months of the German exit from Florence, work began on restoration. Rebuilding bridges was paramount, and by August 1946 Ponte alla Vittoria was up. Ponte San Niccolò was finished in 1949 and Ponte alla Carraia two years later. Ponte Santa Trinita took another seven years, painstakingly reconstructed using copies of 16th-century tools.

Florentine postwar politics were dominated by the colourful *sindaco* (mayor) Giorgio La Pira, a Sicilian with a strong religious inspiration who vowed to govern for the poor. He was a member of the conservative Christian Democrat party, which for decades would remain at the centre of power in Rome. His first electoral victory came in 1951, after a period in which the Communists and other left-wing forces together had dominated the city. La Pira's convictions of the need for world peace and his search to create in Florence a 'better' society won him admirers and detractors. It was difficult to be indifferent about a man whose beatification is now being contemplated.

La Pira, who had been on the committee that wrote the new national constitution promulgated in 1948, was nothing if not controversial. He requisitioned empty buildings to house the homeless, distributed bread to the poor (a stunt in questionable taste) and, oddly enough for a Christian Democrat, sided with factory workers in their struggles with employers.

Such displays were all very well, but critics attacked him for not implementing a proper housing programme. In the meantime, land west of the city was swallowed up and turned into suburban sprawl with virtually no supervision or inspection from the comune. On the other hand, public works programmes were carried out and one of the more visible results was a new bridge, the Ponte Amerigo Vespucci.

Disaster struck in 1966. Torrential rain turned the Arno into a raging torrent that, in

The Monster of Florence

The night of 21 August 1968, a couple was found dead in a car outside Florence, killed by four shots from a Beretta 22 pistol.

The man was later identified as the woman's lover and her husband imprisoned for murder. The Beretta was never found.

In September 1974, another couple was killed with the same make of gun, but this time the killer hung about. The woman was found with knife wounds. No connection was made between the two murders but when, in October 1981, a similar murder was carried out the police began to link all the homicides and the myth of the Mostro di Firenze was born. In the next four years three more murders of similar brutality took place, the last on 7 September 1985.

Unused to the bizarre stories of urban crime that other big cities across the world tend to take more in their stride, Florentines were alarmed, to say the least. Theories abounded as to who the killer might be, but no hard evidence could be found. Since the murderer had the endearing habit of removing bits of his victims, some thought he or she might even be a doctor.

Police inquiries finally led to one Pietro Pacciani. By all accounts not a very nice fellow, the evidence was nevertheless a trifle flimsy – a cartridge that matched those of the murder weapon and an exercise book that might have belonged to the last murder victims. In 1994 Pacciani got life, only to be cleared two years later. This decision was in turn revoked by the Corte di Cassazione, the Supreme Court, which was preparing to start from scratch when Pacciani died on 22 February 1998, taking with him to the grave the secret of the Monster of Florence.

the early hours of 4 November, crashed into Florence. When the flood waters finally subsided, the city was left covered in a mantle of mud, oil and slime. Some 14,000 families were left homeless and the impact on the city's art treasures was incalculable.

In the midst of this calamity, the Florentines pulled together and set about cleaning up their city. It was an arduous process. More complex still was the restoration of monuments, paintings and manuscripts that had been damaged but not lost. Funds and experts poured in from around the world to help out. If anything good can be said to have come of the flood, it was the great advances made in the field of art restoration.

Florence has rarely hit the headlines since, leading the quiet dignified life of a regional capital, under constant siege by a seemingly infinite army of tourists but otherwise caught up in its own little world.

GEOGRAPHY

The Romans founded Florence at the narrowest point on the Arno, about 85km inland from the Tuscan coast. Even this far away from the Mediterranean, the river was still navigable. Since the settlement was also ideally placed to give access to three passes north across the Apennine mountains, Roman Florentia was a significantly strategic location. Being next to a river later proved crucial to the city, as much of its wealth came from the textiles industry, for which a decent water source is indispensable.

The Arno rises in the Tuscan Apennines near Monte Falterona, describes an arc south towards Arezzo and then heads northwest to Florence. From there it winds westward, emptying into the Mediterranean about 11km west of Pisa. In all it is about 240km long. Several minor mountain streams, the most important of which is the Mugnone, feed into the Arno from north of Florence.

When you look down at the pathetic puddle that the Arno is in high summer, it is hard to imagine it thundering down from the east, crashing into the city, sweeping away bridges and leaving countless dead. And yet that is precisely what it has done repeatedly throughout the city's history. In 1177 and 1333 floods swept away the Ponte Vecchio, and some thought the same would happen in the disastrous flood of 1966. Some of the flood control works in place today were designed by Leonardo da Vinci.

The original Roman *castrum* (camp) lay on the northern bank of the river, and the bulk of the city has developed there for the simple reason that the valley is relatively wide and flat on this side of the river. The foothills of the Apennines reach down to within 10km of the Arno and closer still on the eastern side of the city. As a consequence, the bulk of the suburban sprawl has all been channelled westwards towards Prato.

South of the Arno, development is much more limited. Historically the hills crowding up to the river allowed urban spread only within a rough triangle bounded by Porta Romana (Roman Gate), Ponte Vespucci and Ponte alle Grazie. If you take the correct turn-off from the Siena–Florence road you end up at Piazzale Michelangelo – a hill rising just south of the river and affording magnificent views of the city and Arno.

In the past century the westward march of suburban expansion on the northern bank has to some extent been mirrored to the south with the development of areas like the factory zone of Pignone and Isolotto.

CLIMATE

Florence's position in a river basin, walled in by hills to the south and the foothills of the Apennines to the north, largely determines its climate. Summers tend to be torrid, humid affairs. July is the worst month and there are days when not a whisper of air makes itself felt. The average highs hover around 35°C. Occasionally you can enjoy a cracking good thunderstorm and downpour, which brings a little temporary relief.

Winter, on the other hand, is cool and often wet, although mercifully it doesn't last too long. Average temperatures in January hover between 0 and 6°C and snow is a rarity.

ECOLOGY & ENVIRONMENT

The unchecked urban and suburban sprawl, fuelled by land speculation that seemed to leave successive city governments helpless, has all but wiped out any sense of green in Florence. This is particularly so north of the river. As if by a miracle, parts of the Oltrarno are still a haven. South of the walls protecting Via San Niccolò, you can wander almost immediately into what to all intents and purposes is a stretch of countryside, dotted with villas and kept productive with the fruit of the vine.

Florence's single biggest environmental problem is air pollution. Measures to reduce traffic coming into the centre and the introduction of buses running on methane gas have probably helped a little, although on a hot, smoggy day you might be hard pressed to believe it!

Noise, especially in the centre, is another problem. The rattling of two-stroke engines on mopeds is not likely to go away anytime soon!

Another problem is pesky animals. Venice is not the only Italian city plagued by pigeons. Although not as serious, Florence has a fair-sized problem and the town authorities are forever trying to work out how to control the pigeon population. Of greater concern is the *norvegicus* rat, a beast the size of a small cat and weighing up to 3kg. These charmers live in the sewerage pipes and along river banks and streams. How to get rid of them is something of a mystery.

GOVERNMENT & POLITICS

Florence is the capital of Tuscany ('la Toscana' to the Italians), one of 20 regions into which the country is subdivided.

Tuscany is bound to the west by the Tyrrhenian and Ligurian Seas and to the north by the region of Emilia-Romagna,

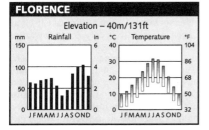

with which it shares a good chunk of the Apennines. To the east and south, Tuscany borders Le Marche, Umbria and Lazio.

The region is further divided into 10 provinces, each named after their respective capitals: Florence (Firenze), Prato, Pistoia, Lucca, Massa, Pisa, Livorno, Siena, Grosseto and Arezzo.

The administrative district of Florence takes in a relatively small area, falling short of the Amerigo Vespucci airport in the west and extending about 4km east of Ponte Vecchio along the Arno. At its southernmost point it reaches only 2km south of the Palazzo Pitti. To the ordinary citizen, such fine distinctions are noticeable only by the signs on roads leading out of the city, which show 'Firenze' with a red line through it. To the north-west, into the comune of Sesto Fiorentino especially, the city sprawl goes on and on. Heading clockwise from Sesto are the districts of Fiesole, Bagno a Ripoli and Scandicci.

From medieval times the city (which until a century ago was largely confined to the area within the last set of city walls) was subdivided in various ways. Up to the end of the 12th century, the city was divided into four administrative units, all of them on the northern side of the river. With expansion beginning to take on more substance on the southern bank, the city was reorganised into six *sestieri*, five on the northern side and one on the southern bank.

In 1343 the comune reverted back to a system of quarters, of which there were three on the northern bank (Santa Maria Novella, San Giovanni and Santa Croce) and one on the southern bank (Oltrarno). Each quarter was further subdivided into districts known as *popoli*.

Nowadays, the comune is made up of five local councils, or *quartieri*. They are: Centro Storico, Campo di Marte, Gavinana-Galluzo, Isolotto-Legnaia and Rifredi-Le Piagge.

The mayor in the driver's seat since July 1999 has been Leonardo Domenici. He fronts a centre-left coalition led by the former communists, the Democratici di Sinistra (DS).

ECONOMY

In 1189 Florence gave the world the silver florin *(fiorino)*, a currency bearing the lily of Florence and the bust of its patron saint, St John the Baptist. By the time the city started to mint the gold version in 1253, the city's banks and currency already had a reputation throughout Europe as being among the most stable in the world of medieval business.

As the inventors of double-entry bookkeeping and a forerunner to the cheque, Florentines were considered the masters of international commerce. All this may sound terribly boring, but Florence was, and is, largely a middle class merchant town, the central Italian equivalent of the burgher towns of Holland.

Of course, banking alone does not an economy make. The central pillar of Florence's prosperity was textiles. Experts in the selection and use of dyes, Florentines often imported the raw materials (especially wool) from northern Europe and then exported the finished products back. Although not a sea power, Florence also did a brisk trade in the export of grain, wines, timber, oil and livestock.

By the 19th century, however, it was clear that Florence was in trouble. Left out of the race to industrialise, as late as 1870 local politicians were still declaring that smokestacks were not for Florence, which should instead rely on artisanal products and tourism. Not everyone agreed, and indeed a big foundry had been operating in the Pignone district since 1842. The optics specialists of the Officina Galilei came into being in 1860 and, now based in Rifredi, is still going strong today. Manetti & Roberts, long famous in Florence for its talcum powder, is another business that continues to thrive.

Overall, however, Florence has proved either unwilling or unable to make itself an important industrial centre. Nowadays, furniture making, food processing, rubber goods and chemicals dominate industrial production in the western suburbs of the city. Various companies have opted to pursue the development and production of precision instruments for use in the fields of space, military and medical technology.

But it will come as no great surprise that tourism plays a huge part in the economic life of Florence. It is estimated that 2.9 million tourists flocked to the city of the Medici in 1998. For the Millennium (Giubileo) year of 2000, the town authorities are expecting a staggering 4.6 million!

On the back of tourism comes the sale of arts, crafts and high fashion (whether locally produced or not).

POPULATION & PEOPLE

With all those people flooding in from all over the world, it is perhaps not so surprising that the average Florentine seems a little on the closed side.

Italians from other parts of the country accuse them of being, above all, slaves to appearance. *Fare bella figura* ('to look good', a broad term encompassing much more than simply dressing well) is of prime importance to many a Florentine. Some foreigners would say that all Italians seem to suffer from this attachment to looks, but to the Italians the Florentines excel.

It appears that this is nothing new. In the days of the Medici rulers, sumptuary laws forbade excessively dressy habits in the interests of bourgeois decorum, although such laws remained largely unenforced. Savonarola railed at the Florentines' vanity at the end of the 15th century. Mind you, his puritan tastes soon lost their appeal and he (literally) went up in smoke. Centuries before him even Dante took his countrymen to task for their excessive attachment to sartorial splendour.

The total population of the Florence area, from the best dressed to the more modestly attired, is 379,000.

EDUCATION

Known to students simply as *la facoltà* (faculty), the Università degli Studi di Firenze is the city's main university. It traces its history back to the Studium Generale established in 1321. Pope Clement VI granted this institution permission to issue full degrees in 1349, after the universities of Bologna and Paris. Italy's first theology faculty was also founded in Florence. In successive centuries the various faculties were split up and spread across the city and Pisa.

In 1860, the Istituto di Studi Pratici e di Perfezionamento (Institute for Practical Studies and Further Education) was established under the auspices of the newly united Italy. It was finally elevated to university status in 1923.

For details on studying in Florence see Universities in the Facts for the Visitor chapter and Courses in the Things to See & Do chapter.

Illiteracy is barely an issue in Tuscany. The national Italian average of 97% literacy can be accepted as standard for this part of the country too.

ARTS

Florence is, with good reason, known above all for the flourishing of all the fine arts known to us as the Renaissance, a period that embraced the better part of the 15th and 16th centuries.

Many of the key characters to bestride the Florentine stage in this period were multi-talented. Architects, painters and sculptors were often masters of more than one medium and several are mentioned in more than one section here.

The definition of a 'Florentine' in this context is equally difficult to settle. Many fine non-Florentine artists left works behind in the city of the red lily. Equally, many Florence-born artists wandered far and wide during their careers. Inevitably the selection will be arbitrary.

The undisputed epicentre of Renaissance painting, Florence can also be considered the heart of Italy's greatest blossoming of sculpture. Although other regions produced capable sculptors, the bulk of them either came from Tuscany or wound up in Florence at some stage of their careers. In construction, equally, the innovations undertaken by such as Brunelleschi helped revolutionise architectural thinking throughout the country.

Why Florence? Although without doubt the history of medieval Florence and on into the Renaissance was characterised by more ups and downs than you might expect from your average yo-yo, the fundamentals, as they would say today, were generally solid. By the time Cosimo de' Medici returned to Florence in 1434, to become its ruler in deed if not in name, the city had already long been one of Europe's most prosperous trading and banking centres.

Those with the dosh were honour-bound to lavish some of their wealth on the prestige of the city, so the great mercantile families subscribed to the building of the great churches – the Duomo, Santa Maria Novella and Santa Croce. They probably hoped to do their souls some good by such beneficence – Cosimo de' Medici once said 'I shall never be able to give God enough to set him down in my books as a debtor'.

The growing magnificence of the city's monuments reflected positively on its leading citizens. Such appearances were good for business too. In the way modern cities try to attract attention to themselves by staging the Olympics or with ambitious new building programs, so the great cities of medieval and Renaissance Italy did the same thing by raising great public and private buildings sumptuously decorated with frescoes, sculpture and paintings.

One essentially fortuitous difference in Florence was, however, a matter of intellectual taste. Far from a perfect democracy, the turbulent rowdy republic was not nevertheless a one-man dictatorship. The taste for rediscovering classical learning had already been awakened in the 12th century in Florence, and while some (such as the Albizis) took a dim view of all this new-fangled thinking, others (such as the Medicis) lapped it up. This curiosity about the past and the consequent rethinking of the present unleashed creative energies that in more conservative, less permissive parts of the land didn't stand a chance. Only as the Florentine masters won acclaim at home did their renown spread and tastes change elsewhere.

The Materials

Geological circumstances seem to have been in collusion with Florence's tradition of artistic patronage. The raw materials for sculpture and building all come from Tuscany. The white marble of Carrara still draws sculptors today, while the green marble used mainly in the facades of great buildings was quarried in the hills near Prato. Pink marble came from the area of Maremma.

Various kinds of stone could be found in abundance around Florence itself, including the dun-coloured *pietra forte* (literally 'strong stone') that characterises the outside of so many great Florentine buildings. From the 13th century it became the most commonly used material in civic and private construction, virtually replacing brick. The Boboli quarry was one of the handiest sources of pietra forte for Florence. The stone *par excellence* of the Renaissance was, however, the grey *pietra serena* ('tranquil stone') used above all for interiors. Brunelleschi propelled the use of this easily worked stone to prominence as a building material. It became common to couple it with plain white-washed stucco *(intonaco)* elements such as window mouldings and the like.

An important innovation in architectural decoration came with Robbia's experiments in glazed terracotta.

Architecture

Architects, in the modern specialised sense, took a while to emerge from anonymity in Italy and the rest of Europe. The first great master-builders in Florence were in the vanguard of those who, from the Gothic period, began to leave their signature on the edifices they raised.

Throughout the Renaissance, however, these masters often combined their architectural skill with prowess in other fields of the arts, such as painting, sculpture and occasionally even writing. Cross-fertilisation of ideas between the disciplines was the norm.

Possibly one of the oddest things about some Florentine architecture – and this goes for many other Italian cities too (Venice is a perfect example) – is that facades were often tacked onto the body of a building as if in afterthought. The Duomo and the Basilica di Santa Croce only got their facades in the 19th century! Many other churches never received theirs – a peculiarly Florentine quirk. It appears builders frequently ran out of money when it came to this final touch.

Romanesque Virtually nothing remains of Roman Florentia. Out of the confusion of the collapse of the Roman empire and the early medieval centuries of barbarian invasion and foreign rule emerged several fairly simple building styles in Italy.

Of course, we are talking about monumental building – churches, government palaces and mansions for the rich and powerful. Your average Giuseppe lived in flimsy, precarious wooden housing so utterly dwarfed by the solid stone and/or brick public edifices that he probably could not conceive what it might be like to live in such sheer luxury.

Byzantine models, drawing on examples in Constantinople and the eastern empire, which in turn looked to the classical Roman heritage, made little impression on Florence.

The Romanesque style, which emerged in the northern Lombard plains of Italy, was characterised by a beguiling simplicity. Few non-religious buildings from this period have survived to modern times, either in Italy or anywhere else in Europe.

The standard ground plan, generally composed of a nave and two aisles, no transept and between one and five apses, topped by a simple bowl-shaped cupola, followed that used in Roman-era basilicas. Initially at any rate, churches tended to be bereft of decoration except for the semicircular arches above doorways and windows. The apses tended to be semicircular too. Such churches were most commonly accompanied by a free-standing square-based bell tower, also adorned with layers of semicircular arched windows.

In Tuscany, the early rediscovery of that favourite of Roman building materials, marble, led to a rather more florid decorative style, the best examples of which can be seen in Pisa and Lucca, to the north-west of Florence. The key characteristics of this

JULIA WILKINSON

The Chiesa di San Miniato al Monte is a fine example of Romanesque architecture.

variant are the use of two-tone marble banding and complex rows of columns and loggias in the facade.

In Florence itself, the main remaining examples of Romanesque building are the Baptistry, the Chiesa dei Santi Apostoli and the Chiesa di San Miniato al Monte. The latter is the finest example of Florentine Romanesque.

Gothic The transition across Europe from Romanesque to the massive forms of the Gothic style was uniformly spectacular but extraordinarily varied in its results. Most of us, when thinking of Gothic, have in mind the improbable lace stonework of the Gothic cathedrals of northern Europe, from the Notre Dame churches of Paris and Amiens to the powerful hulk of the Cologne Dom in Germany. Compared with their humble Romanesque predecessors they are colossal.

Complex structures were perfected using pillars, columns, arches and vaulting of various kinds to support soaring ceilings. Rather than relying on the solidity of mass, and building thick, heavy walls, priority was given to an almost diaphanous light pouring through tall pointed windows. Such fragile structures could not stand the weight of the roof, so outer walls connected by buttressing took the strain. The whole was topped off by an almost obsessive desire to decorate. Such churches are bedecked with pinnacles, statues, gargoyles and all sorts of baubles. The busier the better.

Examples of that northern European style of Gothic are few and far between in Italy, and in Florence non-existent. The city's two great Gothic churches are Santa Croce and Santa Maria Novella, built for the dominant preaching orders of the time, respectively the Franciscans and the Dominicans. Construction of both began in the 13th century but was not completed until well into the 14th century.

In terms of volume they are every bit as impressive as their northern counterparts. Inside Santa Maria Novella, designed by Dominican friars, you can admire the complex ribbed vaulting of the main ceiling above the nave, but there the similarities end. Decoration is minimal. The plastered surfaces of the wall contrast with the bare stone that dominates northern churches. The bicolour banding that edges arches and vaults is a Tuscan touch. Frequently in place of tall Gothic windows in the walls you see small round windows, or oculi. The width of the nave and lack of clutter make up for this and allow in plenty of light.

Santa Croce was designed by the Siena-born Arnolfo di Cambio (1245–probably 1302), the first great master builder in Florentine architectural history. It shares with Santa Maria Novella the broad nave and simplicity of interior decoration. In the privileged place given to uncovered stone it harks to the north and, in contrast to the Dominican church, an A-frame timber ceiling (a carena) obscures the roof vaulting.

More striking because it is something of a one-off is Arnolfo's Palazzo Vecchio (known when it was built as Palazzo dei Priori and later as Palazzo della Signoria). Built of pietra forte with the rusticated surface typical of many grand buildings in Florence, it is one of the most imposing government buildings of the medieval Italian city-states. Its slightly odd shape and the off-centre placing of the distinctive tower lend the structure a brooding but powerful, no-nonsense aspect, no doubt the desired effect in a city continually rent by factional strife.

Arnolfo also designed the Gothic Duomo (also known as the Santa Maria del Fiore) and it is thought that, when he died, construction of the nave had reached the transept. Giotto (see Painting in the special colour section 'Painting & Sculpture in Florence'), although fundamentally a painter, was entrusted with the task of designing the Campanile (bell tower) for the Duomo. It is quirkily unique, betraying Giotto's preference for a soft if graceful simplicity in form and decoration. He only completed the base and was succeeded by Andrea Pisano (c. 1290–1348) and finally Francesco Talenti (active 1325–69). Clearly Gothic elements include the windows (decidedly French), while the dual colour banding is typical of the Tuscan approach to decoration already evident in Romanesque buildings.

Talenti amended Arnolfo's design for the Duomo and added unique polygonal apses, each with five chapels. He drew an octagonal dome between the apses, but had no grander ideas on how to build it than did Arnolfo.

The Chiesa di Orsanmichele, built by Talenti and others between 1337 and 1350, is an outstanding example of florid Gothic. Other important Gothic buildings raised in Florence include: the Bargello, the Ponte Vecchio, the Palazzo Spini-Feroni, the Palazzo Davanzati and the Chiesa della Santa Trinita.

Bad Boy Brunelleschi Enter Filippo Brunelleschi (1377–1446), one of the hotter tempers in the history of Italian architecture. After failing to win the 1401–02 competition to design a set of bronze doors for the Baptistry (see The 15th Century under Sculpture in the special colour section 'Painting & Sculpture in Florence'), Brunelleschi left in a creative huff for Rome. His intention had been to study and continue with sculpture, but his interests slid across to mathematics and architecture. He and his sculptor pal Donatello spent much of their time taking measurements of ancient Roman monuments, storing up knowledge that would later come to spectacular fruition. The locals, however, thought they were using bizarre divining methods to look for buried treasure!

Brunelleschi would launch the architectural branch of the Renaissance in Florence. It manifested itself in a rediscovery of simplicity and purity in classical building, with great attention paid to perspective and harmonious distribution of space and volume.

His single most remarkable achievement was solving the Duomo dome conundrum. He proposed to raise the octagonal-based dome without the aid of scaffolding, unheard of at the time. Although incredulous, the signoria agreed to commission him. Brunelleschi's double-skinned dome, raised in sections, was the greatest feat of its kind since ancient times. In later years Michelangelo, when commissioned to create the dome for St Peter's (San Pietro) in Rome, observed with undisguised admiration, '*io farò la sorella, già più gran ma non più bella* (I'll make its [the Brunelleschi dome's] sister bigger, yes, but no more beautiful)'.

That feat alone was tremendous but Brunelleschi's importance goes beyond the splendid dome. He 'created' the role of architect. Rather than act as a foreman, guiding construction as it progressed and to some extent making it up as he went along, Brunelleschi devised formulae of perspective and balance that allowed him to create a completed concept at the drawing board. Inspired by Roman engineering and Tuscan aesthetics, he launched a new era in construction. In essence, the architectural Renaissance, based on the rational tackling of human and mathematical problems, took flight with him. Other examples of Brunelleschi's keen sense of human proportion are: the portico of the Ospedale (hospital) degli Innocenti (1419), considered the earliest work of the Florentine Renaissance; the Sagrestia Vecchia (Old Sacristy) in San Lorenzo (1428); and the Cappella dei Pazzi in Santa Croce (1430).

Perhaps more importantly, Brunelleschi was also called upon to design the Basilica di San Lorenzo (1420) and the Basilica di Santo Spirito (designed in 1436). San Lorenzo had Medici money behind it, allowing Brunelleschi some latitude in design and choice of materials. Brunelleschi died long before either project reached completion and the supervisors who came after him were not always faithful to his plans.

A quick wander inside both might lead the casual observer to think they are identical. The use of Corinthian columns, simple arches, a coffered ceiling over the wide nave (merely painted in Santo Spirito) and two-tone (grey pietra serena and white intonaco on the trim) colouring are common elements. Closer inspection soon reveals differences. Brunelleschi planned for Santo Spirito to be lined with semicircular chapels jutting out into the square around it – these were walled in. Santo Spirito is an altogether heavier, more massive church in its feel, while San Lorenzo oozes a light elegance. It is not known what, if any, ideas Brunelleschi had for the facades. San Lorenzo still has none.

Brunelleschi had a mean temper and more than once flounced out of meetings and dropped projects if he did not get his own way. But he was good, and most of the time he ended up getting his way. For the Florence we see today, in his monuments and in those of many architects who followed him, we owe a considerable debt of thanks to the genius of Brunelleschi.

Beyond Brunelleschi It is generally accepted that Cosimo de' Medici commissioned Michelozzo di Bartolommeo Michelozzi (1396–1472) to build a new residence in keeping with the family's importance but that didn't stand out too much. Brunelleschi had proposed something altogether too grand for Cosimo's liking, whose policy was to keep his head down while effectively ruling the city. Brunelleschi, predictably, flew into a rage and smashed the model.

Michelozzo's building (now known as Palazzo Medici-Riccardi) was nevertheless no unprepossessing dwarf. Three hefty storeys, with the air somewhat of a fortress, are topped by a solid roof with eaves jutting far out from the walls – a typical trait of Florentine mansions of the period. The lowest storey features rustication (which you can also see on the Palazzo Vecchio). This describes the rough-hewn, protruding blocks of stone used to build it, as opposed to the smoothed stone of the upper storeys. Another of Michelozzo's finer achievements was the library in the former Convento di San Marco.

The acclaimed theorist of Renaissance architecture and art was Leon Battista Alberti (1404–72). Born in Genoa into an exiled Florentine family, he was a true Renaissance figure, learned and multitalented. To his native city he contributed only the facades of the Palazzo Rucellai and Basilica di Santa Maria Novella, both particularly striking and original. His influence on artists, sculptors and architects in Florence and beyond came above all through his many writings.

It is thought that the initial 15th-century core of the Palazzo Pitti (begun in 1458) was built for the powerful if rather mouthy Luca Pitti by a follower of Alberti, the Settignano-born Luca Fancelli (1430–95). Experts are increasingly convinced that Brunelleschi actually provided the design.

Benedetto da Maiano (1442–97) was chosen by Filippo Strozzi to build the Strozzi family mansion. In terms of size alone it outstrips any of the great mansions (*palazzi*) raised during the Medici era. A contemporary of Benedetto, Giuliano da Sangallo (1445–1516) provided the wooden model in which rusticated stone would be used on all three storeys. However, he chose to smooth the surface of the stone in his plan, and also in a building he later built himself, Palazzo Gondi. Benedetto took this lead and went a step further by planning the lengths of stone and their placement. The courtyard, attributed to Simone del Pollaiuolo (1457–1508), better known as Il Cronaca, is considered one of Florence's finest. Il Cronaca also designed other residences and the Chiesa di San Salvatore al Monte. To Benedetto's brother, Giuliano da Maiano (1432–90), is generally attributed another mansion, the Palazzo Pazzi.

Michelangelo Born to a poor family, Michelangelo Buonarroti (1475–1564) got a lucky break early on, entering the Medici household as a privileged student of painting and sculpture. In later years he also turned his attention to building design, although his architectural activities in Florence were not extensive. Called back from Rome in 1516 to design a facade for the Basilica di San Lorenzo, the project was dropped and he ended up working on the Sagrestia Nuova (New Sacristy) for the same church, intended as part of the funerary chapels for the Medici family. Although not completed as planned, this was as close as Michelangelo got to finishing one of his architectural-sculptural whims.

Another of Michelangelo's tasks in the same church was the grand staircase and

JULIET COOMBE

Michelangelo's tomb for Giuliano de' Medici in the Cappelle Medicee

entrance hall for the Laurentian Library (Biblioteca Medicea Laurenziana). Michelangelo never saw it completed, as he returned to Rome beforehand. It is a startling late-Renaissance creation, with columns recessed into the walls (and thus deprived of their natural supporting function) and other architectural oddities since seen as precursors of Mannerism. The reading room he designed was to lead to a strange, triangular, rare-books room that, had it been built, would have been one of the oddest of Renaissance creations.

For more about Michelangelo, see Painting in the special colour section 'Painting & Sculpture in Florence'.

Mannerism Most scholars date the end of the later, or High, Renaissance around 1520. Certainly by 1527, with the sack of Rome, it was all over, if only because war and suffering had snuffed out the funds and desire to continue creating in such quantity.

What followed is generally called Mannerism, though this intermediate phase be-tween the Renaissance and baroque is not easily defined. For many, Michelangelo's work in San Lorenzo is a clear precursor to the Mannerist period. For others, the Mannerists were a fairly unimaginative lot, fiddling around the edges of what had been the core of Renaissance thinking in architecture without making substantive innovations.

Antonio da Sangallo il Giovane (1485–1546), the son of another Florentine architect and sculptor, Antonio da Sangallo il Vecchio, worked mostly in Rome, though he returned briefly to Florence to build the Fortezza da Basso in 1534 for Alessandro de' Medici. It is a menacing fortress aimed more at the Florentines than at external enemies.

Bartolommeo Amannati (1511–92), expanded the Palazzo Pitti into a suburban palace for the Medici dukes and designed the Ponte Santa Trinita. He also had a hand in the design of the Boboli Gardens.

Giorgio Vasari (1511–74), although born in Arezzo, has to be mentioned as the creator of the Uffizi and the Corridoio Vasariano that links Palazzo Vecchio with Palazzo Pitti across the Arno.

Bernardo Buontalenti (1536–1608) succeeded Vasari as architect to the grand duke of Tuscany. He designed the Forte di Belvedere and the Casino Mediceo, near the former Chiesa di San Marco. Both demonstrate the Florentine tendency to retain a certain sobriety in construction, although by now mixed with occasional outbursts of almost misplaced fantasy in decoration. The monkey motifs in the Casino are an example. He also designed the Palazzo Nonfinito on Via del Proconsolo, which differs from its Renaissance predecessors principally in decorative flounces on the facade.

Don't Baroque the Boat The 17th century brought little new construction of note in Florence, although many projects to restructure, expand or finish existing sites were underway. This was the era of baroque, which often had more impact on decor than architectural design. At its most extreme, particularly in Rome, such decoration was sumptuous to the point of giddiness, all curvaceous statuary, twisting pillars and assorted bubbly baubles. In Florence, however, a by now long-established tradition of restraint excluded such excesses, and clear cases of baroque architecture are few and far between.

A couple of notable examples include the Chiesa di San Gaetano and the facade for the Chiesa di Ognissanti. The former, finished by Gherardo Silvani (1579–1675), is considered the finest piece of baroque in Florence and a demonstration of the restraint typical of the city – in stark contrast to the flamboyant baroque of Rome. Silvani was Florence's most prolific architect in this period, having a hand in the construction of several family mansions.

Other edifices dating to this period are Palazzo Corsini and, across the river to the west, the Chiesa di San Frediano in Cestello. Work on the former went on for the best part of a century and comes closest to the more grandiose Roman baroque ideas on the building of family residences.

An imposing example of late-baroque building is the San Firenze complex on the piazza of the same name. Construction was plagued by delays and subject to repeated change, and the final design for the facade was not completed until 1775, although the style was largely faithful to designs of the previous century.

Urban Renewal The trend already set in the 17th century continued into the 18th. Florentines tinkered with their city without troubling themselves over great or worthy additions. Piazza San Marco as we see it today was finalised under Grand Duke Pietro Leopoldo.

After Napoleon's French rulers retired, the process of urban renewal continued. The space around the southern flank of the Duomo was cleared and fronted by neoclassical buildings. The architect behind that project was Gaetano Baccani (1792–1867), who also built the singular Palazzo Borghese in distinctive imperial style on Via Ghibellina. It was around this time that the former Stinche prison, also on Via Ghi-

bellina, was converted into a theatre (now called the Teatro Verdi) in the neoclassical style.

East and west of the town centre two new bridges went up on the Arno, the Ponte San Niccolò and the Ponte alla Vittoria (the names were different then). French engineers raised them and in so doing introduced to Florence the use of metals in construction.

Between the 1840s and the 1870s (ie from the unstable years prior to the Europe-wide uprisings of 1848 through to Florence's limited days as capital of the newly united Italy), a programme of street-widening in the historical centre gathered pace. It may have improved traffic flow and hygiene, but it meant tearing away centuries of history. Neoclassical facades replaced medieval leftovers. In conjunction with that project came the creation of Piazza della Repubblica in the 1890s, for the sake of which much of the heart of old Florence was ripped out. In its place came porticoes and arcades, presumably to reflect a grandeur that Florence could no longer really boast.

Between 1865 and 1869 the city walls north of the Arno were pulled down and replaced by the boulevards (the Parisian influence is unmistakable) you still see today. The *lungarni*, the roads that follow the course of the river, were also laid out in this period.

The Mercato Centrale (finished in 1874) is a rare Florentine example of the late-19th-century passion for iron and glass structures, designed by Giuseppe Mengoni (1829–77), the Bologna-born architect responsible for Milan's Galleria Vittoria Emanuele.

The 20th Century One of the few early 20th-century residences to survive is the Casa Galleria by Giovanni Michelazzi (1879–1920) at Borgo Ognissanti 26. Its facade is quite startling, a sort of imperious Art Nouveau.

The Stazione di Santa Maria Novella (Florence's main train station), completed in 1935, is a fairly typical example of Fascist-era building. Countless Italian cities were blessed with such new stations.

Clearly Mussolini was intent not only on making the trains run on time, but also on giving them a grand reception when they arrived. Sport was almost as important to the Blackshirts as trains, so Florence also got Stadio Franchi in Campo di Marte.

Little of interest has appeared on Florence's skyline since the interwar years and town planning has been haphazard to say the least. The sprawling suburbs to the north and west are a disheartening jumble where the colour green has been submerged beneath a wave of third-rate cheap housing and factories.

Literature

First Stirrings Long after the fall of Rome, Latin remained the language of learned discourse and writing throughout Italy. The elevation of local tongues to literary status was a long and weary process, and the case of Italian was no exception.

In the mid-13th century, Tuscan poets started to experiment with verse and song in the local tongue, inspired by the troubadours of Provence and a Sicilian tradition that had itself grown out of the Provençal experience. Such early poets included Chiaro Davanzati (d. 1303) and Guittone d'Arezzo (c. 1235–94), whose writings also included political and moral treatises in verse. Brunetto Latini (1212–94) was not only recognised as one of Florence's finer poets, he was also Dante's instructor.

The Master All the poetry, song, didactic and religious literature of 13th-century writers in Tuscany, and indeed beyond, would appear as nothing before the genius of the Florentine Dante Alighieri (1265–1321). Dante wrote on many subjects and often in Latin, but when he decided to compose the *Divina Commedia (Divine Comedy)* in the 'vulgar' tongue of his countrymen, he was truly inspired.

Dante himself would not take all the credit. He was full of praise for the poet Guido Cavalcanti (c. 1250–1300), inventor of the *dolce stil nuovo* (sweet new style) in Tuscan that Dante turned into the tool of his most exalted writings.

The protagonist is escorted on a journey through hell, purgatory and heaven in a work so dense with subtext that scholars are still beavering away at it today. At once a religious work and a cautionary tale, it operates on a far more complex level too.

The gloomy circles of Dante's hell do not serve merely to remind his readers of the wages of sin. Far more interestingly, they become an uneasy resting place for a parade of characters, many of them his contemporaries, whom he judged worthy of an uncomfortable time in the next life. Political and religious figures of all persuasions get short shrift. Others come out looking better in his vision of purgatory and heaven.

Dante's extraordinary capacity to construct and tell stories within stories would have ensured him a place in the pantheon of scribblers regardless of his language of delivery. But Dante's decision to write in his Tuscan dialect was a literary coup. In doing so he catapulted Italian, or at least a version of it, to the literary stage. Scholars have been enthusing ever since that Italian was 'born' with Dante's *Commedia*.

Petrarch & Boccaccio Dante does not stand completely alone, and two Tuscan successors form with him the literary triumvirate that laid down the course for the development of a rich Italian literature.

Petrarch (Francesco Petrarca; 1304–74), born in Arezzo to Florentine parents who had been exiled from their city about the same time as Dante, actually wrote more in Latin than in Italian. *Il Canzoniere* is the distilled result of his finest poetry. Although the core subject is the unrequited love for a girl called Laura, the whole breadth of human grief and joy is treated with a lyric quality hitherto unmatched. So striking was his clear, passionate verse, filtered through his knowledge of the classics, that across Europe emerged a phenomenon known as *petrarchismo* – the desire of writers within and beyond Italy to emulate him.

Contemporary and friend of Petrarch was the Florentine Giovanni Boccaccio (1313–75). His masterpiece was the *Decameron*, written in the years immediately following the plague of 1348, which he survived in Florence. His 10 characters each recount a story in which a vast panorama of personalities, events and symbolism are explored.

The Renaissance Even as the Renaissance in fine arts was getting under way in Florence, writers were amusing themselves with language too. Burchiello (1404–49), a barber, would host writers, painters and other creative types in his shop, where they fooled around with verse. The sonnets that have remained often seem to make little sense, leaping from one subject to another, with references to people and events by now unknown even to scholars. The importance of this verse lies more in the extent to which it shows writers actively searching for new forms of expression. Such a search fits in nicely with the age.

Lorenzo the Magnificent dominated the second half of the 15th century in Florence and was handy with a pen himself. His enlightened approach to learning and the arts created a healthy atmosphere for writers.

Angelo Ambrogini (1454–94) was born in Montepulciano but ended up in Florence. Known as Il Poliziano, he is considered one of Italy's most important 15th-century poets in Latin and Italian. His major work in the latter is the allegorical tale *Stanze per la Giostra (Verses for the Joust)* penned to celebrate the victory of Giuliano de' Medici at such a contest.

Another outstanding writer of the Florentine Renaissance is Niccolò Machiavelli (1469–1527). He is known above all for his work on power and politics, *Il Principe* or *The Prince* (see the boxed text 'Machiavelli's Manoeuvres'). But he was a prolific writer in many fields. His *Mandragola* is a lively piece of comic theatre and a virtuoso example of Italian literature.

A little more staid is the principal work of Francesco Guicciardini (1483–1540), a wily statesman and historian. His *Storia d'Italia* might never have been written had Cosimo I not dispensed with his services shortly after becoming duke in 1537.

Back to the Source

The intellectual foundation for the Renaissance lay in what was even then known as Humanism. The term is applied in many contexts philosophically, but in the case of the Umanisti of Florence and northern Italy it refers to the renewed striving for knowledge that came with the rediscovery of the classics.

The term Humanism comes from *studia humanitatis*, a course of studies covering poetry, grammar, rhetoric, history and moral philosophy. The pursuit of such studies was not the activity of mere dilettantes. The goal of the Umanisti was the attainment of *humanitas*, a Latin term that to the 15th-century mind encompassed a gamut of human characteristics. He who truly had humanitas knew to combine knowledge and wisdom with action. The ideal Umanista was compassionate and merciful, but also strong, eloquent and honourable. Action without knowledge and wisdom was barbaric, but the sedentary accumulation of knowledge barren.

Renewed interest in and the availability of the classics from the 14th century spurred students and professors on to pursue new avenues of learning. The translation and distribution of the Greek classics in particular came as a breath of fresh air in the medieval world, still largely caught up in the strictures of Christian teaching.

Rediscovering the ancients' views on morality and ethics, not to mention their ideas on how the physical world worked, opened doors that had long seemed shut. Through the old, teachers, philosophers, writers, artists, sculptors and architects found themselves impelled to reach out for the new, with a greater emphasis on human capacity and responsibility. It is conceivable that without the Umanisti and their enthusiastic rediscovery and reinterpretation of the classics, there may have been no Renaissance.

❖ ❖

Machiavelli's Manoeuvres

JANE SMITH

Born in 1469 into a poor branch of what had been one of Florence's leading families, Niccolò Machiavelli got off to a bad start. His father was a small-time lawyer whose practice had been all but strangled by the city authorities as he was a debtor. Young Niccolò missed out on the best schools and could consider himself lucky that his father was at least rich in books. His prospects were not sparkling.

Somehow he managed to swing a post in the city's second chancery at the age of 29, and so embarked on a colourful career as a Florentine public servant. His tasks covered a range of internal dealings in Florence and some aspects of foreign affairs and defence. Our man must have shown early promise, as by 1500 he was in France on his first diplomatic mission. A couple of years later he married Marietta Corsini, with whom he would have five children in the following 12 years.

Impressed by the marshal success of Cesare Borgia and the centralised state of France, Machiavelli came to the conclusion that Florence needed a standing army. The city, like many others across the length and breadth of the Italian peninsula, had a habit of employing mercenaries to fight its wars. The problem with that system was that mercenaries had few reasons to fight and die for anyone. They took their pay and as often as not did their level best to avoid mortal combat.

Machiavelli managed to convince his rulers of the advantages of an army raised to defend hearth and home and so in 1506 formed a conscript militia. In 1509 he got to try it out on the rebellious city of Pisa, whose fall was in large measure attributed to the troops led by the wily statesman. He was back two years later to dismantle a French-backed schismatic council there.

Florence, however, was not Rome's flavour of the month and troops from the Holy See and its allies marched on the city. Machiavelli was now defending not only his hearth but his future – to no avail.

The return of the Medici family to power was a blow for Machiavelli, who was promptly removed from all posts. Suspected of plotting against the Medici, he was even thrown into the dungeon in 1513 and tortured. He maintained his innocence and was freed, but reduced to penury as he retired to his little property outside Florence.

It was in these years that he produced his greatest writing. *Il Principe (The Prince)* is his classic treatise on the nature of power and its administration. In it he developed his theories not only on politics and power but on history and human behaviour. What was a thoroughly demoralising time Machiavelli thus turned to good account for generations to come. The work and other writings reflect the confusing and corrupt times in which he lived, and his desire for strong and just rule, in Florence and beyond.

He ached to get back into active public life too, but in this he was never to be truly satisfied. He was commissioned to write an official history of Florence, the *Istorie Fiorentine*, and towards the end of his life was appointed to a defence commission to improve the city walls and join a papal army in its ultimately futile fight against imperial forces. By the time the latter had sacked Rome in 1527, Florence had again rid itself of the Medici. Machiavelli hoped that he would be restored to a position of dignity, but by now he was suspected almost as much by the Medicis' opponents as he had been years before by the Medici. He died frustrated and, as in his youth, on the brink of poverty, in 1527.

17th to 19th Centuries Although plenty of lesser scribblers were busy through these centuries, Florence cannot really claim to have produced any outstanding names. There is, as usual, at least one exception to prove the rule. Carlo Lorenzini (1826–90), better known to Italians of all ages under the pseudonym of Carlo Collodi, was the creator of *Le Avventure di Pinocchio*. Outside Italy, Pinocchio has come to be known more in his saccharine Walt Disney guise, but in Italy this best seller has been a source of amusement and instruction for children and adults for generations.

The first signs of change in theatre away from commedia dell'arte (popular comedy), which had become something of a fixture in the Italian repertoire since the early 16th century, emerged in Florence. Giovanni Battista Fagiuoli (1660–1742) was among those who made the first tentative steps away from the old forms, but it would fall to the Venetian Carlo Goldoni to work a true revolution in the theatre.

The Mussolini Years By the 1920s and 30s Florence was bubbling with activity as a series of literary magazines flourished, at least for a while, in spite of the Fascist regime. Magazines such as *Solaria*, which lasted from 1926 to 1934, its successor *Letteratura* (which began circulating in 1937) and *Il Frontespizio* (from 1929 to 40) gave writers from across Italy a platform from which to launch and discuss their work. These were not the easiest of times, and most of the magazines, including Vasco Pratolini's short-lived *Campo di Marte,* fell prey sooner or later to censorship. That some lasted as long as they did is remarkable enough.

To the Present Few Florentine writers this century have gained a particularly high profile. One exception to that rule is Vasco Pratolini (1913–91), son of a manual labourer and self-taught writer who dabbled successfully in theatre and cinema as well as the novel and poetry. Among his most enduring works is the trilogy *Una Storia Italiana (An Italian Story)*, whose first part, *Metello*, set

off a heated debate in Italian literary circles. Those who liked it saw in the novel a mature departure from neorealism to a more robust realism. Pratolini's detractors considered him still caught in a rigid and limited ideological trap. The trilogy follows the lives of working and middle-class Florentines, through whom Pratolini analyses a variety of political, social and emotional issues.

Dacia Maraina (b. 1936) is with little doubt Florence's most prominent contemporary female author, with some 10 novels to her credit. An interesting one is *Voci (Voices)*, in which a woman journalist embarks on the investigation of a murder. The main character has little to go on – the corpse of a young girl and a pair of blue running shoes. Why, she asks herself, do women seem so readily disposed to opening their homes to whoever knocks at the door? A mystery laced with disturbing social comment.

Other Florentine writers of lesser note this century include: Bruno Cicognani (1879–1971); Aldo Palazzeschi (1885–1974); Anna Banti (1895–1985); Emilio Cecchi (1884–1966); Alessandro Bonsanti (1904–84); Romano Bilenchi (1909–89) and Mario Luzi (b. 1914).

Music

The epicentre of the greatest explosion in the world of fine arts and the birthplace of literary Italian, Florence has not made such illustrious contributions to the world of music.

The Rome-born composer Jacopo Peri (1561–1633) moved to Florence in 1588 to serve the Medici court. He and Florentine writer Ottavio Rinuccini (1562–1621) are credited with having created the first opera in the modern sense, *Dafne*, in 1598. They and Giulio Caccini (1550–1618) also wrote *Euridice* a couple of years later. It is the oldest opera for which the complete score still exists. All three were part of a Florentine group of intellectuals known as the Camerata, which worked to revive and develop ancient Greek musical traditions in theatre.

Florence's next musical contribution was a key development, although it came at the hands of a Paduan resident on the Arno. In 1711 Bartolomeo Cristofori (1655–1731) invented the pianoforte.

In 1632, Giovanni Battista Lulli was born in Florence. The name may not ring too many bells until we add that he moved to France where he would dominate the musical life of the court of Louis XIV as Jean-Baptiste Lully. With Molière he created new dramatic forms such as the comedy-ballet. He also gave instrumental suites their definitive form.

Another Florentine export to Paris was the composer Luigi Cherubini (1760–1842) who somehow managed the tricky feat of keeping his head attached to his torso through the French Revolution, the Napoleonic era and the Restoration.

On a quite different note, one of Italy's leading rock bands, Litfiba, happens to be a Florentine product.

Cinema

The Italian cinema has known periods of enormous productivity and contributed some of Europe's proudest gems on film. Most people think of the postwar period of neorealism as the apogee of Italian film-making, and there is no doubting the richness of the output at that time. It didn't end there, and Italy has continued to produce good directors ever since.

Florence, however, has had remarkably little impact on the world of movies, used occasionally as a set and producing only the rare directing or acting talent. Greatness might have come Florence's way. Filoteo Alberini had created his *kinotegrafo* in 1895, a year before the Lumière brothers patented their *cinématographe* (cinematograph) in Paris. No one in Florence was interested, and Alberini moved to Rome, where he created the Cines, which would grow to command the stage in the early years of Italian cinema.

A second chance came in the 1920s when a Florentine gent by the name of Giovanni Montalbano set up studios in Rifredi to produce great historical blockbusters. The enterprise pumped out some pretty poor flicks and soon went belly up.

An early Florentine film-maker of note was Gianni Franciolini (1910–60). After spending about 10 years in France learning journalism and then film, Franciolini returned to Italy in 1940, from which time he turned out a film almost every year until his death. An early flick, *Fari Nella Nebbia* (*Headlights in the Mist*; 1941) shows the French influence on his ideas, but also presages the fecund period of Italian film-making that lay just around the corner – neorealism.

The biggest name to come out of Florence is, with little doubt, Franco Zeffirelli (b. 1923). His varied career took him from radio and theatre to opera productions and occasional stints as aide to Luchino Visconti on several films. His film-directing days began in earnest in the late 1970s. Some of you may remember his TV blockbuster *Jesus of Nazareth* (1977). Many of his productions have been non-Italian. A couple of his more interesting ones were *Young Toscanini* (1988) and *Hamlet* (1990), a British-US co-production. He visited his home town to film *Tea with Mussolini*, starring Maggie Smith, which hit the screens in 1999.

In the genre of TV blockbusters, Franco Rossi (b. 1919) started directing films in the 1950s but moved increasingly to TV. His Italian TV films included *Il Giovane Garibaldi* (*The Young Garibaldi*; 1973), *Quo Vadis?* (1984) and *Un Bambino di Nome Gesù* (*A Baby Called Jesus*; 1988).

Neri Parenti (b. 1950) started directing in 1979. Since 1980 he has been kept busy directing the comedian Paolo Villaggi in a seemingly endless stream of films starring Fantozzi, Villaggio's best-known comic character. Fantozzi is a sort of thinking man's cross between Mr Bean and Benny Hill. The humour can swing pretty low, but he's popular.

Two of Italy's success stories at the moment are Tuscan if not Florentine. Light-hearted comedy is a forte of Leonardo Pieraccioni (b. 1965). His *Il Ciclone* (*The Cyclone*; 1996), about the effects of the arrival of a small flamenco troupe on the lads of a small Tuscan town, was a big hit.

Humour with considerably greater depth is, however, the department of Roberto Benigni (b. 1952). Long established as one of Italy's favourite comedy actors, he must be the first director to try to get a laugh out of the Holocaust – and succeed. He picked up three Oscars in 1999, including Best Actor, an honour rarely bestowed by Hollywood upon anyone but its own, for his *La Vita è Bella* (*Life is Beautiful*; 1998). The film, which he directed and starred in, is the story of an Italian Jewish family that ends up in the camps, where the father tries to hide its horrors from his son by pretending it's all a game. Benigni was already known to cinema-goers outside Italy for his appearances in Jim Jarmusch's *Down by Law* and *Night on Earth*. Charlie Chaplin's daughter, Geraldine, declared months after the Oscars that Benigni had inherited her father's cinematic poetry. Quite an accolade.

Florence as Star

The first movie filmed on location in Florence was Enrico Novelli's *Fiorenza Mia (My Florence)* in 1915. Probably the best Italian films shot in Florence were those based on books by Vasco Pratolini, including *Cronache di Poveri Amanti* (*Stories of Poor Lovers*; 1953), *Le Ragazze di San Frediano* (*The Girls of San Frediano*; 1954), *Cronaca Familiare* (*Family Chronicles*; 1962) and *Metello* (1970).

Roberto Pasolini also included Florence in one of the three episodes that make up his 1946 classic, *Paisà*, which recounts three stages of the Allied campaign in Italy in WWII.

A local researcher, Andrea Vannini, has found that the favourite Florentine locations chosen by film-makers are, in descending order, Piazza della Signoria, Ponte Vecchio, Piazza del Duomo, Piazzale Michelangelo, the steps of San Miniato al Monte and Piazza Santo Spirito.

Perhaps the best-known and most flattering treatment of the city came in James Ivory's 1985 rendition of the EM Forster classic *A Room with a View*, starring Helena Bonham Carter.

SOCIETY & CONDUCT

Florentines, perhaps even more than other Italians, take particular pride in their dress and appearance. To many outsiders such concerns can seem a trifle overdone. In some cases, however, those outsiders seem to abandon the norms they would normally adhere to at home as soon as they hit the holiday trail.

Leaving aside the sartorial spectacle of the loud-shirts-and-shorts brigade, there are those who seem to think walking around with precious little on is the only way to fly. Your average Florentine has grown accustomed to the odd ways of the *stranieri* (foreigners), but in restaurants, cafes and bars it doesn't hurt to at least put your shirt back on!

Most churches (including the Duomo) will not allow you entry if it is deemed you are inadequately attired. No-one's suggesting you bring your Sunday best along, but a little common sense and sensitivity go a long way.

The standard form of greeting is the handshake. Kissing on both cheeks is generally reserved for people who already know one another. There will always be exceptions to these rules, so the best thing on being introduced to locals is probably not to launch your lips in anyone's general direction unless you are pretty sure they are welcome. If this is the case, a light brushing of cheeks will do.

RELIGION

As elsewhere in Italy, Catholicism is the dominant religion, but the history of Florence's relations with the Church is chequered, to say the least. In days when religion and politics were often one and the same thing, Florence sometimes found itself on the receiving end of some nasty papal invective. The rise of the Medici was in no small part due to their power as a European banking dynasty, in turn fuelled by lucrative accounts with the papal curia. This could work both ways, and the Pazzi conspiracy against Lorenzo the Magnificent grew largely out of conflict with the pope. That very conflict, which saw a coalition of forces march on Florence that the city had little hope of withstanding, illustrated clearly just how low relations with the pope could go. After the pope issued a bull of excommunication on the entire city, the city's bishops turned around and issued a counter-bull excommunicating the pope! That particular spat ended only when Lorenzo sailed for Naples to do some horse-trading. The result wasn't wonderful, but better than seeing the city wiped out by the pope and his allies, as surely would otherwise have happened.

Catholicism became the state religion of the new Italian nation when unity was com-pleted in 1870. Only when the 1929 Lateran Treaty between the Vatican and the Italian state was modified in 1985 was Catholicism dropped as the state religion.

Still, as many as 85% of Italians profess to be Catholic, and roughly the same figure can probably be applied to Florence. There is also a small Protestant population, made up of various denominations and consisting mostly of the expat community. Florence, interestingly, is one of the country's biggest centres of Buddhism, which has about 5000 followers throughout Tuscany.

PAINTING & SCULPTURE IN FLORENCE

DAMIEN SIMONIS

The painting to emerge in medieval Europe – and Florence was no exception – was not so much a response to an aesthetic need as a means of keeping alive in the minds of the faithful the stories of the Bible and teachings of the Church. Art was to be devotional and instructive (most people, even among the wealthiest classes, were illiterate or as near as dammit).

For this reason, as you will soon come to notice the more you study the paintings of Florence over the centuries, many themes became standard and crop up again and again. The bulk of Romanesque-, Byzantine- and Gothic-era art was commissioned (though not always paid for) by the Church for churches, monasteries and other religious institutions. The clergy generally had a clear idea of what they wanted depicted and gave precise instructions to painters. The latter were classed as artisans and viewed much as tradespeople are today. There was little exaltation of their skills and until the dawn of the Renaissance few artists even signed their work.

As greater individuality and an aesthetic appreciation of painting, apart from its didactic or devotional purposes, emerged with the Renaissance, so its practitioners gained in social standing.

Oh Madonna!

As so much of the art of medieval and Renaissance Europe falls into distinct thematic groups, the titles of many paintings in particular are nearly always the same. You will rarely see such stock titles translated in English while in Florence, so a handful of clues follow.

A *Crocifissione* (Crucifixion) represents the crucifixion of Christ, one of the most common subjects of religious art. Another is the *Deposizione* (Deposition), which depicts the taking down of the body of Christ from the Cross, while the *Pietà*, a particularly popular subject for sculptors, shows the lifeless body of Christ in the arms of his followers – the characters can vary, but the theme remains the same. Before all the nastiness began, Christ managed to have a Last Supper, or *Ultima Cena*, with the Apostles.

Perhaps the most favoured subject is the *Madonna col Bambino/Bimbo* (Virgin Mary with Christ Child). The variations on this theme are legion. Sometimes they are depicted alone, sometimes with various *santi* (saints), *angeli* (angels) and other figures. The *Annunciazione* (Annunciation) is yet another standard episode, when the Angel Gabriel announces to Mary the strange honour that has been bestowed upon her. When the big event occurred, lots of people, including the *Magi* (Wise Men) came to participate in the *Adorazione* (Adoration) of the newly born Christ.

Title page: Fra Filippo Lippi's *Madonna col Bambino e due Angeli (Madonna with Child and Two Angels)* has been in the Uffizi since 1796.

Above left: Detail from the Duomo

JULIET COOMBE

In Florence especially, but also elsewhere in Italy and beyond, laypeople began to commission art, either for public places or their own homes. This promoted a broadening of themes, but even through the Renaissance and beyond much output remained faithful to a series of frequently stock religious themes. Innovation was not always easy under such conditions.

Still, other genres developed too. Battle scenes, portraits (generally busts) and scenes from classical mythology gained ground during the Renaissance.

Florence as a centre of art began to decline noticeably as the Renaissance receded before the rise of Mannerist, baroque and subsequent genres. While Florence stagnated, the great revolutions in Western art, whether in painting or sculpture, were taking place on other stages. That remains the case to this day.

Above: The intricate mosaic ceiling of the Baptistry

Right: Detail of Michelangelo's *David*

JOHN HAY

PAINTING
Emerging from the Middle Ages

Before the 13th century little of artistic note was happening in Florence. In Tuscany, Pisa was in the ascendant. Master of Sardinia and a busy sea trade, Pisa was more open than Florence to external influences and artistic interchange.

The first artist of note to make an impact in Florence was Cimabue (c. 1240–1302). He, like many others, lived and worked all over Tuscany and beyond. Vasari identifies him as the catalyst for change in painting from the rigidity of Gothic and Byzantine models. In Florence, his *Maestà* (in the Uffizi) amply demonstrates the transition from Byzantine-style iconography to a fresh exploration of expression and life-like dimension.

Giotto

Giotto di Bondone (c. 1266–1337), born in the Mugello north-east of Florence, was the key figure in the artistic revolution that was gathering pace in the run-up to the Renaissance explosion. Most of his Florentine contemporaries were to some degree influenced by him, and he is one of the pivotal names in the Italian artistic pantheon. In Giotto the move from the symbolic, other-worldly representations of Italo-Byzantine and Gothic religious art to something more *real*, more directly inspired by observed truth than the desire to teach conceptual

Left: A Giotto fresco in Santa Croce depicting scenes from the life of St Francis

SCALA

SCALA

truths, is clear. His figures are essentially human and express feeling, something quite alien to earlier phases of art in Christian Europe.

Better known for his work in other towns, such as Assisi (Basilica di San Francesco) and Padua (Cappella degli Scrovegni), he left behind several works in Florence, among the most important of which are the frescoes in the Peruzzi and Bardi chapels in the Basilica di Santa Croce.

Giotto's Successors

Confirmation of Giotto's influence comes in the work of several other painters active at the same time. Maso di Banco, of whom little is known except that he was at work in the eight or so years prior to the plague of 1348, was a student of Giotto. His *Storie di San Silvestro (Stories of St Sylvester)* series (in the Basilica di Santa Croce) reflects in its luminosity and simplicity the long shadow of his master. The human faces also have a fullness and naturalness of expression that one might expect from Giotto, although they retain a Gothic stiffness in movement. Perspective also remains somewhat distorted.

Andrea di Cione Orcagna (active from 1343 to 1368) represents something of a Gothic throwback. His most important remaining works are the tabernacle and other statuary inside the Orsanmichele and a polyptych in the Basilica di Santa Maria Novella. Flattened profiles and garish colouring fly in the face of the groundwork laid by Giotto, and show that Gothic devotional art still had its fans in Florence.

Indeed, Gothic was anything but dead as the new century dawned and the two tendencies appeared in direct competition. One of its principal exponents in the first quarter century in Florence was the Sienese painter Lorenzo Monaco (c. 1370–c. 1424). Several of his works are in the Uffizi.

Above: Maso di Banco's colourful *Storie di San Silvestro (Stories of St Sylvester)* in Santa Croce

Anyone tempted to see in this Gothic revivalism a betrayal of the innovation of Giotto and his followers would be a trifle churlish. Painters delivered what their patrons wanted, and some of the latter clearly remained attached to established styles.

The 15th Century & the Renaissance

The young Masaccio (1401–28) can probably be given a good deal of the credit for the definitive break with Gothic style in Florentine painting, though it persisted for a good 30 years after the artist's death. Born in an Arno village at the dawn of the 15th century (what the Italians call Il Quattrocento, or 'the Four Hundreds'), his brief but dynamic career (he died in Rome at the age of 27) make him for painting what his contemporaries, the older Brunelleschi and Donatello, were for architecture and sculpture.

You don't need to look long and hard at his Florentine masterpieces, such as his frescoes in the Cappella Brancacci (Basilica di Santa Maria del Carmine) or the *Trinità (Trinity)* in the Basilica di Santa Maria Novella, to see what sets Masaccio apart. The relatively new game of perspective dominates his pictorial solution. Colours are subtle and characters brought into relief by the use of light and shadow. His best-known image, the *Cacciata dei Progenitori (Expulsion)* in the Cappella Brancacci, depicts all the anguish and shame of Adam and, especially, Eve. Such raw and believable human emotion was a novelty in painting.

Following in Masaccio's footsteps were two masters who in temperament could not have been more different from one another.

Fra Angelico (c. 1395–1455), a Dominican monk later known as Beato (blessed) Angelico for his noted piety, for a while dominated the Florentine art world. His work, much of it done for the Convento di San Marco, is suffused with a diaphanous light aimed at emphasising the good in humankind. Fra Angelico takes on board the lessons of perspective, depth and foreshortening imparted by Masaccio, but remains faithful to the aims of a religious painter.

Although a friar, Fra Filippo Lippi (c. 1406–69) had an appetite for sex, drink and general carousing that left him the father of two by a

Above: Masaccio's frescoes in the Basilica di Santa Maria del Carmine are considered his greatest works.

nun. Fra Filippo left some fine pieces behind in Florence. A *Madonna col Bambino (Virgin Mary with Child)* in the Uffizi and another in Palazzo Pitti (in the Sala di Prometeo) demonstrate his mastery of light and shadow, a weighty reality about the characters and an eye for detail.

A strange bird if ever there was one was Paolo Uccello (1397–1475). More preoccupied with perspective studies than making a living, Uccello did manage to crank out a few lasting pieces. They include the *Diluvio (Deluge)* fresco in the Basilica di Santa Maria Novella and the *Battaglia di San Romano (Battle of San Romano)* done for the Medici family and now (in part) in the Uffizi.

Andrea del Castagno (c. 1421–57) was born in the Mugello but lived and worked in Florence after stints in Venice. Castagno's style is rugged and muscular. This can be seen in his *Crocifissione* in the Cenacolo di Sant'Apollonia.

Below: Benozzo Gozzoli's *Corteo dei Magi (Procession of the Magi)* fresco series in the Palazzo Medici-Riccardi was commissioned by Cosimo de' Medici

Benozzo Gozzoli (c. 1421–97) brought a cheerfully naive touch to paintings, an element notable by its absence in the often more brooding works of some of his aforementioned confreres. One of the last painters of the International Gothic style, his work is clear confirmation that more than one style or tendency in the arts could happily prosper alongside another. Benozzo's big break in Florence came when the Medici clan commissioned his *Corteo dei Magi (Procession of the*

SCALA

SCALA

Magi) in 1459 for the Palazzo Medici-Riccardi. Full of life, movement and colour, his work is, however, little represented in Florence and he soon slipped out of view. The kind of static detail characteristic of Benozzo Gozzoli could not have been further from the thinking of Antonio del Pollaiuolo (c. 1432–98), whose paintings burst with movement at the expense of clarity of line. He had a predilection for scenes of tension or struggle. His *Ercole e Anteo (Hercules and Anteus)*, now in the Uffizi, amply demonstrates the emphasis on human movement, expressed with a freedom rarely witnessed until then. The grunting and groaning of the adversaries lends a convincingly 'real' feel to the physicality of the fight. The painting of Andrea del Verrocchio (1435–88), who is perhaps better known for his sculpture (see The 15th Century under Sculpture later in the section) presents difficulties as it is often impossible to distinguish his work from that of his pupils. Among the latter was Leonardo da Vinci, with whom Verrocchio did the *Battesimo di Cristo (Baptism of Christ)*, now in the Uffizi.

Mythologised in the 19th century as the embodiment of the Renaissance artist, Sandro Botticelli (1445–1510) has as a result probably been the least understood painter of the period. By most he is remembered for works such as *Nascita di Venere (Birth of Venus)* and *Primavera (Spring)*, in the Uffizi. In these and other paintings of their ilk, wispy, ethereal figures seem to float serenely across the canvas in an idealised evocation of classical Greece. Botticelli faces are striking for their sensitivity, a constant throughout his career. The preaching of Savonarola had a profound effect on the artist who, fired by a new religious fervour, in his later years produced works of greater intensity,

Above: One of Botticelli's best-known pieces, *Nascita di Venere (Birth of Venus)*, can be seen in the Uffizi.

leaving behind the milky dreaminess of earlier days. His *Calunnia de Apelle (Calumny of Apelles)*, finished in 1498 and now also in the Uffizi, is a good example of the transition. Botticelli seemed to fall out of step with his time, however, and in the last 10 years he received few commissions – he died a crumpled and unhappy man.

Filippino Lippi (1457–1504), Fra Filippo's son, worked in Botticelli's workshop for a time but Lippi was more directly influenced by Leonardo da Vinci and Flemish artists. His frescoes of *Storie di San Giovanni Evangelista e San Filippo (Stories of St John and St Phillip)* in the Cappella Strozzi in the Basilica di Santa Maria Novella reveal a move away from the humanist ideals of Quattrocento painting. In one of the frescoes, depicting St Philip exorcising the devil in the temple of Mars, perspective has been flattened and the subject has a disturbing quality absent from other works of the time. The architectural business and attention to detail in people's faces also presages Mannerism.

Domenico Ghirlandaio (1449–94), whose real surname was Bigordi, has fallen in and out of favour with critics over the centuries. While not a great innovator, he was a master of colour and the rendering of human expression. Perhaps his most startling work is the *Strage degli Innocenti (Massacre of the Innocents)* fresco in the Basilica di Santa Maria Novella. The scene is festooned with the mutilated bodies of infants as terrified mothers scramble to escape the blood lust of Herod's soldiers.

Below: Domenico Ghirlandaio's powerful *Strage degli Innocenti (Massacre of the Innocents)* in the Basilica di Santa Maria Novella

SCALA

The Genius from Vinci

Leonardo da Vinci (1452–1519), born in a small town west of Florence, stands apart from all his contemporaries. How do you categorise a man who hardly belonged in his own time? Painter, sculptor, architect, scientist, engineer, Leonardo brought to all fields of knowledge and art an original touch, often opening up whole new branches of thought. If one had to sum up what made him tick, it might be 'seeing is believing'. In the thousands of pages of notes he left behind, he repeatedly extols the virtue of sight and observation. Paying little heed to received wisdoms, either Christian or classical, Leonardo barrelled along with unquenchable curiosity.

His studies took up much of Leonardo's time, but he found plenty more to devote to what he saw as the noblest art, painting.

Leonardo did much of his work outside Florence (he stayed in Milan for 20 years). One of his outstanding early works, *Annunciazione (Annunciation)*, now in the Uffizi (under restoration at the time of writing), already reveals his concern with light and shadow. His techniques were quite different from those of his contemporaries. His unfinished *Adorazione dei Magi (Adoration of the Magi)*, also in the Uffizi, reveals how he first applied a dark wash to the surface, from which he could then extract his figures and shed light upon them. Among his most beguiling portraits are the *Mona Lisa and Madonna col Bambino e Sant'Anna (Madonna with Child and Saint Anna)*, both now in the Louvre in Paris.

SCALA

Left: Detail from Leonardo da Vinci's *Annunciazione (Annunciation)* in the Uffizi

SCALA

Michelangelo

While Leonardo was in Milan, Michelangelo Buonarroti (1475–1564) was asserting himself as a rival painter, albeit of a very different ilk. His primary artistic pursuit was sculpture (see The Fiery Florentine under Sculpture later in the section), but he was no fool with a brush either.

In contrast to Leonardo's smoky, veiled images, Michelangelo demonstrated a greater clarity of line. As a young lad he was taken in by Lorenzo de' Medici, who could spot talent when it presented itself. His greatest painting project was the ceiling of the Sistine Chapel in Rome. In Florence relatively little of his work can be seen, but the *Tondo Doni* in the Uffizi provides stunning insight into his craft.

From High Renaissance to Mannerism

Lesser artists were at work around the turn of the century in Florence, not to mention outsiders like Raphael who stopped in Florence for a while before heading off to pursue their careers elsewhere.

Among the Florentines, Fra Bartolommeo (1472–1517) stands out for such paintings as the *Apparizione della Vergina a San Bernardo (Vision of St Bernard)*, now in the Galleria dell'Accademia. A follower of Savonarola, Fra Bartolommeo's is a clearly devotional art, with virtually all incidental detail eliminated in favour of the central subject. Piero di Cosimo (c. 1462–1521), on the other hand, was interested in nature and mythology. Several of his works can be seen in the Palazzo Pitti.

Above: Michelangelo's elaborately framed *Tondo Doni* in the Uffizi

Michelangelo's almost tormented search for new, more emotionally satisfying ways of representing beauty led him to bend the classical rules that in part lay behind the Renaissance. In this he is often said to have been one of the earliest exponents of the post-Renaissance style known as Mannerism, although he defies simplistic categorisation.

Andrea del Sarto (1486–1530) remained essentially true to the values of High Renaissance painting, turning out works with grace and dignity but none of the torment that would be associated with the likes of Jacopo Pontormo (1494–1556), his student. A quick comparison of frescoes by the two in the atrium of the Chiesa di SS Annunziata is enough to identify the differences. In Pontormo's *Visitazione (Visitation)* his figures seem almost furtive or preoccupied, as indeed they do in his frescoes in the Chiesa di Santa Felicita.

Il Rosso Fiorentino ('the Florentine Redhead'; 1495–1540) also worked on the SS Annunziata frescoes and several other projects elsewhere in Tuscany before heading to Rome. In his works, too, one detects a similar note of disquiet, although his style is different. The flashes of light and dark create an unreal effect in his characters.

A student of Pontormo, Il Bronzino (1503–72) began the move away from Mannerism. Employed by the Medici family, his approach lacked the disquiet evident in his master. Rather he fixes images in a static fashion, reflecting perhaps his masters' desire to convey the sureness of their sovereignty, however spurious. His greatest achievement was Eleonora de Toledo's chapel in the Palazzo Vecchio.

The works of Giorgio Vasari (1511–74) and his students litter Florence, some better than others. His particular boast seems to have been speed – with an army of helpers he was able to plough through commissions for frescoes and paintings with great alacrity, if not always with equal aplomb. He is perhaps most important in the history of Renaissance art as the author of *Lives of the Artists*, a rich compendium of fact and fiction about Italian art until his own day. Vasari & co were largely responsible for the decoration of the Palazzo Vecchio.

Baroque & Neoclassicism

Flocks of artists continued to work in Florence as the new century wore on, but few of enormous note. Giovanni da San Giovanni (1592–1636) was the leading light of the first half of the century, and some of his frescoes remain in the Palazzo Pitti. One much underestimated painter of the period was Francesco Montelatici, or Il Cecco Bravo (1601–60), whose disquieting canvasses betray an unusual mixture of influences, combining Florentine tastes of the period with a rediscovery of the soft smoky colours of Venice's Titian.

The arrival of artists from out of town, such as Pietro da Cortona (1596–1669) and the Neapolitan Luca Giordano (1632–1705), brought the winds of baroque taste to Florence. They and a succession of local and foreign painters worked largely for private families, decorating their residences and occasionally taking on commissions in various churches.

SCALA

Where the Mannerists had searched, often rather stiffly, for ways of breaking with Renaissance conventions, the baroque bounded headlong into a hedonistic riot of colour and movement, leaving any semblance of reality behind – and so always risking a collapse into implausible bathos. Angels, chariots and God knows what else charge at you from the heavens in a voluptuous whirlwind of exaggerated movement.

At any rate, Florence was by now no longer the centre of artistic creation it had been.

Right: Il Cecco Bravo's *San Michele e Angeli Adoranti (St Michael and Adoring Angels)*

The Macchiaioli

By the middle of the 19th century, Florentine art was second-rate and stuck in a rut. Painters produced soulless, academic pieces that, after the excitement of the 1848 Europe-wide revolts, seemed inadequate. Venetian landscape painters began to have an influence, and then in 1855 several Florentines visited Paris for the Universal Exposition. They came back with news of developments in French naturalist painting that proved a precursor to Impressionism.

In Florence anti-academic artists met in the Caffè Michelangelo and declared that painting real-life scenes was the only way forward. The Macchiaioli movement lasted until the late 1860s and received its name (which could be translated as the 'stainers' or 'blotchers') in a disparaging newspaper article in 1862.

The Macchiaioli, whose name stemmed from their technique of splotching various colours onto the canvas to explore effects of tone before proceeding, took at least two important steps to release Florentine, indeed Italian, art from the sclerosis that had set in. They abandoned the religious and historical themes to which painting, no matter how innovative in style, had largely been bound for centuries. Then they dropped chiaroscuro effects in favour of playful use of colour plus light and/or colour plus shade.

Although the hub of their activity was Florence, a good number of the Macchiaioli had come from all over Italy. Many fought in the conflicts leading to the unification of Italy. You can see some of the works of various of these artists, such as Livorno-born Giovanni Fattori

Below: Fattori Giovanni's *Il Campo Italiano dopo la Battaglia di Magenta (The Italian Camp After the Battle of Magenta)* in the Galleria d'Arte Moderna

(1825–1908), Neapolitan Giuseppe Abbati (1836–68) and the Emilian painter Silvestro Lega (1826–95), in the Galleria d'Arte Moderna.

By 1870 the movement had run out of steam. Splinter tendencies emerged separating the realism of subject from questions of style.

The 20th Century

Florence's decline as a centre of artistic ferment seems to have been sealed during the 20th century. Futurism had little impact here in the years before WWI, while the Novecento (the 'Nine Hundreds') movement, which preached a return to order in the wake of various avant-garde tendencies, also bore precious little fruit in Florence.

After WWII, the Arte Oggi (Art Today) group of so-called dissident artists in Florence championed a 'classical abstractism', but by and large the 20th century has passed Florence by. This can probably be explained in part by the fact that, regardless of its history, Florence is little more than a middle-class provincial capital, its conservatism made all the more weighty by the enormity of its cultural golden age – the Renaissance.

Hard Stones & the Art of Restoration

The silver lining on the very dark cloud that constituted the floods of 1966 has been the extraordinary growth in expertise in the field of art restoration in Florence. Indeed it is a world centre for this kind of work, and students from around the globe jostle to get a place either in schools or working on projects here.

In 1975, the Istituto Specializzato per il Restauro was created out of the fusion of the Laboratori di Restauro and one of the city's most venerable organisations, the Opificio delle Pietre Dure. Founded officially in 1796, the Opificio had effectively been working since 1588, when Grand Duke Ferdinando I brought together all the artisans working for the Medici family in one workshop.

For centuries the Opificio's vocation was to produce table tops and other decorative furnishing using semiprecious *pietre dure* (literally 'hard stones'). Mixed in seemingly unlimited colours and hues, veritable works of art came out of this workshop, which soon acquired a worldwide reputation for the exquisite quality of its products.

Today, the Istituto (still known to many as the Opificio) continues the pietre dure tradition, as well as working on the restoration of paintings, frescoes and other works of art.

You can see some fine examples of the Opificio's efforts at its museum in Via degli Alfani 78 (Map 3). It opens from 9 am to 2 pm Monday to Saturday and admission costs L4000.

SCULPTURE
Arnolfo & Co

Among sculptors of note operating in Florence in the 13th century, Nicola Pisano (c. 1215–c. 1278) should be mentioned for his role as a master to others. Born in southern Italy, he worked all over Tuscany and in Rome. In Florence little remains of his sculpture. The Baptistry in Pisa is where to see his work.

Arnolfo di Cambio (d. 1302), a student of Pisano, is best known as the architect of the Duomo and Palazzo Vecchio. He also decorated the Duomo's facade. Some of this sculpture remains in the Museo dell'Opera del Duomo, but the bulk of his work was destroyed in the 16th century.

An outstanding sculptor to sojourn in Florence was Andrea Pisano (c. 1290–1348). He left behind the bronze doors of the south facade of the Baptistry, which he finished in 1336. The realism of the characters combines with the fine linear detail of a Gothic imprint, revealing that the 14th century was one of transition.

The 15th Century

It is tempting to place the launch of the Renaissance at the turn of the century but things are never quite that straight-forward. In 1401, Lorenzo Ghiberti (1378–1455) and the irascible Filippo Brunelleschi (1377–1446) entered a competition for a second set of bronze doors on the Baptistry (now on the northern flank). Ghiberti won in 1402 with an exquisite solution in the International Gothic style, a loose description for the final wave of enthusiasm for Gothic to wash across Europe.

But Ghiberti soon saw which way the wind was blowing. His bronze statue of *San Matteo (St Matthew)* on the Orsanmichele is a visible departure from any residual rigidity evident in the Baptistry doors. He was later called on to do another set of doors on the eastern side and

JOHN HAY

Left: Detail of Ghiberti's bronze doors to the Baptistry

DAMIEN SIMONIS

ended up dedicating 17 years of his career to what an admiring Michelangelo (and it was not his wont to admire anything much) would later dub Porta del Paradiso (Gate of Paradise).

Ghiberti's workshop was a prestige address in Florence, and one of the lucky young hopefuls to be apprenticed there was Donatello (c. 1386–1466). As the Renaissance gathered momentum in the 1420s and 30s, Donatello burst his banks and produced a stream of sculpture hitherto unparalleled in its dynamism and force. A stay in Rome in 1432–33 seems to have been decisive. Armed with his classical knowledge he set to work. The results swing from his rather camp bronze *David*, the first nude sculpture since classical times (now in the Bargello) to the racy *Cantoria (Choir)*, a marble and mosaic tribune where small choirs could gather, done for the Duomo (now in the Museo dell'Opera del Duomo). The *putti* (cherubs) are depicted with such lifelike movement that they seem the result rather of impatient brushstrokes than painstaking stone-cutting.

Although he would subsequently be best known for his decorative, glazed terracotta, Luca della Robbia (c. 1400–82) for a while showed promise as a sculptor, as examination of his exquisite *Cantoria (Choir)*, now in the Museo dell'Opera del Duomo, will reveal. His nephew Andrea (1435–1525) and the latter's son Giovanni (1469–1529) continued the successful family terracotta business. The pretty terracotta medallions and other more complex pieces adorning buildings all over Florence and beyond came to be known as 'robbiane'. A good collection can be admired up close in the Bargello.

Desiderio da Settignano (c. 1430–64), in his brief career, came to be a master of marble. Little of his work remains in Florence aside from the tomb of Carlo Marsuppini in the Basilica di Santa Croce. He sanded down the surface of some of his work to help create a diffused effect in the light hitting his sculpture. His particular talent was the sculpture of children, like the cherubs on Marsuppini's tomb.

A pupil of Desiderio, Mino da Fiesole (1429–84) was busy in Florence and as far afield as Naples. His most important work was a new tomb for Ugo, the early medieval count of Tuscany, in the Badia.

Above: Detail of glazed terracotta by the della Robbia workshop

Other sculptors working in marble at around the same time included Antonio Rossellino (1427–79) and Benedetto da Maiano (c. 1442–97).

In his sculpture as well as his painting (see The 15th Century & the Renaissance under Painting earlier in this section), Antonio del Pollaiuolo brought a hitherto rarely felt wind of movement to his work. None demonstrates this better than the bronze version of his *Ercole e Anteo (Hercules and Anteus)*, in the Bargello.

Although also active as a painter Andrea del Verrocchio is best remembered for his sculpture. His virtuosity can be admired in the tomb monument to Piero and Giovanni de' Medici in the Basilica di San Lorenzo. His masterpiece, however, is the bronze equestrian statue of Colleoni in Venice, which is where he died.

The Fiery Florentine

A passionate republican, Michelangelo Buonarroti was most prolific as a sculptor. And while he painted and built in Florence, his greatest gifts to the city were those he crafted from stone.

Michelangelo was a testy individual, and early on in life got what was coming to him when he made some acid remarks about sculptor Pietro Torrigiani's drawing one day in the Brancacci chapel. Torrigiani thumped the smart-alecky Michelangelo, leaving him with a *very* broken nose. After a stint in Rome, where he carved the remarkable *Pietà*, Michelangelo returned to Florence in 1501 to carry out one of

his most striking commissions ever, the colossal statue of *David*. By now, Michelangelo had long established himself as the champion of full nudity. The body, he argued, was a divine creation and its beauty without peer. Various reliefs and statues, including one of Bacchus and another of Christ crucified (the latter now in the Basilica di Santo Spirito) were full nudes. It is likely the church sacristan covered them up with a loincloth for the sake of public morals.

In 1516, after another long stint in Rome, Michelangelo was back in Florence. Among his last great works, not quite completed, are the statues in the Sagrestia Nuova (New Sacristy) of San Lorenzo. That so many of his works were left unfinished was indicative perhaps of the temperament of an artist incapable of being completely satisfied with his own work. The *Pietà* he began to work on for his own tomb not only left him disappointed enough to abandon work on it, he had such a fit of temper he took to it with a hammer. It was later cobbled back together and stands in the Museo dell'Opera del Duomo.

Above: The full-length statue of *David* is one of the few pieces that Michelangelo ever truly completed.

The 16th Century

Other sculptors active during Michelangelo's lifetime include Benvenuto Cellini (1500–71) and Bartolommeo Amannati (1511–92). The former, trained as a goldsmith, produced the bronze *Perseo e Medusa (Perseus and Medusa)* which stands in the Loggia della Signoria when not undergoing restoration – technically fine, it lacks life. The latter is perhaps best known for the *Fontana del Nettuno (Neptune Fountain)* in Piazza della Signoria, which met more often than not with disapproval. Michelangelo, for one, thought Amannati had ruined a perfectly good block of marble. Another name associated with Florence was Giambologna (Jean de Boulogne, 1529–1608), a Flemish sculptor who arrived in Florence after a study trip to Rome around 1550. Some consider him the herald of baroque. He was at any rate the dominant force in Florentine sculpture towards the end of the 16th century. His *Ratto della Sabina (Rape of the Sabine Woman)*, placed in the Loggia della Signoria, is one of his best-known efforts.

Right: Superstition has it that the figures on the base of Amannati's *Fontana del Nettuno (Neptune Fountain)* come to life on the night of the full moon.

JULIET COOMBE

Lean Centuries

One of Florence's senior court sculptors, Giovanni Battista Foggini (1652–1725), immersed himself in the baroque circles of Rome when sent there by the Medici to copy statues of antiquity. He returned and put to use his new-found knowledge in reliefs and other decoration in several churches, among them the Basilica del Carmine.

The grand man of sculpture in the 19th century was Lorenzo Bartolini (1777–1850). Born in Prato, he studied in France before settling in Florence. He and his contemporaries were to some extent bound up in the rediscovery of the masters of the 15th century, so produced little that was exciting or innovative.

The 20th Century

Perhaps even more so than with painting, Florentine sculpture has remained in the doldrums. Perhaps the awe-inspiring legacy of the great masters has been too great a burden to shake off.

This is not to say activity ground to a complete halt. The Pescia-born Libero Andreotti (1875–1933) and the tormented Florentine Evaristo Boncinelli (1883–1946) were among the prominent figures in the first half of the century, while Pistoia-born Marino Marini (1901–80) is doubtless the torchbearer of 20th-century Tuscan sculpture. You can admire his work in the museum dedicated to him in Florence.

SCALA

Left: Giovanni Battista Foggini decorated the Cappella Feroni in the Chiesa di SS Annunziata

Facts for the Visitor

WHEN TO GO

Stay away from Florence in July and August. Because of its location in a valley, the summer heat and humidity are intensified in a most unpleasant fashion. Strangely enough, a lot of tourists choose just this time to visit, itself an added reason for not doing so. If you hate crowds, avoid Florence during the Easter, Christmas and New Year holidays.

Florence is at its best in spring and autumn. April, May, September and even October are generally the most favourable months, with mild or warm weather and a crisp, clear light. For those who want to avoid fellow tourists as much as possible, the depths of winter have something to be said for them. January and February are quiet months, which means you can generally find a room with little trouble and avoid the hassle of crowds. The downside is the weather, although the cold in Florence is not an enormous hardship.

ORIENTATION

If you enter Florence by train or bus you will arrive at or close to the central train station, Stazione di Santa Maria Novella. This is a good initial reference point. Budget hotels and *pensioni* (small hotels, often with board) are concentrated around Via Nazionale, to the east of the station, and Piazza Santa Maria Novella, to the south. The main route to the city centre is Via de' Panzani and then Via de' Cerretani, about a 10-minute walk. You'll know you've arrived when you first glimpse the Duomo.

Once at the Piazza del Duomo you will find Florence easy to negotiate. Most of the major sights are within easy walking distance – you can stroll from one end of the city centre to the other in about 30 minutes. From Piazza San Giovanni around the Baptistry, Via Roma leads to Piazza della Repubblica and continues as Via Calimala then Via Por Santa Maria to the Ponte Vecchio. Take Via de' Calzaiuoli from Piazza

del Duomo for Piazza della Signoria. The Uffizi is on the piazza's southern edge, opposite the Palazzo Vecchio and near the Arno. Cross the Ponte Vecchio, or the Ponte alle Grazie farther east, and head south-east towards the Piazzale Michelangelo for a fantastic view over the city.

It is not so straightforward for drivers, because much depends on how you enter the city – the choice of initial exits is fairly limited (take Firenze Sud if coming from the south and Firenze Nord from the north). After that, though, you can reach the centre by various routes. Follow the '*centro*' signs. If you are coming from the north and see '*stazione*' signs, you can follow these and use the reasonably priced public parking around the imposing Fortezza da Basso, which is just north of the train station. From there it is a brisk 10-minute walk to the historic centre along Via Faenza.

For more information on parking in Florence see Parking under Car & Motorcycle in the Getting Around chapter.

Street Numbering

Florence has two street-numbering systems: red or brown numbers indicate a commercial premise and black or blue numbers denote a private residence or an entire building. When written, black or blue addresses are denoted by the number only, while red or brown addresses usually carry an 'r' (for *rosso*, or 'red') after the number. Of course, there are exceptions, but check the colouring (the 'red' figures are often faded to murky brown and are generally the smaller numbers) when you are trying to find an address. It can be a little confusing. A further complication is that, in some instances, the blue or black number is subdivided by letters, for example 21a, 21b and 21c.

The only sane advice when looking for a specific address is to keep your eyes on both sets of numbers – and accept that backtracking is sometimes inevitable.

MAPS

You should be able to get by with the maps in the back of this book, but some of the maps on sale are also worthwhile investments. The free one handed out by the tourist office is next to useless.

One of the best maps is the green-covered *Florence* (L15,000), produced by the Touring Club Italiano. It's in a handy pocket-size ring-binder format. The pages covering the city centre are at a scale of 1:5500. The remainder is at 1:11,000. Touring Club Italiano also do a foldout version (L10,000), with the centre covered at 1:6500 and the rest at 1:12,500.

TOURIST OFFICES
Local Tourist Offices

The main APT (Azienda di Promozione Tursitica) office (Map 6; ☎ 055 29 08 32, fax 055 276 03 83) is located just north of the Duomo at Via Cavour 1r and has a Web site at www.firenze.turismo.toscano.it.

It opens from 8.15 am to 7.15 pm Monday to Saturday and from 8.45 am to 1.45 pm on Sunday, between April and October. It is open until 1.45 pm and closed on Sunday in the other months. The branch at Amerigo Vespucci airport (☎ 055 31 58 74) opens from 8.30 am to 10.30 pm daily.

The Comune di Firenze (Florence's city council) operates a tourist office (Map 3; ☎ 055 21 22 45) at the southern end of the series of ATAF (Azienda Trasporti Area Fiorentina) bus stops between Piazza Adua and Piazza della Stazione, just outside the south-east exit of the train station. It generally opens from 8.15 am to 7.15 pm Monday to Saturday in the summer. The hours are cut to 9 am to 1.45 pm in winter. It has another office (Map 7; ☎ 055 234 04 44) at Borgo Santa Croce 29r, which opens the same hours.

Inside the train station, you can also pick up basic information at the Consorzio ITA (Informazioni Turistiche e Alberghiere) office (Map 3; ☎ 055 28 28 93). Their main role is to book hotels. The office is open from 8.30 am to 9 pm daily. For details about this and other hotel booking services, see the Places to Stay chapter.

At all the offices you can pick up a map of the city, a list of hotels and other useful information. Staff at the APT speak English, French, Spanish and German, and have extensive useful information about the city and its services, from language and art courses to car and bike rental.

The police and tourist office combine to operate Tourist Help points for the lost and disoriented at the Ponte Vecchio and Piazza della Repubblica (both Map 6), open from 8.30 am to 7 pm. From April to October, the APT also offers a special service known as Florence SOS Turista (☎ 055 276 03 82). Tourists needing guidance on matters such as disputes over hotel bills can phone from 10 am to 1 pm and 3 to 6 pm Monday to Saturday.

Tourist Offices Abroad

Information on Florence is available from the following branches of the Italian State Tourist Office (Web site at www.enit.at):

Austria
 (☎ 01-505 16 39)
 Kaerntnerring 4, 1010 Vienna
Canada
 (☎ 514-866 7669, ☻ initaly@ican.net)
 Suite 1914, 1 Place Ville Marie, Montreal, Quebec H3B 2C3
France
 (☎ 01 42 66 66 68, ☻ 106616.131@ compuserve.com)
 23 rue de la Paix, 75002 Paris
Germany
 (☎ 030-247 83 97, ☻ enit-berlin@t-online.de)
 Karl Liebknecht Strasse 34, 10178 Berlin
 (☎ 089-53 13 17, ☻ enit.ffm@t-online.de)
 Kaisertrasse 65, 60329 Frankfurt am Main
 (☎ 069-25 93 32)
 Goethestrasse 20, 80336 Munich
Netherlands
 (☎ 020-616 82 44)
 Stadhouderskade 2, 1054 ES Amsterdam
Spain
 (☎ 91 559 9750)
 Gran Via 84, 28013 Madrid
Switzerland
 (☎ 01-211 79 17, ☻ enit@bluewin)
 Uraniastrasse 32, 8001 Zurich
UK
 (☎ 020-7408 1254, toll-free 09001 600 280, ☻ enitlond@globalnet.co.uk)
 1 Princes St, London W1R 8AY

USA
  (☎ 312-644 0996, 🖂 enitch@
  italiantourism.com)
  Suite 2240, 500 North Michigan Ave,
  Chicago, IL 60611
  (☎ 310-820 1898)
  Suite 550, 12400 Wilshire Blvd, Los Angeles,
  CA 90025
  (☎ 212-245 4822)
  Suite 1565, 630 Fifth Ave, New York,
  NY 10111

Sestante-CIT (Compagnia Italiana di Turismo), Italy's national travel agency, has offices throughout the world (known as CIT or Citalia outside Italy). Staff can provide information on travelling in Italy and will organise tours, as well as book individual hotels. CIT can also make train bookings and sell Eurail passes and discount passes for train travel in Italy. Offices include:

Australia
  (☎ 03-9650 5510)
  Level 4, 227 Collins St, Melbourne 3000
  (☎ 02-9267 1255)
  263 Clarence St, Sydney 2000
Canada
  (☎ 514-845 4310, toll-free 800 361 7799)
  Suite 750, 1450 City Councillors St, Montreal,
  Quebec H3A 2E6
  (☎ 905-415 1060, toll-free 800 387 0711)
  Suite 401, 80 Tiverton Court, Markham,
  Toronto, Ontario L3R 0G4
France
  (☎ 01 44 51 39 00)
  5 Boulevard des Capucines, Paris 75002
Germany
  (☎ 0211-69 00 30)
  Geibelstrasse 39, 40235 Dusseldorf
UK
  (☎ 020-8686 0677, 8686 5533)
  Marco Polo House, 3–5 Lansdowne Rd,
  Croydon, Surrey CR9 1LL
USA
  (☎ 310-338 8615)
  Suite 980, 6033 West Century Blvd, Los
  Angeles, CA 90045
  (☎ 212-730 2121)
  10th Floor, 15 West 44th St, New York,
  NY 10036

Italian cultural institutes in major cities throughout the world have extensive information on study opportunities in Italy. See

Cultural Centres later in the chapter for more details.

DOCUMENTS
Passport
Citizens of the 15 European Union (EU) member states can travel to Italy with their national identity cards alone. People from countries that do not issue ID cards, such as the UK, must have a valid passport. All non-EU nationals must have a full valid passport.

If you've had the passport for a while, check that the expiry date is at least six months off, otherwise you may not be granted a visa (if you need one). If you travel a lot, keep an eye on the number of pages you have left in the passport. US consulates will generally insert extra pages into your passport if you need them, but other consulates require you to apply for a new passport.

If your passport is stolen or lost while in Italy, notify the police and obtain a statement, and then contact your embassy or consulate as soon as possible.

Visas
Italy is one of 15 countries that have signed the Schengen Convention, an agreement whereby all EU member countries (except the UK and Ireland) plus Iceland and Norway have agreed to abolish checks at common borders by the end of 2000. The other EU countries are Austria, Belgium, Denmark, Finland, France, Germany, Greece, Luxembourg, the Netherlands, Portugal, Spain and Sweden. Legal residents of one Schengen country do not require a visa for another Schengen country. Citizens of the UK and Ireland are also exempt from visa requirements for Schengen countries. In addition, nationals of a number of other countries, including Canada, Japan, New Zealand and Switzerland, do not require visas for tourist visits of up to 90 days to any Schengen country.

Various other nationals not covered by the Schengen exemption can also spend up to 90 days in Italy without a visa. These include Australian, Israeli and US citizens.

FACTS FOR THE VISITOR

However, all non-EU nationals entering Italy for any reason other than tourism (such as study or work) should contact an Italian consulate, as they may need a specific visa. They should also insist on having their passport stamped on entry as, without a stamp, they could encounter problems when trying to obtain a residence permit, or *permesso di soggiorno* (see Permits later in this section). If you are a citizen of a country not mentioned in this section, you should check with an Italian consulate whether you need a visa.

The standard tourist visa issued by Italian consulates is the Schengen visa, valid for up to 90 days. A Schengen visa issued by one Schengen country is generally valid for travel in all other Schengen countries. However, individual Schengen countries may impose additional restrictions on certain nationalities. It is, therefore, worth checking visa regulations with the consulate of each Schengen country you plan to visit.

Rules for obtaining Schengen visas have been tightened and it's now mandatory that you apply in your country of residence. You can apply for no more than two Schengen visas in any 12-month period and they are not renewable inside Italy. If you are going to visit more than one Schengen country, you are supposed to apply for the visa at a consulate of your main destination country or, if you have no main destination, the first country you intend to visit. It's worth applying early for your visa, especially in the busy summer months.

Permits

EU citizens do not require any permits to live, work or start a business in Italy. They are, however, advised to register with a police station (*questura*) if they take up residence, in accordance with an anti-Mafia law that aims at keeping a watch on everyone's whereabouts in the country. Failure to do so carries no consequences, although some landlords may be unwilling to rent out a flat to you if you cannot produce proof of registration. Those considering long-term residence will eventually want to consider getting a residence permit, a necessary first step to acquiring an ID card (*carta d'identità*). While you're at it, you'll need a tax-file number (*codice fiscale*) if you wish to be paid for most work in Italy. Go to a police station (see the boxed text 'Police Forces' later in this chapter) to obtain precise information on what is required.

For information on visas required for working in Italy, see Work later in this chapter. For information on study visas, see Courses in the Things to See & Do chapter.

Travel Insurance

Medical costs might already be covered through reciprocal healthcare agreements (see Health later in this chapter) but you'll still need cover for theft or loss and for unexpected changes in travel plans (such as ticket cancellation).

You may prefer a policy that pays doctors or hospitals directly rather than you having to pay on the spot and claim later. If you have to claim for anything later, make sure you keep all documentation. Some policies ask you to call back (reverse charge) to a centre in your home country where an immediate assessment of your problem is made.

Check that the policy covers ambulances or an emergency flight home.

Driving Licence & Permits

The pink-and-green driving licences issued in all EU member states (not the old-style UK green licence) are fully recognised throughout Europe, regardless of your length of stay. Those with a non-EU licence are supposed to obtain an International Driving Permit (IDP) to accompany their national licence. These are available from national automobile associations.

For information on paperwork and insurance, see Car & Motorcycle in the Getting There & Away chapter.

Hostel Cards

A valid Hostelling International (HI) card is required if you want to stay in any of the youth hostels (*ostelli per la gioventù*) run by the Associazione Italiana Alberghi per la Gioventù (AIG) in Italy. You can get this by becoming a member of your national Youth Hostel Association (YHA) in your home country or at youth hostels in Italy. In the latter case, you must collect six stamps in the card at L5000 each. You pay for a stamp on each of the first six nights you spend in a hostel, on top of the hostel fee. With six stamps you are considered a full international member. HI has a Web site at www .iyhf.org.

Student, Teacher & Youth Cards

The International Student Identity Card (ISIC), for full-time students, and the International Teacher Identity Card (ITIC), for full-time teachers and professors, are issued by more than 5000 organisations around the world. The cards entitle you to a range of discounts, from reduced museum admission charges to cheap air fares.

Student travel organisations such as STA (Australia, the UK and the USA), Council Travel (the UK and USA) and Travel CUTS/Voyages Campus (Canada) issue these cards. See Air in the Getting There & Away chapter for some addresses, phone numbers and Web sites.

Anyone under aged 26 can get a Euro<26 card. This gives similar discounts to the ISIC and is issued by most of the same organisations. The Euro<26 has a variety of names, including the Under 26 Card in England and Wales and the CartaGiovani in Italy.

CTS (Centro Turistico Studentesco e Giovanile) is the main Italian student and youth travel organisation. The Florence branch (Map 6; ☎ 055 28 95 70) is at Via de' Ginori 25r. They act mainly as a travel agent, but you can also obtain ISIC, Euro<26 and Youth Hostel cards at their branches if you haven't already done so abroad. Note, however, that you will generally be obliged to pay a joining fee of L45,000. For further information, see Travel Agents in the Getting There & Away chapter.

Seniors Cards

Seniors aged over 60 or 65 (depending on the discount they're seeking) can get many discounts simply by presenting their passport or ID card as proof of age.

Copies

Make photocopies of all important documents, especially your passport. This will help speed replacement if they are lost or stolen. Other documents to photocopy might include your airline ticket and credit cards. Also record the serial numbers of your travellers cheques (cross them off as you cash them). All this material should be kept separate from the documents concerned, along with a small amount of emergency cash. Leave extra copies with someone reliable at home.

There is another option for storing details of your vital travel documents before you leave – Lonely Planet's online Travel Vault. Storing details of your important documents in the vault is safer than carrying photocopies. It's the best option if you travel in a country with easy Internet access. Your password-protected travel vault is accessible online at anytime. You can create your own travel vault for free at www.ekno.lonely planet.com.

EMBASSIES & CONSULATES

It's important to realise what your own embassy – the embassy of the country of which you are a citizen – can and can't do to help if you get into trouble.

Generally speaking, it won't be much help in emergencies if the trouble you're in is remotely your own fault. Remember that you are bound by the laws of the country you are in. Your embassy will not be sympathetic if you end up in jail after committing a crime locally, even if such actions are legal in your own country.

In genuine emergencies you might get some assistance, but only if other channels have been exhausted. For example, if you need to get home urgently, a free ticket is exceedingly unlikely – the embassy would expect you to have insurance. If you have all your money and documents stolen, it might assist with getting a new passport, but a loan for onward travel is out of the question.

Italian Embassies & Consulates

The following is a selection of Italian diplomatic missions abroad. As a rule, you should approach the consulate rather than the embassy (where both are present) on visa matters. Also bear in mind that in many of the countries listed below there are further consulates in other cities.

Australia
  Embassy:
  (☎ 02-6273 3333, fax 6273 4223,
  ✉ ambital2@dynamite.com.au)
  12 Grey St, Deakin, Canberra 2600
  Consulates:
  (☎ 03-9867 5744, fax 9866 3932,
  ✉ itconmel@netlink.com.au)
  509 St Kilda Rd, Melbourne 3004
  (☎ 02-9392 7900, fax 9252 4830,
  ✉ itconsyd@armadillo.com.au)
  Level 45, The Gateway, 1 Macquarie Place,
  Sydney, NSW 2000
Austria
  Embassy:
  (☎ 01-712 51 21, fax 713 97 19,
  ✉ ambitalviepress@via.at)
  Metternichgasse 13, Vienna 1030
Canada
  Embassy:
  (☎ 613-232 2401, fax 233 1484,
  ✉ ambital@trytel.com)
  21st Floor, 275 Slater St, Ottawa,
  Ontario KIP 5H9
  Consulates:
  (☎ 514-849 8351, fax 499 9471,
  ✉ consitmtl@cyberglobe.net)
  3489 Drummond St, Montreal,
  Quebec H3G 1X6
  (☎ 416-977 2569, fax 977 1119,
  ✉ consolato.it@toronto.italconsulate.org)
  136 Beverley St, Toronto, Ontario M5T 1Y5
France
  Embassy:
  (☎ 01 49 54 03 00, fax 01 45 49 35 81,
  ✉ stampa@dial.oleane.com)
  47–51 rue de Varenne, Paris 75007
Germany
  Embassy:
  (☎ 0228-82 20, fax 82 22 10,
  ✉ italia.ambasciata.bonn@t-online.de)
  Karl Finkelnburgstrasse 49–51,
  Bonn 53173
  Consulate:
  (☎ 030-25 44 00, fax 25 44 01 00,
  ✉ italcons.berlino@t-online.de)
  Hiroshimastrasse 1–7, Berlin 10785

Ireland
  Embassy:
  (☎ 01-660 1744, fax 668 2759,
  ✉ italianembassy@tinet.ie)
  63–65 Northumberland Rd, Dublin 4
Netherlands
  Embassy:
  (☎ 070-302 1030, fax 361 4932,
  ✉ italemb@worldonline.nl)
  Alexanderstraat 12, 2514 JL The Hague
New Zealand
  Embassy:
  (☎ 04-473 5339, fax 472 7255,
  ✉ ambwell@xtra.co.nz)
  34 Grant Rd, Thorndon, Wellington
Slovenia
  Embassy:
  (☎ 061-126 21 94, fax 125 33 02)
  Snezniska Ulica 8, Ljubljana 61000
Spain
  Embassy:
  (☎ 91 577 6529, fax 91 575 7776,
  ✉ ambitalsp@cempresarial.com)
  Calle Lagasca 98, Madrid 28006
Switzerland
  Embassy:
  (☎ 031-352 4151, fax 351 1026,
  ✉ ambital.berna@spectraweb.ch)
  Elfenstrasse 14, Bern 3006
UK
  Embassy:
  (☎ 020-7312 2200, fax 7312 2230,
  ✉ emblondon@embitaly.org.uk)
  14 Three Kings Yard, London W1Y 2EH
  Consulate:
  (☎ 020-7235 9371, fax 7823 1609)
  38 Eaton Place, London SW1X 8AN
USA
  Embassy:
  (☎ 202-328 5500, fax 328 5593,
  ✉ itapress@ix.netcom.com)
  1601 Fuller St, NW, Washington DC 20009
  Consulates:
  (☎ 213-820 0622, fax 820 0727,
  ✉ cglos@aol.com)
  Suite 300, 12400 Wilshire Blvd, Los Angeles,
  CA 90025
  (☎ 212-737 9100, fax 249 4945,
  ✉ italconsny@aol.com)
  690 Park Ave, New York, NY 10021–5044
  (☎ 415-931 4924, fax 931 7205)
  2590 Webster St, San Francisco, CA 94115

Consulates in Florence

Florence must be a popular posting for diplomats – quite a few countries have consular reps here:

Belgium
(Map 3; ☎ 055 28 20 94)
Via dei Servi 28
Denmark
(Map 3; ☎ 055 21 10 07)
Via dei Servi 13
France
(Map 5; ☎ 055 230 25 56)
Piazza Ognissanti 2
Office hours are from 9 am to noon Monday
to Friday
Germany
(Map 3; ☎ 055 29 47 22)
Lungarno Vespucci 30
Office hours are from 9.30 am to 12.30 pm
Monday to Friday
Netherlands
(Map 3; ☎ 055 47 52 49)
Via Cavour 81
Norway
(Map 4; ☎ 055 247 93 21)
Via Gino Capponi 26
South Africa
(Map 6; ☎ 055 28 18 63)
Piazza Saltarelli 1
Sweden
(Map 3; ☎ 055 49 60 14)
Via Bonifacio Lupi 14
Switzerland
(Map 2; ☎ 055 22 24 34)
Piazzale Galileo 5
UK
(Map 6; ☎ 055 28 41 33)
Lungarno Corsini 2
USA
(Map 2; ☎ 055 239 82 76)
Lungarno Vespucci 38
Office hours are from 9 am to 12.30 pm and
2.30 to 3.30 pm Monday to Friday

Embassies in Rome
Most countries have an embassy in Rome.
Look them up under 'Ambasciate' in the
Pagine Gialle (Yellow Pages). They include:

Australia
(☎ 06 85 27 21)
Via Alessandria 215
Austria
(☎ 06 844 01 41)
Via Pergolesi 3
Canada
(☎ 06 44 59 81)
Via GB de Rossi 27
France
(☎ 06 68 60 11)
Piazza Farnese 67

Germany
(☎ 06 49 21 31)
Via San Martino della Battaglia 4
Ireland
(☎ 06 697 91 21)
Piazza Campitelli 3
Netherlands
(☎ 06 322 11 41)
Via Michele Mercati 8
New Zealand
(☎ 06 441 71 71)
Via Zara 28
Slovenia
(☎ 06 808 12 75)
Via Leonardo Pisano 10
Switzerland
(☎ 06 80 95 71)
Via Barnarba Oriani 61
UK
(☎ 06 482 54 41)
Via XX Settembre 80/a
USA
(☎ 06 4 67 41)
Via Vittorio Veneto 119/a

CUSTOMS
Travellers entering Italy from outside the
EU are allowed to bring in duty-free 1L of
spirits, 2L of wine, 60 mL of perfume and
200 cigarettes.

On 1 July 1999 the sale of duty-free
goods to people travelling within the EU
was abolished. Under the rules of the single market, goods bought in and exported
within the EU incur no additional taxes,
provided duty has been paid somewhere
within the EU and the goods are for personal consumption. 'Guidance levels' on
quantities are set by the EU. At the time of
writing these were: 10L of spirits, 90L of
wine and 800 cigarettes.

MONEY
A combination of travellers cheques and
credit or cash cards is the best way to take
your money.

Currency
Until the euro notes and coins are in circu-
lation (see the boxed text 'Introducing the
Euro'), Italy's currency will remain the *lira*
(plural: *lire*). The smallest note is L1000.
Other denominations in notes are L2000,
L5000, L10,000, L50,000, L100,000 and

Introducing the Euro

Since 1 January 1999, the lira and the euro – Europe's new currency in 11 EU countries – have both been legal tender in Italy. Euro coins and banknotes have not been issued yet, but you can already get billed in euros and opt to pay in euros by credit card. Essentially, if there's no hard cash involved, you can deal in euros. Travellers should check bills carefully to make sure that any conversion has been calculated correctly.

The whole idea behind the current paperless currency is to give euro-fearing punters a chance to limber up arithmetically before euro coins and banknotes are issued on 1 January 2002. The same euro coins (one to 50 cents, €1 and €2) and banknotes (€5 to €500) will then be used in the 11 countries of what has been dubbed Euroland: Austria, Belgium, Finland, France, Germany, Ireland, Italy, Luxembourg, the Netherlands, Portugal and Spain. The lira will remain legal currency alongside the euro until 1 March 2002, when it will be hurled on the scrapheap of history.

Until then, the 11 currencies have been fixed to the euro at the following rates: AS13.76, BF40.34, 5.95 mk, 6.56FF, DM1.96, IR£0.79, L1936, flux40.34, f2.2, 200$48 and 166.39 ptas. The Lonely Planet Web site at www.lonelyplanet.com has a link to a currency converter and up-to-date news on the integration process. Or have a look at europa.eu.int/euro/html/entry.html.

Euro exchange rates include:

Australia	A$1	=	€0.61
Canada	C$1	=	€0.65
Japan	¥100	=	€0.01
New Zealand	NZ$1	=	€0.48
UK	UK£1	=	€1.59
USA	US$1	=	€0.95

L500,000. Coin denominations are L50, L100, L200, L500 and L1000.

Like other continental Europeans, Italians indicate decimals with commas and thousands with points.

country	unit		lira
Australia	AS$1	=	L1172
Canada	C$1	=	L1249
euro	€1	=	L1936
France	1FF	=	L295
Germany	DM1	=	L990
Japan	¥100	=	L1832
New Zealand	NZ$1	=	L933
UK	UK£1	=	L3017
USA	US$1	=	L1836

Exchanging Money

If you need to exchange cash or travellers cheques, be prepared to queue.

You can exchange money in banks, at post offices or in currency exchange booths (bureaux de change). Banks are generally the most reliable option and tend to offer the best rates. However, you should look around and ask about commissions. These can fluctuate considerably and a lot depends on whether you are exchanging cash or cheques. While post offices charge a flat rate of L1000 per cash transaction, banks charge L2500, or even more. Travellers cheques attract higher fees. Some banks charge L1000 per cheque (minimum L3000), while post offices charge a maximum L5000 per transaction.

Keep a sharp eye open for commissions at bureaux de changes. By way of example, Exact Change charges 9.8% on foreign currency travellers cheques. Another booth charges 5% on cash or cheques, along with a set fee (L1000 for cash and L3000 for travellers cheques). Thomas Cook charges 4.5% (minimum L5500) for cash or travellers cheques (except Thomas Cook travellers cheques, which are commission free).

Cash Don't bring wads of cash from home (travellers cheques and plastic are much safer). It is, however, an idea to keep an emergency stash separate from other valuables in case you should lose your travellers cheques and/or credit cards.

You will need cash for some day-to-day transactions (many small pensioni, eateries and shops do not take credit cards).

Travellers Cheques These are a safe way of carrying your money because they can be replaced if they are lost or stolen. They can be cashed at most banks and exchange offices. Amex, Visa and Thomas Cook are widely accepted brands. If you lose your Amex cheques, report the loss by phoning a 24-hour toll-free number (☎ 800 872000).

It doesn't really matter whether your cheques are in lire or in the currency of the country you buy them in. Get most of your cheques in fairly large denominations (the equivalent of L100,000 or more) to save on any per-cheque commission charges. Amex exchange offices do not charge commission to exchange travellers cheques (even other brands).

It's vital to keep your initial receipt, along with a record of your cheque numbers and the ones you have used, separate from the cheques themselves.

Take your passport when you go to cash travellers cheques.

Eurocheques Eurocheques (with guarantee card) were still fairly widely accepted at the time of writing, but the advent of the euro means they are due to be phased out.

Credit/Debit Cards Carrying plastic is the simplest way to organise your holiday funds. You don't have large amounts of cash or cheques to lose, you can get money after hours and at weekends and the exchange rate is better than that offered for travellers cheques or cash exchanges.

Major cards, such as Visa, MasterCard, Eurocard, Cirrus and Eurocheque cards, are accepted throughout Italy. They can be used for many purchases and in hotels and restaurants (although pensioni and smaller trattorie and pizzerie tend to accept cash only). Credit cards can also be used in Automatic Teller Machines (ATMs, or *bancomats*) displaying the appropriate sign, or (if you have no PIN) to obtain cash advances over the counter in many banks – MasterCard and Visa cards are among the most widely recognised for such transactions. Check charges with your bank but, as a rule, there is no charge for purchases on major cards and a 1.5% charge on cash advances and ATM transactions in foreign currencies.

It is not uncommon for ATMs in Italy to reject foreign cards. Don't despair or start wasting money on international calls to your bank. Try a few more ATMs displaying your credit card's logo before assuming the problem lies with your card rather than with the local system.

If your card is lost, stolen or swallowed by an ATM, you can telephone toll-free to have an immediate stop put on its use. For MasterCard the number in Italy is ☎ 800 870 866, or make a reverse-charge call to St Louis in the USA on ☎ 314-275 6690; for Visa, phone ☎ 800 877 232 in Italy. If, by chance, you have a credit card issued in Italy, call ☎ 800 822 056 to have it blocked.

Amex is also widely accepted (although not as commonly as Visa or MasterCard). The office in Florence (see Where to Exchange later in the chapter) also has an express cash machine for cardholders. If you lose your Amex card you can call ☎ 800 864 046.

International Transfers It is inadvisable to send cheques by mail to Italy because of the unreliability of the country's postal service. One reliable way to send money is by 'urgent telex' through the foreign office of a large Italian bank, or through major banks in your own country, to a nominated bank in Italy. The money will always be held at the head office of the bank in the town to which it has been sent. Urgent-telex transfers should take only a few days, while other means, such as telegraphic transfer, or draft, can take weeks. It is important to keep an exact record of all details associated with the money transfer, particularly the exact address of the bank to where the money has been sent.

It is also possible to transfer money through American Express and Thomas Cook. You will be required to produce identification, usually a passport, to collect the money. Take the details of the transaction when you go to collect the money.

Another option is to send money through Western Union. The sender and receiver have to turn up at a Western Union outlet with a passport or other form of ID and the fees charged for the virtually immediate transfer depend on the amount sent. For sums up to US$400, Western Union charges the sender US$20; the money can supposedly be handed over to the recipient within 10 minutes of being sent. This service functions through several outlets in Italy. In Florence try the Exact Change booths (see the following Where to Exchange section). Mail Boxes Etc (Map 3; ☎ 055 26 81 73), Via della Scala 13r, also offers this service.

Another service along the same lines is MoneyGram, which operates mainly through Thomas Cook (for their address in Florence see the following Where to Exchange section). Like Western Union, they are expanding their network of agents. For instance, the Banco di Milano exchange booth (Map 6) at Via de' Cerretani 43r represents them.

Where to Exchange

A number of the main banks are concentrated around Piazza della Repubblica. Hours vary but banks tend to open from 8.30 am to 1.30 pm and 3.30 to 4.30 pm Monday to Friday. They are closed at the weekend (occasionally you may a find a bank open on a Saturday morning).

Thomas Cook has an exchange office (Map 6; ☎ 055 28 97 81) at Lungarno degli Acciaioli 6r, near the Ponte Vecchio. It is open from 9 am to 7 pm Monday to Saturday and from 9 am to 1 pm on Sunday. There's an American Express (Amex) office and travel service (Map 6; ☎ 055 5 09 81) at Via Dante Alighieri 22r. It opens from 9 am to 5.30 pm Monday to Friday and from 9.30 am to 12.30 pm on Saturday.

Exact Change has a booth right by the Ponte Vecchio (Map 6; ☎ 055 28 73 09) at Via Por Santa Maria 3r. It's open daily. A further three branches are at Via dei Calzaiuoli 42r (Map 6), Via Luigi Alamanni 9r (Map 3) and Via Porta Rossa 27r (Map 6).

Security

Keep only a limited amount of money as cash and the bulk in more easily replaceable forms such as travellers cheques or plastic. If your accommodation has a safe, use it. If you have to leave money in your room, divide it into several stashes and hide each in a different place.

When carrying money on the street the safest thing to use is a shoulder wallet or under-the-clothes moneybelt. An external moneybelt tends to attract attention to your valuables. Watch out for people who touch you or seem to be getting unnecessarily close, in any situation. Italy has been rated by one London-based organisation, Card Protection Plan, as second only to Spain for credit card theft among foreign travellers. Florence is one of the worst cities in Italy on this score, with 63% of cards reported missing or stolen rather than lost.

Costs

Florence is expensive – it's as simple as that. Accommodation charges (especially in high season) and high admission fees for many sights keep daily expenditure high. A *very* prudent backpacker might scrape by on around L80,000 a day, but only by staying in a youth hostel, eating one simple meal a day (at the youth hostel), making sandwiches for lunch, walking rather than indulging in local transport (not a great hardship) and keeping the daily museum and gallery intake low.

One rung up, you can get by on L140,000 per day if you stay in the cheapest pensioni or small hotels, and keep sit-down meals and museums to one a day. Lone travellers may find even this budget hard to maintain since single rooms tend to be pricey.

If money is no object, you'll find a plethora of ways to burn it in Florence. There's no shortage of luxury hotels, expensive restaurants and shops. Realistically, a traveller wanting to stay in a comfortable lower- to mid-range hotel, eat two square meals a day, not feel restricted to one museum a day and be able to enjoy the odd drink and other minor indulgences should reckon on a minimum daily average of L250,000.

A basic breakdown of costs per person during an average day for the budget-range traveller could be: accommodation L20,000 (youth hostel) to L60,000 (single in pensione or per person in comfortable double), breakfast L3000 (coffee and brioche), lunch (sandwich and mineral water) L5000, bottle of mineral water L1500, couple of bus rides L3000, admission fee for one museum up to L12,000, and sit-down dinner L20,000 to L50,000.

Ways to Save If you could it would be nice to avoid paying the extra charged by many pensioni for compulsory breakfast – a coffee and brioche in a cafe cost less and are better. The sad reality is that most places only offer the one price on rooms and this automatically includes breakfast.

In bars, prices can double (sometimes even triple) if you sit down and are served at the table. Stand at the bar to drink your coffee or eat a sandwich – or buy a sandwich or slice of pizza and head for the nearest piazza.

Read the fine print on menus (usually posted outside eating establishments) to check the cover charge *(coperto)* and service fee *(servizio)*. These can make a big difference to the bill.

Tipping & Bargaining

You are not expected to tip on top of restaurant service charges, but it is common to leave a small amount. If there is no service charge the customer might consider leaving a 10% tip, but this is by no means obligatory. In bars, Italians often leave any small change as a tip, often only L100 or L200. Tipping taxi drivers is not common practice, but you should tip the porter at higher-class hotels.

Bargaining is common in flea markets but not in shops, although you might find that the proprietor is disposed to give a discount if you are spending a reasonable amount of money. It is quite acceptable to ask if there is a special price for a room in a pensione if you plan to stay for more than a few days.

Taxes & Refunds

A value-added tax (known as Imposta di Valore Aggiunto or IVA) of around 19% is slapped on to just about everything in Italy.

Tourists who are resident outside the EU may claim a refund on this tax if they spend more than a certain amount (L300,000 in 1999) in the same shop on the same day. The refund applies only to items purchased at retail outlets affiliated to the system – these shops display a 'Tax-free for tourists' sign. If you don't see a sign, ask the shopkeeper. You must fill out a form at the point of purchase and have it stamped and checked by Italian customs when you leave the country (you will need to show the receipt and your purchases). At major airports and some border crossings you can then get an immediate cash refund at specially marked booths; alternatively, return the form by mail to the vendor, who will make the refund, either by cheque or to your credit card.

For information call ☎ 0332 87 07 70 or consult the rules brochure available in affiliated stores.

Receipts

Laws aimed at tightening controls on the payment of taxes in Italy mean that the onus is on the buyer to ask for and retain receipts for all goods and services. This applies to everything from a litre of milk to a haircut. Although it rarely happens, you could be asked by an officer of the fiscal police *(guardia di finanza)* to produce the receipt immediately after you leave a shop. If you don't have it, you may be obliged to pay a fine of up to L300,000.

POST & COMMUNICATIONS
Post

Italy's postal service is notoriously slow, unreliable and expensive. Don't expect to receive every letter sent to you, or that every letter you send will reach its destination. Information (in Italian) on postal rates and services can be had by calling ☎ 160.

Stamps *(francobolli)* are available from post offices and authorised tobacconists (look for the official *tabacchi* sign: a big 'T', often white on black). For letters that need to be weighed, what you get at the tobacconist's for international air mail will often be an approximation of the proper rate.

FACTS FOR THE VISITOR

The central post office is at Via Pelliceria, off Piazza della Repubblica (Map 6), and is open from 8.15 am to 7 pm daily. Another big one is on the corner of Via Giuseppe Verdi and Via Pietrapiana (Map 7). Poste restante mail can be addressed to 50100 Florence.

Postal Rates The cost of sending a letter air mail *(via aerea)* depends on its weight and where it is being sent. Postcards and letters up to 20g cost L1400 to Australia and New Zealand, L1300 to the USA and L800 to EU countries (L900 to the rest of Europe). Postcards cost the same. Aerograms are a cheap alternative, costing only L900 to send anywhere. They can be purchased at post offices.

A new service, *posta prioritaria* (priority post, a little like the UK's 1st-class post), began in 1999. For L1200, postcards and letters up to 20g posted to destinations within Italy, the EU, Switzerland and Norway are supposed to arrive the following day. There are no guarantees, however.

Sending letters express *(espresso)* costs a standard extra L3600, but may help speed a letter on its way.

If you want to post more important items by registered mail *(raccomandato)* or by insured mail *(assicurato)*, remember that they will take as long as normal mail. Raccomandato costs L4000 on top of the normal cost of the letter. The cost of assicurato depends on the value of the object being sent (L6000 for objects up to L100,000 value) and is not available to the USA.

Sending Mail If you choose not to use priority post (see Postal Rates in the previous section) an air-mail letter can take up to two weeks to reach the UK or the USA, while a letter to Australia will take between two and three weeks. Postcards can take even longer because they are low-priority mail.

The service within Italy is not much better: local letters take at least three days and up to a week to arrive in another city.

Parcels *(pacchetti)* can be sent from any post office. You can buy posting boxes or padded envelopes from most post offices.

Stationery shops *(cartolerie)* and some tobacconists also sell padded envelopes. There are some strange regulations about how parcels should be sealed and these appear to vary from one post office to another. Don't tape up or staple envelopes – they should be sealed with glue. Your best bet is not to close the envelope or box completely and ask at the counter how it should be done. Parcels usually take longer to be delivered than letters. A different set of postal rates applies.

Express Mail Urgent mail can be sent by the post office's express mail service, known as *posta celere* or CAI Post. Letters up to 500g cost L30,000 in Europe, L46,000 to the USA and L68,000 to Australia and New Zealand. A parcel weighing 1kg will cost L34,000 in Europe, L54,000 to the USA and Canada, and L80,000 to Australia and New Zealand. CAI Post is not necessarily as fast as private services. It will take three to five days for a parcel to reach the USA, Canada or Australia and one to three days to European destinations. Ask at post offices for addresses of CAI Post outlets.

Couriers Several international couriers operate in Italy: DHL has an office at Via della Cupola 243 and a 24-hour toll-free phone line (Map 1; ☎ 800 345 345); Federal Express has offices outside town and can be reached toll-free on ☎ 800 123 800; for UPS, also out of town, call toll-free on ☎ 800 877 877. Note that if you are having articles sent to you by courier in Italy, you might be obliged to pay IVA of up to 20% to retrieve the goods.

Receiving Mail Poste restante is known as *fermo posta* in Italy. Letters marked thus will be held at the counter of the same name in the central post office. Poste restante mail should be addressed as follows:

> John SMITH,
> Fermo Posta,
> Posta Centrale,
> 50100 Florence
> Italy

You will need to pick up your letters in person and present your passport as ID. The counter is through the first door on the left as you enter the post office from Via Pellicceria.

Amex card or travellers cheque holders can use the free client mail-holding service at the Florence office (see Where to Exchange under Money earlier in the chapter).

Telephone

The mostly privatised Telecom Italia is the largest phone company in Italy and its orange public pay phones are liberally scattered all over the country. The most common accept telephone cards (carte/schede telefoniche) only, although you will still find some that accept cards and coins (L100, L200 and L500). Some card phones now also accept special Telecom credit cards and even commercial credit cards. A few send faxes.

You will find Telecom phones in several booths near the ATAF information booth (Map 3) outside the Stazione di Santa Maria Novella. There is an unstaffed phone office with national phone books at Via Cavour 21r (Map 6).

Phonecards can be bought at post offices, tobacconists, newspaper stands and from vending machines in Telecom offices. To avoid the frustration of trying to find fast-disappearing coin telephones, always keep a phonecard on hand. They come with a value of L5000, L10,000 and L15,000. Remember to snap off the perforated corner before using them.

Public phones operated by a new telecommunications company, Infostrada, can be found in airports and train stations. These phones accept Infostrada phonecards (available from post offices, tobacconists and newspaper stands), which come with a value of L3000, L5000 or L10,000. Infostrada's rates are slightly cheaper than Telecom's for long-distance and international calls but you cannot make local calls from these phones.

In 1999 the competition started to heat up. A company called Tiscali put cards on the market to be used with public phones (and separate ones for private phones) with which they claimed you would pay 35% less

on intercity calls. Price wars are, as has long been the case in places like the USA and UK, probably inevitable.

Costs Rates, particularly for long-distance calls, are among the highest in Europe (although they are slowly falling). The cheapest time for domestic calls is from 6.30 pm to 8 am. It is a little more complicated for international calls but, basically, off-peak time is 10 pm to 8 am and all of Sunday, depending on the country called.

A local call (comunicazione urbana) from a public phone will cost L200 for three to six minutes, depending on the time of day. Peak call times are 8 am to 6.30 pm Monday to Friday and 8 am to 1 pm on Saturday.

Rates for long-distance calls (comunicazione interurbana) within Italy depend on the time of day and the distance involved. At most, one minute will cost about L340 in peak periods.

If you need to call overseas, beware of the cost – even a five-minute call to Australia after 10 pm will cost around L10,000 from a private phone (more from a public phone). Calls to most of the rest of Europe (except the UK, which is cheaper) cost L1245 for the first minute and L762 thereafter (and closer to L1200 from a public phone).

Domestic Calls Area codes have become an integral part of the telephone number. The codes all began with 0 and consisted of up to four digits. You must now dial this whole number, even if calling from next door. Thus, any number you call in the Florence area will begin with 055.

Toll-free numbers (numeri verdi) that until February 1999 began with the digits 167 have been changed to 800 numbers, bringing Italy into line with an international trend (although you may still see such numbers advertised as 167).

For directory inquiries call ☎ 12.

Note Not only have area codes become part of the phone number, there are now plans to convert the initial 0 into a 4 by the end of 2000. Thus any number in the Florence area will start with 455.

FACTS FOR THE VISITOR

Emergency Numbers

Military Police (Carabinieri)	☎ 112
Police (Polizia)	☎ 113
Fire Brigade (Vigili del Fuoco)	☎ 115
Highway Rescue (Soccorso Stradale)	☎ 116
Ambulance (Ambulanza)	☎ 118

International Calls Direct international calls can easily be made from public telephones by using a phonecard. Dial 00 to get out of Italy, then the relevant country and city codes, followed by the telephone number.

Useful country codes are: Australia 61, Canada and the USA 1, New Zealand 64, and the UK 44. Codes for other countries in Europe include: Belgium 32, France 33, Germany 49, Greece 30, Ireland 353 and Spain 34. Other codes are listed in Italian telephone books.

To make a reverse-charge (collect) international call from a public telephone, dial ☎ 170.

It is easier and often cheaper to use the Country Direct service. You dial the number and request a reverse-charge call through the operator in your country. Numbers for this service include:

Australia	(Optus)	☎ 172 11 61
	(Telstra)	☎ 172 10 61
Canada	(AT&T)	☎ 172 10 02
	(Teleglobe)	☎ 172 10 01
France		☎ 172 00 33
Germany		☎ 172 00 49
Ireland		☎ 172 03 53
Japan	(IDC)	☎ 172 10 80
Netherlands		☎ 172 00 31
New Zealand		☎ 172 10 64
UK	(BT)	☎ 172 00 44
	(BT Automatic Chargecard Operator)	☎ 172 01 44
USA	(AT&T)	☎ 172 10 11
	(IDB)	☎ 172 17 77
	(MCI)	☎ 172 10 22
	(Sprint)	☎ 172 18 77

For international directory inquiries call ☎ 176.

International Phonecards The Lonely Planet eKno Communication Card (see the Lonely Planet Web site for details) is aimed specifically at travellers and provides cheap international calls, a range of messaging services and free email (though for local calls, you're usually better off with a local card). You can join online at www.ekno.lonely planet.com, or by phone from Italy by dialling ☎ 800 975691. Once you have joined, to use eKno from Italy dial ☎ 800 875683.

Several other private companies now distribute international phonecards, which are mostly linked to US phone companies such as Sprint and MCI. The cards come in a variety of unit sizes and are sold in some bars and tobacconists in the bigger cities.

Telecom has brought out its own Welcome Card, which costs L25,000 for 100 units. It's certainly cheaper than making international calls on a standard phonecard, but may not stand up to some of the competition.

Infostrada sells various cards, some of which are only good in the very limited number of Infostrada phones around. The best for international calls costs L20,000 and can be used from private or public phones (you dial a toll-free access number and then key in a provided code).

A further possibility for long-distance calls are privately run call centres. Yellow Point at Via Santa Elizabetta 5 (Map 6) is a newcomer to Italy; they claim their rates work out cheaper than Telecom's.

Calling Florence from Abroad Dial the international access code (00 in most countries), followed by the code for Italy (39) and the full number, including the initial zero. If you are calling a mobile phone, however, drop the initial 0 of the prefix.

Telegram
These dinosaurs can be sent from post offices or dictated by phone (☎ 186) and are an expensive, but sure, way of having important messages delivered by the same or next day.

Fax
You can send faxes from post offices and private operators in Florence but Italy's high

phone charges make them an expensive mode of communication. To send a fax within Italy expect to pay L3000 for the first page and L2000 for each page thereafter, plus L50 a second for the call. International faxes can cost L6000 for the first page and L4000 per page thereafter, and L100 a second for the call. You can imagine what this could mean with a slow fax machine at peak rates!

The central post office (Map 6) operates a fax poste restante service. You can have faxes sent to you at Fax Fermo Posta. To retrieve the fax you will need a passport or some other photo ID. You pay L2000 for the first page received and L500 for each page thereafter. Ask in the telegrams office (off to the right when you reach the main hall of the post office). Faxes should be sent to ☎ 055 21 49 45.

Email & Internet Access

Travelling with a portable computer is a great way to stay in touch with life back home, but unless you know what you're doing it's fraught with potential problems. If you plan to carry your notebook or palmtop computer with you, remember that the power supply voltage in your hotel may vary from that at home, risking damage to your equipment. The best investment is a universal AC adaptor for your appliance, which will enable you to plug it in anywhere without frying the innards. You'll also need a plug adaptor for Italy (the standard European two round-pin variety), which is easier to buy before you leave home.

Your PC-card modem may or may not work once you leave your home country – and you won't know for sure until you try. The safest option is to buy a reputable 'global' modem before you leave home, or buy a local PC-card modem if you're spending an extended time in Italy.

Increasingly, Italian telephone sockets are being standardised to the US RJ-11 type. If you find yourself confronted with the old-style Italian three-prong socket, most electrical stores can sell you an adaptor. For more information on travelling with a portable computer, see Web sites www.tele adapt.com or www.warrior.com.

Major Internet service providers (ISPs), such as CompuServe at www.compuserve .com, and IBM Net at www.ibm.net, have dial-in nodes throughout Europe; it's best to download a list of the dial-in numbers before you leave home. Some Italian servers can provide short-term accounts for Internet access. Flashnet (☎ 06 66 05 41) offers 20-hour renewable subscriptions for L30,000 (valid for one year); their Web site at www .flashnet.it has a list of authorised sales points in Italy. Agora (☎ 06 699 17 42) has subscriptions for two months for L84,000. Both of these providers have English-speaking staff.

If you intend to rely on cybercafes, you'll need to carry three pieces of information with you to enable you to access your Internet mail account: your incoming (POP or IMAP) mail server name, your account name and your password. Your ISP or network supervisor will be able to give you these. Armed with this information, you should be able to access your Internet mail account from any net-connected machine in the world, provided it runs some kind of email software (remember that Netscape and Internet Explorer both have mail modules). It pays to become familiar with the process for doing this before you leave home. A final option to collect mail through cybercafes is to open a free eKno Web-based email account online. You can then access your mail from anywhere in the world from any net-connected machine running a standard Web browser.

Cybercafes You can expect to pay between L10,000 and L15,000 an hour in any of the growing number of Internet shops and cybercafes dotted about town. They are springing up all over the place, so by the time you read this more are bound to have surfaced.

The cheapest deal in town is Il Cairo Phone Center (Map 7; ☎ 055 263 83 36) Via de' Macci 90r. You can sign up for a block of 10 hours (useable any time) for L50,000. Down the road at No 8r, Net Bar (Map 7; ☎ 055 247 94 65) is open for Internet business until midnight (closed on Sunday). It costs L14,000 per hour (students L10,000).

euro currency converter   L10,000 = €5.16

Internet Train has three branches, at Via dell'Oriuolo 25r (Map 5; ☎ 055 263 89 68), Via Guelfa 24a (Map 3; ☎ 055 21 47 94) and Borgo San Jacopo 30r (Map 6; ☎ 055 265 79 35). It costs L12,000 (students L10,000) to hook up for an hour.

Another option is Intercommunication Centre (Map 5; ☎ 055 267 88 28), Via del Porcellana 20r. Yet another is The Netgate (Map 7; ☎ 055 234 79 67), Via Sant'Egidio 10r. You could also try WWW.Village (Map 4; ☎ 055 247 93 98) at Via degli Alfani 13r. Mondial Net (Map 3; ☎ 055 265 75 84) is at Via de' Ginori 59r. CyberOffice (Map 3; ☎ 055 21 11 03), Via San Gallo 4r, lets you online for L10,000 per hour.

Amex clients can arrange to receive email at their office (see Where to Exchange in the earlier Money section).

INTERNET RESOURCES

The World Wide Web is a rich resource for travellers. You can research your trip, hunt down bargain air fares, book hotels, check on weather conditions or chat with locals and other travellers about the best places to visit (or avoid!).

One of the best places to start your Web explorations is the Lonely Planet Web site at www.lonelyplanet.com. Here you'll find succinct summaries on travelling to most places on earth, postcards from other travellers and the Thorn Tree bulletin board, where you can ask questions before you go or dispense advice when you get back.

Scouring the Internet for a few hours can lead you to some interesting tips about most aspects of the region, from out-of-the-way villas to wine appreciation. Some initial sites you might like to surf include:

ATAF online
www.comune.firenze.it/ataf
All you ever wanted to know, and probably quite a few things you didn't, about Florence's public transport system.

Excitetravel
www.excite.com/travel/countries/italy/florence
Excite's travel Web pages, with farefinder and bookings, and links to maps, restaurant tips and the like.

Ferrovie dello Stato
www.fs-on-line.com
This is the official site of the Ferrovie dello Stato, the Italian railways. You can look up fare and timetable information here, although it can be a little complicated to plough through.

Firenze.net
www.firenze.net/
This site, which is full of more or less useful listings information, is in English and Italian, and includes a host of further links.

Go Tuscany
www.firenze.net/events
This Go Tuscany site is aimed at the expat community and English-speaking visitors to the region. It contains tips on places to stay and eat both in and outside Florence, itineraries in Tuscany, classified ads and an events calendar.

informacittà
www.informacitta.net
Here you can check out the latest in what's happening in and around Florence.

Internet Café Guide
www.netcafeguide.com/
At this sight you can get a list of Internet cafes in Florence (and around Italy). It's not as up-to-date as you might expect such a site to be, but it is a start (see also Cybercafes in the previous Email & Internet Access section).

BOOKS

Most books are published in different editions by different publishers in different countries. Your local bookshop or library is best placed to advise you on the availability of the following recommendations.

For bookshops in Florence, see Books in the Shopping chapter. Remember that books are expensive in Italy. If you can get hold of English-language titles at home, your pocket will be better off.

Lonely Planet

If you are planning on wider travels in the country, get hold of *Italy*. Hikers should take a look at *Walking in Italy*. Other companion titles include *Rome*, *Tuscany* and *Venice*. Also published by Lonely Planet, the *Italian phrasebook* lists all the words and phrases you're likely to need. Lonely Planet's *World Food Italy* is a full-colour book with information on the whole range of Italian food, a culinary dictionary and a useful language section.

The glories of Florence as viewed from Piazzale Michelangelo, south of the Arno

The Neptune Fountain (known locally as 'the Big White Thing') oversees Piazza della Signoria.

To avoid stendhalismo, rest often and well.

Beep beep! Florence is the *motorino* capital of Italy

Modern design catches the eye in this old city.

"Alé Viola!" AC Fiorentina's fans pack the Stadio Franchi.

Guidebooks

If your Italian is good, the single most complete guidebooks to the history, culture and monuments of Italy are the 23 exhaustive hardback volumes published by the Touring Club Italiano. The relevant ones in this instance are *Firenze e Provincia* and *Toscana*.

Italian History & People

Edward Gibbon's *History of the Decline and Fall of the Roman Empire* (available in six hardback volumes, or an abridged, single-volume paperback) remains the masterwork on that subject in English. Other, simpler offerings include: *The Oxford History of the Roman World* edited by John Boardman, Jasper Griffin & Oswyn Murray.

For a general look at Italy, you could do a lot worse than *History of the Italian People* by Giuliano Procacci. Other options to help you get started include *Italy: A Short History* by Harry Hearder and *Concise History of Italy* by Vincent Cronin. *A History of Contemporary Italy: Society and Politics 1943–1988* by Paul Ginsburg, is an absorbing analysis of the country's post-WWII travails.

Florentine History & People

Christopher Hibbert's *The Rise and Fall of the House of Medici* is an acknowledged classic on the fortunes of Florence's most famous family. For a more general history of the city, try his *Biography of Florence*, which sweeps you along at a brisk pace through the political, social and artistic highs and lows of the city. Hibbert has been acclaimed as one of the UK's great popular historians and his racy narrative style makes both books a good initial investment.

Leaning more to the artistic side of Florence's story is Michael Levey's *Florence – A Portrait*. Not as full of intriguing anecdote as Hibbert's books, it is still an excellent and highly readable treatment.

A rather more ponderous general history of the city is Marcello Vanuzzi's multivolume *Storia di Firenze*. The quirky text

FACTS FOR THE VISITOR

The Grand Tour

The guest book of the now extinct Gabinetto Vieussieux, which from its foundation in 1819 in the Palazzo Buondelmonti was something of a cultural institution in Florence, is a veritable who's who of VIPs who have passed through Florence. Some liked it, some hated it. In some respects one of the latter was Mark Twain, who in particular found the Arno a poor excuse for a river (after the Mississippi it must come as a bit of a letdown). Fiodor Dostoyevsky was as beset with financial problems here as anywhere and, although he stayed long enough to write part of *The Idiot*, he felt lonely and cut off since he didn't speak a word of Italian.

Stendhal, it is said, discovered 'stendhalismo' in the Basilica di Santa Croce, overwhelmed by the sheer concentration of art in Florence. Judging by his journal notes, he was somewhat overwhelmed by the need to pay little tips to an unending stream of attendants and small lads to get from one sight to another. His countryman, the Marquis de Sade, found the local women 'tall, impertinent, ugly, dishevelled and gluttonous'.

Percy Shelley composed his *Ode to the West Wind* in the Cascine. Percy and pals, such as Lord Byron, the Brownings and Walter Savage Landor, all resided in Florence for a while, maintaining a haughty distance from the locals and indulging their whims.

Dickens, a little more down to earth, was fascinated by the city, and Anatole France opined that the 'god who created Florence was an artist'.

Mozart popped by with his father as a 14-year-old in 1770. He stayed but a few days, just enough time to waltz from one engagement to the next, wowing all the nobs in town with his genius.

A century later, Queen Victoria visited three times. Not a great lover of museums or art, she preferred to spend her time in the city's parks and gardens and keep a low profile.

The list, as you can imagine, just goes on and on. So you are not in bad company at any rate!

has been condensed into an English version, *The History of Florence*. The information is in there, but the sickly lyrical style is a little peculiar, not to say highly irritating at some points.

Mary McCarthy's *The Stones of Florence*, written in the 1960s, is a more personalised view of the city. McCarthy doesn't pretend to impart history lessons, preferring to weave together facts, figures, anecdotes and her own on-the-spot opinion in an appealing essay-style package. You may not always agree with what she has to say, but her opinions are at the very least thought-provoking. It comes in a large illustrated format or straightforward paperback.

Another highly approachable work is RWB Lewis' *The City of Florence*. Again very personal, it is nevertheless a substantial attempt to get to grips with the city's history and culture to the present day.

Art & Architecture

An attractive coffee-table book with serious content is *History of Italian Renaissance Art* by Frederick Hartt. He concentrates on Florence, but considers the greats of Roman and Venetian art too. Hartt was one of the most distinguished authorities on Renaissance art this century, and if you were to read only one work on the subject, this should probably be it.

A good general reference work covering the Renaissance in all its facets is JR Hale's *Concise Encyclopaedia of the Italian Renaissance*.

Charles Avery's *Florentine Renaissance Sculpture* is a comprehensive study of this aspect of Florence's glittering artistic legacy.

Bruno Nardini's *Incontro con Michelangiolo* has been translated as *Michelangelo – Biography of a Genius*, a compelling account of the artist's life. If you prefer to read about his life in novel form, Irving Stone's *The Agony & The Ecstasy*, which took the author six years to write, could be for you.

If you think you are up to it, you can pick up Giorgio Vasari's classic *Le Vite de' Eccellenti Architetti, Pittori, et Scultori Italiani, da Cimabue, insino a' Tempi Nostri*, better known to English readers simply as *Lives of the Artists*, available in several editions and translations.

Children

Bambini alla Scoperta di Firenze (translated as *Florence for Kids*) is a brightly presented book for young people obliged by their merciless elders to explore the city. It uses an entertaining, informative approach, with quizzes and other learning prompts. Adults can learn quite a lot about the city too. It is published by Fratelli Palomb Editori.

Cuisine

The Food of Italy by Waverley Root is an acknowledged classic, covering Italian cuisine in general. For more specifically Tuscan cooking, you could try *Il Libro della Cucina Fiorentina e Toscana (Book of Florentine and Tuscan Cooking)*, a prettily illustrated job by Elisabetta Piazzesi that has been translated into several languages – you can find it in bookshops in Florence (see Books in the Shopping chapter).

Stephanie Alexander and Maggie Beer's *Tuscan Cooking* is a beautifully illustrated coffee-table tome. Another more suited to the coffee table than the kitchen is Jeni Wright's *Tuscan Food and Folklore*.

For some fine traditional recipes, you will enjoy Slow Food Editore's *Ricette di Osterie di Firenze e Chianti* – if you read some Italian.

Wine buffs may want to get a hold of Luca Maroni's *Guide to Italian Wines* or *Italian Wines*. The latter is published by Gambero Rosso Editore and both books are updated annually.

Residents Guides

People planning to settle in Florence for the long haul may want to invest in some handy local references. *Millevolte Firenze*, by Antonio Tassinari, is a useful guide to all kinds of shops and other addresses in Florence, from barbers to opticians.

For a guide to locally appreciated restaurants, bars and the like in Florence and beyond, a useful supplement to the guide in your hands is the *Guida Locale Firenze e*

Toscana, published by Spettacolo Firenze (L18,000).

Business people may find the *English Yellow Pages in Italy* (L10,000) helpful. Apart from Florence, it covers Rome, Milan, Naples and Genoa.

Walking

For those thinking of exploring the countryside around Florence on foot, there are several possibilities.

Walking and Eating in Tuscany and Umbria by James Lasdun and Pia Davis provides 40 varied itineraries across these two central regions of Italy.

If Italian is not a problem, you might like to consult the *A Piedi...* series. *A Piedi Intorno a Firenze* describes hikes in the vicinity of the city. Other walking guides include: *A Piedi nel Chianti*, *A Piedi in Toscana* and *A Piedi da Firenze a Siena e Roma*.

NEWSPAPERS & MAGAZINES

You can easily find a wide selection of national daily newspapers from around Europe and the UK at news stands all over central Florence. The *International Herald Tribune*, *Time*, *The Economist*, *Le Monde*, *Der Spiegel* and a host of other international magazines are also available.

Italian National Press

There is no 'national' paper as such, but several important dailies are published out of the major cities. These include Milan's *Corriere della Sera*, Turin's *La Stampa* and Rome's *La Repubblica*. This trio forms what could be considered the nucleus of a national press, publishing local editions up and down the country. Politically speaking, they range from centre-left *(La Repubblica)* to establishment-right *(La Stampa)*.

Reading Italian papers is a curious exercise. It is unlikely you will find such a dense and constant coverage of national politics in the press of any other European country. And yet the arcane shenanigans of Italy's political class are so convoluted that even most Italians confess to understanding precious little of what they are bombarded with in the press!

Most daily papers cost L1500, unless there is a weekly magazine *inserto* (supplement) of one sort or another, in which case the cost sometimes rises to L2200.

Local Press

The main local broadsheet is *La Nazione*. Compared with the likes of the *Corriere della Sera* it is pretty poor on both national and foreign news, but if you are more interested in what's happening in Florence and around the region, it's the paper of choice. You will find a fairly decent cinema and theatre listings section in it too.

Useful Publications

In amid the landslide of printed information and disinformation available from the tourist offices is a handy booklet called *Florence – Concierge Information*. It is an advertising vehicle for local enterprises (shops, restaurants, shipping services and the like) aimed at visitors to Florence. The magazine, written in Italian and English, is loaded with all sorts of useful and less useful information on most aspects of the city.

Another magazine (in English) that occasionally has interesting stories on Tuscan themes is the monthly *Vista*. You can generally only find it in the bigger hotels and the occasional bookshop (L3500).

RADIO & TV

You can pick up the BBC World Service on medium wave at 648kHz, short wave at 6195kHz, 9410kHz, 12095kHz, 15575kHz, and on long wave at 198kHz, depending on where you are and the time of day. Voice of America (VOA) can usually be found on short wave at 15205kHz.

There are three state-owned stations: RAI-1 (1332 AM or 89.7 FM), RAI-2 (846 AM or 91.7 FM) and RAI-3 (97.3 FM). They offer a combination of classical and light music with news broadcasts and discussion programmes. RAI-3, in particular, offers a sometimes very attractive mix of classical and contemporary music and interesting talk programmes (for those wanting to improve their Italian).

Many of the local stations are a little bland. For a good mix of contemporary music you could try Controradio on 93.6 AM or Nova Radio on 101.5 FM.

The three state-run TV stations, RAI-1, RAI-2 and RAI-3, are run by Radio e Televisione Italiane. Historically, each has been in the hands of one of the main political groupings in the country, although allegiances are less clear these days.

Of the three, RAI-3 tends to have some of the more interesting programmes. Generally, however, these stations and the private Canale 5, Italia 1 and Rete 4, tend to serve up a diet of indifferent news, tacky variety hours (with lots of near-naked tits and bums, appalling crooning and vaudeville humour) and game shows. Talk shows, some interesting but many nauseating, also abound.

Other stations include Telemontecarlo (TMC), on which you can see CNN if you stay up late enough (starting as late as 5 am), and a host of local channels.

VIDEO SYSTEMS

If you want to record or buy video tapes to play back home, you won't get a picture if the image registration systems are different. TVs and nearly all pre-recorded videos on sale in Italy use the PAL (phase alternation line) system common to most of Western Europe and Australia, incompatible with France's SECAM system or the NTSC system used in North America and Japan. PAL videos can't be played back on a machine that lacks PAL capability.

Ready Made If you're not interested in shooting your own videos, a few local products are available. Vista Video's *Florence* (L40,000) comes in a variety of languages and is a 65-minute journey on film through the city. *Uffizi* (L50,000) is another one you'll see around – no prizes for guessing its subject matter.

PHOTOGRAPHY & VIDEO
Film & Equipment

A roll of 100 ASA Kodak film costs around L7000/8000 for 24/36 exposures. Develop-

ing costs around L11,000/14,000 for 24/36 exposures in standard format. A roll of 36 slides costs L10,000 to buy and L8000 for development.

Numerous outlets sell and process films but beware of poor quality processing. A roll of film is called a *pellicola* but you will be understood if you ask for 'film'. Many places claim to process films in one hour but bear in mind that you may not actually get your photos back that quickly – count on late the next day if the outlet has its own processing equipment, or three to four days if it hasn't. Tapes for video cameras are often available at the same outlets or can be found at stores selling electrical goods.

Technical Tips

Bright middle-of-the-day sun tends to bleach out your shots. You get more colour and contrast earlier and later in the day. This goes both for still photographs and video, and is even more the case in summer, when glare can be a problem – the gentler winter light gives you greater flexibility.

Restrictions

Some museums and galleries ban photography, or at least flash, and the police can be touchy about it. Video is also often not allowed.

Photographing People

It's common courtesy to ask – at least by gesture – when you want to photograph people, except perhaps when they're in some kind of public event, like a procession.

Airport Security

The major Italian airports are all fully equipped with modern inspection systems that do not damage film or other photographic material carried in hand luggage.

TIME

Italy (and hence Florence) is one hour ahead of GMT/UTC during winter and two hours ahead of GMT/UTC during the daylight-saving period from the last Sunday in March to the last Sunday in October. Most other Western European countries have the same time as Italy year-round, the major exceptions being Britain, Ireland and Portugal, which are one hour behind.

When it's noon in Florence, it's 3 am in San Francisco, 6 am in New York and Toronto, 11 am in London, 9 pm in Sydney and 11 pm in Auckland. Note that the changeover to/from daylight saving usually differs from the European date by a couple of weeks in North America and Australasia.

ELECTRICITY
Voltages & Cycles
The electric current in Florence is 220V, 50Hz, as in the rest of continental Europe. Several countries outside Europe (such as the USA and Canada) use 110Hz, which means that some appliances from those countries may perform poorly. It is always safest to use a transformer.

Plugs & Sockets
Plugs have two round-pins, again as in the rest of continental Europe.

WEIGHTS & MEASURES
Italy uses the metric system. Basic terms for weight include *un etto* (100g) and *un chilo* (1kg). Like other continental Europeans, the Italians indicate decimals with commas and thousands with points.

LAUNDRY
The Wash & Dry Laundrette chain (☎ 800 23 11 72) has seven branches across the city. You pay L6000 for 8kg of washing and L6000 for drying. They open from 8 am to 10 pm (last wash at 9 pm). Addresses indicated on the map include: Via Nazionale 49 (Map 3), Via del Sole 52–54r (Map 6), Via dei Servi 105r (Map 3) and Via de' Serragli 87r (Map 5).

There's another coin laundrette at Via Guelfa 33 (Map 3), open from 8 am to 10 pm daily. Another national chain, Onda Blu, has a branch at Via degli Alfani 26r (Map 4). You pay L11,000 to wash and dry 6.5kg of dirty linen.

Another place calling itself Wash & Dry (☎ 055 247 93 13), Via degli Alfani 44r (Map 4), will take your washing and do the business – you pick it up later. The service costs L11,000 a load.

TOILETS
Public toilets are scarce in Florence, but it's OK to wander into most bars and cafes to use their toilet. Common courtesy suggests you order something in exchange for this service, such as a cup of that well-known diuretic, coffee. Make sure the place actually has a loo before committing yourself to more liquid. It's worth carrying some loo paper with you as many toilets lack it.

LEFT LUGGAGE
The left-luggage office at Stazione di Santa Maria Novella (Map 3) is called the Deposito (*deposito bagagli* in full). It is open from 4.15 am to 1.30 pm daily. Each item stored here costs L5000 for 12 hours. You pay the first 12 hours up front and the remaining 12-hour block (or part thereof) when you pick up your belongings.

There is a left-luggage service at Galileo Galilei airport in Pisa but none at Amerigo Vespucci airport in Florence (see Airports in the Getting Around chapter).

Porter Service
A porter (*portabagagli*) service (☎ 055 21 23 19) operates from Stazione di Santa Maria Novella; they charge L4500 per article to escort your luggage to your hotel. You must contact them beforehand and arrange with them to meet your train.

HEALTH
You should encounter no particular health hiccups in Florence. Mild gut problems are a possibility at first, if you're not used to a lot of olive oil, but most travellers experience no problems.

Citizens of EU countries are covered for emergency medical treatment in Italy on presentation of an E111 form. Treatment in private hospitals is not covered and charges are also likely for medication, dental work and secondary examinations, including X-rays and laboratory tests. Ask about the E111 at your local health services department a few weeks before you travel (in the

UK, the form is available at post offices). Australia also has a reciprocal arrangement with Italy so that emergency treatment is covered – Medicare in Australia publishes a brochure with the details.

Medical Kit Check List

Following is a list of items you should consider including in your medical kit – consult your pharmacist for brands available in your country.

☐ **Aspirin** or **paracetamol** (acetaminophen in the USA) – for pain or fever

☐ **Antihistamine** – for allergies, such as hay fever; to ease the itch from insect bites or stings; and to prevent motion sickness

☐ **Antibiotics** – consider including these if you're travelling well off the beaten track; see your doctor, as they must be prescribed, and carry the prescription with you

☐ **Loperamide** or **diphenoxylate** – 'blockers' for diarrhoea; **prochlorperazine** or **metaclopramide** for nausea and vomiting

☐ **Rehydration mixture** – to prevent dehydration, eg due to severe diarrhoea; particularly important when travelling with children

☐ **Insect repellent, sunscreen, lip balm** and **eye drops**

☐ **Calamine lotion, sting relief spray** or **aloe vera** – to ease irritation from sunburn and insect bites or stings

☐ **Antifungal cream** or **powder** – for fungal skin infections and thrush

☐ **Antiseptic** (such as povidone-iodine) – for cuts and grazes

☐ **Bandages, Band-Aids (plasters)** and other wound dressings

☐ **Water purification tablets** or **iodine**

☐ **Scissors, tweezers** and a **thermometer** (note that mercury thermometers are prohibited by airlines)

☐ **Cold** and **flu tablets, throat lozenges** and **nasal decongestant**

☐ **Multivitamins** – consider for long trips, when dietary vitamin intake may be inadequate

Advise medical staff of any reciprocal arrangements *before* they begin treating you. Most travel insurance policies include medical cover. See Travel Insurance under Documents earlier in this chapter.

Travel insurance is still a good idea, however. You should get a policy that covers you for theft, loss and unexpected travel cancellations anyway, and this way you will be covered for the cost of private healthcare as well.

No vaccinations are required for entry into Italy unless you have been travelling through a part of the world where yellow fever or cholera is prevalent.

Medical Services & Emergency

The Italian public health system is administered by local centres generally known as Unità Sanitaria Locale (USL) or Unità Socio Sanitaria Locale (USSL), usually listed under 'U' in the *Pagine Gialle* (sometimes under 'A' for Azienda USL). Under these headings you'll find long lists of offices – look for 'Poliambulatorio' (Polyclinic) and the telephone number for Accetazione Sanitaria. You need to call this number to make an appointment – there is no point in just rolling up. Opening hours vary, with the minimum generally being about 8 am to 12.30 pm Monday to Friday. Some open for a couple of hours in the afternoon and on Saturday mornings too.

For minor health problems, you can head to your local pharmacy *(farmacia)*, where pharmaceuticals tend to be sold more freely without prescription than in places such as the USA, Australia or the UK.

The main public hospital is the Ospedale Riuniti di Careggi (Map 1; ☎ 055 427 71 11), Viale Morgagni 85, north of the city centre. There is also the Ospedale Santa Maria Nuova (Map 3; ☎ 055 2 75 81), Piazza Santa Maria Nuova, just east of the Duomo. In a medical emergency call ☎ 118.

The Tourist Medical Service (Map 2; ☎ 055 47 54 11), Via Lorenzo il Magnifico 59, is open 24 hours and doctors speak English, French and German. An organisation of volunteer translators (English, French and German) called the Associazione Volontari Ospedalieri (☎ 055 234 45 67 or 40 31 26) will provide free translation once you've found a doctor. All public hospitals have a list of volunteers, but you may need to ask for it. The APT has lists of doctors and dentists of various nationalities.

In the USA, the non-profit International Association for Medical Assistance to Travelers (IAMAT; ☎ 716-754 4883, fax 519-836 3412, Center Street, Lewiston, NY 14092) can provide a list of English-speaking doctors in Florence who have been trained in the USA, the UK or Canada.

Should you fall seriously ill in the centre of town, it is perhaps comforting to know that Misericordia di Florence runs ambulances (Map 6; ☎ 055 21 22 22) from Piazza del Duomo.

Pharmacies

Twenty-four hour pharmacies include the Farmacia Comunale (Map 3; ☎ 055 21 67 61) inside the Stazione di Santa Maria Novella, and Molteni (Map 6; ☎ 055 28 94 90), in the city centre at Via de' Calzaiuoli 7r. There's another, All'Insegna del Moro, at Piazza San Giovanni 28 (Map 6).

STDs & AIDS

It is possible to get tests for AIDS and other STDs done (normally you are tested for the lot in one go) at most hospitals, including those listed above. However, it can take ages to arrange and you will probably be charged, even if you are an EU citizen with an E111.

If you seriously feel you might have contracted HIV or another STD, head for the Centro MTS (Malattie a Trasmissione Sessuale; Map 3) at Piazza Brunelleschi 4. It is part of the Clinica Dermatalogica which is in here among the Architecture Faculty buildings. It's open from 8 am to noon, Monday to Friday. This is an anonymous walk-in service at the rear end of the Santa Maria Nuova hospital.

You can also arrange HIV testing and AIDS counselling through Azione Gay e Lesbica Finisterrae (see Gay & Lesbian Travellers later in this chapter).

WOMEN TRAVELLERS

Florence is not a dangerous city but those women travelling alone may find themselves plagued by unwanted attention from men. In bars and discos especially the attention can be more intense than you might like.

If you do get talking but rather you hadn't, reference to your *marito* (husband), *fidanzato* (boyfriend) or even your *figli* (children) may put a brake on your interlocutor's ardour. Otherwise, use whatever methods you use at home to deal with unwanted attention and avoid walking alone in deserted and dark streets.

Recommended reading is the *Handbook for Women Travellers* by M & G Moss.

Organisations

Artemisia (Map 2; ☎ 055 60 13 75) at Via del Mezzetta 1 Interno is a help organisation for women and minors who have been the victims of physical and/or sexual assault. It can provide legal advice and counselling.

To find out about women's groups and social/cultural activities for women, drop in to the Libreria delle Donne (Map 7; ☎ 055 24 03 84), Via Fiesolana 2b. One such group is Giardino dei Ciliegi (Map 3; ☎ 055 28 09 99), Via Sant'Egidio 21.

GAY & LESBIAN TRAVELLERS

Homosexuality is legal in Italy and well tolerated in Florence and the north in general. The legal age of consent is 16. However, overt displays of affection by homosexual couples could attract a negative response in smaller towns.

Gay clubs and discos and the like can be tracked down through local gay organisations (see the following section) or the national monthly gay magazine *Babilonia* which, along with the annual *Guida Gay Italia*, is available at most news stands. You can also read *Il Giglio Fuchsia* (in English, *The Pink Lily*) at www.gay.it/gigliofuchsia/ and www.gay.it/pinklily/ (Italian and English versions) which has extensive information on gay bars, clubs and events in and around Florence.

FACTS FOR THE VISITOR

International gay and lesbian guides that are worth tracking down include the *Spartacus Guide for Gay Men* (the Spartacus list also includes the comprehensive *Spartacus National Edition Italia*, in English and German), published by Bruno Gmünder Verlag, Mail Order, PO Box 11 07 29, D-1000 Berlin 11, Germany, and *Places for Women*, published by Ferrari Publications, Phoenix, AZ, USA.

More information about gay and lesbian clubs and bars can be found in the Entertainment chapter.

Organisations

The national organisations for gay men and lesbians are ArciGay and ArciLesbica (☎ 051 644 70 54, fax 051 644 67 22), at Piazza di Porta Saragozza 2, 40123, Bologna.

You'll find any number of Italian gay Web sites on the Internet. ArciGay, at www.gay.it/arcigay, has general information, mostly in Italian, on the gay scene in Italy and plenty of useful links. For lesbians, the equivalent is ArciLesbica Nazionale at www.women.it/~arciles/. Another interesting site with plenty of links is La comunita'gay/lesbica/bi/trans/italiana. Search for 'itgay' at www.webring.org.

In Florence, Azione Gay e Lesbica Finisterrae (Map 2; ☎/fax 055 67 12 98) is at Via Manara. They have a Web site at www.agora.stm.it/gaylesbica.fi and a phone health-consultation line (☎ 055 48 82 88). It is also possible to arrange to have HIV tests here.

At the Libreria delle Donne (Map 7; ☎ 055 24 03 84), Via Fiesolana 2b, you can get info to tune you into the lesbian scene in Florence.

DISABLED TRAVELLERS

The Italian State Tourist Office in your country may be able to provide advice on Italian associations for the disabled and what help is available in the country. It may also carry a small brochure, *Services for Disabled People*, published by the Italian state railway company, Ferrovie dello Stato, which details facilities at stations and on trains. Some of the better trains, such as the

ETR460 and ETR500, have a carriage for passengers in wheelchairs and their companions.

The Italian travel agency CIT can advise on hotels with special facilities, such as ramps. It can also request that wheelchair ramps be provided on arrival of your train if you book travel through CIT.

The UK-based Royal Association for Disability & Rehabilitation (RADAR) publishes a useful guide called *Holidays & Travel Abroad: A Guide for Disabled People*, which provides a good overview of facilities available to disabled travellers throughout Europe. Contact RADAR (☎ 020-7250 3222), Unit 12, City Forum, 250 City Rd, London EC1V 8AS.

Another UK organisation worth calling is Holiday Care Service (☎ 01293-774535). It produces an information pack on Italy for disabled people and others with special needs.

Mobility International (☎ 02-201 5608, fax 201 5763), 18 Boulevard Baudouin, Brussels, Belgium, organises all sorts of activities and events throughout Europe for the disabled.

In Italy itself you may also be able to get help. Cooperative Integrate (Co.In.) is a national voluntary group with links to the government and branches all over the country. They publish a quarterly magazine for disabled tourists, *Turismo per Tutti (Tourism for All)* in Italian and English. They have information on accessible accommodation, transport and attractions. Co.In. (☎ 06 232 67 505) is at Via Enrico Giglioli 54a, Rome, and has a Web site at andi.casaccia.enea.it/andi/COIN/TUR/turismo.htm.

Promotur – Accessible Italy (☎ 011 309 6363, fax 011 309 1201), Piazza Pitagora 9, 10137 Turin, is a private company specialising in holiday services for the disabled, ranging from tours to hiring of adapted transport. Check out their Web site at www.tour-web.com/accitaly.

The Florence APT publishes a brochure called *Musei, Monumenti, Ville, Giardini di Firenze e Provinca* which gives some details on the accessibility of the sights to those in wheelchairs.

On the public transport front, about 30% of Florence's ATAF buses are equipped for wheelchair access and ATAF expects its fleet of some 500 buses to be modified by about 2005 (depending on finances). The problem, however, is that uneven bus stops sometimes provide obstacles about which the ATAF can do little.

SENIOR TRAVELLERS

Seniors are entitled to discounts on public transport and on admission fees at some museums in Florence. It is always important to ask. The minimum qualifying age is generally 60 years. You should also seek information through seniors organisations and travel agents in your own country on travel packages and discounts for senior travellers.

FLORENCE FOR CHILDREN

The tourist offices have information about child daycare services, courses and special activities for kids (organised for local youngsters, not tourists, so seek advice on those most suitable for your children). These options might come in handy if you are planning a few days of hectic sightseeing and your children have had enough of museums.

Discounts are available for children (usually aged under 12) on public transport and for admission to museums, galleries and other sites.

What To Do with Anklebiters

There is a small playground in Piazza Massimo d'Azeglio (Map 4), about five to 10 minutes' walk east of the Duomo. Beside the Arno, about 15 minutes' walk to the west of Stazione di Santa Maria Novella, is a massive public park *(parco)* called the Cascine (Map 3).

Older children might find the Museo Stibbert (Map 3) entertaining. It features a large collection of antique costumes and armaments from Europe, the Middle East and Asia. It is at Via Federico Stibbert 26, north of the train station, and is open from 10 am to 1 pm and 3 to 5 pm daily except on Thursday (10 am to 4 pm on weekdays and

10 am to 6 pm at weekends in winter). Admission costs L8000.

Before You Go

There are no particular health precautions you need to take with your children in Florence. That said, kids tend to be more affected than adults by unaccustomed heat, changes in diet and sleeping patterns, and just being in a strange place. Nappies, creams, lotions, baby foods and so on are all easily available in Florence, but if there's some particular brand you swear by it's best to bring it with you.

Lonely Planet's *Travel with Children* has lots of practical advice on the subject, and first-hand stories from many Lonely Planet authors, and others, who have done it.

LIBRARIES

If you want to hang out in the local library contact the Biblioteca Comunale Centrale (Map 3 ☎ 055 261 65 12) at Via Sant'Egidio 21. They can tell you where your nearest public lending library is located.

If you need to do research you might try the university faculty libraries or the Biblioteca Nazionale (Map 7; ☎ 055 24 91 91) at Piazza Cavalleggeri 1. The latter won't let you in unless you can produce a letter from your institution detailing your research needs. The cultural centres (see Cultural Centres later in the chapter) also offer library services.

UNIVERSITIES

The main university is the Università degli Studi di Firenze (Map 3 ☎ 055 52 75 71), known to locals simply as *la facoltà* (the faculty). The central administrative offices are at Piazza San Marco 4 and there is a Web site at www.unifi.it. The university offers courses in a wide range of disciplines covering the sciences, medicine, letters, economics, law and so on. Their degrees in art history *(storia dell'arte)* attract students from all over the country.

Several foreign universities have branches here, including Paris, Tokyo, Harvard, New York, Georgetown and Stanford.

Those contemplating serious art studies

FACTS FOR THE VISITOR

Ashen Passion

JANE SMITH

It's amazing what ecstasy people can experience over a few grams of ash. In July 1999, custodians at the Biblioteca Nazionale were doing a little dusting on the 2nd floor in the rare manuscripts section, when they noticed something odd clamped between a couple of books. They dutifully took the small box containing various bits and pieces to the head of the library, who was astonished to find among these objects a small envelope containing a sample of the ashes of the poet Dante.

The envelope was accompanied by a letter covered in seals and dated 1865 that confirmed that the ashes were extracted from the carpet on which the 'coffin and bones' of Dante had rested at one point.

Dante died and was buried in Ravenna in 1321. Over the centuries his remains were shunted about the city a few times, not least, they say, to keep them out of Florentine hands. The Florentines had been keen to keep the living poet from returning to his native city, but now that he was long dead, wanted him to come home. In 1865, the tomb was inspected and it was then that the sculptor Enrico Pazzi collected the ashes and put them in six small envelopes. These he donated to the Biblioteca Nazionale in 1889. In 1929 the ashes, by now in one envelope, were presented in a grand urn at a world librarians' congress and thereafter stored at the Uffizi.

Then they went 'missing' for 70 years. Nobody seems able to explain how or when the ashes got from the urn in the Uffizi to the little box on the bookshelves of the Biblioteca Nazionale.

Judging by the press reports in 1999, Dante experts and other prominent intellectuals seemed to think the discovery of the relics something of a minor miracle. At least one, however, said he simply couldn't understand the fetishism surrounding the ashes.

Let's hope they can find a safe place for these bits of Dante to rest in peace from now on.

---

might want to look into courses offered by the Università Internazionale dell'Arte (Map 2; ☎ 055 57 02 16, fax 055 57 05 08, @ uia@vps.it), Villa Il Ventaglio, Via delle Forbici 24–26, 50133, Florence.

The academic year begins on 1 November. Most of the European students in Florence are on one-year programmes under the Erasmus scheme. They do this as part of their undergraduate studies. You need to approach the Socrates and Erasmus council in your country for more information. Once in Florence, you should go to the office for Erasmus students (Map 3; ☎ 055 275 76 71) at Via La Pira 4. Foreign students looking for help on accommodation and other issues can try Florence Student Point (Map 2; ☎ 055 24 31 30), Viale Antonio Gramsci 9a.

CULTURAL CENTRES

The British Institute (Map 6; ☎ 055 28 40 33), Piazza Strozzi 2, is the main UK centre for English teaching in Florence. The institute also has a library at Lungarno Guicciardini 9 (Map 5) and occasionally screens movies.

If you're after classes in French and Italian, try the Institut Français (Map 5; ☎ 055 28 75 21) in Piazza Ognissanti 2. This is also the best place to see French cinema in the original.

The Deutsches Institut (Map 3; ☎ 055 21 59 93), Via degli Orti Oricellari 10, offers German lessons and lecture programmes, and often stages film cycles and other cultural activities.

The Istituto Italiano di Cultura (IIC), which has branches all over the world, is a government-sponsored organisation aimed at promoting Italian culture and language. They put on classes in Italian and provide a library and information service. This is a good place to start your search for places to study in Italy.

Try the IIC's Web sites at www.iicmelau .org (Australia), www.iicto-ca.org/istituto .htm (Canada), www.italynet.com/cultura/ istcult (France) and www.italcultny.org (USA).

DANGERS & ANNOYANCES

All in all Florence is a fairly secure city, although petty crime (in particular theft) is a problem and its unwitting victims are often strangers in town.

Theft

You need to keep an eye out for pickpockets and bag-snatchers in the most heavily touristed parts of town, especially around the Duomo and the train station. Some of them are *zingari*, bands of gypsy kids who prey on the unsuspecting tourist. The usual gag is to crowd around and shove a piece of cardboard at you. This serves as a distraction while your pockets are emptied.

Prevention is better than cure. Only walk around with the amount of cash you intend to spend that day or evening. Hidden moneybelts or pouches are a good idea. The popular 'bum bags' and external belt pouches people wear around their tummies are like a shining beacon to potential thieves. You may as well wear a neon sign saying: 'Pick Me: I'm a Tourist'.

Never leave anything visible in your car and preferably leave nothing at all. Foreign and hire cars are especially vulnerable.

In hotels and hostels, use the safe if they have one. Try not to leave valuables in your room. If you must, bury them deep in your luggage.

If anything does get lost or stolen, report it to the police and get a written statement from them if you intend to claim on insurance. If your ID or passport disappear, contact your nearest consulate as early as possible to arrange for a replacement (see the earlier Embassies & Consulates section).

Lost & Found Lost property, or *oggetti smarriti* (Map 6; ☎ 055 36 79 43), can be collected (on the assumption it has been found and handed in!) from Via Circondaria 19, north-west of the city centre.

Police Forces

If you run into trouble in Italy, you're likely to end up dealing with the police (*polizia*) or the *carabinieri*. The police are a civil force and take their orders from the Ministry of the Interior, while the carabinieri fall under the Ministry of Defence. There is a considerable duplication of their roles, despite a 1981 reform of the police forces aimed at merging the two. Both forces are responsible for public order and security, which means you can call either in the event of a robbery or violent attack.

The carabinieri wear a dark-blue uniform with a red stripe and drive dark-blue cars with a red stripe. They are well-trained and tend to be helpful. Their police station is called a *caserma* (barracks).

The police wear powder-blue trousers with a fuchsia stripe and a navy-blue jacket, and drive light-blue cars with a white stripe and 'polizia' written on the side. Tourists who want to report thefts and people wanting to get a residence permit will have to deal with them. Their headquarters are the police station (Map 3; ☎ 055 4 97 71), at Via Zara 2. There's another station (Map 6; ☎ 055 29 34 62) at Piazza del Duomo 5. They open from 8 am to 8 pm Monday to Friday, as well as Saturday morning.

Local police (*polizia municipale*) in Italy are known as the *vigili urbani*. One of their main roles is as traffic police, and you will have to deal with them if you get a parking ticket or your car is towed away. They can be reached on ☎ 055 3 28 31.

Lastly, the fiscal police (*guardia di finanza*) are responsible for fighting tax evasion and drug smuggling. It is highly unlikely, but you could be stopped by one of these grey-uniformed fellows if you leave a shop without a receipt for your purchase.

❀ ❀ ❀ ❀ ❀ ❀ ❀ ❀ ❀ ❀ ❀ ❀ ❀ ❀

FACTS FOR THE VISITOR

Drugs

Drug abuse is a visible problem in some parts of town. By and large you may never even realise it is an issue here, but a couple of squares in particular become hangouts for junkies into the evening. One such spot is Piazza SS Annunziata.

It is not a major problem and the people concerned are unlikely to be a direct nuisance to you, but it is worth being aware of the issue.

Emergency

In an emergency call either the carabinieri on ☎ 112 or the police on ☎ 113. In case of fire call the fire brigade (*vigili del fuoco*) on ☎ 115.

LEGAL MATTERS

For some Italians, finding ways to get around the law (any law) is a way of life. They are likely to react with surprise, if not annoyance, if you point out that they might be breaking a law.

Few people pay attention to speed limits, few motorcyclists or drivers stop at red lights – and certainly not at pedestrian crossings. No one bats an eyelid about littering or dogs pooping in the middle of the footpath. But these are minor transgressions when measured up against the country's organised crime, the extraordinary levels of tax evasion and the corruption in government and business.

The average tourist to Florence will probably have a brush with the law only if they are the unfortunate victim of a bag-snatcher or pickpocket.

Drugs

Italy's drug laws are lenient on users and heavy on pushers. If you're caught with drugs that the police determine are for your own personal use, you'll be let off with a warning – and, of course, the drugs will be confiscated. If, instead, it is determined that you intend to sell the drugs in your possession, you could find yourself in prison. It's up to the police to determine whether or not you're a pusher, since the law is not specific about quantities. It's best to avoid drugs.

BUSINESS HOURS

Business laws have become more flexible since opening times were liberalised under new trading hours laws that went into effect in April 1999. Prior to this, the rule of thumb was that, generally, shops opened from around 9 am to 1 pm and 3.30 to 7.30 pm (or 4 to 8 pm) Monday to Friday. Some stayed closed on Monday mornings. Big department stores, such as COIN and Rinascente, and most supermarkets had continuous opening hours, from 9 am to 7.30 pm Monday to Saturday. Some even opened from 9 am to 1 pm on Sunday. Smaller shops were open until about 1 pm on Saturday. At the time of writing it was difficult to determine what effect the new laws would have on day-to-day practice.

Bars (in the Italian sense, that is coffee-and-sandwich places) generally open from 7.30 am to 8 pm, although some stay open after 8 pm and turn into pub-style drinking and meeting places.

For museum and gallery opening hours, see the Things to See & Do chapter. For banking hours see Where to Exchange under Money earlier in the chapter.

PUBLIC HOLIDAYS & SPECIAL EVENTS

The two main holiday periods for Florentines are Settimana Santa (the week leading up to Easter Sunday) and, more noticeably, around the month of August, when tourists seem to take control of the city.

Public Holidays

1 January
  New Year's Day (Anno Nuovo)
6 January
  Epiphany (Befana)
March/April
  Good Friday (Venerdì Santo)
  Easter Monday (Pasquetta/Giorno dopo Pasqua)
25 April
  Liberation Day (Giorno della Liberazione), marking the Allied victory and the end of the German presence and Mussolini
1 May
  Labour Day (Giorno del Lavoro)
15 August
  Feast of the Assumption (Assunzione)

1 November
  All Saints' Day (Ognissanti)
8 December
  Feast of the Immaculate Conception
  (Concezione Immaculata)
25 December
  Christmas Day (Natale)
26 December
  St Stephen's/Boxing Day (Festa di Santo
  Stefano)

Festivals
The APT publishes a list of annual events,
including the many religious festivals staged
by almost every church in the city.

April (Easter)
Explosion of the Cart (Scoppio del Carro)
For centuries, the Florentines have maintained
the annual tradition of 'distributing Holy Fire' to
the populace in this festival on Easter Saturday.
A centuries-old ox-drawn cart, laden with fireworks, is led up outside the Duomo for the ceremony. From the high altar inside the Duomo the
archbishop lights the *colombina* ('little dove'),
virtually a small rocket, which he then launches
along a wire into the cart outside. The subsequent
explosions last for several minutes. They have
been using the same cart since the 18th century,
but the tradition goes back at least to the 15th
century. The origins of the ritual are unclear.
Some say Pazzino de' Pazzi, a hero returned
from the First Crusade, started the tradition on
the day before Easter by lighting a fire with stone
flints from the Holy Sepulchre in Jerusalem
given him for his courage in battle. Others say the
original *carro* was a war cart captured in Fiesole,
made to explode in victory celebrations.

June
Feast of St John (Festa di San Giovanni)
The spectacular fireworks *(fuochi)* let off on 24
June in Piazzale Michelangelo on this feast day
of Florence's patron saint is the culmination of
the city's festivities. In the four or five preceding days, teams from the city's four historical
districts battle it out in the Gioco del Calcio
Storico (Historical Soccer Game). This 'game'
was first played in 1530 as a display of noncha-
lance on the part of the Florentines before
troops of Emperor Charles V, who had the city
under siege. A cross between football (soccer)
and rugby, each team of 27 (!) aims to launch
the ball into the opponents' net. No holds are
barred, so it can get pretty nasty on the field. On
the first day the game is preceded by a proces-

JANE SMITH

**Florentines in traditional dress for the Scoppio
del Carro festival**

sion of hundreds of people in traditional costume on Piazza Santa Croce, which becomes the
pitch for the matches.

August
The Cricket Festival (Festa del Grillo)
The crickets that once featured in this fair held
in the Cascine on 15 August are no longer put
to any pains as a result of environmentalists'
protests.

September
**Festival of the Paper Lanterns (Festa delle
Rificolone)**
A procession of drummers, flag-throwers
(sbandieratori), musicians and others in medieval dress winds its way from Piazza Santa
Croce to Piazza SS Annunziata to celebrate the
eve of Our Lady's supposed birthday on 7 September. Kids with paper lanterns accompany
them. Smaller processions for children and their
families are organised in other quarters of the
city too. On the 8th, the walkway around the
sides and facade of the Duomo is opened to the
public for this one day of the year.
Chianti Wine Harvest Festivals
This is the month of the wine harvest and several Chianti towns celebrate with wine festivals.

euro currency converter L10,000 = €5.16

You need to ask at the APT or keep a close eye on local papers for details.

Arts & Music Festivals
May
Florence's Musical May (Maggio Musicale Fiorentino)
Starting in late April and spilling over into June, Florence's Musical May was inaugurated in 1933. It is a high point on the musical calendar, with top names performing opera, ballet and classical music at venues across the city. Tickets can be hard to come by.

July
Anfiteatro delle Cascine
These free nightly concerts in the Cascine, which keep Florence humming through the summer, largely attract a young crowd. A free shuttle ATAF bus runs every 20 minutes along a route that takes in Piazza San Marco, the train station, Piazzale Vittorio Veneto and Piazza Santo Spirito.

Florence Dance Festival
Piazzale Michelangelo hosts this series of dance performances. There is something for every taste, from classical ballet to modern.

October
International Expo of World Music (Rassegna Internazionale Musica dei Popoli)
Local and international musicians come together to perform traditional and ethnic music from all over the world in this festival, which goes on for most of the month.

Exhibitions
A couple of exhibitions or trade fairs that take place in Florence will be of interest to some tourists in town too. Among them are:

April/May
Mostra Internazionale dell'Artigianato
This prestigious expo of handmade products, of every possible type and colour, is held in Fortezza da Basso. Unfortunately the exhibits aren't for sale!

September/October
Biennale dell'Antiquariato
Every odd-numbered year this prestigious event is held in Palazzo Strozzi. It's an opportunity to search for high-quality antique furniture, paintings, jewellery and a host of other antique objects.

DOING BUSINESS
People wishing to make the first moves towards expanding their business into Italy should get in touch with their own country's Department of Trade (such as the DTI in the UK). The commercial department of the Italian embassy in your own country should also have information – at least on red tape.

In Italy, the trade office of your embassy can provide tips and contacts. The *English Yellow Pages in Italy*, a telephone directory of English-speaking professionals, commercial activities and organisations in Florence (as well as Bologna, Milan and Rome) might be of use. It is available in English-language bookshops.

A GSM mobile phone and a good laptop computer will probably be all you need to do business in Florence. Some of the top hotels have business centres or secretarial assistance for guests.

Companies that can provide business services, such as an email address and secretarial support, are listed in the *Pagine Gialle* under 'Uffici Arredati e Servizi'.

For translators and interpreters look under 'Traduttori ed Interpreti' in the *Pagine Gialle*. You'll also find a couple of dozen listed in the *English Yellow Pages in Italy*. Emynet (Map 5; ☎ 055 21 92 28), Lungarno Soderini 5–9r claims to translate in 82 languages, and also offers specialised legal translations, head-hunting and Website creation.

WORK
It is illegal for non-EU citizens to work in Italy without a work permit *(permesso di lavoro)*, but trying to obtain one through your Italian consulate can be a pain. EU citizens are allowed to work in Italy, but they still need to obtain a residence permit *(permesso di soggiorno)* from a police station. New immigration laws require foreign workers to be 'legalised' through their employers, which can apply even to cleaners and babysitters. The employers then pay pension and health insurance contributions. This doesn't mean that illegal work can't still be found.

A useful guide is *Living, Studying, and Working in Italy* by Travis Neighbor and Monica Larner.

If you intend to look for work in Florence, you should bring any paperwork that might help. English teachers, for instance, will need any certificates they have demonstrating qualifications and references from previous employers. Increasingly, there is cross-recognition of degrees and other tertiary qualifications, so it may be worthwhile bringing these as well. Translations validated by the Italian embassy in your country wouldn't hurt either.

Opportunities

Working Holidays The best option, once you're in the country, is trying to find work in a bar, nightclub or restaurant during the tourist season. Another possibility is au pair work, organised before you come to Italy. A useful guide is *The Au Pair and Nanny's Guide to Working Abroad* by S Griffith & S Legg (Vacation Work, paperback). By the same publisher is *Work Your Way Around the World* by Susan Griffith.

Language Teaching The easiest source of work for foreigners is teaching English (or another foreign language), but even with full qualifications a non-EU citizen might find it difficult to secure a permanent position. Most of the larger, more reputable schools will only hire people with work permits, but their attitude can become more flexible if demand for teachers is high and they come across someone with good qualifications.

The more professional schools will require a Teaching English as a Foreign Language (TEFL) certificate. It is advisable to apply for work early in the year, in order to be considered for positions available in October (language school years correspond roughly to the Italian school year: late September to the end of June).

Numerous schools hire people without work permits or qualifications, but the pay is usually low (around L15,000 an hour). It is more lucrative to advertise your services and pick up private students (though rates vary wildly, ranging from as low as L15,000 up to L50,000 an hour), but of course this takes time to develop. The average rate is around L30,000.

Most people get started by placing advertisements in shop windows and on university or school notice boards.

Restaurants Non-EU citizens, even if they have no kitchen experience and little Italian, can sometimes get 'cooking' work. This might be little more than assembling pre-prepared pizzas. Even qualified cooks can expect to be paid little more than L10,000 an hour and to work long hours. We are talking about the tourist trap restaurants that are quite happy to serve up deep-frozen, pre-cooked stuff. What's worse? Eating it or preparing it?

Getting There & Away

Although not an international hub, Florence is reasonably well served by air from the rest of the country and Europe. It is also linked by regular fast trains to major centres such as Rome, Milan and Bologna. Plenty of buses run into the hinterland.

AIR

It pays to shop around for your flight to Florence. A plethora of options ranging from cheap charter deals and standard scheduled flights through to weekend getaway deals is on offer. From outside Europe, your flight will almost certainly involve changing in either Rome or Milan (Italy's main intercontinental gateways) or in another major European hub such as London, Frankfurt or Paris. This depends largely on the airline. Often it is Alitalia's European rivals that come up with the better deals.

The nearest airport to town is Amerigo Vespucci, but if you are on an international flight there is a good chance you will arrive at the more important Galileo Galilei airport outside Pisa. This airport is linked to Florence by direct trains and occasional buses.

For more detailed information on airport facilities and transport, see Airports in the Getting Around chapter.

Travellers with Special Needs

If you are on crutches, are a vegetarian or require a special diet (such as kosher food), are travelling in a wheelchair or have some other special need, let the airline know so that they can make any necessary arrangements. You should call to remind them of your requirements at least 72 hours before departure and again when you check in at the airport. It may also be worth ringing round the airlines before you make your booking to find out how they can handle your particular needs. Some airlines publish brochures on the subject. Ask your travel agency for details.

Guide dogs for the blind will often have to travel in a specially pressurised baggage compartment and are subject to quarantine laws when entering, or returning to, countries currently free of rabies, such as the UK or Australia. Quarantine laws in Britain were due to change at the time of writing; check the current situation with the Ministry of Agriculture, Fisheries and Food (☎ 0645 33 55 77).

Travellers with a hearing impairment can ask for airport and in-flight announcements to be written down for them.

Children aged under two travel for 10% of the standard fare (or free on some airlines), as long as they don't occupy a seat. They don't get a baggage allowance. Skycots, baby food and nappies (diapers) should be provided by the airline if requested in advance. Children aged between two and 12 can usually occupy a seat for half to two-thirds of the full fare and do get a baggage allowance. Pushchairs (strollers) can often be carried as hand luggage.

Departure Tax

Airport departure taxes are factored into ticket prices and vary according to the destination and whether you are buying a one-way or a return ticket.

Other Parts of Italy

Travelling by plane is expensive within Italy and it makes much better sense to use the efficient and considerably cheaper train and bus services. In any case, only a handful of domestic airports are served by direct flights from Florence. The domestic lines are Alitalia (☎ 800 050350) and Meridiana (☎ 0789 6 93 00); their Web sites are at www.alitalia.it and www.meridiana.it respectively. In Florence, call ☎ 055 3 29 61 for Meridiana. It has a booking office at Lungarno Soderini 1 (Map 5).

From Florence's Amerigo Vespucci airport Alitalia has flights to Bari, Cagliari, Milan and Rome. From Pisa you can get to

Air Travel Glossary

Cancellation Penalties If you have to cancel or change a discounted ticket, there are often heavy penalties involved; insurance can sometimes be taken out against these penalties. Some airlines impose penalties on regular tickets as well, particularly against 'no-show' passengers.

Courier Fares Businesses often need to send urgent documents or freight securely and quickly. Courier companies hire people to accompany the package through customs and, in return, offer a discount ticket which is sometimes a phenomenal bargain. However, you may have to surrender all your baggage allowance and take only carry-on luggage.

Full Fares Airlines traditionally offer 1st class (coded F), business class (coded J) and economy class (coded Y) tickets. These days there are so many promotional and discounted fares available that few passengers pay full economy fare.

Lost Tickets If you lose your airline ticket an airline will usually treat it like a travellers cheque and, after inquiries, issue you with another one. Legally, however, an airline is entitled to treat it like cash and if you lose it then it's gone forever. Take good care of your tickets.

Onward Tickets An entry requirement for many countries is that you have a ticket out of the country. If you're unsure of your next move, the easiest solution is to buy the cheapest onward ticket to a neighbouring country or a ticket from a reliable airline which can later be refunded if you do not use it.

Open-Jaw Tickets These are return tickets where you fly out to one place but return from another. If available, this can save you backtracking to your arrival point.

Overbooking Since every flight has some passengers who fail to show up, airlines often book more passengers than they have seats. Usually excess passengers make up for the no-shows, but occasionally somebody gets 'bumped' onto the next available flight. Guess who it is most likely to be? The passengers who check in late.

Promotional Fares These are officially discounted fares, available from travel agencies or direct from the airline.

Reconfirmation If you don't reconfirm your flight at least 72 hours prior to departure, the airline may delete your name from the passenger list. Ring to find out if your airline requires reconfirmation.

Restrictions Discounted tickets often have various restrictions on them – such as needing to be paid for in advance and incurring a penalty to be altered. Others are restrictions on the minimum and maximum period you must be away.

Round-the-World Tickets RTW tickets give you a limited period (usually a year) in which to circumnavigate the globe. You can go anywhere the carrying airlines go, as long as you don't backtrack. The number of stopovers or total number of separate flights is decided before you set off and they usually cost a bit more than a basic return flight.

Transferred Tickets Airline tickets cannot be transferred from one person to another. Travellers sometimes try to sell the return half of their ticket, but officials can ask you to prove that you are the person named on the ticket. On an international flight tickets are compared with passports.

Travel Periods Ticket prices vary with the time of year. There is a low (off-peak) season and a high (peak) season, and often a low-shoulder season and a high-shoulder season as well. Usually the fare depends on your outward flight – if you depart in the high season and return in the low season, you pay the high-season fare.

euro currency converter L10,000 = €5.16

Catania, Milan and Rome. Domestic flights can be booked through any travel agency. Milan and Rome are both cheaper and almost just as easily reached by train. Taking into account the hassle of airports, your time saving is not likely to be great either, especially given that most of the flights require a change.

Alitalia offers a range of discounts for young people, families, the elderly and weekend travellers, as well as occasional special promotional fares. One-way fares and standard returns (basically just two one-way tickets) are expensive. If you get a return, purchasing an Apex (or even better a Super Apex) fare will bring the price down considerably in exchange for respecting certain conditions.

One-way fares from Florence on Alitalia include:

destination	fare (L)	duration
Bari	270,000	1½ hours direct/ 3 hours via Rome
Cagliari	260,000	3½ hours via Rome
Milan	165,000	55 minutes
Rome	165,000	1¼ hours

A return Apex fare to Rome, however, comes to L180,000. To Cagliari it costs L310,000. In the case of the Rome trip it is much simpler to get the train (which can take as little as 1½ hours)!

One-way fares from Pisa on Alitalia include:

destination	fare (L)	duration
Catania	315,000	1½ hours direct/up to 4 hours via Rome
Milan	165,000	1¼ hours
Rome	165,000	1 hour 10 minutes

Meridiana has flights to Catania and Palermo from Florence and Pisa, as well as flights to Cagliari from Florence. Meridiana also has a handful of international flights from Florence to Amsterdam, Paris and London. Meridiana operates a similar fare system to that of Alitalia and is just as expensive.

Other Countries

The UK Most British travel agents are registered with ABTA (the Association of British Travel Agents). If you have paid for your flight with an ABTA-registered agent who then goes bust, ABTA will guarantee a refund or an alternative. Unregistered bucket shops are riskier but sometimes cheaper.

One of the more reliable, but not necessarily cheapest, agencies is STA Travel (☎ 020-7361 6161 for European flights). STA has several offices in London, as well as branches throughout the UK. A similar place is Trailfinders (☎ 020-7937 5400 for European flights); its short-haul booking centre is at 215 Kensington High St. It also has branches in Birmingham, Bristol, Glasgow, Manchester and Newcastle-upon-Tyne. Usit Campus (European flights on ☎ 020-7730 3402), 52 Grosvenor Gardens, London SW1W 0AG, is in much the same league and has five other branches in London, as well as many more throughout the UK. These agencies' Web sites are at www.sta-travel.com, www.trailfinder.com and www.usitcampus.co.uk respectively.

The two principal airlines linking the UK and Italy are British Airways (BA; ☎ 020-7434 4700; local rate ☎ 0345 222111, 24 hours), 156 Regent St, London W1R 6LB, and Alitalia (☎ 020-7602 7111), 4 Portman Square, London W1H 9PS. High-season fares on a scheduled Alitalia flight to Pisa range from UK£119 to UK£169 return (plus UK£27 departure tax). The cheaper the ticket the shorter the validity. A standard one-way ticket costs around UK£260 and it's hard to think of any reason for buying one. Alitalia has no direct flights to Florence. To fly there you must change in Milan. Return fares range from UK£119 to UK£199. A standard one-way ticket costs UK£268. Similar fares are available with BA.

BA's low-budget subsidiary, Go, flies to four Italian destinations from London Stansted, including Bologna (the closest it gets to Florence). It offers two kinds of return fare, Standard and Flexible. The former allows no changes and is non-refundable, while the latter permits you to alter your plans (although probably charging you for the pleasure). Standard returns start at UK£100 including taxes, while flexible fares start at UK£150. You can book online (www.go-fly.com) or by phone (☎ 0845 6054321 in the UK; ☎ 147 887766 in Italy). From Bologna you can get the train down to Florence.

The Irish budget airline Ryanair (☎ 0541 569569) has two flights a day (except Saturday, when only one goes) from London to Pisa. At the time of writing the fare was UK£85 return, but Ryanair has a habit of making silly offers. For further information look at its Web site at www.ryanair.ie.

Charter flights are an option. Italy Sky Shuttle (☎ 020-8748 1333), 227 Shepherd's Bush Rd, London W6 7AS, specialises in these to 22 destinations in Italy, including Pisa. Prices are largely determined by availability and ranged from UK£169 to UK£209 at the time of writing. It can also organise one-week fly/drive deals, which, in high season, cost UK£159 for a small car (Fiat Punto or similar) on top of the air fare.

The Charter Flight Centre (☎ 020-7565 6755), 15 Gillingham St, London SW1V 1HN, has return flights to Pisa valid for up to four weeks in high season from UK£149 (including taxes). It has a direct flight to Florence with Meridiana, which costs UK£259 plus taxes. You're better off with the cheaper flights into Pisa.

Another specialist in flights and holidays to Italy is Skybus Italia (☎ 020-7631 3444), 37 Harley Street, London W1 1DB.

The Air Travel Advisory Bureau (☎ 020-7636 5000) can provide further details of discount travel agencies.

You needn't necessarily fly from London, as many good deals are as easily available from other major UK centres.

You can also hunt for fares on Teletext and the Internet.

Youth Passes Alitalia offers people under 26 (and students under 31 with a valid ISIC) a Europa Pass from London and Dublin. The pass is valid for up to six months and allows unlimited one-way flights to all the airline's European and Mediterranean destinations for UK£62 per flight, with a min-

imum of four flights. The first flight has to be *to* Italy and the last flight back to the UK or Ireland *from* Italy. Internal flights in Italy on this pass cost UK£45 a pop.

Continental Europe Short hops can be expensive, but for longer journeys you can often find air fares that beat overland alternatives on cost.

France Occasionally you can dig up a good flight deal from Paris. One low-season option at the time of writing was a return to Florence for FF1414, flying with Meridiana. You needed to book 10 days ahead and stay at least one weekend. This could work out better than the train, and it's certainly quicker.

STA Travel's outlet in France is Voyages Wasteels (☎ 08 03 88 70 04, in France only), 11 rue Dupuytren, 75006 Paris.

Germany Munich is a haven of bucket shops and more mainstream budget-travel outlets. Council Travel (☎ 089-39 50 22), Adalbertstrasse 32, near the university, is one of the best. STA Travel (☎ 089-39 90 96), Königstrasse 49, is also good.

In Berlin, Kilroy Travel-ARTU Reisen (☎ 030-310 00 40), at Hardenbergstrasse 9, near Berlin Zoo (with three branches around the city), is a good travel agent. In Frankfurt am Main, you could try STA Travel (☎ 069-70 30 35), Bockenheimer Landstrasse 133.

The Netherlands Amsterdam is a popular departure point. The student travel agency NBBS Reiswinkels, Rokin 38 (☎ 020-620 5071), offers reliable and reasonably low fares. Compare with the bucket shops along Rokin before deciding. NBBS has branches throughout the city and in Brussels, Belgium.

The USA Council Travel (☎ 800 226 8624) and STA (☎ 800 777 0112) have offices in major cities across the USA. Their Web sites are at www.counciltravel.com and www.statravel.com respectively. Discount travel agencies, known as consolidators, can be found in the weekly travel sections

GETTING THERE & AWAY

euro currency converter L10,000 = €5.16

of the *New York Times*, the *Los Angeles Times*, the *Chicago Tribune* and the *San Francisco Examiner*.

Flights from the USA to either Florence or Pisa are possible with such European airlines as Lufthansa and Air France, and sometimes work out cheaper and more convenient than getting an Alitalia flight.

At the time of writing you could get return (round-trip) fares from Los Angeles to Florence for as little as US$525 with United Airlines and Lufthansa via Frankfurt in low season (roughly January to March). A more commonly quoted price from San Francisco was US$650. Strangely enough, you are unlikely to do much better from the east coast.

After March, prices begin to rise rapidly and availability declines. In high season you would typically be looking at from US$1350 to US$1600. Again, it doesn't seem to make much difference whether you leave from the east or west coast.

Given that Florence is a fairly easy train ride from Rome, you could consider looking at flight options to the capital (if you find any significantly cheaper) and making the connection by train.

Discount and rock-bottom options from the USA include charter flights, stand-by fares and courier flights. Stand-by fares are often sold at 60% of the normal price for one-way tickets. Airhitch (☎ 212-864 2000, 800-326 2009 toll-free), 2641 Broadway, 3rd floor, #100, New York, NY 10025, specialises in this. You will need to give a general idea of where and when you need to go, and a few days before your departure you will be presented with a choice of two or three flights. Airhitch has several other offices in the USA, including Los Angeles (☎ 310-726 5000, 888-AIRHITCH toll-free), and its Web site is at www.airhitch.org. You can contact their Rome representative on ☎ 06 772 08 655.

Courier flights are where you accompany freight or a parcel to its destination. A New York–Rome return on a courier flight can cost about US$300 (more from the west coast). Generally, courier flights require that you return within a specified period (sometimes one or two weeks, but often up to a month). You will need to travel light, as luggage is usually restricted to what you can carry onto the plane (the parcel or freight you carry comes out of your luggage allowance). You may have to be a US resident and apply for an interview before they will take you on.

A good source of information on courier flights is Now Voyager (☎ 212-431 1616), Suite 307, 74 Varrick St, New York, NY 10013. This company specialises in courier flights, but you must pay an annual membership fee (around US$50), which entitles you to take as many courier flights as you like. Phone after 6 pm to listen to a recorded message detailing all available flights and prices. The Colorado-based Air Courier Association (☎ 303-215 9000) also does this kind of thing. You join the association (for US$64), which is used by international airfreight companies to provide the escorts.

Prices drop as the departure date approaches. It is also possible to organise the flights directly through the courier companies. Look in your *Yellow Pages* under Courier Services.

If you can't find a particularly cheap flight, it is always worth considering getting a cheap transatlantic hop to London and prowling around the bucket shops there. See the UK section earlier in the chapter.

Canada Both Alitalia and Air Canada have direct flights to Rome and Milan from Toronto and Montreal. Direct flights to Florence are less likely. Scan the budget travel ads in the *Toronto Globe & Mail*, the *Toronto Star* and the *Vancouver Province*.

Travel CUTS (☎ 800 667 2887), called Voyages Campus in Quebec, has offices in all major cities in Canada; its Web site is at www.travelcuts.com.

See the USA section for information on courier flights. For courier flights originating in Canada, contact FB on Board Courier Services (☎ 514-631 7925 in Montreal and ☎ 604-278 1266 in Vancouver). BCS no longer flies to continental Europe but a return courier flight to London costs around $525 from Toronto and C$590 from Vancouver.

Australia STA Travel (fast fares on ☎ 1300 360 960) and Flight Centres International (☎ 131600) are major dealers in cheap air fares. Their Web sites are at www.sta travel.com.au and www.flightcentre.com.au respectively. Heavily discounted fares can also be obtained through travel agencies. Some agencies, particularly smaller ones, advertise cheap fares in the travel sections of weekend newspapers, such as the *Age* in Melbourne and the *Sydney Morning Herald.*

Alitalia, Qantas and several other airlines fly more or less direct to Rome.

Discounted return air fares on mainstream airlines through reputable agents can be surprisingly cheap. Low-season fares from Sydney or Melbourne to Rome average around A$1800 return but can go as low as A$1400 with airlines like EgyptAir. An add-on to Florence may not cost too much more, although the train may prove as good an option. A train from the airport in Rome goes right to Termini train station, from where you can board regular services to Florence (see also the later Train section).

On some flights between Australia and destinations like London, Paris and Frankfurt, a return ticket between that destination and another major European city is thrown in – you could use this to get to Florence.

For courier flights try Jupiter (☎ 02-9317 2230), Unit 3, 55 Kent Rd, Mascot, Sydney, NSW 2020.

New Zealand As with Australia, STA Travel (☎ 09-309 0458, Auckland office) and Flight Centres International (☎ 09-309 6171, Auckland office) are popular agents, with branches throughout the country. Their Web sites are at www.statravel.com.au and www.flightcentre.com.au respectively. The *New Zealand Herald* has a travel section in which travel agencies advertise fares. A round-the-world (RTW) ticket is sometimes cheaper than a normal return. Otherwise, you can fly from Auckland to pick up a connecting flight in Melbourne or Sydney. Return fares from New Zealand to Rome are around NZ$2400 but airlines such as Thai International or Malaysia Airlines may offer cheaper deals.

Asia Hong Kong can be a good place to buy tickets. Its bucket shops are at least as unreliable as those of other cities. A one-way fare to Europe can cost about US$660 but shop around. Bucket shops in Bangkok can get you a one-way fare for about US$460.

STA Travel has branches in Hong Kong, Tokyo, Singapore, Bangkok and Kuala Lumpur.

Airline Offices in Florence

You can find airlines listed under 'Linee Aeree' in the *Pagine Gialle (Yellow Pages)*. Many no longer maintain offices in the city.

Air France
  (☎ 147 884466)
Alitalia
  (Map 6; ☎ 055 2 78 88) Lungarno degli
  Acciaiuoli 10–12r
British Airways
  (☎ 147 812266, 050 4 08 66) There is a desk
  at Pisa's Galileo Galilei airport.
Lufthansa
  (Map 6; ☎ 055 21 79 36) c/o City Center
  Intertravel, Via de' Lamberti 39r
Meridiana
  (Map 5; ☎ 055 230 23 14) Lungarno Soderini 1
TWA
  (Map 6; ☎ 055 239 68 56) Via de' Vecchietti 4

BUS

The bus is generally cheaper than the train, but less comfortable for the long haul. For shorter trips around some parts of Tuscany, especially where train services are limited or non-existent, it can be more convenient or even the only option. Buses leave from a variety of terminals scattered about the main train station, Stazione di Santa Maria Novella.

The SITA bus terminal (Map 3; ☎ 055 21 47 21), Via Santa Caterina da Siena 15, is just to the west of Stazione di Santa Maria Novella. Several bus companies, including CAP (Map 3; ☎ 055 24 46 37) and COPIT (Map 3; ☎ 055 21 54 51), operate from Largo Fratelli Alinari, at the southern end of Via Nazionale.

Lazzi (Map 3; ☎ 055 21 51 55, 166 84 50 10), Piazza Adua 1, next to the train station, runs services to Tuscan destinations and across the country. Lazzi forms part of the Eurolines network of international bus services and can provide a detailed Eurolines brochure.

Other Parts of Italy

Tuscany SITA operates bus services from Florence to central Tuscany, north into the Mugello region, south-east to Arezzo and beyond and some services west. It has regular runs to Siena, some of them fast services along the *superstrada* or expressway (others make more stops en route). You can also get buses to Poggibonsi, where you connect for San Gimignano, or to Colle di Val d'Elsa, where you change for Volterra (there is one direct Florence–Volterra service). A few direct services run to Arezzo, several towns in the Chianti region, Borgo San Lorenzo and other towns in the Mugello.

The CAP and COPIT companies serve towns such as Prato and Pistoia in the north-west. Lazzi also has buses to north-western Tuscany, including Lucca, Pisa and Viareggio. All three companies pool resources to main destinations, while CAP and COPIT have networks taking in towns around Prato and Pistoia respectively.

Some sample one-way fares are:

destination	fare (L)	duration
Arezzo	L9900	2 hours 10 minutes
Greve in Chianti	L5000	1 hour five minutes
Lucca	L8600	1¼ hours
Pisa	L11,200	3 hours
Pistoia	L5000	50 minutes
Poggibonsi	L5800	1 hour 20 minutes
Prato	L3500	45 minutes
Radda in Chianti	L6200	1 hour 40 minutes
San Gimignano	L10,000	around 1½ hours
Siena	L7800	up to 2 hours 10 minutes
Siena (rapid)	L11,000	1¼ hours
Volterra	L7800	2 hours 10 minutes
Volterra (rapid)	L11,000	1¼ hours

Warning Always compare travel times on the bus and train for your destination. A classic example is the Florence–Pisa run. On the bus you can be travelling for three hours (because of intermediate stops), while on the train you get there in just over an hour (and the fare is lower too!). Such bus services are really designed for people getting on and off along the way at intermediate stops not served by train.

There are other factors to consider. The train to Siena costs less than the fast bus and is only marginally slower. But bus services are frequent and trains intermittent. In addition, the bus takes you into the heart of town, while the train leaves you way downhill, from where you have to plod up in a local bus.

Rest of Italy Lazzi is responsible for long-haul bus services to other parts of Italy, mostly on routes south where train services are either non-existent or painfully slow. Destinations include Potenza and Matera (Basilicata) and some in Puglia and Calabria. SITA also offers a handful of long-distance services, all to southern Italy. Generally you must book these tickets in advance. A one-way fare will cost around L80,000 for the most distant destinations and the trip can take 12 hours.

In collaboration with SITA, Lazzi also operates a service called Alpi Bus, which serves an extensive range of destinations in the Alps. These buses depart from numerous cities and towns throughout Lazio, Umbria, Tuscany and Emilia-Romagna for most main resorts in the Alps. A brochure detailing the service is available at the Lazzi office.

Destinations likely to interest visitors to Florence are hardly numerous. Lazzi has a bus to Perugia at 5 pm from Monday to Saturday. The fare is L19,000 and the trip takes about 1¾ hours. It also goes to Assisi.

The same company also operates the Freccia dell'Appennino (Apennine Arrow) service, with buses connecting Florence, Siena and Montecatini with destinations in Le Marche (such as Ascoli Piceno) and Abruzzo (like Chieto and Pescara). These services tend to stop in Perugia, where sometimes you have to change bus.

Other Countries

Eurolines, in conjunction with local bus companies across Europe, is the main international carrier. Its Web site at www.eurolines.com provides links to the sites of all the national operators.

The UK Eurolines (☎ 0990 143219), 52 Grosvenor Gardens, Victoria, London SW1W 0AU (the terminal is a couple of blocks away), runs buses to Florence (and on to Rome) via Milan on Wednesday and Saturday (up to three extra buses operate in summer). The trip takes 30 hours. The one-way and return fares are, respectively, UK£88 and UK£125 (UK£78 and UK£112 for those under 26 and senior citizens). The standard one-way adult fare going the other way is L222,000. Fares rise in the peak summer season (July and August) and in the week before Christmas.

France Eurolines has offices in several French cities. In Paris it's at the Paris Galliéni international terminal (☎ 08 36 69 52 52), 28 ave du Générale de Gaulle, 93170 Bagnolet, and on the left bank at 55 rue St Jacques, 75005 Paris (off blvd St Germain). UK passengers may have to change buses here. The standard one-way/return fare to Florence from Paris is FF830.

Rest of Europe Eurolines also has services at least twice weekly between Florence and Amsterdam, Barcelona, Brussels, Budapest, Frankfurt am Main, Montpellier, Nice, Perpignan and Warsaw. In Florence, go to the Lazzi bus terminal (see the start of this section).

SITA also handles a few international services, such as to Zagreb in Croatia.

TRAIN

Florence is an important rail hub and from the city's main train station, Stazione di Santa Maria Novella (Firenze SMN for short; Map 3), you can get direct trains heading in most directions. It lies on the line connecting Milan, Bologna and Rome. Trains also fan out to various parts of Tuscany, although in some cases you will find it more convenient to use the bus for exploring the region around Florence.

Eurail, InterRail, Europass and Flexipass tickets are valid on the national rail network Ferrovie dello Stato (FS).

Information

There is a rail travel information office in the main vestibule of the Stazione di Santa Maria Novella where the ticket windows are located. It opens from 7 am to 9 pm daily. For information on trains you can also call ☎ 147 88 80 88. In the waiting room a couple of doors up from the vestibule and facing the platforms you can sometimes find the handy *In Treno Toscana* booklet of timetables, which covers journeys in Tuscany and to other parts of Italy from Florence.

Timetables are posted at the station. The main timetable *(orario)* displays arrivals *(arrivi)* on a white background and departures *(partenze)* on a yellow one. Impending arrivals and departures also appear on electronic boards. You will notice a plethora of symbols and acronyms on the main timetables, some of which are useful for identifying the kind of train concerned (see also Types of Train in the following Other Parts of Italy section).

It is possible to get a paperback-sized timetable with all the main train services listed from selected outlets outside Italy. In the UK, for instance, you can find it at Italwings (☎ 020-7287 2117), 162–168 Regent St, London W1R 5TB. The same timetable is available at many newsstands in Italy.

At the Stazione di Santa Maria Novella, you will also find a tourist information office (which can book hotels; see the Places to Stay chapter), currency exchange offices, a bank (with ATM), an automatic banknote exchange machine (in the main ticket hall), phones and left-luggage facilities. The latter is called the Deposito (Map 3) and is open from 4.15 am to 1.30 am daily. You pay L5000 per item per 12 hours or fraction thereof – the first 12 hours you pay for in advance, the remainder on picking up your luggage.

euro currency converter   L10,000 = €5.16

Other Parts of Italy

Types of Train A wide variety of trains circulates around Italy. They start with slow all-stops *locali*, which generally don't travel much beyond their main city of origin or province. Next come the *regionali*, which also tend to be slow but cover greater distances, sometimes going beyond their region of origin. *Interregionali* cover greater distances still and don't necessarily stop at every last station.

From this level there is a qualitative leap upwards to InterCity (IC) trains, faster long-distance trains operating between major cities for which you pay a *supplemento* on top of the normal cost of a ticket. EuroCity (EC) trains are the international version. They can reach a top speed of 200km/h (but rarely get the chance!).

Comfort and speed on the most important lines have for the past few years been provided by the *pendolino* trains, so-called because they 'lean' up to 8° into curves to increase the overall speed of a standard IC by up to 35%.

Pendolini and other top-of-the-range services, which on high-speed track can zip along at more than 300km/h, are now collectively known as Eurostar Italia (ES). ES trains connect Florence with Rome (1¾ hours) up to 25 times a day and Milan (2¾ hours) 16 times daily. Seven Eurostar trains proceed from Rome to Naples and five others connect Florence with Venice (one goes on to Trieste). Other main lines for this premier service include one connecting Milan with Venice and another from Milan to Ancona (on the Adriatic) via Bologna.

Other train types you may encounter are the *diretto* (D) and *espresso* (E). They are slow and gradually disappearing.

Night trains *(notturne)* are either old *espressi* or, increasingly, InterCity Notte (ICN) services. You generally have the option of *cuccette* (couchettes) – four or six fold-down bunkbeds in a compartment – or a proper bed in a *vagone letto* (sleeping car). A place in the latter tends to be much more expensive than a simple *cuccetta*. The international version is the EuroNight (EN) service.

Tickets The cost of train travel is lower in Italy than in most of the rest of Western Europe. Fares are generally calculated according to distance travelled. All this may change, as the national government has announced sweeping changes in fare calculation and hefty price rises for 2000.

There are many ticketing possibilities. Apart from the standard division between 1st and 2nd class *(prima classe* and *seconda classe)* on the faster trains (generally you can only get 2nd-class seats on locali and regionali), you pay a supplement for being on a fast train. As with tickets, the price of the supplement is in part calculated according to the length of the journey. You can pay the supplement separately from the ticket. Thus if you have a 2nd-class return ticket from Florence to Rome you might decide to avoid the supplement one way and take a slower train, but pay it on the return trip to speed things up a little. Whatever you decide, you need to pay the supplement before boarding the train.

You can buy rail tickets (for major destinations on fast trains at least) from most travel agents. If you choose to buy them at the station, there are automatic machines that accept credit cards.

It is advisable, and in some cases obligatory, to book long-distance tickets in advance, whether international or domestic. In 1st class, booking is often mandatory (and free). Where it is optional (which is more often, but not always, the case in 2nd class), you may pay a L5000 booking fee. Tickets can be booked at the windows in the station or at most travel agencies.

The following prices are approximate, standard, 2nd-class, one-way fares (plus supplement) on IC trains. ES fares are higher.

destination	fare (L)	duration
Bologna	8200 (+5500)	1 hour
Milan	25,500 (+13,000)	3 hours 20 minutes
Naples	42,000 (+17,500)	4 hours
Rome	25,500 (+13,000)	1 hour 55 minutes
Venice	22,000 (+12,000)	3 hours

Other long-haul destinations within Italy for which there is at least one direct connection from Florence include Bolzano, Palermo, Reggio di Calabria, Siracusa, Trieste and Udine.

When you buy a ticket you are supposed to stamp it in one of the yellow machines scattered about all stations (usually with a *convalida* sign on them). Failure to do so will be rewarded with an on-the-spot L40,000 fine by the conductor. If you buy a return ticket, you must stamp it each way (each end of the ticket).

The ticket you buy is valid for two months until stamped. Once stamped it is valid for 24 hours if the distance of the journey (one-way) is greater than 200km (six hours if it is less). The time calculated is for each one-way journey (so on a short return trip you get six hours from the time of stamping the way out and the same on the way back).

Seats on ES trains on Friday and Sunday must be booked. On other days wagons for unbooked seats are set aside. If you board an ES train on Friday or Sunday without a booking, you pay a L10,000 fine.

Tuscany Rail services to destinations around Tuscany are uneven. Train is the better option for the north-west but places like Siena are more easily reached by bus. A wide range of trains, from slow little locali to relatively fast IC trains, can get you around where rail is the transport of choice. Remember that for short journeys on IC and ES trains the supplement will often as much as double the cost of the fare – it is up to you to decide to what extent time is money.

Some sample one-way fares and journey times within Tuscany include:

destination	fare (L)	duration
Arezzo	8000	1 hour 25 minutes
Borgo San Lorenzo	5700	55 minutes
Lucca	7300	1 hour 25 minutes
Pisa	8000	1 hour five minutes via Empoli
Pistoia	4200	40 minutes
Prato	2400	25 minutes
Siena	8800	1 hour 25 minutes

Other Countries

The UK The Channel Tunnel allows for land transport links between Britain and Continental Europe. The Eurostar passenger train service (☎ 0990 186186) travels between London and Paris and London and Brussels. Visit its Web site at www.eurostar.com. The Eurotunnel vehicle-carrying service (☎ 0990 353535) travels between terminals in Folkestone and Calais. Its Web site is at www.eurotunnel.com.

Alternatively, you can get a train ticket that includes the Channel crossing by ferry, SeaCat or hovercraft. After that, you can travel via Paris and southern France or by swinging from Belgium down through Germany and Switzerland. As a rule, however, it is quicker to travel via Paris.

The cheapest standard fares by train and ferry to Florence on offer at the time of writing were UK£74/143 one-way/return for students and those under 26, while the full adult fares were UK£93/153.

Always ask about discounts. As a rule, toddlers under four go for free and kids aged four to 11 travel for half the adult fare. Seniors can get a Rail Europe Senior card (valid for a year only for trips that cross at least one border). You pay UK£5 for the card, but you must already have a Senior Citizens Rail Card (UK£18), available to anyone who can prove they are over 60 (you are not required to be a UK resident). The pass entitles you to roughly 30% off standard fares. The card is known in Italy as Carta Rail Europe Senior, where it costs L33,000. Groups often qualify for discounts too.

For international train-travel information (if you intend to use Eurostar) try the Rail Europe Travel Centre (☎ 0990 848 848), 179 Piccadilly, London W1V 0BA. For rail travel to Italy using cheaper train-ferry combinations, go to Wasteels travel agency (☎ 020-7834 7066), opposite platform 2 at Victoria train station in London.

France Your quickest choice from Paris to Florence is a morning departure on a TGV to Milan (8.12 am or 11.12 am), changing there for the onward trip. You are looking at

GETTING THERE & AWAY

about 10½ hours' travel and FF652 one way in 2nd class. Some 2½ hours slower is the trip via Lausanne (Switzerland), also starting with a TGV. About the cheapest one-way ticket available from Paris is FF496, for people under 26. You have to add a little for the couchette, as the ticket is for the overnight sleeper train. As many as three trains do an overnight run from Paris, one direct but the others involving early morning changes in either Milan or Pisa. Some of these arrive at Florence's Rifredi station, not Santa Maria Novella.

Switzerland, Germany & Austria The comfiest way to rail into Switzerland is with one of the modern Cisalpino (CiS) services. The bulk of these start in Milan, from where you can reach Basle, Bern, Geneva and Zurich. One service connects Florence directly with Zurich, via Milan. That trip costs L142,800 one way and takes a little less than seven hours. From Switzerland it is then possible to connect with fast services into Germany, to destinations such as Stuttgart, Frankfurt am Main and Cologne.

Up to three daily direct trains connect Florence with Innsbruck and Munich via the Brenner Pass. Three other trains go to Vienna via Bologna and Venice. For other destinations in Germany, you will generally have to make connections along the way (although there is one overnight train between Florence and Dortmund).

Spain Direct overnight trains run from Milan to Barcelona (12¾ hours) from three to seven days a week, depending on the season. The cheapest bed costs 29,000 ptas, or you can get a seat for 22,000 ptas. From Barcelona you can connect with trains to other points in Spain. From Florence, you need to allow at least 17 hours (including the change of trains in Milan).

CAR & MOTORCYCLE

To give you an idea of how many clicks you'll put behind you travelling with your own wheels, Florence is 1235km from Berlin, 1555km from London, 1138km

from Paris, 1665km from Madrid, 605km from Geneva, 296km from Milan and 267km from Rome.

Coming from the UK, you can take your car across to France by ferry or the Channel Tunnel car train, Eurotunnel (☎ 0870 5353535). The latter runs around the clock, with up to four crossings (35 minutes) an hour between Folkestone and Calais in the high season. You pay for the vehicle only and fares vary according to time of day and season. The cheapest economy fare (January to May) is around UK£200 return (valid for a year) and the most expensive (May to late September) around UK£290, if you depart during the day Friday to Sunday.

The main points of entry to Italy are: the Mont Blanc tunnel from France at Chamonix (closed at the time of writing following a fire in March 1999 and not due to reopen until autumn 2000 at the earliest), which connects with the A5 for Turin and Milan; the Grand St Bernard tunnel from Switzerland (Sfr27), which also connects with the A5; and the Brenner pass from Austria (AS130), which connects with the A22 to Bologna. Mountain passes in the Alps are often closed in winter and sometimes in autumn and spring, making the tunnels a less scenic but more reliable way to arrive in Italy. Make sure you have snow chains in winter.

Europe is made for motorcycle touring and Italy is no exception. Motorcyclists swarm into the country in summer to tour the winding, scenic roads. Motorcyclists rarely have to book ahead for ferries.

An interesting Web site loaded with advice for people planning to drive in Europe is at www.ideamerge.com/motoeuropa. If you want help with route planning, try out www.shell.com/euroshell/routeplanner.

Florence is connected by the A1 to Bologna and Milan in the north, and Rome and Naples in the south. The Autostrada del Mare (A11) connects Florence with Prato, Lucca, Pisa and the coast, and a superstrada joins the city to Siena. Exits from the *autostrade* (four- to six-lane motorways) into Florence are well signposted and there are tourist offices on the A1 both north and south of the city. From the north on the A1, exit at Firenze Nord and then simply follow the bull's-eye 'centro' signs; if approaching from Rome, exit at Firenze Sud. The more picturesque SS67 connects the city with Pisa to the west and Forlì and Ravenna to the east.

Paperwork & Preparations

Vehicles must be roadworthy, registered and insured (third party at least). The Green Card, an internationally recognised proof of insurance, is compulsory. A European breakdown assistance policy, such as the AA Five Star Service or the RAC Euro-cover Motoring Assistance in the UK, is a good investment.

For information on driving licences, see Driving Licences & Permits under Documents in the Facts for the Visitor chapter.

For details of driving conditions in Florence itself, as well as the hire or purchase of vehicles, see Car & Motorcycle in the Getting Around chapter.

Driving in Italy

Road Rules In general, standard European road rules apply. In built-up areas the speed limit is usually 50km/h, rising to 90km/h on secondary roads, 110km/h on main roads (80km/h for caravans) and up to 130km/h (100km/h for caravans) on autostrade.

Motorcyclists must use headlights at all times. Crash helmets are obligatory on bikes of 125cc or more.

Vehicles already on roundabouts *often* have right of way. However, this is not always the case and working out which type you are confronted with is best done by paying careful attention to local example!

The blood-alcohol limit is 0.08%. Random breath tests are conducted – penalties range from on-the-spot fines to confiscation of your driving licence.

Petrol Italy is among the most expensive place in Western Europe for petrol *(benzina)*; the price has been increasing steadily of late with the runaway dollar fuelling the problem. Super costs L2050 per litre, un-leaded *(senza piombo)* L1965 per litre and diesel *(gasolio)* L1610 a litre. These prices can drop by up to L50 in some service stations, especially those with *fai da te* promotions, where you serve yourself rather than wait for an attendant. Stations on motorways charge about L20 more per litre.

If you are driving a car that uses liquid petroleum gas (LPG), you will need to buy a special guide to service stations that have *gasauto* (GPL in Italy). By law these must be located in nonresidential areas and are usually in the country or on city outskirts, although you'll find plenty on the autostrade. GPL costs around L960 per litre (although it can come down to L850).

You can pay with most credit cards at most service stations. Those on the autostrade open 24 hours a day. Otherwise, opening hours are generally from around 7 am to 12.30 pm and 3.30 to 7.30 pm (7 pm in winter). Up to 75% are closed on Sunday and public holidays; others close on Monday. Don't assume you can't get petrol if you pass a station that is closed. Quite a few have self-service pumps that accept banknotes. It is illegal to carry spare fuel in your vehicle.

Toll Roads & Highways Many of Italy's autostrade are toll roads, and the tolls *(pedaggi)* tend to be expensive. Some reasonable *superstrade* are toll-free. More often than not you will have the choice between a toll road and busy *strada statale*. These tend to pass right through towns and can as much as double your travel time. The SS435 from Florence to Lucca via Prato and Pistoia is a perfect example. Smaller roads are known as *strade provinciali* (SP).

You can pay tolls with a credit card (including Visa, MasterCard, AmEx and Diners Club) on most autostrade in northern Italy. Another way to pay is to buy a Viacard (at toll booths and some service stations and tourist offices). You present it for payment to the attendant or insert it into the appropriate Viacard machine as you exit an autostrada. Leftover credit is not refundable on leaving Italy.

Sign Language

You can save yourself some grief in Florence and elsewhere by learning what some of the many road signs mean:

ENTRATA	ENTRANCE (eg to autostrada)
INCROCIO	INTERSECTION/CROSSROADS
LAVORI IN CORSO	ROADWORKS AHEAD
PARCHEGGIO	CAR PARK
PASSAGGIO A LIVELLO	LEVEL CROSSING
RALLENTARE	SLOW DOWN
SENSO UNICO	ONE-WAY STREET
SENSO VIETATO	NO ENTRY
SOSTA VIETATA	NO STOPPING/PARKING
SOSTA AUTORIZZATA	PARKING PERMITTED (during times displayed)
SVOLTA	BEND
TUTTE LE DIREZIONI	ALL DIRECTIONS (useful when looking for town exit)
USCITA	EXIT (eg from autostrada)

Road Assistance As a rule, members of foreign motoring organisations, such as the RAC, AA (both UK) and AAA (USA), and people who arrange car insurance through them will be provided with an emergency assistance number to use while travelling in Italy. You can also get roadside assistance from the Automobile Club Italia by calling ☎ 116. Your insurance may cover this. Otherwise, you'll pay a minimum fee of L150,000. In any case, it is likely that, whichever number you use, an ACI truck will arrive.

Spot Checks Theft of foreign cars is a problem in Italy, so you may well find yourself being pulled over, usually by the *carabinieri* (military police), to have your papers checked. If the car isn't yours, you need a letter from the owner granting permission to drive it (unless they're with you), otherwise you risk having the car impounded.

BICYCLE

If you plan to bring your own bike, check with the airline about any hidden costs. It will have to be disassembled and packed for the journey.

Once in Italy, it is possible to transport your bicycle on many trains. Those marked

with a bicycle symbol on timetables have a carriage set aside for the transport of bicycles. Otherwise you need to dismantle it and pack it. You cannot take your bike on ES services requiring a booking. In all cases where you can take your bike, you must pay a supplement of L5000 to L10,000.

For details on cycling around Florence and Tuscany see the Activities section of the Things to See & Do chapter.

HITCHING

Hitching is never entirely safe and we don't recommend it. Travellers who decide to hitch should understand that they are taking a small but potentially serious risk.

To get out of Florence you need to start at one of the highway exits. The chances of anyone stopping for you on autostrade are low – try the more congested toll-free highways (such as the SS2 heading south towards Siena, the SS65 north to Bologna or the SS435 west to Lucca).

ORGANISED TOURS

There are many options for organised travel to Italy. The Italian Tourist Office can sometimes provide a list of tour operators noting what each specialises in. It is always worth shopping around for value, but such tours rarely come cheap. Tours can save you some hassles but they do rob you of independence.

A couple of big specialists may be worth investigating initially, if only for the variety of tours they present: Magic of Italy (☎ 020-8748 7575), 227 Shepherd's Bush Rd, London W6 7AS, and Alitalia's subsidiary, Italiatour (☎ 01883-621900). Between them they offer a wide range of tours, city breaks, resort-based holidays and the like covering most of the country. Sestante-CIT (also known as CIT or Citalia), with offices worldwide (see the Tourist Offices section of the Facts for the Visitor chapter), organises many types of tour.

Kirker Travel Ltd (☎ 020-7231 3333), 3 New Concordia Wharf, Mill St, London SE1 2BB, specialises in short breaks from London. Such trips start at about UK£390 per person for three nights in twin accommodation with air fare, transfers and breakfast included. Depending on the hotel you choose, the price can rise considerably. Prices also rise in summer.

Shopping around usually pays off. It is not unheard of for different operators to offer the same thing for considerably different prices. Hotel packages are the easiest to compare, and there's nothing worse than finding out you got the same holiday as someone else but paid much more for the pleasure.

TRAVEL AGENCIES

Florence can hardly be considered one of Europe's discount-flight capitals. If you need to organise a flight you could start

Warning

The information in this chapter is particularly vulnerable to change: prices for international travel are volatile, routes are introduced and cancelled, schedules change, special deals come and go, and rules and visa requirements are amended. Airlines and governments seem to take a perverse pleasure in making price structures and regulations as complicated as possible. You should check directly with the airline or a travel agent to make sure you understand how a fare (and ticket you may buy) works. In addition, the travel industry is highly competitive and there are many lurks and perks.

The upshot of this is that you should get opinions, quotes and advice from as many airlines and travel agents as possible before you part with your hard-earned cash. The details given in this chapter should be regarded as pointers and are not a substitute for your own careful, up-to-date research.

with the following agents, but there is no substitute for shopping around.

Sestante has offices at Via Cavour 56r (Map 6; ☎ 055 29 43 06) and CIT at Piazza della Stazione 51r (Map 3; ☎ 055 28 41 45). At either you can book train and air tickets, organise guided tours and so on.

A branch of CTS (Map 6; ☎ 055 28 95 70), the national youth-travel organisation, is at Via de' Ginori 25r. Otherwise, you can call its telephone sales department on ☎ 055 21 66 60. CTS is about the best source of discounted flight deals.

Getting Around

THE AIRPORTS

Those flying to Florence will probably arrive at Pisa's Galileo Galilei airport, about an hour by train or car from Florence. Some domestic and European flights use Florence's Amerigo Vespucci airport.

Galileo Galilei Airport

Galileo Galilei is one of northern Italy's main international and domestic airports and has regular connections to London, Paris, Munich and major Italian cities.

The airport (flight information at ☎ 055 21 60 73, Florence Air Terminal at Stazione di Santa Maria Novella) terminal lies a short way south of Pisa on the SS1 highway to Rome.

The long, low terminal building is divided into *arrivi* (arrivals) on the left (if you are looking in from the outside) and *partenze* (departures) on the right.

In the arrivals sector you will find Informazioni Turistiche (tourist information) at the end of the hall. It opens from 10.30 am to 5.30 pm daily. It also handles left luggage between 7 am and 10 pm. You can buy bus and train tickets here as well.

About where the arrivals and departures sectors intersect is the Cassa di Risparmio bank, open from 7 am to 10 pm daily. Outside it you'll find an ATM and a foreign-cash changing machine. The post office is open from 8.15 am to 1 pm Monday to Saturday.

Car rental agencies, including Avis, Eurodollar, Europcar, Hertz, Maggiore and others, are all represented in the terminal building.

To/From the Airport There are several options for getting into Florence.

Bus The local No 3 bus runs into central Pisa about every 15 minutes. Tickets cost L1500 and can be bought at tobacconists (they are not sold on the bus). If you can't get one, you can probably get away without the ticket.

A taxi between central Pisa and the airport will cost from L8000 to L13,000.

For Florence, get the train (see the next section). A few bus services run to meet flights for which there are no trains. Two of these are run by SITA (VOLAinBUS), departing at 11.15 am and 9.20 pm from near the taxi rank. The fare is L20,000 and you are dropped at the SITA terminal (Map 3) in Via Santa Caterina da Siena, just by the train station. The railways run a third bus at 12.49 am for late arrivals, which goes to the train station in Florence after a stop in Empoli.

Train Turn left out of the departures hall and walk onto the railway platform, from which you can pick up a train to Florence.

Trains for the airport depart from platform No 5 at Stazione di Santa Maria Novella. Check in your luggage at the station 15 minutes before the train departs.

Trains run roughly hourly from 7.51 am to 5.05 pm from Florence, and from 10.44 am to 5.44 pm from the airport (only until 4.44 pm at weekends). Tickets cost L7400 and the trip takes 80 minutes.

Taxi You'd have to be seriously well-lined to want to get a cab to or from Galileo Galilei airport. There's no guarantee you'll get from central Florence to the airport much quicker than with the train, and it'll cost you around L220,000. It might be an option if you are in imminent danger of missing your flight and are a long way from the train station.

Parking Three parking areas operate at the airport. The P1 parking area is for short-term parking. It's free for the first 30 minutes or L2000 for the first hour; thereafter it's L6000 per hour. There's free long-term parking (unguarded) at the P2 car park. Otherwise try the multi-storey P3 park, which costs up to L20,000 per 24 hours. The P4 park is for buses.

Amerigo Vespucci Airport

The airport (☎ 055 37 34 98) is a few kilometres north-west of the city centre at Via del Termine 11. The main building serves as the Partenze (Departures) hall, while Arrivi (Arrivals) is in a smaller building just to the rear.

When you emerge in the arrivals hall you will find a tourist office, which is open from 8.30 am to 10.30 pm daily. There's also an office for lost luggage *(bagagli smarriti)*, an ATM and a cash changing machine. Car rental agencies, including Avis, Europcar, Hertz, Maggiore, Sixt and Thrifty are all represented in the arrivals hall.

If you want a bank with people in it (to exchange travellers cheques, for example), go to the departures hall (it's open from 7.15 am to 5.30 pm). Aside from the bank (and another ATM and cash-changing machine), you'll also find police, phones, a bar and a first-aid centre in the departures hall.

There is no left-luggage service at this airport.

To/From the Airport There are no trains to Amerigo Vespucci airport.

Bus The No 62 bus runs approximately every 20 minutes from outside Stazione di Santa Maria Novella to/from Amerigo Vespucci airport. The service from the airport runs from 6.30 am to 10.45 pm; from the train station the service runs from 6 am to 10.20 pm. The trip is meant to take 15 minutes but can often be much longer with traffic. Buy a normal city bus ticket (L1500). A ticket vending machine is by the exit in the arrivals hall. The ticket is valid for one hour.

Alternatively, you can get the faster SITA Navetta (Shuttle) to the SITA terminal in Via Santa Caterina da Siena, near the main train station. It costs L6000.

Taxi A taxi to/from Amerigo Vespucci airport will take about half an hour depending on traffic and set you back L25,000 to L30,000.

Parking You may park briefly outside the terminal building to set down or pick up passengers. Otherwise you pay L1500 for an hour in the car park, L8000 for 12 hours and L12,000 for 24 hours.

PUBLIC TRANSPORT

To negotiate the bulk of the city centre you won't need to use the public transport system. It will only come in useful if you need to reach places beyond the centre or are simply too tired to keep going on foot. Traffic in the centre is still a problem and the local administration has all sorts of grand ideas to reduce it by radically altering the public transport situation. On the wish list are tram and underground train systems. In the meantime, to reduce air pollution buses are increasingly being converted from petrol to methane.

Bus

ATAF (Azienda Trasporti Area Fiorentina) buses serve the city centre, Fiesole and other areas in the city's periphery. For information, call ☎ 055 565 02 22.

Useful Lines You'll find several main bus stops for most routes around Stazione di Santa Maria Novella. Some of the most useful lines operate from a stop (Map 3) just outside the south-east exit of the station below Piazza Adua. Many lines stop operating by 9 pm or so. Useful buses leaving from here include:

No 7, for Fiesole
No 13, for Piazzale Michelangelo
No 62, for Amerigo Vespucci airport
No 70 (night bus), for the Duomo and the Uffizi

A network of dinky little minibuses *(bussini)* operates around the centre of town. They can be handy for those getting tired of walking around or needing to backtrack right across town. Only Linea D operates from 8 am to 9.20 pm daily. The others run from 8 am to 8.20 pm Monday to Saturday.

Linea A
    This line runs from the Stazione di Santa Maria Novella to Piazza della Repubblica, along Via Ghibellina and Borgo la Croce to Piazza Beccaria, and passes back along Via dell'Agnolo

and Via Condotta to Piazza della Repubblica and back to the train station via Piazza dell' Unità.

Linea B
From Piazza Vittorio Veneto, this line runs along Lungarno Vespucci to the Uffizi and eastwards to Piazza Piave before turning around and heading back to Piazza Vittorio Veneto via Via de' Neri and the Uffizi.

Linea C
Starting at Piazza San Marco, this line passes through Piazza SS Annunziata, Via Alfani, Piazza Santa Croce, Corso dei Tintori, Ponte alle Grazie, Piazza di Santa Maria Soprarno and then back across Ponte alle Grazie, past the Biblioteca Nazionale, Piazza Santa Croce, Borgo Allegri, Piazza Ciompi, Piazza Sant'Ambrogio, up to Via Colonna and finally back to Piazza San Marco.

Linea D
This line starts at the Stazione di Santa Maria Novella and weaves its way down to Ponte di Vespucci, from where it passes on to Borgo San Frediano, Lungarno Gucciardini, Lungarno Torrigiani, Via dei Renai and on to Piazza Ferrucci and Via Orsini. On the return leg it passes the Palazzo Pitti, Piazza San Felice, Piazza Santo Spirito and Piazza del Carmine before heading back north across the Arno.

Night Buses Of the four so-called night-bus lines, three operate only between 9 pm and 1 am. The only true night bus *(autobus notturno)* is No 70, which is a circle line starting at Stazione di Santa Maria Novella and passing through Piazza San Marco, Piazza del Duomo, Campo di Marte, Ponte Rosso and back to the train station. It operates about every 30 minutes from 12.30 to 6 am.

Tickets Bus tickets should be bought at tobacconists or automatic vending machines at major bus stops before you get on the bus and must be validated in the machine as you enter. You can buy tickets and pick up a useful routes brochure at the ticket office (Map 3) in among the series of ATAF bus stops on Largo Alinari just outside the south-east exit of the train station.

Tickets cost L1500 for 60 minutes or L2500 for three hours. A 24-hour ticket costs L6000. A four-ticket set *(biglietto multiplo)* for night buses (valid for one hour each) costs L5800. You are supposed to

stamp these in the machine when you get on your first bus. If you are hanging around Florence longer, you might want to invest in a monthly ticket *(mensile)* at L55,000 (L36,000 for students). Yearly *(annuale)* tickets are also available. If you just hop on the bus without a ticket, you can get one for L3000 (double the normal price).

There is a special 30-day ticket for using the bussini (lines A to D) only. It costs L25,000.

Fines The fine for being caught without a ticket on public transport is L75,000 – in addition to the price of the ticket, of course.

CAR & MOTORCYCLE
Rule number one: don't bother driving around central Florence. The one-way streets, the pedestrian-only areas and a labyrinth of rules mean that to get from one place to another within 10 minutes' walking distance can involve driving right around most of the city. And then comes the fun of looking for a parking space – even illegal ones are hard to come by!

Traffic is restricted in the city centre, to the extent that only the chosen few with special permits may even contemplate entering it. Of course, not everyone respects this, and the city government is considering setting up barriers around the centre. Only people with appropriate electronic cards would be able to open these barriers.

A no-parking regime (except for residents) rules from 7.30 am to 6.30 pm Monday to Friday. Non-residents may only stop in the centre to drop off or pick up luggage from hotels or park in hotel or public garages (the latter will cost you a fortune).

Parking
Several major car parks and numerous smaller parking areas can be found around the fringes of the city centre. If you are planning to spend the day in Florence, one option is to park at the Fortezza da Basso, which costs L2000 per hour. If you are arriving by car from the north you will eventually end up at the Fortezza – you just park your car and pay the attendant in advance.

Brunelleschi's dome was built without scaffolding.

The Baptistry is one of Florence's oldest buildings.

The cluttered Ponte Vecchio remains much as it did when it was first constructed in 1345.

DAMIEN SIMONIS

Giotto's Campanile dates from 1334.

JOHN HAY

Popular with the birds: a bust of Cellini on the Ponte Vecchi

JULIET COOMBE

Gone fishing: *Neptune* in the Boboli Gardens

JULIET COOMBE

Detail of Pisano's south door of the Baptistry

JULIET COOMBE

The modern face of art outside the Palazzo Pi

From here it is a brisk 10-minute walk to the Duomo.

Closer to the centre are more expensive underground car parks at Piazza del Mercato Centrale (much too expensive for periods longer than a few hours) and Piazza della Stazione (L2000 for the first hour and from L2000 to L5000 for each consecutive hour). For shorter visits, there are several parking areas along the Arno river, which cost L2000 an hour for the first two hours and L3000 for each consecutive hour. As a rule, metered street parking is in use from 8 am to 8 pm Monday to Saturday.

Paid parking is also available along the inside of the city wall between Porta Romana and Piazza Tasso.

To park for free, you need to be prepared to leave the car away from the centre and have a little patience. Streets with non-metered parking begin on the boundaries of the centre. On the northern side of the Arno this means the area ringed by Viale Fratelli Rossi, Viale Strozzi, Viale Lavagnini, Piazza della Libertà, Viale Matteotti, Viale Gramsci and Viale Amendola. Along some sections of this internal 'ring road' you can find parking spots. Uninterrupted white lines on the road mean you are OK. Blue means metered parking. Yellow usually means you may not park.

You can also find such free parking along stretches of the Lungarno beyond the limit marked by these roads. Finally, some (but by no means all) side streets offer such free parking. In some cases it will be free on one side of the road but not on the other (except sometimes for local residents).

Across the Arno things are a little easier. From Ponte alle Grazie east, for example, it is possible to find free parking in some of the side streets.

If you intend to park for days on end, keep an eye out for signs displaying a street-sweeping vehicle. The signs indicate the day of the week and time that cars must be moved to allow street sweepers through. This is usually between midnight and 6 am; thus 'Sabato 0 a 6' indicates that from midnight on Friday until 6 am on Saturday the street needs to be clear. Your car will be towed if left in such a zone. In areas where they don't do this so regularly temporary signs announcing the next day it will be done are posted a few days before the street sweepers appear.

If your car is towed away, call ☎ 055 30 82 49 for the Deposito Comunale (car pound; Map 2) at Viale Strozzi by the Fortezza da Basso. You will have to pay L90,000 to recover it plus whatever fine you are charged. Fines vary depending on the offence.

Warning Talk of free parking needs to be tempered with a warning. Until you are miles from the city centre pretty much all such parking is technically reserved for local residents with permits. Statistics suggest you risk receiving a fine, but it doesn't seem to happen too often – if yours is not an Italian car, no-one will be able to enforce the fine anyway unless you are truly chosen for evil things and you run into the traffic cop at the wrong time!

Rental

Avis (Map 3; ☎ 055 239 88 26) is at Borgo Ognissanti 128r, Europcar (Map 5; ☎ 055 29 04 38) at Borgo Ognissanti 53r and Hertz (Map 3; ☎ 055 239 82 05) at Via Maso Finiguerra 33r.

Alinari (see Bicycle & Moped later in this chapter) rents out motorcycles for up to L180,000 a day.

If you decide to rent a motorhome while in Florence, one of Italy's few rental outlets specialising in these is based about 20km south of the city. Laika Viaggi (☎ 055 805 82 00, fax 055 805 85 00) is at Via B Cellini 210/214 at Tavarnelle Val di Pesa. Its low-season rates for a week's rental start at L204,000 with unlimited kilometres. Note that you have to pay a L2,500,000 deposit. Its Web site is at www.laikaviaggi.com.

Purchase

Only people legally resident in Italy may purchase cars or motorbikes. If you are not resident, about the only way around this is to purchase a vehicle and put it in the name of a friend who is.

Greasy Riders

JANE SMITH

Florence is the *motorino* capital of Italy. With one scooter for every five inhabitants, it has the greatest per capita density of the nippy two-wheelers. Essential for weaving about the complex old centre and choking traffic of so many Italian cities, these cute vehicles are in some respects little monsters. Studies in Florence show that more than half the hydro-carbons polluting the city's air come from *motorini*, along with about 40% of the cancer-causing benzene and 9% of the car-bon monoxide. Not to mention that clattering two-stroke racket (often worsened by delib-erate tinkering).

In 1999 two new laws came into effect, one national and one from Brussels, lowering emission limits and effectively outlawing most two-stroke motorini. Technically, the 10 mil-lion scooters zipping around Italy's streets are supposed to meet the new EU directive's re-quirements. The Italian law applies to scoot-ers sold after it came into effect. So far there hasn't been any noticeable change on the streets. After all, laws were already in place limiting emissions and noise pollution and no-one really seemed to take the trouble to either respect or enforce them. Why should it be any different now?

TAXI

Taxis are found outside Stazione di Santa Maria Novella, or call ☎ 055 42 42, ☎ 055 47 98 or ☎ 055 43 90. The flagfall is L4400, on top of which you pay L1430 per kilo-metre within the city limits (L2540 per kilometre beyond). You are charged at the rate of L200 every 20 seconds while sta-tionary. There is a night-time surcharge (from 10 pm to 6 am) of L5100. On public holidays you pay an extra L3100 (but not if you are already paying the night surcharge). Each piece of luggage costs L1000.

BICYCLE & MOPED

Florence is an ideal city for zipping about on either a moped or a human-powered two-wheeler. It is largely flat and the centre is in any case nearly impossible to navigate by car (see the previous Car & Motorcycle section). Traffic is as chaotic as anywhere else in Italy (with the exception of such all-time favourites as Naples), but not overly unfriendly to cyclists. Hell, the town hall has even laid out a few bike lanes along one-way streets (such as the Arno bridges) allowing cyclists to cross *either* way, much like pedestrians.

Rental

Alinari (Map 3; ☎ 055 28 05 00), Via Guelfa 85r, hires out scooters, larger mopeds and bicycles. In summer it also sets up shop at several camping grounds – check at the APT for details (see Tourist Offices in the Facts for the Visitor chapter). Mopeds/scooters cost from L28,000 to L50,000 for five hours, or from L35,000 to L80,000 per day.

You can rent a bicycle for L12,000 for five hours, L20,000 per day or L40,000 per weekend. A mountain bike costs L20,000 for five hours, L30,000 per day or L60,000 for a weekend.

Motorent (Map 3; ☎ 055 49 01 13), Via San Zanobi 9r, also hires out bikes and scooters. The latter can cost L50,000 a day plus 20% IVA (value-added tax), while a pushbike comes in at L20,000 plus IVA.

Florence by Bike (Map 3; ☎ 055 48 89 92) is at Via San Zanobi 120/122r. You can hire anything from a standard bicycle for getting around town (up to L20,000 a day) to a scooter (L120,000 a day). Its Web site is at www.florencebybike.it.

WALKING
The city's sights are largely concentrated in and around the centre. Walking is definitely the only way to get around and get to know this city.

ORGANISED TOURS
Sestante, CIT and American Express offer tours of the city. Call into one of their offices for information. The SITA bus company (☎ 055 21 47 21) also organises several tours round the city and in the area surrounding Florence.

CAF Tours (Map 6; ☎ 055 21 06 12, fax 055 28 27 90), Via Roma 4, offers a variety of one-day tours of the city and beyond, including to Siena and San Gimignano. Prices range from L34,000 for a Medieval Florence walk to L175,000 for an excursion to Venice (now that's a *long* day!).

Walking Tours of Florence (☎ 055 234 62 25) organises walks of the city led by historians (or at least graduates in art history). It does an introductory walk three days a week for L50,000 starting at 10 am in Piazza della Repubblica. You can organise all sorts of specific walks to suit your own needs and tastes – at a price. Its Web site is at www.artviva.com.

The Comune di Firenze (Florence's council) also has a program of guided tours around the city that goes by the name of Le Piazze di Firenze (Florence's Squares). For more information you can call ☎ 055 262 59 55 or contact the APT office (see Tourist Offices in the Facts for the Visitor chapter). Guides can also be contacted through the APT office.

A little more unusual are the 40-minute tours along a stretch of the Arno in traditional rowing boats. They start at Lungarno Diaz and take you west under the Ponte Vecchio and Ponte Santa Trinita. The boats hold eight to 12 people and leave from 6 pm onwards. You need to book ahead by calling ☎ 0347 7982356, or try your luck by just turning up at the boat landing (Map 6). These trips are organised from May to September and cost L15,000 per person (children aged up to 14 pay L5000).

Florence by Bike (see the earlier Bicycle & Moped section) organises cycle tours in and beyond the city. I Bike Italy (☎ 055 234 23 71) offers reasonably priced full and half-day guided mountain-bike rides in the countryside around Florence, including in the picturesque hills around Fiesole, northeast of the city. All you need is a reasonable amount of energy and a hardy backside.

For guided tours of the Uffizi, you could approach the Associazione Mercurio (☎ 055 21 84 13). For L60,000 a head you will be given an expert sweep of the most important works in the gallery. Tours start at 5.45 pm on Tuesday, Thursday and Saturday and last two hours. You can book at the Amici del Turismo travel agency at Via Cavour 36r (Map 6).

If you want to arrange to have your own guides, you can do so with the Associazione Guide Turistiche (☎ 055 504 83 59), the Associazione Guide Turistiche Fiorentine (☎ 055 422 09 01) or the Centro Guide Turistiche Fiorentine (☎ 055 28 84 48).

Things to See & Do

Highlights

- Gorge yourself on the art collections of the Uffizi (if you can deal with the crowds)

- Climb to the top of Giotto's Campanile for a bird's eye view of the centre of Florence

- Marvel at the magnificence of Michelangelo's *David* in the Galleria dell'Accademia

- Hang out in one of the city's *enoteche* or *osterie* and sample fine Tuscan wines

- Visit the Bargello for the city's finest collection of sculpture

- Dig into a fortifying slab of Fiorentina steak

- Explore the Palazzo Vecchio and Palazzo Pitti, seats of Florentine power and treasure chests of Renaissance art

- Abandon yourself to the joys of stylish (window) shopping

- Drink in the views of the city from Piazzale Michelangelo or the Forte di Belvedere

- Admire the grandeur of the Cappelle Medicee in the Basilica di San Lorenzo

Florence is the proverbial chocolate cake. All cliches apply. Like 'all good things come in small packages'. We won't even try to compete with the battalions of literary greats and other important persons who have spilled rivers of ink in the search for an original superlative. Florence is jammed with monuments and sights, most of them mercifully confined to a small area.

It might be objected that what follows gives insufficient space to the great art and best known of the city's monuments. Within the limits of this book, we have preferred to communicate more of the flavour of the city, often noting less-known corners and characters of Florence's tumultuous past. We certainly do not ignore any of the 'biggies', but those looking for detailed treatment of the main sights should consider investing in some of the books dedicated solely to these subjects. They abound, in several languages, in bookshops in central Florence.

In one sense, 1999 was a lousy year to research a guide to Florence. Many monuments were closed or partly obscured by the restorers' scaffolding in preparation for the fun and games of the Millennium, when as many as 30 million more tourists than usual are expected to flood into the country. Hopefully, by the time you read this, much of the scaffolding will have come down.

Opening Times

Museums and monuments tend to be closed on Monday in Italy. Given the hordes of tourists that pour into Florence year-round, quite a few places *do* open on Monday – you can get a list of them from the APT tourist office (see Tourist Offices in the Facts for the Visitor chapter).

Opening times vary throughout the year, though many monuments stick to a vague summer/winter timetable. In the case of state museums, summer means the six months between 1 May and 31 October. For other sights it can be more like Easter to the end of September. It is impossible to be overly precise, if only because many of the timetables change from year to year anyway.

Details of further variations at some of the most important sights are given in the course of the chapter but be warned that a considerable amount of confusion reigns. Many museums alter the timetables each year, so that even a detailed account of the 1999 summer and winter timetables could easily reveal itself wide of the mark in the following year (and perhaps even more so in the case of the Millennium year 2000). Museum staff members themselves only find out about changes at the last minute.

Warning At most sights the ticket window shuts up to 30 minutes before the advertised closing time. Also, in some of these places (the Uffizi and Cappella Brancacci, to name a couple of the culprits) staff actually shuffle you out at least 15 minutes before closing time. It would seem in such instances that closing time means not when you have to start heading out the door, but when the door has to be bolted shut.

Carnet dei Musei Fiorentini

If you intend to see a good number of the museums in Florence, this carnet (actually a set of 10 vouchers) for L10,000 is worth considering. You get an explanatory booklet and discounts of up to 50% on 10 sights. Some of these are pretty minor, but others you will probably want to visit. They are (in order of interest): Palazzo Vecchio, Cappella Brancacci; the museum and cloisters in the Basilica di Santa Maria Novella; Museo Stibbert; Museo Bardini; Museo di Firenze; Museo Marino Marini; Fondazione Romano (Cenacolo di Santo Spirito); Raccolta Alberto della Ragione; and Galleria Rinaldo Carnielo. The carnet is valid for a year from the date of purchase.

For information on phone and Internet bookings to major sights, see the 'Queue Jumping' boxed text.

PIAZZA DEL DUOMO & AROUND
The Duomo (Map 6)
The Exterior When you first come upon the Duomo from the crowded streets around the square, you will likely stop momentarily in your tracks, taken aback by the ordered vivacity of its pink, white and green marble facade (slowly but surely getting a long overdue clean, as the modest bits of scaffolding attest). You had probably already espied Brunelleschi's sloping, red-tiled dome – the predominant feature of Florence's skyline.

On 25 March 1436 the pope set off from his apartments in the monastery of Santa Maria Novella along a specially raised wooden walkway that had been laid out to the Duomo. Behind him in solemn procession followed cardinals, bishops and the city's leading figures, including the *priori* (governors) led by the *gonfaloniere* (standard-bearer). They arrived at the Duomo to render homage to Brunelleschi's remarkable feat of engineering, the **dome**, which had just been completed.

Brunelleschi had won a public competition to design the enormous dome, the first of its kind since antiquity. Although now severely cracked and under restoration, it remains a remarkable achievement of design.

For the record, the great temple's full name is Cattedrale di Santa Maria del Fiore. It was begun in 1296 by Arnolfo di Cambio

Queue Jumping

If time is precious and money is not a prime concern, you can skip some of the museum queues in Florence by booking ahead.

For a L2000 fee, you can book a ticket to the Uffizi by phoning Firenze Musei (☎ 055 29 48 83). You are given a booking number and agree the time you want to visit. When you arrive at the gallery, follow the signs to a separate entrance for those with pre-booked tickets, which you pick up and pay for on the spot without queuing. You can book to any of the state museums this way. They include the Palazzo Pitti, the Bargello, Galleria dell'Accademia and Cappelle Medicee.

If you prefer the electronic age, Weekend a Firenze is an online service for booking museums, galleries, shows and tours. For this you pay L8270 on top of the normal ticket price. You must book at least five days in advance. You will get an email confirmation that you will have to print out and present at the cashier's desk on the day you go. Check out the service at www.weekendafirenze.com.

Many of the bigger hotels will also book these tickets for you.

When you go to the Uffizi or other sights with prepaid tickets, email confirmation or whatever, head for the designated entrance for those with booked tickets and smile smugly at the suffering hordes lined up outside the other entrance.

A Recipe for Stendhalismo

Any list of 'must sees' in Florence is going to incite cries of protest. How can you recommend that a tour cover the Uffizi, the Duomo and the Baptistry, without including the Museo del Bargello, the Convento di San Marco and the churches of Santa Maria Novella, Santa Croce and SS Annunziata? And what about Masaccio's fresco cycle in Basilica di Santa Maria del Carmine? Or Michelangelo's *David* in the Galleria dell'Accademia and his Medici tombs in the family chapel attached to the Basilica di San Lorenzo?

Plan carefully, or you could end up with a severe case of 'stendhalismo'. The French writer Stendhal was so dazzled by the magnificence of the Basilica di Santa Croce that he was barely able to walk for faintness. He is apparently not the only one to have felt thus overwhelmed by the beauty of Florence – they say Florentine doctors treat a dozen cases of stendhalismo, or *'sindrome di Stendhal'* (Stendhal syndrome), a year.

Oh, and by the way, make sure you carry plenty of L100, L200 and L500 coins for the machines to illuminate the frescoes in the churches.

and took almost 150 years to complete. It is the world's fourth-largest cathedral. It is 153 metres long and 38 metres wide, except the transept, which extends 90 metres. The cathedral it replaced, dedicated to Santa Reparata, fit into an area extending less than halfway down from the entrance to the transept.

The first 'disappointment', if you will, comes from the facade. To all intents and purposes it appears to blend perfectly well with the cathedral's flanks and the Romanesque facing of the Baptistry and the Gothic work on the Campanile (for both see the following section), but the truth of the matter is that it was only raised in the late 19th century. Its architect, Emilio de Fabris, was in fact inspired by the design of the flanks, which largely date from the 14th century.

Arnolfo had begun to raise a facade before his death, but it remained incomplete and was finally stripped away in 1587 because it was considered old hat. The cathedral remained, as it were, exposed for the next three centuries, largely because no one could decide how they would like the facade, nor find the money to finance it.

From the facade, do a circuit of the cathedral to take in its splendour before heading inside.

The southern flank is the oldest and most clearly Gothic of the Duomo. The second doorway here, the **Porta dei Canonici** (Canons' Door) is a mid-14th-century High-Gothic creation (you enter here to climb up inside the dome). Wander around the trio of apses, designed to appear as the flowers on the stem that is the nave of the cathedral (and so reflecting its name – Santa Maria del Fiore – St Mary of the Flower). The first door you see on the northern flank after the apses is the early-15th-century **Porta della Mandorla** (Almond Door), so named because of the relief of the Virgin Mary contained within an almond-shaped frame. Much of the decorative sculpture that graced the flanks of the cathedral has been removed, for its own protection, to the Museo dell'Opera del Duomo, in some cases to be replaced by copies.

The Interior The Duomo's vast and spartan interior comes as a surprise after the visual assault outside.

Down the left aisle you will see two immense frescoes of equestrian statues dedicated to two mercenaries, or *condottieri*, who fought in the service of Florence (for lots of dosh of course). The one on the left is Niccolò da Tolentino (by Andrea del Castagno) and the other Giovanni Acuto, better known to the English as Sir John Hawkwood (by Paolo Uccello). The Florentines made his acquaintance in rather unpleasant circumstances in 1375, when he and his merry band of bloodthirsty marauders gave Florence two options: pay a huge ransom or we'll lay waste to Tuscany. The bankers coughed up and Hawkwood from that point on remained the city's leading soldier.

Although Florence had exiled him, Dante and the world he created in the *Divina Commedia (Divine Comedy)* fascinated subsequent generations of Florentines, who revered him. Domenico di Michelino's *Dante e I Suoi Mondi (Dante and His Worlds)*, the next painting along the left aisle, is one of the most reproduced images of the poet and his verse masterpiece.

The festival of colour and images that greets you as you arrive beneath Brunelleschi's dome is the work of Giorgio Vasari and Frederico Zuccari. The fresco series depicts the *Giudizio Universale (Last Judgement)*. Below it is the octagonal *coro* (choirstalls). Its low marble 'fence' also encloses the altar, above which hangs a crucifix by Benedetto da Maiano.

From the choirstalls, the two wings of the transept and the rear apse spread out, each containing five chapels. The pillars delimiting the entrance into each wing and the apse are fronted by statues of Apostles, as are the two hefty pillars just west of the choirstalls.

Between the left (northern) arm of the transept and the apse is the **Sagrestia delle Messe** (Mass Sacristy), whose panelling is a marvel of inlaid wood created by Benedetto and Giuliano da Maiano. The fine bronze doors were executed by Luca della Robbia, showing he could turn his hand to other material as well as glazed terracotta. That said, the top of the doorway is decorated with one of his 'robbiane', as is the **Sagrestia Nuova** (New Sacristy) by the right transept (no access). By the way, it was through della Robbia's doors that Lorenzo de' Medici fled in the uproar following the assassination by the Pazzi conspirators of his brother Giuliano during Mass in 1478 (see Piero de' Medici & Lorenzo the Magnificent under History in the Facts about Florence chapter).

Some of the finest stained-glass windows in Italy, by Donatello, Andrea del Castagno, Paolo Uccello and Lorenzo Ghiberti, adorn the windows.

A stairway near the main entrance of the Duomo leads down to the 'crypt', actually the site where excavations have unearthed parts of the 5th-century Chiesa di Santa Reparata. Brunelleschi's tomb is also in here. Admission to the excavations costs L5000. Apart from the surviving floor mosaics, typical of early Christian churches in Italy and recalling their Roman heritage, the spurs and sword of Giovanni de' Medici were dug up here. Otherwise the remains give only a vague idea of what the Romanesque church might have been like, and a still dimmer clue of what the church's Roman predecessor might have been.

You can enter the Duomo and 'crypt', except during Mass, from 10 am to 5 pm daily (1 to 5 pm on Sunday).

The Dome You can climb up into the dome to get a closer look at Brunelleschi's engineering feat. You enter by the Porta dei Canonici from outside the southern flank of the cathedral. The view from the summit over Florence is breathtaking.

The dome is open from 8.30 am to 6.20 pm Monday to Friday and until 5 pm on Saturday. The climb costs L10,000.

On 8 September every year, a walkway that stretches around the sides and facade of the dome is opened to the public. You access it by the same entrance as to the dome.

Campanile (Map 6)

Giotto designed and began building the unusual and graceful Campanile (bell tower) next to the Duomo in 1334, but died only three years later.

Andrea Pisano and Francesco Talenti continued the work. The first tier of bas-reliefs around the base, carved by Pisano but possibly designed by Giotto, depicts the Creation of Man and the Arts and Industries (Attività Umane). Those on the second tier depict the planets, cardinal virtues, the arts and the seven sacraments. The sculptures of the prophets and sibyls in the niches of the upper storeys are actually copies of works by Donatello and others – the originals are in the Museo dell'Opera del Duomo.

The Campanile is 84.7m high and you can climb its 414 stairs between 8.30 am and 6.50 pm daily (9 am and 5.20 pm in October; 9 am and 4.20 pm from November to March). Admission costs L10,000.

Warning People with heart conditions or who are otherwise unfit should not undertake this climb. There is no lift should you get into difficulties.

Museo dell'Opera del Duomo (Map 6)

This museum, behind the cathedral at Piazza del Duomo 9, features most of the art treasures from the Duomo, Baptistry and Campanile and is definitely worth a visit.

Displays include the equipment used by Brunelleschi to build the dome, as well as his death mask. Perhaps its best piece is Michelangelo's *Pietà*, which he intended for his own tomb. Vasari recorded in his *Lives of the Artists* that, unsatisfied with the quality of the marble or his own work, Michelangelo broke up the unfinished sculpture, destroying the arm and left leg of the figure of Christ. A student of Michelangelo later restored the arm and completed the figure of Mary Magdalene.

The collection of sculpture is considered the city's second best after that in the Museo del Bargello. Note in particular Donatello's carving of the prophet Habakkuk (taken from the Campanile) and his wooden impression of Mary Magdalene.

Ghiberti's original doors (the 'Gate of Paradise') from the Baptistry were also due to go on display in late 1999.

The museum is usually open from 9 am to 6.50 pm (6.20 pm in winter) Monday to Friday. Admission costs L8000. At the time of writing, restoration and reorganisation works still had not been completed and the museum was tightly shut.

Baptistry (Map 6)

The Exterior The Romanesque Baptistry (Battistero) may have been built as early as the 5th century on the site of a Roman temple. It is one of the oldest buildings in Florence and dedicated, as indeed was often the case with baptistries in Italy, to St John the Baptist (San Giovanni Battista). Dante was among those to be baptised here.

The present structure, or at least its facade, dates from about the 11th century. The stripes of white and green marble that be-

deck the octagonal structure are typical of Tuscan Romanesque style.

More striking still are the three sets of bronze doors, conceived as a series of panels in which the story of humanity and the Redemption would be told.

The earliest set of doors, now on the southern side, was completed by Andrea Pisano in 1336. The bas-reliefs on its 28 compartments deal predominantly with the life of St John the Baptist. If you take time to look at the scenes, you will see that Pisano's work is still largely rooted in the Gothic. Stiff, expressionless people communicate a didactic message with little or no human emotion.

Lorenzo Ghiberti tied with Brunelleschi in a competition in 1401–02 to see who would do the north doors. Brunelleschi was so disgusted he went to Rome, leaving Ghiberti to toil away for the next 20 years in an effort to get the doors just right. The top 20 panels recount episodes from the New Testament, while the eight lower ones show the four evangelists and the four fathers of the Church.

Good as this late-Gothic effort was, Ghiberti returned almost immediately to his workshops to turn out the east doors. Made of gilded bronze, they took 28 years to complete, largely because of Ghiberti's intransigent perfectionism. The bas-reliefs on their 10 panels depict scenes from the Old Testament. So extraordinary were his exertions that, many years later, Michelangelo stood before the doors in awe and declared them fit to be the 'Porta del Paradiso' (Gate of Paradise), which is how they remain known to this day. Certainly the difference between them and Pisano's doors is evidence of the extraordinary shift towards Renaissance ideals. The scenes seem more lifelike, full of movement and depth. It is instructive to spend a little time comparing the two sets of doors.

Most of the doors are copies. The original panels are being removed for restoration and are due to be placed in the Museo dell'Opera del Duomo as work is completed.

The Roman-era north gate was close by here, about where Via de' Cerretani hits

Piazza di San Giovanni. That street marks the line of the Roman north wall.

The Interior Inside, one is reminded of the Pantheon in Rome. The two-coloured marble facing on the outside continues within and is made more arresting by the geometrical flourishes above the Romanesque windows. The inlaid marble designs of the floor, reminiscent of those in the Chiesa di San Miniato in the Oltrarno (see Oltrarno later in the chapter) are equally delightful. Look in particular for the sun and zodiac designs on the side opposite the apse.

The single most arresting aspect of the decoration are the mosaics. Those in the apse were started in 1225 and are looking a little jaded. The glittering spectacle in the dome is, however, a unique sight in Florence. It was carried out by Venetian experts over 32 years from 1270 to designs by Tuscan artists, including Cimabue.

Around the northern, eastern and southern sides of the dome stories of the Old and New Testaments unfold, including Genesis, the Visitation, the Last Supper and the death of Christ. The western side is dominated by the marvellous figure of Christ Pantocrator enthroned. Around him takes place the Last Judgement. Anyone who has had the fortune to see the 12th- and 13th-century Byzantine mosaics in the Chiesa di Santa Maria Assunta on the Venetian lagoon island of Torcello will notice uncanny similarities. It becomes clear that only artisans steeped in the same artistic tradition could have produced such a masterpiece of the Middle Ages.

Donatello carved the tomb of Baldassare Cossa, better known as John XXIII the Antipope, which takes up the wall to the right of the apse.

The Baptistry is open from noon to 6.30 pm daily. Admission costs L5000.

Loggia del Bigallo (Map 6)

This elegant marble loggia was built in the second half of the 14th century for the Compagnia del Bigallo, which had been formed in 1244 to help elderly people, orphans and beggars. Lost and abandoned children were customarily placed here so that they could be reclaimed by their families. At the time of writing the loggia was completely hidden by scaffolding. Across Via dei Calzaiuoli you'll notice Florence's ambulance station, the Misericordia di Firenze. The Arciconfraternita della Misericordia started work here in 1244, its task to transport the sick to hospital and bury the dead in times of plague. The latter problem is hopefully permanently relegated to the past, but the ambulance vocation at this site remains.

Museo di Firenze (Map 5)

This is mildly interesting for those who want to get an idea of how the city developed, particularly from the Renaissance to the modern day. Paintings, models, topographical drawings (the earliest dating from 1594) and prints help explain the history of the city. The sketches and other pictures of the Mercato Vecchio (Old Market) and the old Jewish ghetto area are intriguing (and a little sad), showing as they do something of what was the bustling heart of the city before the town fathers had it all torn down to make way for the Piazza della Repubblica. A fine diorama and some maps complete the picture of destruction.

A relatively new section is dedicated to the evolution of the site from the times of the earliest-known settlement to Roman days, also providing information on what excavations have revealed about the city. Interspersed between explanatory panels is a sparse collection of Roman and Etruscan remains which were dug up in and around Florence.

The museum can be found behind the Duomo at Via dell'Oriuolo 24 and is open from 9 am to 2 pm daily except Thursday (8 am to 1 pm on Sunday and holidays). Admission costs L5000.

FROM THE DUOMO TO PIAZZA DELLA SIGNORIA

What follows is a rather serpentine meander across the heart of old Florence. You could do it in a million ways, so don't take the following order too much to heart.

Via del Proconsolo (Map 6)

Bernardo Buontalenti started work on the **Palazzo Nonfinito** (Map 6), a residence for the Strozzi family, in 1593. The area had been occupied by a series of smaller houses, all swept aside for the grand new structure. Buontalenti and others completed the 1st floor and courtyard, which is Palladian in style, but the upper floors were never completely finished, hence the building's name. Buontalenti's window designs and other details constitute a Mannerist touch that take the building beyond the classicist rigour of the Renaissance. The obscure **Museo dell'Antropologia e Etnologia** is housed here. It opens from 10 am to noon every day except Tuesday, and admission costs L6000.

Across Borgo degli Albizi stands the equally proud **Palazzo dei Pazzi**, which went up a century earlier than the Palazzo Nonfinito and is clearly influenced by the Palazzo Medici-Riccardi. The main, striking difference is in the sumptuous sculpting of the cornices on the windows, a departure that places the building's design, attributed to Giuliano da Maiano, in the late 15th century. It now houses offices. You can wander into the courtyard.

La Badia (Map 6)

The 10th-century Badia Fiorentina (Florence Abbey) was built on the orders of Willa, mother of one of the early Margraves of Tuscany, Ugo, on Via del Proconsolo. Willa was inspired to this act by calls for greater piety in the Church, which at the time was coming under hefty attack from some quarters for corruption of all kinds. Ugo continued the work of his mother, investing considerably in the Benedictine monastery and church. He was eventually buried here. It is particularly worth a visit to see Filippino Lippi's *Appearance of the Virgin to St Bernard*, to the left of the entrance. You could wander into the Renaissance cloister were the church not shut for major restoration works.

Palazzo del Bargello (Map 6)

Just across Via del Proconsolo from the Badia is this grand mansion, also known as the Palazzo del Podestà. Started in 1254, the palace was originally the residence of the chief magistrate and then a police station. During its days as a police complex, many people were tortured near the well in the centre of the medieval courtyard. Indeed, for a long time the city's prisons were located here.

It now houses the **Museo del Bargello** and the most comprehensive collection of Tuscan Renaissance sculpture in Italy. The museum is absolutely not to be missed.

You enter the courtyard from Via Ghibellina and turn right into the ticket office. From here you end up in the ground-floor **Sala del Cinquecento** (16th-Century Room), dominated by early works by Michelangelo. His drunken *Bacco (Bacchus)*, executed when the artist was 22, a marble bust of *Brutus*, a tondo of the *Madonna col Bambino (Madonna and Child)* are among his best here. Other works of particular interest are Benvenuto Cellini's rather camp marble *Ganimede (Ganymede)* and *Narciso (Narcissus)*, along with Giambologna's *Mercurio Volante (Winged Mercury)*.

Among the statues lining the courtyard is Giambologna's powerful *Oceano* (on the Via della Vigna Vecchia side). Cross the courtyard to the small **Sala del Trecento** (14th-Century Room) where, among other pieces, you can see Arnolfo's very Gothic group of *Acoliti (Acolytes)*.

Head now up the grand staircase to the 1st floor. In the gallery (which in the days when the building was a prison was closed off and divided into cells) are a series of statues and bronzes destined for fountains and gardens. They include a series of animal and bird bronzes by Giambologna.

Turn right into the majestic **Salone del Consiglio Generale** (Hall of the General Council). At the far end, housed in a tabernacle, is Donatello's famed *San Giorgio (St George)*, which once graced the Orsanmichele. David (as in David and Goliath) was a favourite subject for sculptors. In this hall you can see both a marble version by Donatello and the fabled bronze he executed in later years. The latter is extraordinary – more so when you consider it was the first freestanding naked statue sculpted since classical times. This *David* doesn't appear terribly warrior-like. He looks rather like he is mincing up to the bar for a drinkie. This might well have been part of the point, as Donatello succeeds in transmitting a range of human sentiment in the statue's gesture and demeanour.

Another Donatello of note here is the *Marzocco*, the lion propping up the standard of Florence (a red lily on a white background). This originally stood on Piazza della Signoria, where it has been replaced with a copy.

From this hall you pass into a room given over to Islamic tapestries, ceramics and other items. There follows the Carrand collection, a mixed bag of items collected by a 19th-century French antiquarian in Florence. At the far end of this hall is the **Cappella di Santa Maria Maddalena** (Mary Magdalene's Chapel). The frescoes were created around 1340 by Giotto's workshop. The back-wall fresco depicting *Paradiso (Heaven)* includes a portrait of Dante.

You head back into the Carrand hall and then left into a room containing exquisite ivory pieces, some dating from Carolingian times. The closer you look at these miniature sculptures, the more astounding the workmanship appears.

Up on the 2nd floor you arrive in a room filled with glazed terracotta sculptures by the della Robbia family and others. The simplest and yet most captivating is the bust of a *Fanciullo (Boy)* in the annexe room to the left.

From that room you enter another filled with small bronzes. Among them, the two masterpieces are Antonio Pollaiuolo's *Ercole e Anteo (Hercules and Anteus)* and Cellini's *Ganimede*. Backtrack through the small room with the *Fanciullo* and continue into the next hall. Reliefs and sculptures by Mino da Fiesole and others play second fiddle to Verrocchio, among whose best efforts here is the bust of the *Madonna del Mazzolino*.

The museum is less popular than the Uffizi and Accademia galleries and attracts smaller crowds. It is open from 8.30 am to 1.50 pm Tuesday to Saturday and on alternating Sundays and Mondays. Admission costs L8000.

Palazzo Borghese (Map 5)

This long, low building occupying a whole block between Via Ghibellina and Via de' Pandolfini is an early-19th-century neoclassical pile put up for the family of the same name.

San Firenze (Map 6)

From as early as 1645, the Oratorian Fathers wanted to expand the small parish church of San Firenze. For the next century, architects and finances came and went, and the design continued to change. The original church, which stood on the right flank of the present building, was to have a chapel and convent added. In the end, a new church, dedicated to St Philip Neri (San Filippo Neri), was built on the left flank and the San Firenze church reduced to an oratory. The two were then linked and the whole complex became known, erroneously, as Chiesa di San Firenze. The late-baroque facade that unites the buildings was completed in 1775. Today most of the building is occupied by law courts.

Across the piazza (on the western side) is the main facade of **Palazzo Gondi**, once the site of the merchants tribunal, a court set up to deal with their quarrels. Off Via de' Gondi you can enter a beautiful courtyard with fountain and staircase in *pietra serena* ('tranquil stone'). The whole courtyard is now crammed with the tourist tat on sale in the shops that have nested in the ground floor of the building. What would Leonardo da Vinci, who as a young lad was apprenticed to a painter's workshop that stood here before Palazzo Gondi, think of it all?

Casa di Dante & Around (Map 6)

From Piazza San Firenze you can turn west along Via della Condotta, which in medieval times was one of the main shopping streets for clothes and fabrics. Take Via dei Magazzini north and you'll arrive at Via Dante Alighieri.

On the corner of this street and Via Santa Margherita is a house touted as Casa di Dante (Dante's House). It is in fact an early-20th-century structure built on a site that more or less corresponds to the location of the great poet's lodgings. In other words, it's a fake.

Inside, over several floors, is a museum tracing Dante's life. It consists principally of photocopied documents, some pictorial material and a written commentary that follows Dante's peregrinations and the history of Florence. On the top floor are old copies of the *Divina Commedia* in every language from Chinese to Russian. Some of the explanations are in Italian and English, but most of the commentary is in Italian only. It will really only interest Dante fans, and even then it is a trifle bogus. If you want to poke your nose in, it is open from 10 am to 4 pm daily except Tuesday (until 6 pm from May to September; until 2 pm on Sunday and holidays). Admission costs L5000.

Just up Via Santa Margherita is the small **Chiesa di Santa Margherita**, which dates at least from 1032. Some claim that it was in this small single nave church with a timber ceiling that Dante met his muse, Beatrice Portinari, though he himself said he bumped into her in the Badia. However, he may have married Gemma Donati in Santa Margherita. Members of both families, and conceivably Beatrice and Gemma themselves, are buried here.

Heading back south down the lane, you run into the **Torre della Castagna**, all that remains of the palazzo where the republic's leaders, the priori, met until the Palazzo della Signoria (nowadays the Palazzo Vecchio) was built. Facing the tower across Via dei Magazzini is the **Oratorio di San Martino**, which occupies the site of the former Chiesa di San Martino, Dante's parish church.

Orsanmichele (Map 6)

Continuing along Via Dante Alighieri, which leads into Via dei Tavolini, you come across the Chiesa di Orsanmichele. Originally a grain market, the church was formed when the arcades of the granary building

were walled in during the 14th century and the granary moved elsewhere. The granary was built on a spot known as Orsanmichele, a contraction of Orto di San Michele (St Michael's Garden). Under the Lombards a small church dedicated to St Michael and an adjacent Benedictine convent had indeed been graced with a pleasant garden. The *signoria* (the city's government) cleared the lot to have the granary built. It was destroyed by fire 20 years later and a finer replacement constructed. This was considered too good to be a mere granary so it was converted into a church.

The signoria ordered the guilds to finance the decoration of the oddly shaped house of worship, and they proceeded to commission sculptors to erect statues of their patron saints in tabernacles placed around the building's facades.

The statues, commissioned over the 15th and 16th centuries, represent the work of some of the Renaissance's greatest artists. Some of the statues are now in the Museo del Bargello. Many splendid pieces remain, however, including Giambologna's *San Luca* (*St Luke*, third on the right on Via dei Calzaiuoli), a copy of Donatello's *San Giorgio* (*St George*, last on the right on Via Orsanmichele), and Ghiberti's bronze *San Matteo* (*St Matthew*, first on the left on Via Arte della Lana).

The main feature of the interior is the splendid Gothic tabernacle, decorated with coloured marble, by Andrea Orcagna. It is an extraordinary item; to look at the convulsed, twisting columns you could swear you are looking at a scale prototype for the Duomo in Orvieto (Umbria). Classical music recitals are held here occasionally.

The church is open from 9 am to midday and 4 to 6 pm (closed the first and last Monday of the month). There is also a small museum inside, for which you have to join a tour at 9, 10 or 11 am. Admission is free.

Opposite Orsanmichele on Via dei Calzaiuoli is the humble little **Chiesa di San Carlo dei Lombardi**. The church, built in the 14th century, though technically Gothic, still bears Romanesque trademarks in its simple, squat facade.

At Via Orsanmichele 4 is the **Arte dei Beccai**, the 14th-century headquarters of the Butchers' Guild.

Arte della Lana (Map 6)

Far more important was the Arte della Lana (Wool Guild) whose medieval headquarters still stands proudly on the corner of Via Orsanmichele and Via Calimala. It is made up of a tower-house, echoing that Florentine preoccupation with self-defence that clearly affected the guilds almost as much as it did feuding families.

The street gave the **Arte dei Mercatanti** (Merchants' Guild) its alternative name, Arte di Calimala, which emerged as the most powerful force in medieval Florentine politics. Unfortunately, little remains of the building apart from bits of the facade. The front of the building is at Piazza della Signoria 4a. The guild's symbol, an eagle clutching a bundle, is embossed in stone in several places along the wall on Via Calimaruzza. The biggest one sits above a doorway.

Just south of where Via Calimaruzza runs into Via Calimala is where the Roman city's south gate stood. By the way, some think the name 'Calimala' was a distortion of *callis maius*, itself a badly pronounced version of the Roman *cardo maximus*, the standard main cross street in a Roman garrison town.

Piazza della Repubblica (Map 6)

A short way north along Via Calimala is Piazza della Repubblica. When you first come across this broad, breezy square, you might be forgiven for thinking it perfectly acceptable as squares go. The more you look at it the more you realise it probably is not an ancient public space, but for all that it still may fail to offend.

But ever since this square was ruthlessly gouged from the city centre in the years following Italian unity in 1861, all and sundry have continued to execrate it.

On the western flank of the square a huge memorial plaque atop a bombastic triumphal arch proclaims stridently *'l'antico centro della città da secolare squallore a nuova vita restituito'* ('the ancient city centre returned to new life after centuries of squalor'). This was a polite way of saying: 'Hey, look! We've managed to rip out the heart of the old city and replace it with a soulless void!' Even today more sensitive Florentines remain embarrassed by this masterstroke of middle-class 19th-century fatheadedness.

To create the piazza and restructure the surrounding areas, 26 ancient streets and a further 18 lanes disappeared, along with 341 residential buildings, 451 stores, 173 warehouses and other buildings and services...5822 residents were forcibly relocated to other parts of the city. The entire Mercato Vecchio, which had inherited its function as central market from the Roman forum, and the nearby lanes of the small Jewish ghetto were simply wiped from the map. Nice one.

Just off the north-western tip of Piazza della Repubblica, where the Cinema Gambrinus is, excavators found a Roman ramp leading down to what must have been one of the Roman town's main cisterns, from which the populace would have drawn its fresh water.

If you want to get some idea of what this part of town looked like before the 'squalor' was wiped away, the Museo di Firenze has a model, maps and late-19th-century pictures of the area.

Mercato Nuovo (Map 6)

If you stroll back south down Via Calimala you arrive at this loggia, built to cover the merchandise (including wool, silk and gold) traded here at the 'New Market' under Cosimo I in the mid-16th century. Nowadays the goods on sale are aimed exclusively at tourists and range from trashy statuettes and other souvenirs to leather goods of mixed quality.

At its southern end is a bronze statue of a boar known as the **Fontana del Porcellino** (Piglet's Fountain), an early-17th-century copy of the Greek marble original that is now in the Uffizi. They say that if you chuck a coin into the small basin and rub the critter's snout you will return to Florence. Does that mean you won't if you don't?

Smack in the middle of the market is a stone symbol in the shape of a cartwheel (visible if it has not been covered up with bags and other junk) in the pavement. In times of war, the city's old medieval war cart (*carroccio*) was placed here as a symbol of impending hostilities. On a less serious note (except perhaps for those on the receiving end), this was also the spot where dodgy merchants were punished. According to the law they were to drop their trousers, 'exposing the pudenda', and receive a sound thrashing on the bare buttocks. No doubt some disgruntled shoppers will wish the law were still on the books today.

Palazzo dei Capitani di Parte Guelfa (Map 6)

Just off to the south-west of the Mercato Nuovo, this 'Palace of the Guelph Faction's Captains' was built in the early 13th century and later tinkered with by Brunelleschi and Vasari. The leaders of the Guelph faction raised this fortified building in 1265, taking up land and houses that had been confiscated from the Ghibellines.

Palazzo Davanzati (Map 6)

About a block west is this remarkable 14th-century mansion at Via Porta Rossa 13. One could perhaps be a little put out that it has been closed for restoration since 1995, but sometimes restoration is a good thing.

Indeed, that the building has survived intact in its medieval state is largely due to the intervention of an antiquarian, Elia Volpi, who bought the building in 1904. By that time it had come down in the world, having been divided into small flats and shops and been run down to a pathetic state. Volpi had it restored to its former glory and it eventually became the seat of the **Museo dell'Antica Casa Fiorentina**, which aims to transmit an idea of what life was like in a medieval Florentine mansion.

Chiesa degli SS Apostoli (Map 6)

This modest 11th-century church is dwarfed by the houses built on and around it in Piazza del Limbo. If the repairers' scaffolding ever comes down, you will be able to see that the facade is a 16th-century addition. Inside, columns of green Prato marble set apart two aisles from the considerably higher central nave. At the end of the left aisle is a brightly glazed terracotta tabernacle by Giovanni della Robbia.

Chiesa di Santo Stefano (Map 6)

If you hike back east to Via Por Santa Maria, cross into the little square presided over by the part-Romanesque part-Gothic facade of this now deconsecrated church. It's only ever open when concerts are held, in which case you could get a look at the rather heady baroque interior.

Ponte Vecchio (Map 6)

See Oltrarno later in this chapter.

PIAZZA DELLA SIGNORIA
The Piazza (Map 6)

The hub of the city's political life through the centuries and surrounded by some of its most celebrated buildings, the piazza has the appearance of an outdoor sculpture gallery. Just to the east, stretching in a semicircle from Via de' Gondi to the junction of Via de' Castellani and Via dei Neri, was Roman Florentia's first theatre, built in the 1st century AD.

Throughout the centuries, whenever Florence entered one of its innumerable political crises, the people would be called here as a people's plebiscite (*parlamento*) to rubber-stamp decisions that frequently meant ruin for some ruling families and victory for others. Often one side or the other would make sure the square was cordoned off with loyal troops, just to hint in which direction votes should go. Here too the Ciompi rampaged in Florence's only true proletarian uprising in the 14th century. Scenes of great pomp and circumstance alternated with others of terrible suffering – here the preacher-leader Savonarola was hanged and fried along with two supporters in 1498. A bronze plaque towards the centre of the piazza marks the spot of his execution.

Amannati's huge *Fontana di Nettuno (Neptune Fountain)* sits beside the Palazzo

JULIET COOMBE

'The king reigns and the Lord reigns supreme' – wise words in Piazza della Signoria

Vecchio. Although the bronze satyrs and divinities frolicking about the edges of the fountain are quite delightful, Il Biancone ('the Big White Thing'), as locals derisively refer to it, is pretty universally considered a bit of a flop. Michelangelo couldn't believe that Amannati had ruined such a nice block of marble.

Flanking the entrance to the palace are copies of Michelangelo's *David* (the original is in the Galleria dell'Accademia) and Donatello's *Marzocco*, the heraldic Florentine lion (the original is in the Museo del Bargello). To the latter's right is a 1980 copy of Donatello's bronze *Giuditta e Oloferne (Judith Slays Holofernes)* – the original is in the Sala dei Gigli inside the palace.

A bronze equestrian statue of Cosimo I de' Medici, rendered by Giambologna in 1594–98, stands towards the centre of the piazza.

Palazzo Vecchio (Map 6)

Formerly known as the Palazzo della Signoria and built by Arnolfo di Cambio between 1298 and 1314, this is the traditional seat of Florentine government. Its **Torre d'Arnolfo** is 94m high and, with its striking crenellations, is as much a symbol of the city as the Duomo.

Built for the priori who ruled Florence in two-month turns, the mansion came to be known as the Palazzo della Signoria as the government took on this name. The fortress-like pile is a strange rhomboid

shape, in part due to a government decree that nothing should be built on the razed land (now part of Piazza della Signoria near the palazzo) on which the Uberti family's residences had stood. The Uberti had been declared traitors.

In 1540, Cosimo I de' Medici moved from the Palazzo Medici into this building, making it the ducal residence and centre of government. Cosimo commissioned Vasari to renovate the interior, creating new apartments and decorating the lot. In a sense it was all in vain, because Cosimo's wife, Eleonora de Toledo, was not so keen on it and bought Palazzo Pitti.

The latter took a while to expand and fit out as Eleonora wanted (she died before the work was finished), but the Medici family moved in anyway in 1549. Thus the Palazzo Ducale (or della Signoria for those with a nostalgic bent) came to be called the Palazzo Vecchio (Old Palace) as it still is today. It remains the seat of the city's power, as this is where the mayor does his thing.

Coming in from Piazza della Signoria, you arrive first in the courtyard, reworked in early Renaissance style by Michelozzo in 1453. The decoration came more than a century later when Francesco de' Medici married Joanna of Austria. The cities depicted are jewels in the Austrian imperial crown. The poor woman was much neglected by her unpleasant husband, who made no secret of his preference for various mistresses. The thin, pale and haughty Joanna, not much liked by anyone in Florence, died in this bitter golden cage at the age of 30.

From here you pass into the **Cortile della Dogana** (Customs Courtyard), off which you'll find the ticket office.

A stairway leads upstairs to the magnificent **Salone dei Cinquecento**, also known more simply as the Sala Grande (Big Hall). It was created within the original building in the 1490s to accommodate the Consiglio dei Cinquecento (Council of 500) called into being in the republic under Savonarola. History takes some funny twists, and Cosimo I de' Medici turned the hall, whose council had symbolised the end of Medici family rule, into a splendid expression of his own power. The elevated tribune at one end was where Cosimo held audiences. In the 1560s the ceiling was raised 7m and Vasari added the decorations. Vasari operated with a vast workshop of apprentices and boasted of the speed with which he could turn out paintings, frescoes and whatever else might be required. Michelangelo once quipped that you could tell by the results.

Vasari & co slapped on the two sets of three panels depicting famous battles between Florence and Pisa (on the side you enter the hall) and Siena (on the opposite side). On the same side as the Siena painting is a statue, *Genio della Vittoria (Genius of Victory)*, by the acid-tongued Michelangelo.

On the same side as the entrance, another door leads off to the small, windowless *studiolo* (little study) of Francesco I de' Medici, a little Mannerist gem whose design was again directed by Vasari. The best you can hope for is to get a peek inside if a museum employee leaves the door open. Once every three or four years it is opened to the public, which must be quite a sight.

Opposite the studiolo, you enter the **Quartiere di Leone X** by another door. The so-called 'Leo X Area' is named after the Medici pope. You can only see the one room as the others are given over to offices. Upstairs is the **Quartiere degli Elementi** (Elements Area), a series of rooms and terraces dedicated to pagan deities. The original *Putto col Delfino (Cupid with Dolphin)* sculpture by Verocchio (a copy graces the courtyard of the building) is in the Sala di Giunone. Have a look at Vasari's Venus in the central Sala degli Elementi and compare it with Botticelli's version. Michelangelo might have had a point.

From here a walkway takes you across the top of the Salone dei Cinquecento into the **Quartiere di Eleonora**, the apartments of Cosimo I's wife. The room most likely to catch your attention is Eleonora's chapel just off to the right as you enter the apartments. Bronzino's decoration represents the acme of his painting career (pity this is a copy of the original).

You pass through several more rooms until reaching the **Sala dell'Udienza** (Audience Room), where the priori administered medieval Florentine justice. The following room is the **Sala dei Gigli**, named after the lilies of the French monarchy that decorate three of the walls (the French were traditionally well-disposed to Florence). Domenico Ghirlandaio's fresco on the far wall was supposed to be matched by others. Donatello's restored bronze of *Giuditta e Oloferne* stands in here. A small, bare study off this hall is the chancery, where Machiavelli worked for a while. The other room off the hall is a wonderful map room. The walls are covered by 16th-century maps of all the known world.

Exit the Sala dei Gigli and climb the stairs to the **battlements**, from where you have fine views of the city. As you then follow the stairs down towards the exit you'll see, at the mezzanine level, the **Loeser collection** of minor Tuscan art from the 14th–16th centuries.

The palace is open from 9 am to 7 pm daily (to 2 pm on Thursday). Admission costs L10,000.

Loggia della Signoria (Map 6)

Built in the late 14th century as a platform for public ceremonies, this loggia eventually became a showcase for sculptures. It also became known as the Loggia dei Lanzi, as Cosimo I used to station his Swiss mercenaries (or *Landsknechte*), armed with lances, in it to remind people who was in charge around here.

To the left of the steps normally stands Benvenuto Cellini's magnificent bronze statue of Perseus holding the head of Medusa. It has been under restoration since 1997. To the right is Giambologna's Mannerist *Ratto delle Sabine (Rape of the Sabine Women)*, his final work. Inside the loggia proper is another of Giambologna's works, *Ercole col Centauro Nesso (Hercules with the Centaur Nessus)*, in which the centaur definitely appears to be coming off second best. The statue originally stood near the southern end of the Ponte Vecchio. Among the other statues are some Roman representations of women.

JANE SMITH

A triumphant Perseus holds Medusa's head
aloft in Cellini's bronze sculpture.

Raccolta d'Arte Contemporanea Alberto della Ragione (Map 6)

The collection (raccolta) of contemporary art may awaken mild interest in the art buff with a passion for the Italian 20th-century product. Most of the painters on view worked in the first half of the 20th century. A few Giorgio Morandis in Room IX are worth a quick look. There's even a modest De Chirico in the same room. Fans of Carlo Levi's classic book, *Cristo si è Fermato ad Eboli (Christ Stopped at Eboli)*, may be curious to see the trio of paintings he did while in exile in southern Italy (on the 1st floor). Well represented are Mario Mafai, Ottone Rosai (among whose works figure some dreamscapes of Florence) and Virgilio Guidi.

The collection was donated to Florence by the Genoese collector Alberto della Ragione on his death in 1970.

The museum is open from 8.30 am to 1.30 pm every day except Tuesday. Admission costs L4000.

THE UFFIZI

Designed and built by Vasari in the second half of the 16th century at the request of Cosimo I de' Medici, the Palazzo degli Uffizi, south of the Palazzo Vecchio, originally housed the city's administrators, judiciary and guilds. It was, in effect, a government office building (*uffizi* means offices).

Vasari also designed the private corridor that links the Palazzo Vecchio and the Palazzo Pitti, through the Uffizi and across the Ponte Vecchio. Known as the **Corridoio Vasariano**, it was recently opened to the public (see Corridoio Vasariano later in the chapter).

Cosimo's successor, Francesco I, commissioned the architect Buontalenti to modify the upper floor of the Palazzo degli Uffizi to house the Medicis' growing art collection. Thus, indirectly, the first steps were taken to turn it into an art gallery.

The Galleria degli Uffizi (Uffizi Gallery) now houses the family's private collection, bequeathed to the city in 1743 by the last of the Medici family, Anna Maria Ludovica, on condition that it never leave the city. Over the years sections of the collection have been moved to the Museo del Bargello and the city's Museo Archeologico. In compensation, other collections, such as that put together by the Count Augusto Contini-Bonacossi in the 1930s, have joined the core group. Paintings from Florence's churches have also been moved to the gallery. It is by no means the biggest art gallery around (this is no Louvre), but all in all, the Uffizi still houses the world's single greatest collection of Italian and Florentine art.

Sadly, several of its artworks were destroyed and others badly damaged when a car bomb planted by the Mafia exploded outside the gallery's west wing in May 1993. Six people died in the explosion. Documents cataloguing the collection were also destroyed. A massive clean-up enabled the gallery to reopen quickly.

Partly in response to the bombing, but even more to the gallery's immense popularity (a staggering 1.5 million visitors marched through in 1998, compared with 100,000 in 1950!), restoration and reorganisation will lead to what promoters have dubbed the 'Grandi Uffizi'. It is hoped that by 2001 all the damaged rooms and others previously closed off will be open to the public.

While these changes are made the displays remain in a state of flux. However, the principal lines remain the same – the gallery is arranged to illustrate the evolving story of Italian and, in particular, Florentine art. Those rooms marked with an asterisk were closed at the time of writing.

It has to be said that, especially when crowded in summer, visiting the Uffizi can be a singularly unpleasant experience. The gallery tends to be hot and stuffy and the crowds render the chances of enjoying anything of what is on display a challenge, to say the least. To queue and then suffer inside seems more like a modern-day act of religious abnegation than a desirable opportunity to contemplate beautiful art. On the other hand, the queuing is in part due to an effort to limit the maximum number inside at any time to 660 people.

To avoid some of the pain, try to arrive in the morning when the gallery first opens, or during lunchtime or the late afternoon. Alternatively, book ahead (see the boxed text 'Queue Jumping' earlier in this chapter).

The extraordinary wealth of the collection and the sheer number of famous works means one visit is not enough – if you are going to come down with stendhalismo, it might as well be here! If you are in Florence for three or four days and can afford the additional cost, try to spend at least two blocks of three or so hours in the gallery, spread over a few days.

Several guidebooks to the gallery are on sale at vendors all over the city, and outside the entrance.

The Gallery (Map 6)

Before heading upstairs, visit the restored remains of the 11th-century **Chiesa di San Piero Scheraggio**. The church's apse was

incorporated into the structure of the palace but most of the rest destroyed. At the time of writing it was closed, but you can get a fractional idea from what remains on the exterior of the northern wall of the palace. Room 1, devoted to archaeological finds, was also closed.

On the 1st floor is a small **Galleria dei Disegni e delle Stampe** (Drawing and Print Gallery), in which sketches and initial draughts by the great masters are often shown. They tend to rotate the display frequently, as prolonged exposure can damage the drawings.

Upstairs in the gallery proper, you pass through two vestibules, the first with busts of several of the Medici clan and other grand dukes, the second with some Roman statuary.

The long corridor has been arranged much as it appeared in the 16th century. Below the frescoed ceilings is a series of small portraits of great and good men, interspersed with larger portraits, often of Medici family members or intimates. The statuary, much of it collected in Rome by the Medicis' agents, is either Roman or at least thought to be.

The first rooms feature works by Tuscan masters of the 13th and early 14th centuries. Room 2 is dominated by three paintings of the *Maestà* by Duccio di Buoninsegna, Cimabue and Giotto. All three were altarpieces in Florentine churches before being placed in the gallery. To look at them in this order is to appreciate the transition from Gothic to the precursor of the Renaissance. Also in the room is Giotto's polyptych *Madonna col Bambino Gesù, Santi e Angeli (Madonna with Baby Jesus, Saints and Angels)*.

Room 3 traces the Sienese school of the 14th century. Of particular note is Simone Martini's shimmering *Annunciazione*, considered a masterpiece of the school, and Ambrogio Lorenzetti's triptych *Madonna col Bambino e Santi (Virgin Mary and Child with Saints)*. Room 4 contains works of the Florentine 14th century.

Rooms 5 and 6 house examples of the International Gothic style, among them Gentile da Fabriano's *Adorazione dei Magi (Adoration of the Magi)*.

Room 7 features works by painters of the early-15th-century Florentine school, which pioneered the Renaissance. There is one panel (the other two are in the Louvre and London's National Gallery) from Paolo Uccello's striking *La Battaglia di San Romano (Battle of San Romano)*. In his efforts to create perspective he directs the lances, horses and soldiers to a central disappearing point. Other works include Piero della Francesca's portraits of *Battista Sforza* and *Federico da Montefeltro*, and a *Madonna col Bambino* painted jointly by Masaccio and Masolino. In the next room is Fra Filippo Lippi's delightful *Madonna col Bambino e due Angeli (Madonna with Child and Two Angels)*. One of those angels has the cheekiest little grin. Have you ever noticed how rarely anyone seems to be smiling in the religious art of this or other periods?

The Botticelli Room, Nos 10 to 14, is considered the gallery's most spectacular. Highlights are the *La Nascita di Venere (Birth of Venus)* and *Allegria della Primavera (Joy of Spring)*. *Calunnia (Calumny)* is a disturbing reflection of Botticelli's loss of faith in human potential that came in later life.

Room 15 features Da Vinci's *Annunciazione*, painted when he was a student of Verrocchio. Perhaps more intriguing is his unfinished *Adorazione dei Magi*. Rooms 16* and 17* are fairly minor.

Room 18, known as the Tribuna, houses the celebrated *Medici Venus*, a 1st-century BC copy of a 4th-century BC sculpture by the Greek sculptor, Praxiteles. The room also contains portraits of various members of the Medici family.

The great Umbrian painter, Perugino, who studied under Piero della Francesca and later became Raphael's master, is represented in Room 19, as well as Luca Signorelli. Room 20 features works from the German Renaissance, including Dürer's *Adorazione dei Magi*. Room 21 has works by Giovanni Bellini and his pupil, Giorgione. Peek through the railings to see the 15th- to 19th-century works in the Minia-

tures Room and then cross into the west wing, which houses works of Italian masters dating from the 16th century.

The star of Room 25 is Michelangelo's dazzling *Tondo Doni*, which depicts the Holy Family. The composition is highly unusual, with Joseph holding Jesus on Mary's shoulder as she twists around to watch him. The colours are so vibrant, the lines so clear as to seem almost photographic. This masterpiece of the High Renaissance leaps out at you as you enter, demanding attention.

In the next room are works by Raphael, including his *Leo X* and *Madonna del Cardellino*. The former is remarkable for the richness of colour (especially the reds) and detail. Room 27 is dominated by the sometimes disquieting works of Florence's two main Mannerist masters, Pontormo and Rosso Fiorentino.

Room 28 boasts seven Titians, including *Venere d'Urbino (Venus of Urbino)*. His presence signals a shift in the weighting here to representatives of the Venetian school. Rooms 29 and 30 contain works by comparatively minor painters from northern Italian, but Room 31 is dominated above all by Venice's Paolo Veronese, including his *Sacra Famiglia e Santa Barbara (Holy Family and St Barbara)*. In Room 32 it is Tintoretto's turn. He is accompanied by a few Jacopo Bassano canvasses. Rooms 33 and 34 were open but still being organised at the time of writing. Room 35 is closed pending reorganisation.

For some reason the counting starts at No 41* after this. This room is given over mostly to non-Italian masters such as Rubens and Van Dyck. The beautifully designed Room 42, with its exquisite coffered ceiling and splendid dome, is filled with Roman statues.

Caravaggio dominates Room 43*, while Rembrandt and Jan Breughel the Elder feature in Room 44*. In Room 45* are 18th-century works by Canaletto, Guardi and Crespi, along with a smattering of foreigners such as the Spaniard Goya.

Between Rooms 25 and 34 is an entrance (not open to the public) into the Corridoio Vasariano, which at the time of writing could be visited in a guided tour from Palazzo Vecchio (see Corridoio Vasariano).

Admission

The gallery is open from 8.30 am to 10 pm Tuesday to Saturday (to 6.30 pm in winter) and to 8 pm on Sunday (to 1.50 pm in winter). Admission costs L12,000. The ticket office closes 55 minutes before the gallery closes.

Corridoio Vasariano (Maps 5 & 6)

When Cosimo I de' Medici's wife bought the Palazzo Pitti and the family moved into their new digs, they wanted to maintain their link – literally – with what from then on would be known as the Palazzo Vecchio. And so Cosimo commissioned Vasari to build an enclosed walkway between the two palaces that would allow the Medicis to wander between the two without having to deal with the public. Vasari originally envisaged that it would take five years to complete. Cosimo had other ideas. His son Francesco was to be married soon and father wanted everything ready in time. Vasari always boasted about being fast with a canvas. Now he and his workshop managed to turn out this singular architectural feat in just five months – the kind of efficiency Florentines can only dream about nowadays.

The corridor, lined with phalanxes of largely minor artworks, has changed considerably over the years. Its present aspect dates from 1923, but it is possible that many of the paintings hung here will be moved to the Grandi Uffizi (see the previous sections) in the coming years.

Be that as it may, the corridor was opened to the public in a rather limited fashion in 1999. Let's say right away that, given the difficulty and cost of getting in here, many visitors are likely to be disappointed. To appreciate it at all you will want to have a genuine interest in Florentine history and/or a hunger for relatively obscure art. Your average three-day visitor who has done little or no reading on Florence will *not* be interested in this.

In 1999 it opened from March to May and again from September to October. It was unclear what the situation would be in coming years. People seem to have caught Vasari Fever – the September to October period was fully booked by the *beginning* of September. During those months it was open Tuesday to Thursday and on Saturday. Visits are by guided tour (generally in Italian), which lasts a long 2½ hours. Tours start at 9 am, 10.30 am, 1 pm and 2.30 pm. A maximum of 35 people go through in any one visit. You start in the Corte Dogana in the Palazzo Vecchio and emerge in Palazzo Pitti. You need to book ahead for this by calling ☎ 055 265 43 21 between 8.30 am and 1.30 pm Monday to Saturday. You can also book online (see the boxed text 'Queue Jumping' earlier in the chapter). You pick up your tickets (which cost a whopping L38,500) at the pre-booked ticket desk in the Uffizi.

What you can expect is the following. The first hour or so of the tour takes you through to the Salone dei Cinquecento in the Palazzo Vecchio. From here the tour follows a route upstairs via the Quartiere di Leone X and into the Quartiere di Eleonora. With much unbolting of doors and ceremony you are then ushered in through the first part of the corridor (which houses offices) across to the Uffizi, where you emerge at the beginning of the gallery. Here the tour continues, stopping at certain points of the Uffizi (but without scope for looking at the art) until another door is unlocked to allow you into the main stretch of the corridor. This first part of the tour takes an hour, and for those who have already visited the Palazzo Vecchio and the Uffizi and done some research, you can get the feeling that you'll never get down to business.

What of the corridor? You descend a staircase and follow the corridor's twists and turns along the Arno, over the Ponte Vecchio, around the Torre dei Marsili (whose owners refused to allow Cosimo to bulldoze through the medieval tower house), across the road and past the Chiesa di Santa Felicita (where an enclosed balcony allowed the Medici to hear Mass without being seen) and on into the Palazzo Pitti, where you emerge by the Grotta del Buontalenti in the Boboli Gardens (Giardino di Boboli), which your ticket allows you to visit. Along the way you can peer out for unusual views of Florence and various paintings are explained. A long corridor of self-portraits of artists starts with one of Leonardo (at least, it is believed to be genuine) through to one by Chagall. But for most of us the paintings are a little yawn-inducing. Apart from a couple of Rubens and Dürer there is precious little in the way of first-class art on view. In all, it is a long time for a smoker to go without a fag.

Museo di Storia delle Scienze (Map 6)

Telescopes that look more like works of art, the most extraordinarily complex-looking instruments for the measurement of distance, time and space, and a room full of wax and plastic cutaway models of the various stages of childbirth are among the highlights in this odd collection in the Museum of the History of Science.

Given the admission price, you may want to think twice about it. If you have a genuine interest in the history of science, then you will almost certainly find at least some of the exhibits intriguing. Many, such as Samuel Morland's mechanical calculator, are from other parts of Europe. Indeed, after the golden age personified by the likes of Galileo, science in Florence and the rest of Tuscany declined.

The centre of Room VIII, filled with globes of the world, is occupied by a huge solar-system globe with Earth at the centre and the moon, sun and other known planets, as well as astrological symbols, represented by wooden rotating 'spheres'.

Other instruments on display in 21 rooms over two floors include astrolabes, clocks, microscopes, pumps, surgical instruments and the like.

The museum is open from 9 am to 1 pm every day except Sunday. In winter it opens from 2 to 5 pm as well on Monday, Wednesday and Friday. Admission costs L10,000.

SANTA MARIA NOVELLA & AROUND
Basilica di Santa Maria Novella (Map 6)

Just south of the main train station, Stazione di Santa Maria Novella, in the piazza of the same name, this church was begun in the late 13th century as the Florentine base for the Dominican order. Although mostly completed by around 1360, work on its facade and the embellishment of its interior continued well into the 15th century.

The lower section of the green and white marble facade is transitional from Romanesque to Gothic, while the upper section and the main doorway were designed by Alberti and completed in around 1470. The highlight of the Gothic interior is Masaccio's superb fresco of the *Trinità* (1428), one of the first artworks to use the then newly discovered techniques of perspective and proportion. It is about halfway along the north aisle.

The first chapel to the right of the choir, the **Cappella di Filippo Strozzi**, features lively frescoes by Filippino Lippi depicting the lives of St John the Evangelist and St Philip the Apostle. Another important work is Domenico Ghirlandaio's series of frescoes behind the main altar, painted with the help of artists who may have included the young student Michelangelo. Relating the lives of the Virgin Mary, St John the Baptist and others, the frescoes are notable for their depiction of Florentine life during the Renaissance. Brunelleschi's crucifix hangs above the altar in the **Cappella Gondi**, the first chapel on the left of the choir.

To reach the **Chiostro Verde** (Green Cloister), exit the church and follow the signs to the 'Museo'. The porticoes' arches are propped up by massive octagonal pillars. Three of the four walls are decorated with fading frescoes recounting Genesis. The cloister actually takes its name from the green earth base used for the frescoes. The most interesting artistically, by Paolo Uccello, are those on the party wall with the church. Outstanding is *Il Diluvio Universale (The Great Flood)*.

Off the next side of the cloister is the

THINGS TO SEE & DO

JULIA WILKINSON

The welcome shade of the Chiostro Verde in the Basilica di Santa Maria Novella

Cappellone degli Spagnoli, or Spanish Chapel (Map 3), which was set aside for the Spanish retinue that accompanied Eleonora de Toledo, Cosimo I's wife, to Florence. It contains well-preserved frescoes by Andrea di Bonaiuto and his helpers.

On the western side of the cloister is the **museum** itself, which in two rooms that used to be the convent's foyer and refectory contains vestments, relics and some art belonging to the Dominicans.

The church was closed for most of 1999 for restoration. The museum is open from 9 am to 2 pm daily except Friday (8 am to 1 pm on Sunday and holidays). Admission costs L5000.

Chiesa di Ognissanti (Map 5)

This 13th-century church was much altered in the 17th century and has a baroque facade, but inside are 15th-century works by Domenico Ghirlandaio and Botticelli. Of interest is Ghirlandaio's fresco above the second altar on the right of the *Madonna della Misericordia*, protector of the Vespucci family. Amerigo Vespucci, who gave

his name to the American continent, is supposedly the young boy whose head appears between the Madonna and the old man.

Ghirlandaio's masterpiece, the *Ultima Cena (Last Supper)*, covers most of a wall in the former monastery's refectory, or *cenacolo*. The church is usually open from 8 am to midday and 4 to 6 pm daily, but at the time of writing was closed for restoration. Access to the refectory is from 9 am to noon only.

The Cascine (Map 2)

Before we turn our steps back to the centre of Florence, you might want to bear in mind that about 10 minutes' walk to the west along Borgo Ognissanti brings you to the **Porta al Prato**, part of the walls that were knocked down in the late 19th century to make way for the ring of boulevards that still surrounds the city.

A short walk south from here towards the Arno brings you to the eastern tip of Florence's great green lung, the Cascine. The Medici dukes made this a private hunting reserve, but Peter Leopold opened it to the public in 1776, with boulevards, fountains and bird sanctuaries (Le Pavoniere, now a swimming pool). In the late 19th century horse racing began here (a British import it seems, since the locals referred to the sport as *le corse inglesi* – the English races). Queen Victoria was a fan of Florence and toddled along to the Cascine during her stays – whether or not she had a flutter at the races we don't know.

At the extreme west end of the park is a monument to Rajaram Cuttiputti, an Indian maharajah who, while holidaying in Florence in 1870, managed to get a severe bout of gastro-enteritis and die. His retinue requested, and surprisingly obtained, permission to cremate him by the river. This was quite a spectacle for the locals, who didn't understand a word of the ritual but were thoroughly fascinated by it. Four years later he got a statue and memorial designed by British artisans. At its opening the British imperial anthem sounded across the green expanses. To this day, the spot is called Piazzetta dell'Indiano. The nearby bridge is named after him too.

Casa Galleria (Map 5)

Giovanni Micheluzzi breathed a rare moment of originality into Florentine architecture of the 20th century with a couple of townhouses. This one, a few doors east of Ognissanti at Borgo Ognissanti 26, is a pleasing Art-Nouveau house whose facade, liberally laced with glass and iron, has curves and circles forged into it in a striking manner. Most other buildings and villas built around Florence at this time have since been pulled down.

Palazzo Rucellai (Map 6)

Designed by Alberti, the Palazzo Rucellai is in Via della Vigna Nuova. The palace houses a photographic museum dedicated to the vast collection compiled by the Alinari brothers. It was closed at the time of writing. The facade is curious for a few reasons, not least for the seating originally intended for employees of the Rucellai family but now quite handy for anyone passing by. Across the small triangular square is the family loggia, also designed by Alberti and now used for occasional exhibits. Any family worth its salt aimed to have a loggia in addition to the family residence.

Chiesa di San Pancrazio & Museo Marino Marini (Map 6)

As early as the 9th century a church stood here. The shabby-looking version you see today is what remains of the building from the 14th and 15th centuries. The church was deconsecrated in the 19th century and now houses the museum donated to the city of Florence by the Pistoia-born sculptor Marino Marini (1901–80).

Among the 200 works the artist left behind are sculptures, portraits and drawings. The overwhelmingly recurring theme seems to be man and horse, or rather man on horse. The figures are, in some cases, simple-looking chaps in various poses suggesting rapture or extreme frustration; the horses too seem to express a gamut of emotion. On the other extreme, man and horse seem barely distinguishable from one another.

The museum opens from 10 am to 5 pm daily except Tuesday (to 1 pm Sunday and

holidays). It closes all of August. In the other summer months (from May to September) it remains open until 11 pm on Thursday. Admission costs L8000, which is rather a lot unless you are particularly taken with this guy.

Via de' Tornabuoni & Around (Map 6)

If from Palazzo Rucellai you skittle on down Via del Purgatorio and make a right down the narrow Via Parioncino you reach Via Corsini on the Arno.

For the best view of the Arno-side of the **Palazzo Corsini**, head across the bridge. This grandiose late-baroque edifice will probably seem a little curious – the u-shaped courtyard isn't in the middle. It would have been had the project been completed. The wing nearest Ponte alla Carraia was originally supposed to mirror the right wing. The building had belonged to the Medici family but they sold it in 1640. From then until 1735 work on the exterior (the mighty facade on Via del Parione is a worthy counterpoint to the Arno frontage) dragged on at a snail's pace. By the time it was completed, the Corsini family was in the ascendant, with Lorenzo Corsini in the driving seat in Rome as Pope Clement XII. The most interesting feature of the inside is the spiral staircase known as the *lumaca* (literally, the 'slug').

Head east for the **Ponte Santa Trinita**. It is a harmonious and charming crossing for the river, but its recent history is in many respects more remarkable than the story of its construction. Cosimo I de' Medici put Vasari in charge of the project and he in turn asked Michelangelo for advice. In the end, the job was handed over to Amannati, who finished it in 1567. The statues of the seasons are by Pietro Francavilla. The bridge was one of those blown up by the Germans as they pulled out in 1944. Rather than throw some slapdash number back over the river after the war, engineers rebuilt it as it had been, using copies of 16th-century tools and stone from the Boboli quarry. The statues were fished out of the Arno and the bridge completed in 1958.

All that was missing was the head from Francavilla's *Primavera (Spring)* statue on the northern bank. The fate of the head was long a source of anguished debate in Florence. Some eyewitnesses swore they had seen an Allied soldier make off with it after the city was liberated. Ads were even placed in New Zealand newspapers (New Zealanders were among the first Allied troops to enter the city in 1944) asking for whoever had made off with the head to send it back – no questions asked and a US$3000 reward! Needless to say, no one owned up. Then, three years later, the missing head was discovered by chance in the riverbed of the Arno and finally restored to its rightful place.

Turning inland to the piazza of the same name, you arrive at the 13th-century **Chiesa della Santa Trinita**. Although rebuilt in the Gothic style and later graced with a Mannerist facade of indifferent taste, you can still get some idea of what the Romanesque original looked like by looking at the facade wall from the inside. Among its more eye-catching art are the frescoes depicting the life of St Francis of Assisi by Domenico Ghirlandaio in the **Cappella Sassetti** (in the right transept). The altarpiece of the Annunciation in the fourth chapel of the south aisle is by Lorenzo Monaco, who was Fra Angelico's master. Monaco also painted the frescoes on the walls of that chapel.

Across Via de' Tornabuoni is the forbidding **Palazzo Spini-Ferroni**, built in the 14th century with Guelph battlements and now owned by the Ferragamo shoe empire (see the boxed text 'Ferragamo' in the Shopping chapter). The street itself, often referred to as the 'Salotto di Firenze' (Florence's Drawing Room) follows the original course of the Mugnone tributary into the Arno. The Mugnone was diverted to the present-day Via dei Fossi and then again to the Cascine.

Piazza Santa Trinita is faced by **Palazzo Buondelmonti**. The Buondelmonte family was at the heart of the Guelph-Ghibelline feud in Florence (see Guelphs & Ghibellines under History in the Facts about Florence chapter). More imposing is the **Palazzo Bartolini-Saltimbeni**, an example of High Renaissance with a Roman touch (columns flanking the main door and triangular tympana).

By far the most impressive of the Renaissance mansions is the earthy-coloured **Palazzo Strozzi**, a great colossus of rusticated *pietra forte* ('strong stone'). The Strozzi family rivalled the Medici, but Filippo Strozzi was no fool. Before setting about the building of a structure greater than the Medici residence, he consulted Lorenzo de' Medici on some rather modest plans. Lorenzo advised Filippo to go for something grander, more befitting his family and the city. This Filippo took as carte blanche to massage his own ego and so the stage was set for the construction of the city's greatest, if only in dimensions, Renaissance residence. It now houses offices and is occasionally used for art exhibitions.

Two blocks north stands the clearly baroque facade in pietra forte of the **Chiesa di San Gaetano**. The church had been around since the 11th century, but from 1604 it was rebuilt. The facade only went up in 1683. Opposite and a few strides north, the **Palazzo Antinori** was built in the 15th century by Giuliano da Maiano.

SAN LORENZO AREA
Basilica di San Lorenzo (Map 6)
The Medici family commissioned Brunelleschi to rebuild this church in 1425, on the site of a 4th-century basilica. It is considered one of the most harmonious examples of Renaissance architecture. Michelangelo prepared a design for the facade that was never executed, which is why this, as so many other Florentine churches, appears unfinished from the outside.

It was the Medici parish church and many family members are buried here. The church is a masterstroke of Brunelleschi's style. The nave is separated from the two aisles by columns in pietra serena and crowned with Corinthian capitals. It is interesting to visit this church in tandem with the Basilica di Santo Spirito (see under Oltrarno later in the chapter) in the Oltrarno district, as Brunelleschi designed both. The materials are the same, as is the maintenance of spartan, classical harmony in the proportions in each.

The differences are also noteworthy. The beautiful coffered ceiling here is mirrored in Santo Spirito by a frescoed trompe l'oeil 'fake'. The latter is admirable, but the real thing splendid.

The inside facade was done by Michelangelo, and above the main entrance is the Medici family coat of arms with the six balls. Rosso Fiorentino's *Sposalizio della Vergine (Marriage of the Virgin Mary)* dominates the second chapel on the right aisle after you enter. As you approach the transept, you will see two pulpits, or *pergami* (they look like treasure chests on Ionic columns), in dark bronze – or at least what appears to be dark bronze. Some of the panels on each have been attributed to Donatello. Others, added later, are supposedly made of wood (money was obviously running short) made to seem like bronze.

You enter the **Sagrestia Vecchia** (Old Sacristy) to the left of the altar. It was designed by Brunelleschi and mostly decorated by Donatello.

From the main body of the church you can also enter the peaceful cloisters, off the first of which a staircase leads up to the **Biblioteca Medicea Laurenziana**. It was commissioned by Cosimo de' Medici to house the Medici library and contains 10,000 volumes. The real attraction is Michelangelo's magnificent vestibule and staircase. He also designed the main reading hall, but the project would have been more striking still had he been able to finish it (see The Fiery Florentine in the 'Painting & Sculpture in Florence' section). The library is normally open from 9 am to 1 pm Monday to Saturday. At the time of writing it was, however, closed for restoration work. Admission is free.

The entrance to the church is in the busy Piazza San Lorenzo, off Borgo San Lorenzo. The church is open from 7 am to midday and 3.30 to 6.30 pm daily.

Cappelle Medicee A separate entrance on via Piazza Madonna degli Aldobrandini takes you to the Medicean chapels. After buying your ticket you first enter a crypt.

JANE SMITH

The figure of *Dawn* takes it easy on Lorenzo the Magnificent's tomb in the Cappelle Medici.

The stairs from this take you up to the **Cappella dei Principi** (Princes' Chapel), which comes as something similar to a blow over the head with a mallet.

Conceived not as a place of religious reflection, the so-called chapel is rather the triumphalist mausoleum of some (but by no means all) the Medici rulers.

It is sumptuously decorated top to bottom with various kinds of marble, granite and other stone. Breaking up the colossal splendour of the stone are the decorative tableaux made from painstakingly chosen and cut semiprecious stones, or *pietre dure*. It was for the purpose of decorating the chapel that Ferdinando I ordered the creation of the Opificio delle Pietre Dure.

Statues of the grand men were supposed to be placed in the still empty niches, but no one quite got around to finishing the project. Only the bronze of Ferdinando I and partly gilt bronze of Cosimo II were done.

A corridor leads from the Cappella dei Principi to the **Sagrestia Nuova** (New Sacristy), so-called to distinguish it from the Sagrestia Vecchia. In fact it was the Medicis' funeral chapel.

It was here that Michelangelo came nearest to finishing an architectural commission. His haunting sculptures, *Notte e Giorno (Night and Day), Aurora e Crepusculo*

(*Dawn and Dusk*) and the *Madonna col Bambino*, adorn Medici tombs including that of Lorenzo the Magnificent. Michelangelo's sculptures are interesting for many reasons. A subdued melancholy emanates from all of them. In Giorno, whose face remains barely hinted at, Michelangelo goes to town in his study of human musculature. He liked boys so much that the female figures were modelled by lads. In the case of Notte this is especially evident in the upper torso – the breasts seem to have been added as an afterthought.

The chapels are open from 8.30 am to 5 pm Monday to Saturday and until 1.50 pm on Sunday and holidays. Admission costs L13,000.

Palazzo Medici-Riccardi (Map 6)

When Cosimo de' Medici felt fairly sure of his position in Florence, he decided it was time to move house. He asked Brunelleschi to design him a new residence, but rejected the result as too ostentatious. Cosimo had learned that the secret to long life in the politically fickle atmosphere of Florence was to keep a relatively modest profile. With this in mind, he entrusted Michelozzo with the design in 1444.

What Michelozzo came up with was ground-breaking and would continue to influence the construction of family residences in Florence for years to come. The fortress townhouses with their towers that characterised Gothic Florence were no longer necessary. Cosimo's power was more or less undisputed. Instead Michelozzo created a self-assured, stout but not inelegant pile on three storeys.

The ground floor is characterised by the bulbous, rough surface (known as rustication) in pietra forte. The upper two storeys are less aggressive, maintaining restrained classical lines, which were already a feature of an emerging Renaissance canon, and topped with a heavy timber roof whose eaves protrude well out over the street below.

The Medicis stayed here until 1540 and the building was finally acquired and somewhat remodelled by the Riccardi family in the 17th century.

You can wander inside to the courtyard and to some of the rooms upstairs, though much of the building is now given over to public administration offices. The main hall you will want to inspect is the **Galleria** on the 1st floor. It is a rather sumptuous example of late baroque designed for the Riccardi family. The room glisters with gold leaf and bursts with curvaceous figures looming out at you, especially from the ceiling frescoes by Luca Giordano, after whom the room is now usually named the **Sala Luca Giordano**.

The highlight, however, is the **Cappella dei Magi**, a chapel with striking frescoes by Benozzo Gozzoli. Buy a ticket first from the office off the second internal courtyard. Staff rotate 15 people through the chapel every 15 minutes as it is rather squeezy inside.

Make an effort to see this jewel. Gozzoli never got a break like this again. Although he worked at a time when the Renaissance had taken off in Florence, Gozzoli remained rooted in the International Gothic style. This magnificent fresco depicting the arrival of the Wise Men and a procession of the faithful to adore the newborn Christ betrays all sorts of jarring qualities. On the rear wall he captures the natural essence of the Tuscan countryside (for despite the subject, this is a very Florentine painting, filled with Medici family members and medieval dress), and yet on the side walls that same countryside seems bizarrely unreal. His characters mostly lack the realism and movement you might expect from greater Renaissance painters, and yet some of them are strikingly human. The men in the lower right-hand corner on the left wall as you enter are exquisitely rendered, particularly the one with creased brow and quizzical expression. The colours are joyful and Gozzoli ensures immortality by penning his own name on one of the paraders' caps. He's the one looking straight out at you towards the back of the procession on the left side of the right-hand wall.

The palace is open from 9 am to 1 pm and 3 to 6 pm Monday to Saturday (closed Wednesday, open in summer from 9 am to

7 pm daily) and to 1 pm on Sunday and holidays. Admission to the chapel costs L6000, but the remainder is free.

Mercato Centrale (Map 3)

Built in 1874, the city's central produce market seems to disappear amid the confusion of makeshift stands of the clothes and leather market that fill the surrounding square and streets during the day. At night all of this disappears, replaced instead by the contented munching of punters at the various eateries (which vary considerably in quality, just by the way) around about. The iron and glass architecture was something of a novelty in Florence when the market was first built.

SAN MARCO AREA
Galleria dell'Accademia (Map 3)

Take Via Cesare Battisti from Piazza SS Annunziata to Piazza San Marco; the entrance to the gallery is to the left on Via Ricasoli. For many visitors to Florence, the gallery is pretty much unavoidable, if only because it contains the original of one of the greatest (and most trumpeted) masterpieces of the Renaissance, Michelangelo's giant statue of *David*.

When you enter the museum you are obliged to turn left into a long hall, at the end of which you can make out the *David*. Try to contain the urge to hurtle off in the giant-slayer's general direction and have a look at the four *Prigioni* ('prisoners' or 'slaves') and the statue of *San Matteo (St Matthew)* between the two Prigioni on the right. The latter was sculpted about 1506, and the four others in 1530. The *Prigioni* were supposed to decorate the tomb of Pope Julius II, but ended up in the Boboli Gardens. All five have in common the feature of not being completed. The experts will tell you completion is in the eye of the beholder. In the case of Michelangelo in particular, it is said he left many works 'unfinished' deliberately. Thus the observer is engaged in the process of creation, being obliged to 'complete' the work left undone by the master. It has been said that with Michelangelo this was in

part due to his perfectionism. He could *stop* working on a project, but never truly finish.

Whatever you make of all these arguments, they are interesting if only because they show us a little of how the artist went about extracting such beauty from lumps of marble. Some of us will continue to think the sculptures are in fact unfinished, if only because old Michelangelo had an irascible streak in him and a tendency to abandon blocks of stone he considered bungled or in any way deficient.

Now, the *David* is finished. Carved from one block of marble and weighing in at 19 tonnes, it's an exquisite, powerful figure that beggars description. While the statue still stood in Piazza della Signoria, the left arm actually fell off and killed a peasant. Cosimo I de' Medici happened to be there at the time and is said to have been rather taken aback by the incident. You can see the break still, as well as one on the middle finger on the right hand.

In the wing to the right of the *David* are various paintings by Florentine contemporaries of Michelangelo.

In the wing to the left are more paintings of secondary importance. At the end of that wing, a hall hosts the **Gipsoteca Bartolini**. Lorenzo Bartolini was a major Italian sculptor of the 19th century. The works in here are plaster models created to help with the production of sculptures.

Another series of rooms off the left wing contains 13th- and 14th-century works of art. A triptych by Andrea Orcagna, which once hung in the Chiesa degli SS Apostoli, is particularly striking.

In the grand **Sala del Colosso**, dominated by a plaster model of Giambologna's *Ratto delle Sabine (Rape of Sabine)*, are several interesting paintings, including a fresco of the *Pietà* by Andrea del Sarto.

Upstairs is a further collection of 13th- and 14th-century art and Russian icons.

The gallery is open from 8.30 am to 9 pm Tuesday to Friday (to midnight on Saturday and 8 pm on Sunday). Closing time is usually 6.50 pm (1.50 pm at the weekend) in winter. Admission costs L12,000.

Museo di San Marco (Map 5)

The museum is housed in the now deconsecrated Dominican convent and the Chiesa di San Marco. Back in 1481 a rather ugly and intense little Dominican friar, Girolamo Savonarola, turned up in Florence with a post as *lector* at the Chiesa di San Marco. His fire and brimstone thunderings soon had the people of Florence crowding to the church in unprecedented numbers, enthralled and horrified at the same time by Savonarola's calls for repentance. He became the de facto head of a short-lived theocracy in Florence but ended up on an Inquisitorial bonfire. Subsequently the Medici family returned to reclaim control of the city.

The piazza is the centre of the university area. The church was founded in 1299, rebuilt by Michelozzo in 1437, and again remodelled by Giambologna some years later. It features several paintings, but they pale in comparison to the treasures contained in the adjoining convent.

Famous Florentines who called the convent home include the painters Fra (or Beato) Angelico and Fra Bartolommeo. Fra Angelico, who painted the radiant frescoes on the convent walls, and Savonarola were of the same religious order – the latter arriving in Florence almost 30 years after the painter's death in 1455.

The convent now serves as a museum of Fra Angelico's works, many of which were moved there in the 1860s, and should be up there on every art lover's top-priority hitlist.

You find yourself in the **Chiostro di Sant'Antonio** (St Anthony's Cloisters), designed by Michelozzo in 1440, when you first enter the museum. Turn immediately to the right and enter the **Sala dell'Ospizio**. Paintings by Fra Angelico that once hung in the Galleria dell'Accademia and the Uffizi have been brought together here. Among the better known works are the *Deposizione di Cristo* and the *Pala di San Marco*, an altarpiece for the church paid for by the Medici family. It did not fare well as a result of 19th-century restoration.

More of Angelico's works, including a *Crocifissione*, are on display in the **Sala del Capitolo** (Chapter House) on the opposite side of the cloister. In here is also La Piagnona, the bell rung the night Savonarola was arrested on 8 April 1498.

The east wing of the cloister, formerly the monks' rectory, contains works by various artists from the 14th to the 17th centuries. Paintings by Fra Bartolommeo are on display in a small annex off the refectory rooms. Among them is a celebrated portrait of Savonarola.

You reach the upper floor by passing through the bookshop. This is in a sense the real treat. Fra Angelico was invited to decorate the monks' cells with devotional frescoes aimed as a guide to the friars' mediation. Some were done by Fra Angelico, others by aides under his supervision. You can peer into them today and wonder what sort of thoughts would swim through the minds of the monks as they prayed before these images.

The true masterpieces up here are, however, on the walls in the corridors. Already at the top of the stairs you climbed to the 1st floor is an *Annunciazione*, faced on the opposite wall with a *Crocifisso* featuring San Domenico (St Dominic). One of Fra Angelico's most famous works is the *Madonna delle Ombre (Virgin of the Shadows)*, to the right of cell No 25.

The museum is open from 8.30 am to 1.50 pm Tuesday to Saturday (as well as alternating Mondays and Sundays). Admission costs L8000.

Cenacolo di Sant'Apollonia (Map 3)

A quick detour two blocks west, you could duck into this, the former refectory of a Benedictine monastery. It was decorated with fine frescoes by Andrea del Castagno, among them the *Ultima Cena (Last Supper)*, a Crucifixion and Resurrection. The refectory is open from 8.30 am to 1.50 pm daily except Monday. Admission is free.

Opificio delle Pietre Dure (Map 3)

Just around the corner from the Galleria dell'Accademia, the Opificio delle Pietre Dure is now renowned throughout the world for its work in art restoration, which has been carried out here since it was fused with the Laboratori di Restauro in 1975. Its new title became the Istituto Specializzato per il Restauro, but it is still know to many as the Opificio.

But the Opificio started life as a very different institution, when Ferdinando I established it in 1588 to create decorative pieces in pietre dure for the Cappella dei Principi in the Basilica di San Lorenzo. In the museum you can see a fine selection of works in pietre dure, or *scagliola*, which is a method that looks like pietre dure. The museum is open from 9 am to 2 pm daily except Sunday. Admission costs L4000.

Piazza della SS Annunziata (Map 4)

Giambologna's equestrian statue of the Grand Duke Ferdinando I de' Medici commands the scene from the centre of this square. Some observers find it the city's loveliest square. Certainly part of Florence's junkie community seems to like it in the evening.

Chiesa di SS Annunziata The church that gives the square its name was established in 1250 by the founders of the Servite order and rebuilt by Michelozzo and others in the mid-15th century. It is dedicated to the Virgin Mary and in the ornate tabernacle, to your left as you enter the church from the atrium, is a so-called miraculous painting of the Virgin.

The painting, no longer on public view, is attributed to a 14th-century friar, and legend says it was completed by an angel. Also of note are frescoes by Andrea del Castagno in the first two chapels on the left of the church, a fresco by Perugino in the fifth chapel and the frescoes in Michelozzo's atrium, particularly the *Nascita della Vergine (Birth of the Virgin)* by Andrea del Sarto and the *Visitazione* by Jacopo Pontormo. The church is open from 7.30 am to 12.30 pm and 4 to 6.30 pm daily.

Spedale degli Innocenti This 'hospital of the innocents' was founded on the south-

east side of the piazza in 1421 as Europe's first orphanage.

Brunelleschi designed the portico, which Andrea della Robbia then decorated with terracotta medallions of a baby in swaddling cloths. Under the portico to the left of the entrance is the small revolving door where unwanted children were left. A good number of people in Florence with surnames such as degli Innocenti, Innocenti and Nocentini, can trace their family tree only as far back as the orphanage. The idea of the orphanage was in itself no novelty – this place was built in response to the growing numbers of foundlings. Undoubtedly life inside was no picnic, but the Spedale's avowed aim was to care for and educate its wards until they turned 18.

A small gallery on the 2nd floor features works by Florentine artists. If you are already overdosing on the seemingly endless diet of art in Florence, you could skip this stop. Those truly interested will find it worthwhile.

The most striking piece is Domenico Ghirlandaio's *Adorazione dei Magi* at the right end of the hall. This is one of those paintings that truly repays close inspection. The main image of the Wise Men come to adore the Christ child distracts most observers from such secondary scenes as Herod's massacre of the innocents. The city and port detail in the background is remarkable. Also in here is a *Madonna in Trono col Bambino e Santi* by Piero Cosimo and a glazed terracotta *Madonna col Bambino* by Luca della Robbia. Watch out also for the muted tones of Botticelli's *Madonna col Bambino e un Angelo*.

The gallery is open from 8.30 am to 2 pm daily except Wednesday. Admission costs L5000.

Museo Archeologico (Map 4)

About 200m south-east of the piazza along Via della Colonna is the Museo Archeologico, considered one of Italy's best. A good deal of the Medici family's hoard of antiquities ended up here. Further collections have been added in the centuries since. In each room you will find detailed explanatory sheets in several languages. You'd have the beginnings of a book if you were to take a copy of each home – which, in the interests of saving paper, you might perhaps refrain from doing.

For those interested in antiquity, this museum offers a surprisingly rich collection of finds. Many items were damaged in the floods of 1966 and even today parts of the museum are still being worked on. All up, the museum is well worth the effort.

On the 1st floor you can either head left into the ancient Egyptian collection, or right into the section on Etruscan and Greco-Roman art.

The former is an impressive collection of tablets inscribed with hieroglyphics, statues and other sculpture, various coffins and a remarkable array of everyday objects – it is extraordinary to ponder on how sandals, baskets and all sorts of other odds and ends have survived to this day.

In the Etruscan section you pass first through two rooms dominated by funeral urns. Particularly noteworthy is the marble Sarcofago delle Amazzoni (Amazons' Sarcophagos) from Tarquinia and the alabaster Sarcofago dell'Obeso (Sarcophagos of the Fat Man) from Chiusi. People often ask themselves what the difference is between Etruscan and Roman art. If you study the scenes on many of these urns a little while you will notice a distinctly oriental touch in the depiction of battle and other scenes. Frequently the appearance of the characters and their attire is anything but Roman or classical. Of course, even from the early days of Roman expansion, there had been cross-fertilisation between the Greeks, Romans and Etruscans, and just as the Romans tended to ape the artists of Hellas, so too the Etruscans appear to have been influenced to a greater or lesser extent by them.

From the funerary urns you pass into a hall dedicated to bronze sculptures, ranging from miniatures depicting mythical beasts through to the life-size *Arringatore (Orator)*. Dating from the 1st century BC, the figure, draped in clearly Roman garb, illustrates the extent to which the empire had come to dominate the Etruscans at this point. By the time the statue was made, Etruria had been under the Roman thumb for a good 200 years. Other outstanding works include the statue of *Minerva* from Arezzo, a Roman copy of a Greek original, and the *Chimera*, a beast of classical mythology.

From this display you enter an enclosed corridor lined on one side by ancient rings, pendants and amulets, many made of chalcedony. When you reach the end you swing left and walk back along another corridor with windows overlooking the museum's gardens. Here you can admire a selection of the museum's treasure of ancient gold jewellery.

Thre is space downstairs for temporary exhibits.

The 2nd floor is taken up with an extensive collection of Greek pottery from various epoques. Again it is surprising for its sheer extent. Although most of the exhibits have had to be meticulously reassembled from the shards discovered on excavation sites, the collection is varied and certainly intriguing to anyone interested in this kind of thing.

It is open from 9 am to 2 pm Tuesday to Saturday and to 1 pm on Sunday. Admission costs L8000.

Rotonda del Brunelleschi (Map 3)

If you end up walking down towards the Duomo from Piazza della SS Annunziata along Via dei Fibbiai, you will stumble across this rather sad-looking hectagonal building. It was going to be the Rotonda di Santa Maria degli Angioli and, lined with chapels, would have been one of the architect's most original buildings had money not run out. What stands today was finished off in 1936 so that the building might at least be useable. The university uses it now for offices.

SANTA CROCE AREA
Piazza di Santa Croce (Map 7)

The Franciscan Basilica di Santa Croce stands haughty watch over the piazza of the same name. The square was initially

JON DAVISON

Santa Croce is the final resting place of Michelangelo, Dante, Galileo and Machiavelli.

cleared in the Middle Ages primarily to allow hordes of the faithful to gather when the church itself was full (Mass must have been quite an event in those days). On a more sober religious note, the piazza was used in Savonarola's day for the execution of heretics.

Such an open space inevitably found other uses and from the 14th century on it was often the colourful scene of jousts, festivals and 'Calcio Storico' matches. The latter was like a combination of football (soccer) and rugby with no rules. They still play it today (see Festivals in the Facts for the Visitor chapter). Below the gaily frescoed facade of the **Palazzo dell'Antella**, on the southern side of the piazza, is a marble stone embedded in the wall – it marks the halfway line on this, one of the oldest football pitches in the world. Today the square is lined with the inevitable souvenir shops.

Curiously enough, the Romans used to have fun in much the same area centuries before. The city's 2nd-century amphitheatre took up the area facing the west end of Piazza di Santa Croce. To this day, Piazza de'

Peruzzi, Via Bentaccordi and Via Torta (Map 5) mark the oval outline of the theatre's northern, western and southern sides.

Basilica di Santa Croce (Map 7)

Attributed to Arnolfo di Cambio, Santa Croce was started in 1294 on the site of a Franciscan chapel but not completed until 1385. The name stems from a splinter of the Holy Cross donated to the Franciscans by King Louis of France in 1258. Today the church is known as much for the celebrities buried here as its captivating artistic treasures.

The magnificent facade is actually a neo-Gothic addition of the 19th century, as indeed is the bell tower. The architect, Niccola Matas, had a hard time even getting his facade design passed. Rather austere compared with the contemporary job done on the Duomo, the main source of jollity is the variety of colour in the different types of marble used. A commission set up in 1837 to study the urgent question of dressing the front of the church, apparently loath to make any decision, was finally moved to do so when

Matas produced the old designs for a facade by Il Cronaca, found in the church's archives. Matas was a clever fellow, for it seems he created these designs in the hope of finally getting some action, and it worked!

The statue in front of the left end of the facade is of Dante.

The church's massive interior is divided into a nave and two aisles by solid octagonal pillars. The ceiling is a fine example of the timber A-frame style used occasionally in Italy's Gothic churches.

You could easily spend an hour or more wandering inside. Pity is it no longer as it was in the days when EM Forster's heroine and hero stumbled across one another in here in *A Room with a View*. Today you'll be lucky to squeeze through the seemingly mindless hordes of tour groups that mill at the front end of the church before being raced through by their tour leaders. Try to get here early in the morning or leave it to late in the day.

Heading down the right aisle you see first, between the first and second altar, Michelangelo's tomb, designed by Vasari. The three muses below it represent his three principal gifts – sculpting, painting and architecture. Next up is a cenotaph to the memory of Dante, followed by a tomb sculpted by Antonio Canova in 1810. After the fourth altar is Machiavelli's tomb.

After the next altar is an extraordinary piece of sculpture of the *Annunciazione* by Donatello. You won't see many other sculptures in grey pietra serena, brightened here by some gilding. Between the sixth and seventh altars you can peer out the doorway into the cloister and get a look at Brunelleschi's Cappella de' Pazzi (see the following section).

Dogleg round to the right as you approach the transept and you find yourself before the delightful frescoes by Agnolo Gaddi in the **Cappella Castellani**. By the way, the church is covered in more than 2500 square metres of frescoes. Taddeo Gaddi did the frescoes, depicting the life of the Virgin, and the stained-glass window in the adjacent **Cappella Baroncelli**. Next, a doorway designed by Michelozzo leads into

a corridor off which is the **Sagrestia**, an enchanting 14th-century room dominated on the right by Taddeo Gaddi's fresco of the *Crocifissione*.

Through the next room, which now serves as a bookshop, you can get to the **Scuola del Cuoio**, or School of Leather (see Leather in the Shopping chapter). At the end of the Michelozzo corridor is a Medici chapel, featuring a large altarpiece by Andrea della Robbia.

Back in the church, the transept is lined by five minor chapels on either side of the **Cappella Maggiore**, or Major Chapel. The two chapels nearest the right side of the Cappella Maggiore are decorated by partly fragmented frescoes by Giotto. In the ninth chapel along, you can see a glazed terracotta altarpiece by Giovanni della Robbia, while the final chapel is frescoed by Maso di Banco. These frescoes, among them the *Miracolo del Santo che Chiude le Fauci del Drago e Risuscita due Maghi Uccisi Dall'Alito del Mostro* (*Miracle of the Saint who Shuts the Dragon's Jaws and Brings Back to Life the Magi Killed by the Monster's Breath* – how's that for a title), burst with life.

In the central chapel of the northern transept (also a Bardi chapel) hangs a wooden crucifix by Donatello. Brunelleschi thought it ugly and, to get his point across, went and sculpted another for the Basilica di Santa Maria Novella.

From the entrance, the first tomb in the left aisle is Galileo Galilei's. You will also have noticed by now that the floor is paved with the tombstones of famous Florentines of the past 500 years. Monuments to the particularly notable were added along the walls from the mid-16th century.

Cloisters & Cappella de' Pazzi Brunelleschi designed the serene **cloisters** just before his death in 1446. Brunelleschi's **Cappella de' Pazzi**, at the end of the first cloister, is a masterpiece of Renaissance architecture. The **Museo dell'Opera di Santa Croce**, off the first cloister, features a partially restored crucifix by Cimabue, which was badly damaged during the disastrous 1966 flood, when the Santa Croce area

DAMIEN SIMONIS

o *Commedia* here: Dante in Piazza di Santa Croce

DAMIEN SIMONIS

The 14th-century Certosa monastery

JULIET COOMBE

s best side? Another view of *David*

BETHUNE CARMICHAEL

Della Robbia's babes adorn the Spedale degli Innocenti.

DAMIEN SIMONIS

Light and shadow draw the eye to a simple building facade.

Michelangelo took three years to sculpt his *David*.

Hercules and Cacus in the Piazza della Signoria

Giambologna's equestrian statue of Grand Duke Cosimo I graces Piazza della Signoria.

was inundated. Donatello's gilded bronze statue of *San Ludovico di Tolosa (St Ludovich of Toulouse)* was originally placed in a tabernacle on the Orsanmichele facade.

In summer the church is open from 8 am to 6.30 pm Monday to Saturday (closed from 12.30 to 3 pm in winter) and from 3 to 6 pm on Sunday. The museum is open from 10 am to 12.30 pm and 2.30 to 6.30 pm daily except Wednesday (3 to 5 pm in winter). Admission costs L5000.

Museo del Rinascimento (Map 7)

Guess it was inevitable that Florence should get its own wax museum. Dummies in period costume include Dante with his beloved Beatrice in the heaven he described in the *Divina Commedia*, Masaccio hard at work in the Cappella Brancacci, Leonardo with Mona Lisa, Amerigo Vespucci with his navigational charts and so forth. In all, some 50 characters of Florentine greatness from the year 1000 to 1700 are brought to waxy life in this 'Museum of the Renaissance'. If you like this sort of thing it's all right, but with so much genuine material to marvel over in this city, you may find it hard to justify the L12,000 outlay. It opens from 10 am to 7 pm daily.

Museo Horne (Map 5)

Herbert Percy Horne was one of those eccentric Brits abroad with cash. He bought this building on Via de' Benci in the early 1900s and installed his eclectic collection of 14th- and 15th-century Italian paintings, sculptures, ceramics, coins and other odds and sods. Horne renovated the house in an effort to recreate a Renaissance ambience. Although the occasional big name pops up among the artworks, such as Giotto, Luca Signorelli and Giambologna, most of the stuff is minor. Perhaps more interesting than many of the paintings is the furniture, some of which is exquisite. On the top floor is the original kitchen. Kitchens tended to be on the floor to reduce the risk of fire.

The museum is open from 9 am to 1 pm daily except Sunday and holidays. Admission costs L8000.

Ponte alle Grazie (Map 5)

In 1237, Giorgio Villani tells us, Messer Rubaconte da Mandella, a Milanese then serving as external martial *(podestà)* in Florence, had this bridge built. It was swept away in 1333 and on its replacement were raised chapels, one of them dubbed Madonna alle Grazie, from which the bridge then took its name. Eventually the chapel, at one end of the bridge, was expanded into a small convent whose Benedictine nuns lived in isolation. Their food was passed to them through a small window and so the nuns came to be known as Le Murate ('the Walled-in Ones'). In 1424 they left for larger premises on Via dell'Agnolo, which took on their name, Le Murate (Map 7). Much later it was turned into a women's prison and nowadays is used in summer as a bar (see the boxed text 'Summer Frolics' in the Entertainment chapter).

The bridge, in the meantime, had filled up with chapels, shops and other buildings much in the manner of the Ponte Vecchio. These were demolished in 1876 to allow street-widening across it. The Germans then blew up the bridge in 1944, and the present version was constructed in 1957.

Teatro Verdi (Map 7)

Rather than cross the bridge at this point, we will head back north along Via de' Benci (which becomes Via Giuseppe Verdi after Piazza Santa Croce). At the intersection with Via Ghibellina stands this 19th-century theatre on the site of the 14th-century prison, Le Stinche, which had also been used as a horse-riding school. The theatre was built in 1838. We now head east along Via Ghibellina.

Casa Buonarroti (Map 7)

Three blocks from the Teatro Verdi at No 70 is the Casa Buonarroti, which Michelangelo owned but never lived in. Upon his death, the house went to his nephew and eventually became a museum in the mid-1850s.

Although not uninteresting, the collections are a little disappointing given what you pay to get in. On the ground floor on the left is a series of rooms used for temporary exhibitions, usually held once a year from May to September. To the right of the ticket window is a small archaeological display. The Buonarroti family collected about 150 pieces over the years, many of which were long in the Museo Archeologico (see San Lorenzo Area earlier in the chapter). The last of them were returned to this house in 1996. The most interesting items are the Etruscan urns – though if you have seen the collection in the Museo Archeologico you don't really need to come here.

Beyond this room are some paintings done in imitation of Michelangelo's style, along with some fine glazed terracotta pieces by the della Robbia family.

Upstairs you can admire a detailed model of Michelangelo's design for the facade of the Basilica di San Lorenzo – as close as the church came to getting one. By Michelangelo also are a couple of marble bas reliefs and a crucifix. Of the reliefs, *Madonna della Scala (Madonna of the Steps)* is thought to be his earliest work.

Otherwise, a series of rooms designed by Michelangelo Il Giovane, the genius' grandnephew, are intriguing. The first is full of paintings and frescoes that together amount to a kind of apotheosis of the great man. Portraits of Michelangelo meeting VIPs of his time predominate.

The museum is open from 9.30 am to 1.30 pm every day except Tuesday. Admission costs L12,000.

Piazza Sant'Ambrogio & Around (Maps 4 & 7)

From the Casa Buonarroti, turn north up Via Michelangelo Buonarroti and proceed to **Piazza dei Ciompi** (Map 7) cleared in the 1930s and named after the textile workers who used to meet in secret in the Santa Croce area and whose 14th-century revolt, which had seemed so full of promise, came to nothing. Nowadays it is the scene of a busy flea market called Mercato dei Pulci (see Markets in the Shopping chapter).

The **Loggia del Pesce** (Fish Market) was designed by Vasari on the orders of Cosimo I de' Medici for the Mercato Vecchio (Old Market), which was at the heart of what is

now Piazza della Repubblica. The loggia was moved to the convent at San Marco when the Mercato Vecchio and heart of the town were wiped out towards the end of the 19th century to make way for Piazza della Repubblica. Then in 1955 it was set up here.

A block east along Via Pietrapiana the plain **Chiesa di Sant'Ambrogio** presents an inconspicuous 18th-century facade on the square of the same name. The first church here was raised in the 10th century, but what you see inside is a mix of 13th-century Gothic and 15th-century refurbishment. The name comes from Sant'Ambrogio (St Ambrose), the powerful 4th-century archbishop of Milan who stayed in an earlier convent on this site when he visited Florence. The church is something of an artists' graveyard too. Among those who rest in peace here are Mino da Fiesole, Il Verrocchio and Il Cronaca.

Nearby is the local produce market, the **Mercato di Sant'Ambrogio** on Piazza Ghiberti.

A quick nip up Via de' Pilastri off Piazza Sant'Ambrogio and right up Via Luigi Carlo Farini brings us to the **Sinagoga** (Map 4), the late 19th-century synagogue. It is a fanciful structure with playful Moorish and even Byzantine elements. In the **Museo Ebraico** you can see Jewish ceremonial objects and some old codices. The synagogue and museum are open from 10 am to 1 pm and 2 to 5 pm daily except Friday afternoon and Saturday (to 4 pm in winter). Admission costs L6000.

The shady **Piazza Massimo d'Azeglio**, a block north, was the result of late-19th-century urban planning. The area was one of the few within the city walls (knocked down around the same time) that had not already been built on. The buildings around the square were constructed in the early years of the 20th century.

OLTRARNO
Ponte Vecchio (Map 6)

The first documentation of a stone bridge here, at the narrowest crossing point along the entire length of the Arno, dates from 972. The Arno looks placid enough, but when it gets mean, it gets very mean. Floods in 1177 and 1333 destroyed the bridge, and in 1966 it came close again. Newspaper reports of the time highlight how dangerous the situation was. One couple who owned a jewellery store on the bridge described afterwards the crashing of the waters just below the floorboards as they tried to salvage some of their goods. Carabinieri on the river bank excitedly warned them to get off, but they retorted that the forces of law and order should *do* something. They did get off in the end, fearful they'd be swept away by the torrential onslaught.

Those jewellers were among several who have inherited the traditional business on the bridge since Grand Duke Ferdinando I de' Medici ordered them here in the 16th century to replace the rather malodorous presence of the town butchers. The latter tended to jettison unwanted leftovers into the river.

The bridge as it stands was built in 1345 and those of us who get the chance to admire it can thank...well, someone...that it wasn't blown to smithereens in August 1944. The retreating German forces blew up all the other bridges on the Arno, but someone among them must have decided that sending the Ponte Vecchio to the bottom would have been a bridge too far. Instead they mined the areas on either side of the bridge.

As you reach the southern bank, this becomes pretty obvious. Take a halfway careful look at the buildings around Via de' Guicciardini and Borgo San Jacopo – they ain't exactly ancient heritage sites.

It was on this side of the bridge that Buondelmonte dei Buondelmonti was assassinated beneath the statue of Mars that stood here then, sparking the Guelph-Ghibelline conflict that subsequently tore the city and Tuscany apart. Mars was washed away by the 1333 flood.

A couple of buildings to survive the Nazi's mines are two medieval towers. The first, **Torre dei Mannelli**, looks very odd, as the Corridoio Vasariano was built *around* it, not simply straight through it as the Medici

would have preferred. Across Via de' Bardi as your eye follows the Corridoio you can espy **Torre degli Ubriachi**, the Drunks' Tower. Nice surname! On the intersection of Borgo San Jacopo and Via de' Guicciardini you will see an unassuming fountain, the Fontana di Bacco (Bacchus). Giambologna's *Ercole col Centauro Nesso (Hercules with the Centaur)* statue was here until transported to the Loggia della Signoria (see Piazza della Signoria earlier in the chapter).

Chiesa di Santa Felicita (Map 6)

About the most captivating thing about the facade of this 18th-century remake of what had been Florence's oldest (4th century) church is the fact that the Corridoio Vasariano passes right across it. The Medici could stop by and hear Mass without being seen by anyone!

Inside, the main interest is in the small **Cappella Barbadori**, designed by Brunelleschi, immediately on the right as you enter. Here Pontormo left his disquieting mark with a fresco of the Annunciation and a *Deposizione*. The latter depicts the taking down of Christ from the Cross in disturbingly surreal colours. The people engaged in this operation look almost as if they have been given a fright by the prying eyes of the onlooker.

The good thing about coming into a 'minor' church like this is that you'll probably find it empty, with one or two seniors perhaps muttering a few prayers in the silence. Shame it's not like that all over town! It is open from 9 am to noon and 3 to 6 pm on weekdays and from 9 am to 1 pm on Sunday and holidays.

Around Piazza de' Pitti (Maps 5 & 6)

Various important persons lived around here at some time. At Via de' Guicciardini 18 (Map 6), Machiavelli had his Florentine residence. Exiled for a time, he ended up back in Florence and breathed his last here.

A little further down the road, at No 15 is **Palazzo Guicciardini** (Map 5), one of several mansions belonging to the family. In this one the 16th-century intriguer and historian, Francesco, had his home. On Piazza de' Pitti itself, at No 22, is a house where the Russian novelist Fiodor Dostoyevsky stayed to write *The Idiot* in 1868–69. A few doors down was the home of Paolo dal Pozzo Tosca-nelli (1397–1482), cosmographer, scientist, engineer and all-round extremely clever chap. They say his theoretical maps were used by Columbus on his explorations that led to the discovery of the Americas.

Palazzo Pitti (Map 5)

When the Pitti, a wealthy merchant family, asked Brunelleschi to design the family home, they did not have modesty in mind. Great rivals of the Medici, there is not a little irony in the fact that their grandilo-quence would one day be sacrificed to the bank account.

Begun in 1458, the original nucleus of the palace took up the space encompassing the seven sets of windows on the second and third storeys.

In 1549 Eleonora de Toledo, wife of Cosimo I de' Medici, finding Palazzo Vec-chio too claustrophobic, acquired the palace from a by-now rather skint Pitti family. She launched the extension work, which ended up crawling along until 1839! Through all that time the original design was respected and today you would be hard-pressed to dis-tinguish the various phases of construction.

After the demise of the Medici dynasty, the palace remained the residence of the city's rulers, the dukes of Lorraine and their Austrian and (briefly) Napoleonic successors.

When Florence was made capital of the nascent kingdom of Italy in 1865, it became a residence of the Savoy royal family, who graciously presented it to the state in 1919.

The Museums The palace houses five museums. The **Galleria Palatina** (Palatine Gallery) houses paintings from the 16th to 18th centuries, which are hung in lavishly decorated rooms. The works were collected mostly by the Medici and their grand ducal successors.

After getting your ticket you head up a grand staircase to the gallery floor. The first rooms you pass through are a seemingly haphazard mix of the odd painting and period furniture.

The gallery proper starts after the **Sala della Musica** (Music Room). The paintings hung in the succeeding rooms are not in any particular order. Among Tuscan masters you can see work by Fra Filippo Lippi, San-dro Botticelli, Giorgio Vasari and Andrea del Sarto. The collection also boasts some important works by other Italian and for-eign painters. Foremost among them are those by Raphael, especially in the Sala di Saturnio. A close second is Titian, one of the greatest of the Venetian school. Other important artists represented include Tin-toretto, Paolo Veronese, Ribera, Rubens and Van Dyck. Caravaggio is represented with the striking *Amore Dormiente (Love Sleep-ing)* in the **Sala dell'Educazione di Giove**.

From the gallery you can pass into the **Appartamenti Reali** (Royal Apartments), a series of rather sickeningly furnished and decorated rooms, where the Medici and their successors slept, received guests and generally hung about. The style and div-ision of tasks assigned to each room is rem-iniscent of Spanish royal palaces.

At the time of writing some of the minor rooms of the gallery (not mentioned above) and a good many of the royal apartments were closed.

The other galleries are worth a look if you have plenty of time. The **Galleria d'Arte Moderna** (Modern Art Gallery) covers mostly Tuscan works from the 18th until the mid-20th century, and the **Museo degli Ar-genti** (Silver Museum), entered from the garden courtyard, has a collection of glass-ware, silver and semi-precious stones from the Medici collections. The **Galleria del Costume** (Costume Gallery) has high-class clothing from the 18th and 19th centuries, while the **Museo delle Carrozze** (Coach Museum) contains ducal coaches and the like.

Opening Times The Galleria Palatina is open from 8.30 am to 9 pm (6.50 pm in winter) Tuesday to Friday, until midnight on Saturday (6.50 pm in winter) and to 8 pm on Sunday (1.50 pm in winter).

The Museo degli Argenti and the Galleria d'Arte Moderna open from 8.30 am to 1.50 pm Tuesday to Saturday and on alternating Sundays and Mondays. The other two galleries were closed at the time of writing.

Admission Prices A L20,000 cumulative ticket *(biglietto cumulativo)* will get you entry into everything that is open and the Boboli Gardens (see the following section). But watch the times, as you may be too late for some of the museums.

L12,000 gets you into the Galleria Palatina and Appartamenti Reali alone. Admission into each of the other museums costs L4000. As you can see, the cumulative ticket only makes sense if you plan to see the lot on the same day.

Boboli Gardens (Maps 2 & 5)
Take a break in the palace's Renaissance Boboli Gardens (Giardino di Boboli), which were laid out in the mid-16th century and based on a design by the architect known as Il Tribolo. Buontalenti's noted artificial grotto (Grotta del Buontalenti), with a *Venere (Venus)* by Giambologna, is interesting.

Inside the garden is the **Museo delle Porcellane** (Map 2) which houses a varied collection of the fine porcelain collected over the centuries by the illustrious tenants of Palazzo Pitti, from Cosimo I de' Medici and Eleonora de Toledo on. The exhibits include some exquisite Sèvres and Vincennes pieces. You could skip the museum if the tupperware of the rich and famous leaves you cold. On the other hand, since you have already paid to get into the garden, it can't hurt to get a glimpse of how the other half must have lived in this town.

You can get into the Forte di Belvedere (Map 2; see Forte di Belvedere later in the chapter) from the south-eastern end of the garden. Also near here is the **Kaffeehaus** (Map 5), a late-19th-century conceit where you can sit down for a L4500 espresso.

The garden is open from 9 am to 4.30 pm

daily in winter and to 8 pm at the height of summer. Admission costs L4000, which includes access to the Museo delle Porcellane. The latter keeps the same timetable as the Museo degli Argenti (see the preceding section).

Chiesa di San Felice (Map 5)
This unprepossessing church has been made over several times since the Romanesque original went up in 1066. The simple Renaissance facade was done by Michelozzo. Inside you can admire an early-14th-century crucifix by Giotto's workshop. Opening hours are irregular.

At No 8 on this square is Casa Guidi, where the Brownings lived. It is possible to stay in this house (see Landmark Trust in the Places to Stay chapter).

Museo Zoologico La Specola (Map 5)
A little further down Via Romana from Piazza San Felice, this rather fusty museum, apart from the stuffed animal collection, offers for your delectation a collection of wax models of various bits of human anatomy in varying states of bad health. An offbeat change from all that art and history anyway! It opens from 9 am to 1 pm daily except Wednesday and admission costs L6000. It sometimes closes on public holidays, but second guessing on this is a hazardous exercise.

To Porta Romana (Map 2)
Pilgrims to Rome headed down Via Romana as they left Florence behind them. The end of the road is marked by the Porta Romana, an imposing city gate that was part of the outer circle of city walls knocked down in the 19th century. A strip of this wall still stretches to the north from the gate. If you head along the inside of this wall (the area is now a car park) you will soon come across an entrance that allows you to get to the top of Porta Romana.

The square below was traditionally a fairground for peasants in the surrounding county *(contado)*. By far the most curious of these fairs was the Fiera dei Contratti

(Contracts Fair), when country folk from near and far dragged sons and daughters along to contract marriage. They would haggle keenly over dowries and, much to the amusement of the none-too-respectful city folk who had taken the day off to come and gawk, compel prospective brides to walk up the hill towards the Poggio Imperiale (see Poggio Imperiale under South of the Old City later in the chapter), to see how well they swayed their hips!

Via Maggio (Map 5)

No, it doesn't mean May St, but rather Via Maggiore (Main St). In the 16th century this was a rather posh address, as the line-up of fine Renaissance mansions duly attests. **Palazzo di Bianca Cappello**, at No 26 has the most eye-catching facade, covered as it is in *graffiti* designs. Bianca Cappello was Francesco I de' Medici's lover and eventually wife. Across the street, a series of imposing mansions more or less follow the same Renaissance or Renaissance-inspired style. They include the **Palazzo Ricasoli-Ridolfi** at No 7, **Palazzo Martellini** at No 9, **Palazzo Michelozzi** at No 11, **Palazzo Zanchini** at No 13 and **Palazzo di Cosimo Ridolfi** at No 15. All were built and fiddled around with over the 14th, 15th and 16th centuries. Another impressive one is the **Palazzo Corsini-Suarez** at No 42.

Basilica di Santo Spirito (Map 5)

From Via Maggio you can turn into Via de' Michelozzi to reach Piazza Santo Spirito. If you wander into the square late on a summer afternoon you could almost be in Spain. The bars are grunge cool, attracting a mixed and largely local crowd of students, layabouts, artists, misfits and the odd foreigner. The feel is laid-back in the bars with their tables tumbling out on to the square, music always humming from one corner or another. It gets more animated as the night sets in.

During WWII, the Deutsches Institut (German Institute) had its offices and library in a building on this square. The staff had a risky habit of sheltering anti-Fascists in its library.

At its northern end, the square is fronted by the flaking facade of the Basilica di Santo Spirito, designed by Brunelleschi. It's a shame they couldn't get their act together to provide it with a dignified front, but don't let this put you off. The inside is a masterpiece of Florentine Renaissance design.

The church was one of Brunelleschi's last commissions. The entire length of the church inside is lined by a series of 40 semicircular chapels. Unfortunately, the architects who succeeded the master were not entirely faithful to his design. He wanted the chapels to form a shell of little apses right around the church, which clearly would have been a revolutionary step. Instead they chose to hide them behind a rather ad-hoc looking wall, flattening off the flanks of the church in an unsatisfying and untidy fashion.

More than the chapels, the colonnade of 35 columns in pietra serena is particularly striking inside. Not only do they separate the aisles from the nave, they continue around into the transept, creating the optical impression of a grey stone forest. Look closely at the high coffered ceiling above the nave. It is simply painted (funds were limited). Remember the similar-looking ceiling in the Basilica di San Lorenzo? There the coffered effect was real.

One of the most noteworthy works of art is Filippino Lippi's *Madonna col Bambino e Santi* in one of the chapels in the right transept. The main altar, beneath the central dome, is a voluptuous baroque flourish rather out of place in the spare setting of Brunelleschi's church. The sacristy *(sagrestia)* on the left side of the church is worth a look, particularly for its barrel-vaulted vestibule.

Santo Spirito is open from 8 am to midday and 4 to 6 pm daily, but not on Wednesday afternoon.

Next door to the church is the refectory, **Cenacolo di Santo Spirito**, which is home to the Fondazione Romano. Andrea Orcagna decorated the refectory with a grand fresco depicting the Last Supper and the Crucifixion. In 1946 the Neapolitan collector Salvatore Romano left his sculpture collection to Florence's council, the Comune di Firenze. Among the most intriguing pieces are rare pre-Romanesque sculptures and other works by Jacopo della Quercia and Donatello. Only those with a genuine interest in pre-Romanesque and Romanesque sculptures need enter.

It is open from 9 am to 2 pm Tuesday to Saturday, and from 8 am to 1 pm on Sunday and holidays. Admission costs L4000.

Basilica di Santa Maria del Carmine (Map 5)

As you walk south across Piazza Santo Spirito you will notice a fine Renaissance residence, the **Palazzo Guadagni**, on the south-east corner.

We instead turn west and head to Piazza del Carmine, an unkempt square used as a car park. On its southern flank stands the Basilica di Santa Maria del Carmine, high on many art-lovers' Florentine list of must-sees because of the **Cappella Brancacci**.

This chapel is a treasure of paintings by Masolino da Panicale, Masaccio and Filippino Lippi. Above all, the frescoes by Masaccio are considered among his greatest works, representing a definitive break with Gothic art and a plunge into new worlds of expression in the early stages of the Renaissance. His *Cacciata dei Progenitori (Expulsion of Adam and Eve)*, on the left side of the chapel, is the best-known work. His depiction of Eve's anguish in particular lends the image a human touch hitherto little seen in European painting. In times gone by prudish church authorities had Adam and Eve's privates covered up. Masaccio painted these frescoes in his early 20s and interrupted the task to go to Rome, where he died aged only 28. The cycle was completed some 60 years later by Filippino Lippi.

That you can even see these frescoes today is little short of miraculous. The 13th-century church was nearly destroyed by a fire in the late 18th century. About the only thing the fire spared was the chapel.

The church interior is something of a saccharine baroque bomb. Look up at the barrel-vaulted ceiling above the single nave. It fairly drips with excessive architectural trompe l'oeil fresco painting, with arches, pillars, columns, tympana all colliding into one another in a frenzy of movement. Opposite the Cappella Brancacci is the **Cappella Corsini**, one of the first (and few) examples of the extremes of Roman baroque executed in Florence. The billowy statuary is all a bit much.

The chapel is open from 10 am to 5 pm daily except Tuesday (1 to 5 pm on Sunday and holidays), but you will be thrown out by 4.45 pm. Admission costs L6000. You enter by a side door that takes you through the cloister.

Should you arrive after the chapel has closed but find the church open you can wander in and get a distant look at it from behind barriers – but the close-up inspection is what you need to appreciate the staggering detail.

Borgo San Frediano (Map 2)

Heading north from Piazza del Carmine you come across Borgo San Frediano. The street and surrounding area retain something of the feel of what they have always been, a working-class quarter where small-scale artisans have been beavering away over the centuries.

At the west end of the street stands the lonely **Porta San Frediano**, one of the old city gates left in place when the walls were demolished in the 19th century. Before you reach the gate, you'll notice the unpolished feel of the area neatly reflected in the unadorned brick walls of the **Chiesa di San Frediano in Cestello**, whose incomplete facade hides within a fairly bland, restrained version of a baroque church interior.

The church is open from 9 to 11.30 am and 5 to 6 pm on weekdays; and from 5 to 6 pm only on Sunday and holidays. The western side of Piazza di Cestello is occupied by granaries built under Cosimo III de' Medici.

Back to Ponte Vecchio (Maps 5 & 6)

From the front of Chiesa di San Frediano in Cestello you can wander along the river back towards the Ponte Vecchio.

Along the way you pass several grand family mansions, including **Palazzo Guicciardini** (Map 5) at Lungarno Guicciardini 7 and the 13th-century **Palazzo Frescobaldo** (Map 6) on the square of the same name. The latter played host to Charles de Valois in 1301, when he came to mediate peace between the Bianchi and Neri.

Round this palazzo you continue east along Borgo San Jacopo, on which still stand two 12th-century towers, the **Torre dei Marsili** and **Torre de' Belfredelli**. On Via de' Ramaglianti once stood the old Jewish synagogue.

Ponte Vecchio to Porta San Niccolò

Continuing east away from the Ponte Vecchio, the first stretch of Via de' Bardi shows clear signs of its recent history. This entire area was flattened by German mines in 1944 and hastily rebuilt in questionable taste after the war.

The street spills into **Piazza di Santa Maria Soprarno** (Map 6), which takes its name from a church that has long ceased to exist. Follow the narrow Via de' Bardi (the right fork) away from the square and you enter a pleasantly quieter corner of Florence. The Bardi family once owned all the houses along this street, but by the time the chubby Cosimo de' Medici married Contessina de' Bardi in 1415, the latter's family was well on the decline. They were among the banking dynasties ruined by the habit of debtors such as England's King Edward III of defaulting on huge loans. Cosimo and Contessina moved into a Bardi mansion on this street, but it was later pulled down. Buying up the street had clearly been a medieval bargain, as until the de' Bardi family built their mansions the street had been known as Borgo Pidiglioso (Flea St), one of the city's poorer quarters.

A couple of 15th-century mansions on the left, the **Palazzo Capponi delle Rovinate** at No 36 and **Palazzo Canigiani** at No 28 (Map 2), are typically Renaissance structures with their heavy pietra forte facades and jutting eaves.

A little further on, the **Chiesa di Santa Lucia dei Magnoli** (Map 2) has a striking glazed terracotta relief above the portal of Santa Lucia in the style of the della Robbia workshop.

Via de' Bardi expires in **Piazza de' Mozzi** (Map 5) which is also surrounded by the sturdy facades of grand residences belonging to the high and mighty. No 2, the southern flank of the piazza, is occupied by the **Palazzi de' Mozzi**, where Pope Gregory X stayed when brokering peace between the Guelphs and Ghibellines. The western side is lined by the 15th-century **Palazzo Lensi-Nencioni**, **Palazzo Torrigiani-Nasi** (with the graffiti ornamentation) and **Palazzo Torrigiani**.

Across the square, the long facade of the **Museo Bardini** is the result of an eclectic 19th-century building project by its owner, the collector Stefano Bardini. The collection is a broad mix ranging from Persian carpets to Etruscan carvings, from paintings by many lesser and occasionally well-known artists through to sculptures in stone and wood from a wide variety of artists and periods. It was closed for refurbishment at the time of writing.

From here turn east down Via dei Renai past the leafy **Piazza Demidoff**, dedicated to Nicola Demidoff, a 19th-century Russian philanthropist who lived nearby in Via San Niccolò. The 16th-century **Palazzo Serristori** (Map 7) at the end of Via dei Renai was home to Joseph Bonaparte in the last years of his life (he died in 1844). At the height of his career he had been made king of Spain under Napoleon.

Turn right and you end up in Via San Niccolò. The bland-looking **Chiesa di San Niccolò Oltrarno** (Map 7) is interesting if for nothing else than the little plaque indicating how high the 1966 flood waters reached – about 4m. If you head east along Via San Niccolò you emerge at the tower marking the **Porta San Niccolò**, all that is left of the city walls here.

To get an idea of what the walls were like walk south from the Chiesa di San Niccolò Oltrarno through **Porta San Miniato** (Map 7). The wall extends a short way to the east and quite a deal further west up a steep hill that leads you to the Forte di Belvedere (see the following section).

Less strenuous are the back roads, such as **Via dell'Erta Canina**, that meander off southwards into a mini-bucolic paradise of olive groves and vineyards. The people who live in the few villas scattered about in what is virtually Florence's back garden must know people in the right places to keep developers out. Good on them.

Forte di Belvedere (Map 2)
Bernardo Buontalenti helped design the rambling fortifications here for Grand Duke Ferdinando I towards the end of the 16th century. From this massive bulwark soldiers could keep watch on four fronts, and indeed it was designed with internal security in mind as much as foreign attack. Set high on a hill, the views across the city are, for this writer's money, better than the much-touted ones from Piazzale Michelangelo (see the following section).

The main entrance is near **Porta San Giorgio**, and you can approach, as we have, from the east along the walls or by taking Costa San Giorgio up from near the Ponte Vecchio. If you take the latter, you will pass, at Nos 17–21 (Map 5), one of the houses where Galileo Galilei lived while in Florence. You can also visit the fort from the Boboli Gardens, which is in fact what most people do (see Boboli Gardens earlier in the chapter).

As you take in the sweep of the view south of the fort, you can identify clearly the marble Romanesque facade of the Chiesa di San Miniato al Monte to the south-east. More or less directly south on a distant height you can make out what appears to be another fort with watch tower. It is known as the **Torre del Gallo** (Map 2). It belonged to the Galli clan, a Ghibelline family. They say Galileo carried out his astronomical observations from the tower here. What you see today is a bit of a travesty – a medieval-style reconstruction built in 1906.

Admission to the fort is free – in fact there's no-one to disturb you as you wander around inside.

If you feel like a long walk, you could follow Via San Leonardo south to Viale Galileo Galilei (about 1.5 km) and then turn left to head another couple of kilometres towards the Chiesa di San Miniato al Monte (or catch a bus back into the centre of town). Along Via San Leonardo you'll pass the medieval **Chiesa di San Leonardo**, whose 13th-century marble pulpit was taken from another church, San Piero Scheraggio (largely demolished to make way for the Uffizi). They say the likes of Dante and Boccaccio spoke from that pulpit. The church is only open for occasional services. Shortly before you reach Viale Galileo Galilei, you pass a villa on your right where Tchaikovsky resided for a while.

The street brings you to Viale Galileo Galilei. Turn left down the viale and you will eventually reach Piazzale Michelangelo, passing the Chiesa di San Miniato al Monte on the way. We're going to take a quicker approach.

Piazzale Michelangelo (Map 2)
From Porta San Miniato (Map 7) you could turn east instead of following the climb up to the Forte di Belvedere. A few twists and turns and you find yourself looking over Porta San Niccolò (Map 7). Several paths and stairways lead up from here to Piazzale Michelangelo, a favoured spot for viewing the city. Buses arriving from Siena often pass this way, and for those who are arriving in Florence for the first time, this initial glimpse of the place usually elicits a little leap of joy in even the hardest of hearts.

Local bus No 13, which leaves from Stazione di Santa Maria Novella and crosses Ponte alle Grazie, stops at the piazzale.

Chiesa di San Salvatore al Monte (Map 2)
A short steep climb up from the piazzale brings you to this spartan church, which you will probably find closed. That is no great disaster as this early-16th-century structure ain't that fascinating inside either.

The World Turns

'*Eppur si muove*' Galileo is supposed to have muttered after having been compelled to recant his teachings on astronomy before the Inquisition in Rome in 1633. 'And yet it *does* move.' He was referring to the Earth, whose exalted position at the centre of the universe he so inconveniently maintained was a falsehood. The Earth, along with other planets, rotated around the Sun, just as Copernicus had sustained.

As long ago as 1616 he had been ordered not to push this theory, which conservative Vatican elements not overly well-disposed to the 'new learning' saw as a potential threat to the very Church. If teachings long held dear about the position of the world in God's universe were accepted as balderdash, might not the whole edifice be open to the kind of unforgiving inquiry that Galileo and others were engaged in to better understand the world around them? The growing insistence on humankind's capacity to reveal what makes things tick, rather than simply remaining awestruck by the divine majesty of it all, was singularly inconvenient to those intent on maintaining the Church's position of pre-eminence in worldly and spiritual affairs.

Galileo was born in Pisa on 15 February 1564, the son of a musician. He received his early education at the monastery of Vallombrosa near Florence and later studied medicine at the University of Pisa. During his time there he became fascinated by mathematics and the study of motion, so much so that he is regarded as the founder of experimental physics. He became teacher of mathematics in Pisa and then moved to Padua for 18 years to teach and research there.

Having heard of the invention of the telescope in 1609, he set about making his own version, the first used to scan the night skies. In the coming years he made discoveries that led him to confirm Copernicus' theory that the planets revolve around the Sun. In 1610 he moved to Florence, where the grand duke had offered him permanent residence to continue his research. Galileo had many supporters, but not enough to prevent his works on the subject being placed on the index of banned books in 1616.

For the next seven years he continued his studies in Florence, where he lived mainly at Bellosguardo. The 1616 edict declaring his teachings on astronomy blasphemous was softened in 1924 to the extent that he was given permission to write an 'objective study' of the various proposed systems. His study was a triumph of argumentation in favour of his own theory, culminating nevertheless in the obligatory disclaimer that remained imposed on him. It was in the wake of this that the Inquisition summoned him to Rome in 1632. From then on he was confined to internal exile in Florence until his death in 1642. Until his last days, even after blindness had beset him in 1637, he continued to study, experiment, correspond with other scientists across Europe and write books. He lies buried in the Basilica di Santa Croce.

JANE SMITH

Chiesa di San Miniato al Monte (Map 2)

The real point of your exertions is about five minutes further up, at this wonderful Romanesque church, surely the best surviving example of the genre in Florence. The church is dedicated to St Minius (San Miniato), an early Christian martyr in Florence who is said to have flown to this spot after his death down in the town.

The church was started in the early 11th century, and the typically Tuscan marble facade features a mosaic depicting Christ between the Virgin and St Minius added 200 years later. The eagle at the top represents the Arte di Calimala, which financed the construction.

Inside you will see 13th- to 15th-century frescoes on the right wall, intricate inlaid marble designs down the length of the nave and a fine Romanesque crypt at the back, below the unusual raised presbytery *(presbiterio)*. The latter boasts a fine marble pulpit replete with intriguing geometrical designs. The sacristy, to the right of the church (they suggest you donate L1000 to get in), features marvellously bright frescoes. The four figures in the cross vault are the Evangelists.

The **Cappella del Cardinale del Portogallo** to the left side of the church, features a tomb by Antonio Rossellino and a ceiling decorated in terracotta by Luca della Robbia. It is possible to wander through the cemetery outside. Some of Michelangelo's battlements remain standing around here too.

The church is open from 8 am to noon and 4 to 6.30 pm daily. Bus No 13 stops nearby.

NORTH OF THE OLD CITY
Fortezza da Basso (Map 3)
Alessandro de' Medici ordered this huge defensive fortress built in 1534 and the task went to a Florentine living in Rome, Antonio da Sangallo il Giovane. The Medici family in general and Alessandro in particular were not flavour of the month in Florence at the time and construction of the fortress was an ominous sign of oppression. It was not designed to protect the city from invasion – Alessandro had recently been put back in the saddle after a siege by papal-imperial forces. The idea of this fort was to keep a watchful eye over the Florentines themselves. Nowadays it is sometimes used for exhibitions and cultural events.

Chiesa Russa Ortodossa (Map 2)
A couple of blocks east of the fortress, the onion-shaped domes are a bit of a giveaway on this Russian Orthodox church. Built in 1902 for the Russian populace resident here, it was designed in the northern Russian style, with two interior levels decorated in part by Florentine artists but mostly by Russians expert in iconography.

Museo Stibbert (Map 2)
Frederick Stibbert was one of the grand wheeler-dealers on the European antiquities market in the 19th century and unsurprisingly had quite a collection himself. He bought the Villa di Montughi with the intention of creating a museum exuding the atmosphere of the various countries and periods covered by his collections. The result is an intriguing mix.

An eye-opener is his collection of armour and arms. In one room, the **Sala della Cavalcata** (Parade Room), are life-size figures of horses and their soldierly riders in all manner of suits of armour from Europe and the Middle East. The exhibits also include clothes, furnishings, tapestries and paintings from the 16th to the 19th centuries.

The museum is at Via Federico Stibbert 26, north of the Fortezza da Basso. In summer it is open from 10 am to 1 pm and 3 to 6 pm daily except Thursday. In winter it opens from 10 am to 6 pm at the weekend and 10 am to 2 pm on weekdays (closed Thursday). Admission costs L8000.

The No 4 bus from Stazione di Santa Maria Novella takes you as close as Via Vittorio Emanuele II, from where you have a fairly short walk.

SOUTH OF THE OLD CITY
Bellosguardo (Map 2)
A favourite spot for 19th-century landscape painters was the hill of Bellosguardo (Beautiful View) south-west of the city centre. A narrow winding road leads up past a couple of villas from Piazza Tasso to Piazza Bellosguardo. You can't see anything from here, but if you wander along Via Roti Michelozzi into the grounds of the Albergo Torre di Bellosguardo, you'll see what the fuss was about. The hotel is the latest guise of what was once a 14th-century castle.

Try to get a look at things before you are not so kindly requested to be on your way. The hotel is great if you are staying there (see Oltrarno under Places to Stay – Top

End in the Places to Stay chapter) but otherwise they won't even let you spend money at the bar. No buses run here.

Poggio Imperiale (Map 1)

From Porta Romana a straight boulevard, Viale del Poggio Imperiale, leads directly to this once-grand Medici residence, the 'Imperial Hill'. The neoclassical appearance is due to changes wrought in the 18th and 19th centuries. It is now home to a high school and girls boarding school. If you turn up alone you will probably be able to wander around this somewhat neglected pile. Bus No 38 from Porta Romana stops here.

Certosa di Galluzzo (Map 1)

Instead of the road to Poggio Imperiale from Porta Romana, you could follow Via Senese south about 3km to the village of Galluzzo, which is home to a quite remarkable 14th-century monastery, the Certosa. The Carthusian order of monks once had 50 monasteries in Italy. Of these, only two are now inhabited by monks of that order. The Certosa di Galluzzo passed into Cistercian hands in 1955.

The guide will take you first to the Gothic hall of the **Palazzo degli Studi**, now graced by a small collection of art, including five somewhat weathered frescoes by Pontormo. The **Basilica di San Lorenzo**, with 14th-century origins, has a Renaissance exterior. To one side of it is the **Colloquio**, a narrow hall with benches. Here the Carthusian monks were permitted to break their vow of silence once a week, though they got a second chance on Mondays when allowed to leave the monastery grounds for a gentle stroll. You end up in the **Chiostro Grande**, the biggest of the complex's three cloisters. It is flanked by 18 monks' cells and decorated with busts from the della Robbia workshop.

The Certosa is open daily except Monday and can be visited only with a guide (reckon on about 45 minutes) from 9 am to midday and from 3 to 6 pm (to 5 pm in winter). To get there catch bus No 37 from Stazione di Santa Maria Novella. Payment is by offer (try not to be overly stingy).

Activities

CYCLING

Cycling around Florence and across Tuscany is becoming increasingly popular. UK-based cyclists planning to do some of this during their time in Florence might want to contact the Cyclists' Touring Club (☎ 01483-417217), Cotterell House, 69 Meadrow, Godalming, Surrey GU7 3HS. It has a Web site (www.ctc.org.uk) and can supply information to members on cycling conditions, itineraries and cheap insurance. Membership costs UK£25 per annum.

Once in Florence, ask for a copy of *Viaggio in Toscana – Discovering Tuscany by Bike* at the APT office. For details of where to rent a bike or join cycling tours of Florence and surrounds, see Bicycle & Moped in the Getting Around chapter.

SWIMMING

The Piscina Nannini (Map 2; ☎ 055 67 75 21) is 3.5km east of the Ponte Vecchio along Lungarno Aldo Moro in Bellariva (bus No 14 from Piazza dell'Unità and the Duomo takes you closest to the pool). In summer, when they pull back the movable roof over the Olympic-size pool it becomes a watery haven on those torrid Florentine days. Opening times tend to change from month to month, but as a rule of thumb it opens from 9 am to 6.30 pm, and from 8 to 11.30 pm daily in summer. Standard adult admission costs L10,000, or you can become a member *(socio)* for L10,000 and get blocks of 10 tickets for L71,000. A block of tickets for non-members costs L75,000.

The Piscina Le Pavoniere pool (Map 2; ☎ 055 35 83 27) at Viale degli Olmi in the Cascine opens from May to September. It opens late into the night on some evenings and has a pizzeria and bar.

From mid-September to June is winter for Florentine pools and it all becomes much more complicated. You have to take out one-month (or longer) subscriptions and access is restricted to certain times on no more than four days a week. Pathetic, as most Florentines would agree.

Courses

Florence has more than 30 schools offering courses in Italian language and culture. Numerous other schools offer courses in art, including painting, drawing, sculpture and art history, and there are also plenty of schools offering cooking courses.

While Florence is one of the most attractive cities in which to study Italian language or art, it is one of the more expensive. You may want to check out the options in places like Siena, Perugia and Urbino. Also, as far as learning the language is concerned, Florence is a poor choice – for English speakers at any rate – as most Anglo students find themselves hanging out with other Anglos and never speaking a word of the language. If you are serious about learning Italian, you may want to think about picking a less touristed town.

Brochures detailing courses and prices are available at Italian cultural institutes throughout the world (see Cultural Centres in the Facts for the Visitor chapter). Florence's APT also has lists of schools and courses, which it will mail on request. You can write in English to request information and enrolment forms – letters should be addressed to the '*segretaria*' (secretary).

Non-EU citizens who want to study at a university or language school in Italy must have a study visa. These visas can be obtained from your nearest Italian embassy or consulate. You will normally require confirmation of your enrolment, payment of fees and proof of adequate funds to support yourself before a visa is issued. The visa will then cover only the period of the enrolment. This type of visa is renewable within Italy but, again, only with confirmation of ongoing enrolment and proof that you are able to support yourself – bank statements are preferred.

LANGUAGE COURSES

The cost of language courses in Florence depends on the school, the length of the course (one month is usually the minimum duration) and its intensity. Local authorities sometimes run irregular courses, generally for free and aimed at impecunious migrants, for a couple of hours a week.

Schools in Florence offering language course include:

Istituto Europeo
(Map 6; ☎ 055 238 10 71) Piazzale delle Pallottole 1, 50122. Courses here start at L370,000 for two hours (one week). A much better deal is to hang around for four weeks (L840,000).
Istituto di Lingua e Cultura Italiana per Stranieri Michelangelo
(Map 7; ☎ 055 24 09 75) Via Ghibellina 88, 50122. At this institute you will pay L890,000 for four weeks' tuition, but the school will also organise private one-on-one courses, starting at L6,230,000 for two weeks (which includes lunch with the teacher – so you'd better hope you like your teacher!).
Dante Alighieri School for Foreigners
(Map 5; ☎ 055 234 29 86) Via de' Bardi 12, 50125. Another well-known school for language and culture classes.
Centro Lingua Italiana Calvino
(Map 3; ☎ 055 28 80 81) Viale Fratelli Rosselli 74, 50123. You have the option of standard and intensive courses here, the latter totalling 30 hours a week. The problem with this place is the location around the back end of Stazione di Santa Maria Novella – hardly the most romantic little niche of Florence.
Scuola Leonardo da Vinci
(Map 3; ☎ 055 29 44 20) Via Bufalini 3, 50122. Courses offered range from two to 24 weeks, usually averaging four hours' class a day. Basic course costs start at L800,000 for four weeks.
Scuola Toscana
(Map 7; ☎ 055 24 45 83) Via de' Benci 23, 50122. This school tends to pitch for business customers.
Centro Linguistico Sperimentale
(Map 6; ☎ 055 21 05 92) Via del Corso 1, 50122. This school has a reasonable reputation.
Centro Lorenzo de' Medici
(Map 3; ☎ 055 28 73 60) Via Faenza 43, 50122. This school is popular with American students wishing to learn the Italian language.

OTHER COURSES

Many of the schools already listed also offer a programme of courses on art history, cooking, art, music and the like.

Some schools specialise in these sorts of course. Art courses range from one-month summer workshops (costing from L500,000 to more than L1,000,000) to longer-term professional diploma courses. These can be expensive; some cost more than L6,500,000 a year. Schools will organise accommodation for students, on request and at added cost, either in private apartments or with Italian families.

Istituto per l'Arte e il Restauro
(Map 7; ☎ 055 24 60 01) Palazzo Spinelli, Borgo Santa Croce 10, 50122. Here you can learn to restore anything from paintings to ceramics, interior and graphic design, gilding and marquetry.

Accademia Italiana
(Map 5; ☎ 055 28 46 16) Piazza de' Pitti 15, 50125. This school offers a wide range of design programmes. They include one-month courses for dilettantes and more rigorous semester courses in painting, graphic arts, fashion design and related fields.

Cordon Bleu
(Map 7; ☎ 055 234 54 68) Via di Mezzo 55r, 50123. This is the place to go to learn some stylish cooking methods.

Florence Dance Center
(Map 5; ☎ 055 28 92 76) Borgo della Stella 23r (www.florencedance.org). This centre offers a range of courses in classical, jazz and modern dance.

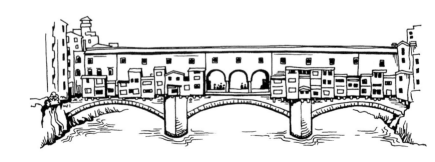

Places to Stay

The city has hundreds of hotels in all categories and a good range of alternatives, including hostels and private rooms. There are more than 200 one- and two-star hotels in Florence, so even in the peak season it is generally possible – although not always easy – to find a room *(camera)*.

You are, however, advised to book ahead in summer (from mid-April on) and for the Easter and Christmas to New Year holiday periods, and, frankly, it's not a bad idea at any time.

Things are likely to get more difficult in the coming years too. As the numbers of visitors to Florence continue to grow (see Economy in the earlier Facts about Florence chapter), the city's number crunchers have found themselves faced with a growing dilemma – where to put them all. With about 26,500 beds available in the city, things can get a little squeezy. In addition to the hotels, about 175 houses have been registered as *affittacamere* – basically offering beds in private houses. The authorities are taking it a step further, inviting Florentines looking to make a few euros on the side to enter into the 'bed and breakfast' game. The breakfast part is relatively new to Italy, and Florence's town council hopes it will prove effective in helping to deal with the rising tourist tide.

Hotels generally go by the name of *hotel* or *albergo*, essentially the same thing. A *pensione* is generally a smaller, cheaper family-run affair. That said, you will sometimes find that even the tiniest places refer to themselves as hotels. The one- to five-star system is indicative only of the facilities and services available in a hotel – although the rating may give some idea of quality and prices, it is all rather arbitrary. Hoteliers are under little or no obligation to charge any particular rate.

Hotels and pensioni are concentrated in three areas: near the main train station, near Piazza di Santa Maria Novella and in the old city between the Duomo and the Arno.

If you arrive at the main train station,

Stazione di Santa Maria Novella, without a hotel booking, head for the Consorzio ITA office (Map 3; ☎ 055 28 28 93). Using a computer network, the office can check the availability of rooms and make a booking for a small fee; there are no phone bookings. The fee charged ranges from L4500 to L15,000 (for one- to five-star places). The office is open from 8.30 am to 9 pm daily. Several other hotel associations offer booking services for a range of hotels registered with them. See Hotel Associations for a list.

You can also contact the APT (Azienda di Promozione Tursitica) for a list of private rooms, which generally cost from L25,000 per person in a shared room and from L35,000 in a single room. Most fill with students during the school year (from October to June), but are a good option if you are staying for a week or longer.

When you arrive at a hotel, always ask for the full price of a room before putting your bags down. Florentine hotels and pensioni are notorious for their bill-padding, particularly in summer. Some may require up to L10,000 extra for compulsory breakfast and others will charge L3000 or more for a shower. Contact the APT's SOS Turista (see Local Tourist Offices in the Facts for the Visitor chapter) if you have any problems.

Prices listed here are for the high season and, unless otherwise indicated, are for rooms without bathroom. A bathroom will cost from L10,000 to L30,000 extra; sometimes all this means is a shower cubicle. Many places, especially at the lower end, offer triples and quads as well as the standard single/double *(singola/matrimoniale)* arrangement. If you are travelling in a group of three or four, these bigger rooms are generally the best value.

High season for those hotels that lift their prices (which is most of them) starts on 15 April and fizzles out by mid-October. Some hotels have an intermediate stage starting on 1 March. Others don't bother changing prices much at any time of the year.

It follows that low season (mid-October to the end of February, and for some places also March) is the thinnest time for tourists and so the best for getting the cheapest hotel rates.

Hotel Associations

The following organisations can book you into member hotels. They usually offer a fair range of possibilities, but rarely drop below two stars.

Associazione Gestori Alloggi Privati (AGAP)
(☎/fax 055 28 41 00)
Via dei Neri 9
This organisation can get you a room in an affittacamere, which is basically a type of bed-and-breakfast-style accommodation but usually without the breakfast.
Consorzio Finestre Sull'Arno
(☎ 800 292773)
c/o Hotel Augustus, Vicolo dell'Oro 5
COOPAL
(☎ 055 21 95 25, fax 055 29 21 92)
Via Il Prato 2r
Florence Promhotels
(☎ 055 57 04 81 or ☎ 800 866022, fax 055 58 71 89, ❷ info@promhotels.it)
Viale Volta 72
Top Quark (incorporating Family Hotels and Sun Ray Hotels)
(☎ 055 462 00 80, fax 055 48 22 88, ❷ top-quark.fi@mbox.it.net)
Via Trieste 5

PLACES TO STAY – BUDGET
Camping

The closest camping ground to the city centre is *Campeggio Michelangelo (Map 2; ☎ 055 681 19 77, Viale Michelangelo 80)*, just off Piazzale Michelangelo, south of the Arno. It opens from April until the end of October. Take bus No 13 from the main train station. The *Villa Camerata* camping ground *(Map 2; ☎ 055 61 03 00, Viale Augusto Righi 2–4)* is next to the HI hostel of the same name (see under Hostels for more details).

There is a camping ground at Fiesole, *Campeggio Panoramico (☎ 055 59 90 69, Via Peramonda 1)*, which also has bungalows. Take bus No 7 to Fiesole from the Stazione di Santa Maria Novella.

Hostels

The Hostelling International (HI) *Ostello Villa Camerata (Map 2; ☎ 055 60 14 51, fax 055 61 03 00, Viale Augusto Righi 2–4)* is considered one of the most beautiful hostels in Europe. B&B is L24,000, dinner L14,000, and there is a bar. Only members are accepted and the hostel is part of the International Booking Network (IBN), the online booking system for HI (see www.iyhf.org for more details). It's open from 7 am to midnight, with a break from 9 am to 2 pm. Take bus No 17B, which leaves from the right side of the main train station as you leave the platforms. The trip takes 30 minutes.

The private *Ostello Archi Rossi (Map 3; ☎ 055 29 08 04, Via Faenza 94r)* is another good option for a bed in a dorm room (L24,000), and it is close to the train station. A bed in a smaller room costs L30,000. *Ostello Santa Monaca (Map 5; ☎ 055 26 83 38, Via Santa Monaca 6)* is another private hostel. It is a 15- to 20-minute walk south from the train station, through Piazza Santa Maria Novella, along Via de' Fossi, across the Ponte alla Carraia and directly ahead along Via de' Serragli. Via Santa Monaca is a few blocks from the river, on the right. A bed costs L23,000, and sheets and meals are available.

The *Ostello Spirito Santo (Map 3; ☎ 055 239 82 02, Via Nazionale 8)* is a religious institution near the main train station. The nuns accept only women and families, and charge L40,000 per person or L60,000 for a double. They seem cagey about accepting bookings over the phone – but try in any case. The hostel is open from July to October.

Istituto Gould (Map 5; ☎ 055 21 25 76, Via de' Serragli 49) has clean doubles for L39,000. A bed in a quad costs L33,000, while one in a quintuple comes in at L28,000.

Hotels
East of Stazione di SM Novella Many of the hotels in this area are very well-run, clean and safe, but there are also a fair number of seedy establishments. The area includes the streets around Piazza della

Stazione and east to Via Cavour. If you have nothing booked and don't wish to tramp around town, the area has the advantage of being close to the main train station. The hotels in this section can be found on Map 3, unless specified.

At the start of Via Nazionale, the **Pensione Bellavista** (☎ *055 28 45 28, Largo Alinari 15)* is small, but a bargain if you can manage to book one of the two double rooms with balconies and a view of the Duomo and Palazzo Vecchio – they cost L130,000. At the time of writing staff at the pensione said they had no singles.

Albergo Azzi (☎ *055 21 38 06, Via Faenza 56)* has a helpful management, who will arrange accommodation for you in other Italian cities. Simple, comfortable singles/doubles are L70,000/100,000, or L140,000 for a double with bathroom. Ask for a room away from the noisy Via Faenza and enjoy breakfast on the hotel's terrace. The same management runs *Albergo Anna* (☎ *055 239 83 22)* upstairs, where prices are similar. Several other budget *pensioni* in the same building are all habitable.

At No 24 is the *Pensione Ausonia & Rimini (Map 3;* ☎ 055 49 65 47), run by an obliging young couple. Singles/doubles are L70,000/105,000, or L95,000/125,000 with own bath. The price includes breakfast.

Hotel Globus (Map 6; ☎ *055 21 10 62, Via Sant'Antonino 24)* is a handy little place with reasonable if unspectacular rooms going for up to L80,000/130,000. You can snag a single for L60,000 in low season, which is about as cheap as this kind of place gets around here. Everything is kept spotlessly clean.

Around Piazza di SM Novella This area is just south of the Stazione di Santa Maria Novella and includes Piazza di Santa Maria Novella, the streets running south to the Arno and east to Via de' Tornabuoni.

Via della Scala, which runs north-west off the piazza, is lined with pensioni. It is not the most salubrious part of town, but if you want to find a place to put your head down quickly after arriving, at least you have plenty of choice. *La Romagnola*

(Map 3; ☎ *055 21 15 97)* at No 40 has large, clean rooms and a helpful management. Singles/doubles cost L48,000/84,000. Add L8000 for a room with private bath.

Hidden away on a tiny, quiet intersection is the modest *Pensione Ferretti (Map 6;* ☎ *055 238 13 28, Via delle Belle Donne 17).* Simple but quiet rooms start at L66,000/ 105,000 without private bath or L85,000/ 125,000 with bath.

A simple but well-maintained establishment is the *Hotel Abaco (Map 6;* ☎*/fax 055 238 19 19, Via dei Banchi 1).* Doubles start at L105,000 with bathroom in the corridor. For a room with your own shower you are looking at around L120,000. They have no singles, though in low season they will rent a double out for L65,000.

Fancy staying on Florence's posh shopping strip and paying only L60,000/90,000 for the pleasure? *Albergo Scoti (Map 6;* ☎*/fax 055 29 21 28, Via de' Tornabuoni 7)* has perfectly good rooms (with shower off the corridor).

Hotel Fiorentina (Map 5; ☎ *055 21 95 30, fax 055 28 71 05, Via de' Fossi 12)* is a good deal. Singles/doubles cost L60,000/ 110,000. Rooms have phones but only three doubles have their own shower. Breakfast is included in the price.

Between the Duomo & the Arno This area is a 15-minute walk south from Stazione di Santa Maria Novella in the heart of old Florence. The hotels mentioned in this section can be found on Map 6, unless specified.

One of the best deals is the small *Aily Home* (☎ *055 239 65 05, Piazza Santo Stefano 81),* just near the Ponte Vecchio. Rooms cost L35,000/60,000. It has five large rooms, three overlooking the bridge, and accepts bookings. The singles are tiny, but this has to be about the cheapest hotel option in Florence.

Pensione Maria Luisa de' Medici (☎ *055 28 00 48, Via del Corso 1)* is in a mansion dating from the 17th century. The pensione has large rooms and caters for families. Doubles/triples cost L101,000/140,000 without own bath and L139,000/179,000 with. Prices include breakfast.

euro currency converter L10,000 = €5.16

PLACES TO STAY

Just south of the Duomo is **Albergo Firenze** (☎ 055 21 42 03, *Piazza de' Donati 4*), which has singles/doubles for L90,000/130,000 with breakfast. **Brunori** (☎ 055 28 96 48, *Via del Proconsolo 5*) charges up to L102,000 for doubles with a shower. Singles without start at L48,000.

Albergo Bavaria (*Map 5;* ☎ 055 234 03 13, *Borgo degli Albizi 26*) is housed in the fine Palazzo di Ramirez di Montalvo, built around a peaceful courtyard by Amannati. The hotel has singles/doubles for up to L90,000/120,000. A double with bathroom is L150,000.

Pensione TeTi & Prestige (☎ 055 239 84 35, *Via Porta Rossa 5*) has singles/doubles for L90,000/130,000 with own shower and a few doubles with full private bathroom for L150,000. The manager is willing to chop off about L20,000 per room at slack times.

The **Maxim** (☎ 055 21 74 74, *Via dei Medici 4*) has singles/doubles/triples from L105,000/140,000/180,000 and offers substantial discounts in the low season.

Elsewhere If things are looking tough in the centre of town, a few suggestions a little further out are worth considering.

Pensione Losanna (*Map 4;* ☎ 055 24 58 40, *Via Vittorio Alfieri 9*) lies a few blocks east of the Museo Archeologico as the crow flies and is a well-run establishment where rooms cost L70,000/95,000. If there is no room at that inn, try upstairs a flight at **Pensione Donatello** (*Map 4;* ☎ 055 247 74 16, *Via Vittorio Alfieri 9*). The place is a little tattier, but the rooms are spacious, clean and quiet. The bathrooms are on the corridor. The price, which includes breakfast, is L60,000/100,000. If no singles are left, the lady running the place will give you a double for L70,000 (which the lady downstairs will not).

PLACES TO STAY – MID-RANGE
East of Stazione di SM Novella
The **Pensione Le Cascine** (*Map 3;* ☎ 055 21 10 66, *Largo Alinari 15*), near the train station, is a two-star hotel with nicely furnished rooms, some of them with balconies. Singles/doubles with bathroom cost L140,000/300,000, including breakfast.

Nuova Italia (*Map 3;* ☎ 055 26 84 30, *Via Faenza 26*) is a good choice. Its singles/doubles with bathroom cost up to L125,000/185,000. **Pensione Accademia** (*Map 6;* ☎ 055 29 34 51, *Via Faenza 7*) has pleasant rooms and incorporates an 18th-century mansion with magnificent stained-glass doors and carved wooden ceilings. The only single costs L130,000 (without bathroom), while doubles with bathroom go for L200,000, breakfast and television included.

Hotel Bellettini (*Map 6;* ☎ 055 21 35 61, *Via de' Conti 7*) is a delightful small hotel with well-furnished singles/doubles with bathroom for L140,000/190,000. Try for one of the rooms with a view of the Basilica di San Lorenzo.

The **Giotto** (*Map 6;* ☎ 055 28 98 64, *Via del Giglio 13*) has doubles with bathroom for L160,000. The **Giada** (*Map 6;* ☎ 055 21 53 17*) is in the middle of the open-air leather market at Via del Canto de' Nelli 2. The rooms with bathroom are OK, and you have the rare luxury of breakfast in your room. Rates are L120,000/180,000. **Hotel Le Casci** (*Map 6;* ☎ 055 21 16 86, *Via Cavour 13*) has good rooms for L140,000/190,000, with bathroom, breakfast and TV.

Between the Duomo & the Arno
The **Hotel Alessandra** (*Map 6;* ☎ 055 28 34 38, *Borgo SS Apostoli 17*) has lots of character. Singles/doubles are L100,000/150,000, or L150,000/200,000 with bathroom. The **Pendini** (*Map 6;* ☎ 055 21 11 70, *Via degli Strozzi 2*) is another excellent choice. Its rooms are furnished with antiques and reproductions, and singles/doubles with bathroom cost L170,000/250,000. **Hotel Porta Rossa** (*Map 6;* ☎ 055 28 75 51, *Via Porta Rossa 19*) has large singles/doubles for L170,000/285,000.

Oltrarno
A good choice if you want to stay south of the river is the **Pensione la Scaletta** (*Map 6;* ☎ 055 28 30 28, *Via de' Guicciardini 13*). It has a terrace with great views. Rooms with

bathroom are L140,000/200,000, including breakfast. Some of the rooms looking onto the street cost a little less.

Pensione Bandini *(Map 5;* ☎ *055 21 53 08, fax 055 28 27 61, Piazza Santo Spirito 9)* is overpriced but a pretty hip address. They don't do singles and the doubles come in at a hefty L159,000, or L194,000 with private bathroom.

Set in a charming old palazzo in one of the most attractive (and, thankfully, comparatively little-touristed) parts of Florence is ***Hotel Silla*** *(Map 7;* ☎ *055 234 28 88, fax 055 234 14 37, Via dei Renai 5)*. Pleasant and impeccably maintained rooms cost L180,000/250,000.

PLACES TO STAY – TOP END

In this category appear a handful of choices where a single can cost from L200,000 a night up to more than L620,000 at the very top end of the scale.

Around Stazione di SM Novella

Machiavelli Palace *(Map 3;* ☎ *055 21 66 22, Via Nazionale 10)* is in a 17th-century mansion. Many of its beautiful rooms have terraces. Singles/doubles are worth the price at L240,000/390,000. The four-star ***Albergo Majestic*** *(Map 6;* ☎ *055 26 40 21, Via del Melarancio 1)* has very comfortable singles/doubles up to L330,000/450,000.

Grand Hotel Baglioni *(Map 6;* ☎ *055 2 35 80, Piazza dell'Unità Italiana 6)* has rooms starting from L320,000/428,000. Some rooms fall into the 'superior' category and cost an extra L40,000. All rooms have TV, phone, air-con and heating.

East of Stazione di SM Novella

Tucked away in a fine Renaissance palazzo, ***Hotel Monna Lisa*** *(Map 4;* ☎ *055 247 97 51, Borgo Pinti 27)* has a mix of rooms for L300,000/505,000. The best of them are good value and some look out over the private garden where you can eat breakfast in summer.

Hotel Le Due Fontane *(Map 4;* ☎ *055 21 01 85, Piazza SS Annunziata 14)* is in a fine old building right on this square. The well-presented rooms cost L200,000/290,000, in-

cluding breakfast. It's one of the few hotels at this level to have a baby-sitting service.

Hotel Il Guelfo Bianco *(Map 3;* ☎ *055 28 83 30, fax 055 29 52 03, Via Cavour 57r)* has 29 attractively laid-out and comfortable rooms. If you are alone, see if you can get the charming single with its own private terrace. Rooms cost L205,000/335,000.

Another of the handful of five-star hotels in town is the ***Hotel Regency*** *(Map 4;* ☎ *055 24 52 47, fax 055 234 67 35, Piazza Massimo D'Azeglio 3)*. Facing a leafy park, the hotel is a quiet, understated place with 49 modern, well-appointed rooms. They range in cost from L380,000/500,000 for a single/double through to L620,000 for a deluxe double, excluding 10% in IVA (value added tax). You can check out the hotel and make online reservations at www.regency-hotel.com.

Around Ognissanti

The most expensive hotels in town face each other in self-assured style on Piazza d'Ognissanti. ***Grand Hotel*** *(Map 5;* ☎ *055 28 87 81, fax 055 21 02 78, Piazza d'Ognissanti 1)* is every bit as grand as the name suggests. Marble bathrooms and regal furnishings characterise the best rooms, which have river views. A wander around the glorious ground floor, with its bars and restaurant, is almost nauseating. You are looking at a minimum in high season of L620,000/860,000 for singles/doubles. Deluxe doubles with river views cost L1,062,000.

Hotel Excelsior *(Map 5;* ☎*/fax 055 26 42 01, Piazza d'Ognissanti 3)* is the haughtier of the two hotels. Luxury is again the key in the 158 rooms. Prices for singles/doubles in high season start at L566,000/860,000, rising to L1,100,000 for a double with river views.

Between the Duomo & the Arno

An excellent hotel in a historic building is ***Bernini Palace*** *(Map 6;* ☎ *055 28 86 21, Piazza San Firenze 29)*. Its luxurious rooms cost L340,000/500,000 for singles/doubles.

If you fancy sleeping (almost) in the round tower of a one-time medieval prison, the place to stay is the ***Hotel Brunelleschi***

(Map 6; ☎ 055 2 73 70, fax 055 21 96 53, Piazza Santa Elisabetta 3). Good, modern rooms with satellite TV, air-con and hairdryers cost L380,000/510,000, including breakfast. Suites bordering on the tower itself cost L800,000 but the bulk of the tower's floor space is taken up with convention rooms. Check out the Web site and make online reservations at www.hotel brunelleschi.it.

Oltrarno

Its location away from the busy centre makes the ***Hotel Villa Liberty*** *(Map 6; ☎ 055 681 05 81; fax 055 681 25 95, Viale Michelangelo 40)* a choice worth considering. The Art-Nouveau decor and leafy surroundings are highly agreeable, although traffic on the main road can be a trifle irritating. High season prices are L250,000/ 310,000 but in off-season you can be fairly sure of a 15% drop. For more information and to make online reservations take a look at www.hotelvillaliberty.com.

It's worth considering the ***Albergo Torre di Bellosguardo*** *(Map 2; ☎ 055 229 81 45, fax 055 22 90 08, Via Roti Michelozzi 2, @ torredibellosguardo@dada.it)*, if only for its position. Long appreciated as a bucolic escape from the simmering heat of summertime Florence, the Bellosguardo hill to the south-west of the city centre offers not only enchanting views but enticing accommodation in what started life as a small castle in the 14th century. The strategically placed hotel pool is the best spot to drink in the views. Rooms cost L340,000/450,000 year-round, and breakfast an extra L35,000. There are also a couple of suites at L550,000 and L650,000.

LANDMARK TRUST

If you fancy staying in the poet Browning's house, *Casa Guidi (Map 5)*, in Piazza San Felice, contact the Landmark Trust in the UK. Established as a charity in 1965, the trust restores and conserves a host of architectural marvels in the UK, as well as several abroad. Casa Guidi has been restored and is owned by Eton College. It sleeps six and can cost around UK£1300 a week.

For further information, get in touch with The Landmark Trust (☎ 01628-825 925) at Shottesbrooke, Maidenhead, Berkshire SL6 3SW, UK,

SHORT-TERM RENTAL

If you are travelling in a group and plan to stay in Florence for at least a week or more, it may be worth considering renting an apartment or villa. This is obviously an even more popular option for those choosing to stay in the surrounding countryside. Any Italian tourist office abroad will be able to supply you with mountains of brochures for companies brokering such arrangements. The problem is knowing what you are going to get – not always easy to judge, even if you get to see photos. Remember to find out exactly what the facilities are and what costs extra (such as heating and use of a swimming pool).

One major Italian company with villas in Tuscany is Cuendet. This reliable firm publishes a booklet listing all the villas in its files, many with photos. Prices for a villa for four to six people range from around US$400 a week in winter up to US$1200 a week in August. For details, write to Cuendet & Cie spa (☎ 0577 57 63 10, fax 0577 30 11 49, @ cuede@tin.it), Strada di Strove 17, 53035 Monteriggioni, Siena, and ask them to send you a copy of their catalogue (US$15).

In the UK, you can order Cuendet's catalogues and make reservations by calling ☎ 0800 891 573 toll-free. In North America, Cuendet is represented by Rentals In Italy – and Elsewhere! (☎ 805-987 5278, fax 805-482 7976), 1742 Calle Corva, Camarillo, California. They have a Web site at www.rentvillas.com. In Australia, try Cottages & Castles (☎ 03-9853 1142, fax 9853 0509, @ cottages@vicnet.net.au), 11 Laver St, Kew 3101, Victoria.

LONG-TERM RENTAL

If you want an apartment in Florence, save your pennies and, if you can, start looking well before you arrive, as apartments are difficult to come by and can be very expensive. A one-room studio with kitchenette in the city centre will generally cost around L1,000,000 a month. Firenze & Abroad (Map 3; ☎ 055 48 70 04), Via Zanobi 58, deals with rental accommodation.

If you decide while in Florence to start looking, be prepared for some degree of frustration. You can look for rental ads in advert rags such as *La Pulce* (L2800; three times a week) and *Il Mercato della Toscana* (L2500). You'll find few ads for share accommodation, though.

Another obvious route to follow, especially if you are looking for share housing, is the language and other schools frequented by foreigners in Florence. You can put up your own ad or hopefully get lucky and find some likely candidates to share with.

Other places to look for ads include English bookshops (such as the Paperback Exchange), cybercafes, laundrettes and faculty buildings of the Università degli Studi di Firenze (Map 3).

Places to Eat

FOOD

For some visitors, arrival in Tuscany means having reached the pearly gates of food heaven. For others, Tuscan cuisine is rather overrated.

The truth lies somewhere between the two. As with many (but not all) of the Mediterranean cuisines, Tuscan cookery is essentially the result of poverty. Simple, wholesome ingredients have traditionally been thrown together to produce healthy but hardly fascinating meals. The extraordinary excesses we read about of the tables of medieval barons or later on of the Medici and their pals were not passed down to us through the ages. One can only drool and dream about what extraordinary concoctions such private festivals of Bacchus must have been like.

Most common folk had to make do with limited ingredients. *That* is what has come down to us today. It has been refined and enriched, particularly with other dishes and combinations from more widely flung parts of Italy. And all told it is very good – one of the keys remains the quality and freshness of the ingredients, upon which great store is placed. The use of herbs such as basil, thyme, parsley and rosemary is liberal.

Some gourmands will miss something though – adventure. In Tuscany, as elsewhere in Italy, tradition still controls much of what the cook does. S/he can tweak and fiddle (perhaps best exemplified in a growing daring in the preparation of pasta sauces) but all in all must remain faithful to the old ways. There are those in Tuscany (and again, throughout the country) who can solemnly state exactly what kind of sauce will go with which kind of pasta – any deviation from the rules meets with scorn. Undoubtedly many of these 'rules' are sound, but at times they are merely oppressive and unimaginative.

Although not always exactly cheap, it is possible to dine well without doing undue harm to your savings account in Florence. What you need to be especially wary of are the phalanxes of tourist rip-off restaurants that predictably congregate in the city centre and near the main tourist sights.

Carping aside, it is difficult to get sick of Tuscan cuisine and other Italian dishes on offer in Florence. Add to your meal some of the finest wines produced in the country and you will want to come with your taste buds fully braced for action.

When to Eat

Breakfast *(colazione)* is generally a quick affair taken on the hop in a bar on the way to work.

For lunch *(pranzo)*, restaurants usually operate from 12.30 to 3 pm, but many are not keen to take orders after 2 pm.

In the evening, opening hours for dinner *(cena)* vary but people start sitting down to eat around 7.30 pm. You will be hardpressed to find a place still serving after 10.30 pm.

Bars (in the Italian sense, that is coffee-and-sandwich places) and cafes generally open from 7.30 am to 8 pm, although some stay open after 8 pm and turn into pub-style drinking and meeting places.

Many restaurants and bars shut one or two days a week. In some parts of Italy at least one day off is mandatory but ultimately the decision on whether or not to enforce that rule rests with the council. The Florence council does not seem to care what restaurateurs do (unless they close for three days or more in a week). As a result, the closing days given throughout this chapter, and the Entertainment chapter, are subject to change.

Where to Eat

Bars Some bars, known as *vinai*, are good places to either snack or put together a full meal from a range of enticing options on display. This is more of a lunchtime option than for your evening meal.

Restaurants, Trattorie & Osterie, Fiaschetterie & Pizziccherie The standard name for a restaurant is *ristorante*. Often you will come across something known as a *trattoria*, by tradition at least a cheaper, simpler version of a ristorante. On pretty much the same level is the *osteria*. The *pizzeria* needs no explanation.

A *fiaschetteria* may serve up snacks, sandwiches and the like, usually at the bar while you down a glass of wine or two. It is a particularly Tuscan phenomenon, as indeed is the *pizziccheria*, which traditionally sold cheeses and sausages (and in many cases still does). A *tavola calda* (literally 'hot table') usually offers cheap, pre-prepared meat, pasta and vegetable dishes in a self-service style.

Wine lovers should look out for the local *enoteca*. These places offer snacks and sometimes full meals to accompany a selection of wines. Their business is the latter – food is viewed as an accompaniment to your chosen tipple(s). Generally the idea is to try the wines by the glass.

The problem with all this is that nowadays all the names seem to have become interchangeable. It would appear restaurant

Fast Food Florence-Style

Some habits die hard. When Florentines feel like a fast snack instead of a sit-down lunch, they might well stop by a *trippaio* for a nice tripe burger (well, tripe on a bread roll). It may sound a little nauseating to the uninitiated but it's really not that bad. McDonalds has very definitely arrived in Florence, but the American giant fronted by the silly-looking clown has yet to snuff out local preferences. But then, who knows what a generation fed on the Big Mac might think of tripe rolls in years to come?

Savouring fine wines is one of the great pleasures of the palate in Florence, and for many there is nothing better than a couple of glasses of a good drop accompanied by simple local snacks – sausage meats, cheeses, *ribollita* (vegetable stew) and the like. And the good news is that the tradition of the *vinaio* has won new life in the past few years in Florence. You may never see the word 'vinaio' on the doorway, but the idea remains the same. The old traditional places still exist – often dark little grog shops where you can get a bite to eat too. Look out for the sign 'Mescita di Vini' (roughly, 'wine outlet').

At **Enoteca Fuoriporta** (Map 2; ☎ 055 234 24 83, Via Monte alle Croci 10r) the wine list comprises hundreds of different wines (and an impressive roll-call of Scotch whiskies and other liquors). You can order from a limited list of *primi* ('first dishes') for a pleasant evening meal. The desserts are also good. It is closed on Sunday.

Hidden deep in the San Frediano area **Le Barrique** (Map 5; ☎ 055 22 41 92, Via del Leone 40r) offers a limited *menù del giorno* (menu of the day) or, for those just stopping in for a quick drink or two, snacks at the bar. Again the emphasis is on wine, although the pasta dishes are good. It also offers a selection of Tuscan and French cheeses. It is closed on Monday.

At **Fiaschetteria** (Map 5; ☎ 055 21 74 11, Via dei Neri 17r) you can drop by for an excellent ribollita for L11,000, accompanied by a few glasses of wine. It is closed on Monday.

It seems barely conceivable that within about 10 seconds' walk off Piazza della Signoria, which is lined with tourist rip-off restaurants, one of the city centre's last surviving, more or less genuine, osterie should remain. In **Vini e Vecchi Sapori** (Map 6; ☎ 055 29 30 45, Via dei Magazzini 3r) there is barely room to swing a Florentine rat, but you can eat decently and taste some solid local wines for about L25,000 a head. They also import *fragolino*, a strawberry-flavoured wine made in the north-east of Italy.

Another choice is **Le Volpi e l'Uva** (Map 3; ☎ 055 239 81 32, Piazza dei Rossi 1r), hidden away off the Oltrarno end of the Ponte Vecchio, where you can sample cheeses, have a *tramezzino* (sandwich) and try out new wines. It is closed on Sunday and holidays.

owners consider it more enticing for punters to call their places osterie (or even *hostarie*, the olde worlde version). In all cases, it is best to check the menu, usually posted by the door, for prices.

Don't judge an eatery by its tablecloth. You may well have your best meal at the dingiest little establishment you can find.

Occasionally you will find places with no written menu. This usually means they change the menu daily. Inside there may be a blackboard or the waiter will tell you what's on – fine if you speak Italian, a little disconcerting if you don't. Try to think of it as a surprise. If you encounter this situation in an overtly touristy area, you should have your rip-off antenna out.

Most eating establishments have a cover charge, which ranges from L1500 up to L10,000(!). You usually have to factor in a service charge *(servizio)* of 10% to 15%.

Where Not to Eat

You may not wish to know this but many of the touristy restaurants – especially in the centre of town – have a rather ruthless attitude to food, their customers and their employees. How does it make you feel to know that a number of pizzerie employ foreigners without papers at slave rates to churn out pre-prepared pizzas? The base and sauce are ready to go, just tip canned mushrooms on the top, heat and serve. Delicious. The process with other dishes in some trattorie (perhaps they should be called 'trap-orie') is similar. Mountains of precooked pasta get the reheat treatment – you can be sure most if not all ingredients are canned and your hosts will do their best to make sure the elements of your salad have been well aged.

Didn't want to spoil your appetite, but this is the state of affairs. How to recognise these places before it's too late? It's not always easy. Many of the places on the most touristed squares and streets, especially if they have outdoor dining, tend to fall roughly into this category. If no locals are eating in the place you are considering, ask yourself why. If you see tour groups gobbling down identical meals – stay away! Places that need to advertise themselves

loudly or that display menus in a variety of languages are often suspect. Unfortunately, there are some noble exceptions to these rules, so at the end of the day you need something of a sixth sense and a small portion of good luck.

What to Eat

Breakfast Italians rarely·eat a sit-down breakfast. They tend to drink a cappuccino, usually *tiepido* (warm), and eat a croissant *(cornetto)* or other type of pastry (generically known as a *brioche*) standing at a bar.

Snacks A few bars serve filling snacks with lunchtime and pre-dinner drinks. At others you can pick up reasonable *panini* (filled rolls or sandwiches). Otherwise snack food is more the preserve of the *trippai* and occasional vinai (see the boxed text 'Fast Food Florence-Style' on the previous page). You'll also find numerous outlets where you can buy pizza by the slice *(al taglio)*.

Another option is to go to an *alimentari* (delicatessen) and ask them to make a panino with the filling of your choice. At a *pasticceria* you can buy pastries, cakes and biscuits.

Lunch & Dinner Lunch *(pranzo)* is traditionally the main meal of the day and some shops and businesses close for two or three hours every afternoon to accommodate it.

A full meal will consist of an *antipasto*, which can vary from vegetables to a small offering of fried seafood. Next comes the *primo piatto*, usually a pasta or risotto, followed by the *secondo piatto* of meat or fish. This Italians usually accompany with a *contorno* (vegetable side-dish), though in some cases these latter are eaten separately. Salads *(insalate)* have a strange position in the order here. They are usually ordered as separate dishes and in some cases served as a replacement for the primo. Although there's nothing to stop you ordering a salad as a side order to a main (second) course, Italians as a rule do not seem to do so.

Although most restaurants offer a range of desserts, Italians sometimes prefer to round off the meal with fruit and *caffè*, the latter often at a bar on the way back to work.

Numerous restaurants offer a *menù turistico* or *menù a prezzo fisso*, a set-price lunch that can cost as little as L10,000 to L15,000 (usually excluding drinks). Generally the food is breathtakingly unspectacular (and sometimes just plain bad), with choices limited. From your tastebuds' point of view (if you are not overly hungry) you'd be better off settling for a good plate of pasta, some salad and wine at a decent restaurant. On the other hand, if you look at lunch as a mere refuelling stop, this could be the way to go.

The evening meal *(cena)* was traditionally a simpler affair, but habits are changing because of the inconvenience of travelling home for lunch every day.

Gelati At the tail end of lunch and dinner you can opt for a house dessert, but at least once or twice you should head for the nearest *gelateria* (ice-cream parlour) to round off the meal with some excellent *gelati*, followed by a *digestivo* (digestive liqueur) at a bar. Many Italians skip the gelato altogether. They tend to see it as a summertime treat and/or something for the kids.

Food Vocabulary

For a list of essential food vocabulary, see Food in the Language chapter towards the end of this book.

Florentine & Tuscan Cuisine

Staples In the dark years of the barbarian invasions of what was left of the Roman empire, times got exceedingly difficult for the bulk of Tuscans. Salt was scarce and *pane sciocco* (unsalted bread) became the basis of nutrition. Unsalted bread has remained a feature of local cooking ever since. Another basic product is olive oil – some of the best extra virgin olive oil, with its limpid emerald appearance, looks good enough to drink.

The main Tuscan cheese is *pecorino*, made with ewe's milk. It can be eaten fresh or after up to a year's maturing, when it is tangier.

Antipasti (Starters) You have the option of starting a meal with a 'pre meal'. The classic antipasti in Tuscany are *crostini*, lightly grilled slices of unsalted bread traditionally covered in a chicken-liver pate. Other toppings have become equally popular – the diced tomato with herbs, onion and garlic is a popular version virtually indistinguishable from the Pugliese *bruschetta*.

The other classic is *fettunta*, basically a slab of toasted bread rubbed with garlic and dipped in olive oil.

Another favourite, *prosciutto e melone* (ham and melon), is known well beyond the confines of Tuscany. Other cured meats and sausages are also popular.

Primi Piatti (First Courses) You may be surprised to learn that pasta does not occupy a place of honour in traditional Tuscan menus. Some believe it was the Arabs who introduced pasta to Sicily in the early Middle Ages. By the 14th century its use had definitely spread to Florence, but without displacing local favourites.

A light summer dish is *panzanella*, basically a cold mixed salad with breadcrumbs. Tomato, cucumber, red onions and lettuce are tossed into a bowl with stale bread that has been soaked and broken up. Mix in lots of oil, vinegar and basil and stick it in the fridge.

The winter equivalent is *ribollita*, another example of making use of every last scrap. Basically a vegetable stew, again with bread mixed in, it is a hearty dish for cold winter nights. *Pappa di pomodoro* is a bread and tomato paste served hot.

Pasta did take hold in Tuscany and among the dishes that have long kept locals munching happily are: *pappardelle sulla lepre* (ribbon pasta with hare), *pasta e ceci* (a pasta and bean broth) and *spaghetti allo scoglio* (spaghetti with seafood – pretty much a national dish). Ravioli and tortelli, both kinds of filled pasta, are also popular.

Note It appears certain culinary stereotypes have gone too far. Many people seem to believe that *parmigiano* (parmesan cheese) should be scattered atop all pasta dishes, no

PLACES TO EAT

matter what the sauce. Nothing could be further from the truth. You should never use it with any kind of seafood sauce, for the simple reason that the cheese kills the flavour instead of enhancing it! If your waiter doesn't offer you the cheese, 99 times out of 100 there will be a perfectly good reason.

Secondi Piatti (Second Courses) In keeping with the simplicity for which local cuisine is known, meat and fish tend to be grilled. Meat eaters will sooner or later want to try *bistecca alla fiorentina*, a slab of Florentine steak. It should not cost more than L50,000–60,000 a kilogram, which is usually sufficient for two. Traditionally the meat was taken from bovines in the Val di Chiana, but often this is no longer the case.

Cuisines born of poverty found a use for everything. As a result, animal innards became an integral part of the local diet. *Rognone*, a great plate of kidneys, is one fave, although you might find it a little much. Tripe is particularly prized by some, and you can get it at roadside stands (in the Cascine park for example). *Trippa alla fiorentina* is prepared with a kind of carrot, celery, tomato and onion mix. For the true tripe fans, locals distinguish between various bits of the gut – one particular part of the tripe is also known as *lampredotto*, just in case you are contemplating having some on a roll without knowing what it is.

Tuscany is hunting territory and wild boar *(cinghiale)*, along with other game meats, finds its way to many restaurant tables.

Main meals are accompanied by side dishes *(contorni)*. Among the possible choices are *fagiolini alla fiorentina*, little beans prepared with tomatoes, fennel seeds, onion and garlic.

Dolci (Desserts) Apart from the classic gelati (see Gelati earlier in the chapter), you will find no shortage of house desserts.

Tiramisù, a rich mascarpone dessert, has become something of a worldwide favourite among lovers of Italian food. It is actually a Venetian speciality, but is not too hard to stumble across in Florence.

More in the Tuscan tradition are almond-based biscuits, such as Siena's *cantucci* or *biscottini di Prato*, best chomped while you sip sweet Vin Santo. Lighter but also using almonds are *brutti ma buoni* ('ugly but good') pastries. *Schiacciata con l'uva* is a flat pastry covered in crushed red grapes.

Foreign & Vegetarian Cuisine

The availability of ethnic cuisine in Florence is limited, aside from the ubiquitous Chinese option. Still, a few possibilities do present themselves, including Japanese, Indian, Cuban, Mexican, Israeli and a couple of felafel and shawarma bars.

Seriously vegetarian restaurants are thin on the ground, but this shouldn't create too much hardship, as the salads and many first courses should meet most vegetarians' requirements.

DRINKS
Nonalcoholic

Water While tap water is reliable, most Italians prefer bottled mineral water *(acqua minerale)*. It will be either sparkling *(frizzante/gasata)* or still *(naturale/ferma)* and you will be asked in restaurants and bars which you would prefer. If you want a glass of tap water, ask for *acqua del rubinetto*.

Coffee The first-time visitor is likely to be confused by the many ways in which the locals consume their caffeine. As in other Latin countries, Italians take their coffee seriously. Consequently they also make it complicated!

First is the pure and simple *espresso* – a small cup of very strong black coffee which you will get by just asking for *caffè*. A *doppio espresso* is a double shot of the same. You could also ask for a *caffè lungo*, but this may end up being more like the watered-down version with which Anglos will be more familiar. If you want to be quite sure of getting the watery version, ask for a *caffè americano*.

Enter the milk. A *caffè latte* is coffee with a reasonable amount of milk. To most locals it is a breakfast and morning drink. The stronger version is a *caffè macchiato*, an espresso with a dash of milk. Alternatively, you can have *latte macchiato*, a glass of hot milk with a dash of coffee. The *cappuccino* is a frothy version of the caffè latte. You can ask for it *senza schiuma* (without froth), in which case the froth is scraped off the top. It tends to come lukewarm, so if you want it hot, ask for it to be *molto caldo*.

In summer, the local version of an iced coffee is a *caffè freddo*, a long glass with cold coffee, sometimes helped along with ice cubes.

To warm up on winter nights, a *corretto* might hit the spot – an espresso 'corrected' with a dash of grappa or some other spirit. Some locals have it as a morning heart-starter.

After lunch and dinner it wouldn't occur to Italians to order either caffè latte or a cappuccino – espressos, macchiatos and correttos are perfectly acceptable. Of course, if you want a cappuccino there's no problem – but you might have to repeat your request a couple of times to convince disbelieving waiters that they have heard correctly.

An espresso or macchiato can cost from an Italy-wide standard of L1400 or L1500 standing at a bar to L5000 sitting outside at the Gilli cafe (see Places to Eat – Top End later in the chapter).

Tea Italians don't drink a lot of tea *(tè)* and, if they do, generally only in the late afternoon, when they might take a cup with a few *pasticcini* (small cakes). You can order tea in bars, though it will usually arrive in the form of a cup of warm water with an accompanying tea bag. If this doesn't suit your taste, ask for the water molto caldo or *bollente* (boiling). Good-quality packaged teas, such as Twinings tea bags and leaves, as well as packaged herbal teas, such as camomile, are often sold in grocery stores and some bars. You can find a wide range of herbal teas in a herbalist's shop *(erboristeria)*.

Granita A drink made of crushed ice with fresh lemon or other fruit juices, or with coffee topped with fresh whipped cream, *Granita* is a Sicilian speciality but you'll see it in Florence in the summer months too.

Soft Drinks The usual range of international soft drinks are available in Florence, though they tend to be expensive. There are some local versions too, along with the rather bitter, acquired taste of Chinotto.

Alcoholic Drinks

Beer The main Italian labels are Peroni, Dreher and Moretti, all very drinkable and cheaper than the imported varieties. If you want a local beer, ask for a *birra nazionale*. Italy also imports beers from throughout Europe and the rest of the world. You can find anything from Guinness to Australia's XXXX on tap *(alla spina)* in *birrerie* (bars specialising in beer).

Wine Of course, wine *(vino)* is an essential accompaniment to any meal, and liqueurs *(digestivi)* are a popular way to end one. Italians are justifiably proud of their wines and it would be surprising for dinnertime conversation not to touch on the subject at least for a moment.

Prices are reasonable and you will rarely pay more than L15,000 for a good bottle of wine, though prices range up to more than L40,000 for the better stuff. An exceptional *riserva* (reserve) can cost you L150,000.

If you just want something to wash down your meal, you will generally be safe spending L8000 or even less in a supermarket. Don't expect too much at this level though.

You will often see many wines from other Italian regions on sale, but only rarely from beyond Italy.

Since the 1960s, Italian wine has been graded according to four main classifications. *Vino da tavola* (table wine) indicates no specific classification; IGT *(indicazione geografica tipica)* means that the wine is typical of a certain area; DOC *(denominazione di origine controllata)* wines are produced subject to certain specifications (regarding grape types, method and so on); and DOCG *(denominazione di origine controllata e garantita)* shows that the wine is subject to the same requirements as normal DOC but that it is also tested by government inspectors. These indications appear on labels.

A DOC label can refer to wine from a single vineyard or an area. DOC wines can be elevated to DOCG after five years' consistent excellence; they can also be demoted.

Further hints come with indications such as *superiore*, which can denote DOC wines above the general standard (perhaps with greater alcohol content or longer ageing). 'Riserva' is applied only to DOC or DOCG wines that have aged for a specified time.

In general, however, the presence or absence of such labels is by no means a cast-iron guarantee of anything. Many notable wines fly no such flag. Many a vino da tavola is so denominated simply because its producers have chosen not to adhere to the regulations governing production. These sometimes include prestige wines.

Your average trattoria will generally only stock a limited range of bottled wines, but better restaurants (some listed later in the chapter) present a carefully chosen selection from around the country. Wine shops and some osterie concentrate on presenting a range of fine wines rather than on the food, which is almost seen as an accompaniment to the drink.

Generally if you simply order the house wine (*vino della casa*, by the glass, half litre or litre) you will get a perfectly acceptable table wine to accompany your food. Otherwise, look at the wine list.

Tuscan Wines Tuscany, perhaps surprisingly to some readers, actually ranks third (behind Il Veneto and Piedmont) in the production of classified wines. In total volume it comes eighth of the 20 regions, largely because the lie of the land is restrictive.

Six of Italy's DOCG wines come from Tuscany. They are Brunello, Carmignano, Chianti, Chianti Classico, Vernaccia di San Gimignano and Vino Nobile di Montepulciano.

There was a time when the bulk of wine coming out of Tuscany was the rough and ready, if highly palatable, Chianti in flasks. The Chianti region remains the heartland of Tuscan wine production but for a good generation now vintners have been concentrating on quality rather than quantity.

The best of them, Chianti Classico (a red), comes from seven zones in many different guises. The base for all is the Sangiovese grape, though other grape types are added in varying modest quantities to produce different styles of wine. Chianti Classico wines share the Gallo Nero (Black Cockerel) emblem that once symbolised the medieval Chianti League (a league of Chianti towns that cooperated in defence and similar matters). Chianti in general is red and dry, though ageing requirements differ from area to area and even across vineyards.

The choice doesn't stop in the Chianti. Among Italy's most esteemed and priciest drops is the Brunello di Montalcino (in Siena province). Until not so long ago only a handful of established estates produced this grand old red, but now everyone seems to be at it. At one reckoning some 60 producers turn out a good product, which as usual varies a great deal in style depending on soil, microclimate and so on. Like the Chianti reds, the Sangiovese grape is at the heart of the Brunello. It is aged in casks for four years and then for another two years in bottles. Another Sangiovese-based winner is Vino Nobile di Montepulciano, named after a hilltop town in Siena province. The grape blend and conditions here make this a quite distinctive wine too, but it is not aged for as long as the Brunello.

Tuscany is not all about reds. Easily the most widely known white is the Vernaccia di San Gimignano. Some of the best is aged in *barriques* (small barrels), while others are sometimes oaked.

A regional speciality that will appeal to the sweet tooth is Vin Santo (Holy Wine), a dessert wine also used in Mass. Malvasia and Trebbiano grape varieties are generally used to produce a strong, aromatic and amber-coloured wine, ranging from dry to very sweet (even the dry retains a hint of sweetness). A good one will last years and is traditionally served with almond-based Cantucci biscuits.

For hints on particular vineyards you might want to invest in a wine guide. Burton Anderson's *Wines of Italy* is a handy little tool to have in your back pocket.

Liqueurs After dinner try a shot of *grappa*, a strong, clear brew made from grapes. It originally comes from the Grappa area in the Veneto region of north-eastern Italy, although plenty is also produced locally. Or you could go with an *amaro*, a dark liqueur prepared from herbs. If you prefer a sweeter liqueur, try an almond-flavoured *amaretto* or the sweet aniseed *sambuca*.

PLACES TO EAT – BUDGET

Eating at a good trattoria can be surprisingly economical – a virtue of the competition for customers' attention. The definition of budget eating is as solid as a bowl of soup, so what follows is an arbitrary division. Anywhere you can fairly safely assume you will pay below about L40,000 for a full meal has been classed as 'budget' – ranging from sandwich joints (where you might pay around L5000 for a filling roll) through trattorie serving respectable and good-value set meals (menù del giorno or menù turistico) and upwards into the modest categories of restaurant. Anything from around L40,000 up to L80,000 is classed here as mid-range, and everything beyond that as top end. Obviously in that category the sky's the limit.

City Centre

The streets between the Duomo and the Arno harbour many pizzerie where you can buy takeaway pizza by the slice for around L2000 to L3000, depending on the weight. Unless otherwise states, All restaurants mentioned in this section are on Map 6.

When it comes to eating a full meal while you pinch pennies, it's hard to go past *Ristorante Self-Service Leonardo (☎ 055 28 44 46, Via de' Pecori 35r)*, where mains cost L7500 for lunch or dinner. It is closed on Saturday.

Hostaria il Caminetto (☎ 055 239 62 74, Via dello Studio 34), south of the Duomo, has a small, vine-covered terrace. Pasta costs around L7000 and a main from L9000 to L10,000. It is closed on Wednesday.

Trattoria Le Mossacce (☎ 055 29 43 61, Via del Proconsolo 55r) serves pasta for around L9000 and a full meal with wine

will cost up to L40,000. It is closed at the weekend.

Trattoria del Pennello (☎ 055 29 48 48, Via Dante Alighieri 4r) is popular but not as cheap as it once was. Pasta starts at L10,000. The place has been serving up food for the past four centuries! It is closed on Sunday evening and Monday. *Ristorante Paoli (☎ 055 21 62 15, Via dei Tavolini 12)* has magnificent vaulted ceilings and walls covered with frescoes, and food to match. It offers a L36,000 set menu and pasta from L12,000. It is closed on Tuesday.

A tiny but welcoming little corner is *Trattoria Pasquini (☎ 055 21 89 95, Via Val di Lamona 2r)*. The cheerful guy who runs it, Giacinto, offers a varied menu that includes Tuscan meals such as tripe or bistecca alla fiorentina, and a mix of other national dishes. Great wreaths of garlic and tomato grace the little bar, while the simple timber furnishing and dimly lit, vaulted ceiling all help to create a cosy atmosphere. It is closed on Wednesday.

Trattoria da Benvenuto (☎ 055 21 48 33, Via Mosca 16r), on the corner of Via dei Neri, is hardly an ambient dining experience, but the food is reliable and modestly priced. Mains include several Florentine favourites, including lampredotto and bistecca, while the pasta dishes are an interesting mix, including a decent *rigatoni alla siciliana*. A full meal can cost around L35,000. It is wise to reserve a table. The trattoria is closed on Sunday.

Among the great little treasures of Florence is *Angie's Pub (☎ 055 239 82 45, Via dei Neri 35r)*, east of the Palazzo Vecchio, which offers a vast array of panini and focaccia, as well as hamburgers, Italian-style with mozzarella and spinach, and real bagels. A menu lists the panini, but you can design your own from the extensive selection of fillings; try one with artichoke, mozzarella and mushroom cream. Prices start at around L4000. It is closed on Sunday.

Virtually on Piazza San Pier Maggiore is a pleasant, reasonably priced little trattoria, *Osteria Natalino (Map 7; ☎ 055 28 94 04, Borgo degli Albizi 17r)*. It is closed on Monday.

euro currency converter L10,000 = €5.16

East of Stazione di SM Novella

The restaurants mentioned in this section can be found on Map 3.

Mario (☎ *055 21 85 50, Via Rosina 2r)*, a small bar and trattoria near Piazza del Mercato Centrale, is open only for lunch and serves pasta for around L6000 to L8000 and mains for L7000 to L9000. It is very busy. It is closed on Sunday. A few doors down is *Ristorante ZàZà* (☎ *055 21 54 11, Piazza del Mercato Centrale 20)*, so popular that it's growing. Try the *ravioli al pesto* – an unusual combination that works well. Prices are similar to those at Mario's. The restaurant is closed on Sunday.

Trattoria Il Messere (☎ *055 47 19 67, Via Guelfa 52 or 98r)* is a pleasant little place with first courses for up to L15,000 and mains ranging from L14,000 to L25,000. It is closed on Tuesday.

Vegetarian One of the few vegie options in town is *Il Vegetariano* (☎ *055 47 50 30, Via delle Ruote 30r)*. It is an unassuming little place with a limited (but changing) menu. A meal with wine can cost under L30,000 per head. It is closed on Monday and it opens for dinner only at the weekend.

Stazione di SM Novella to Ognissanti

Snacks Those wanting to spend little *and* switch from Italian fare should make a bee-line for *Amon* (Map 3; ☎ *055 29 31 46, Via Palazzuolo 6)*. Here you can pick up cheap Egyptian sandwiches such as felafel or *foul* (fava beans) for around L4000 – a couple of these will fill most reasonable paunches. It is closed on Sunday.

Restaurants At *La Grotta di Leo* (Map 3; ☎ *055 21 92 65, Via della Scala 41)*, a pleasant trattoria with a L20,000 set menu, pizzas and pasta cost from L8000. *Trattoria il Contadino* (Map 3; ☎ *055 238 26 73, Via Palazzuolo 71r)* offers a L15,000 set menu, including wine. The food is no great culinary exploit, but it is perfectly edible and at a price hard to beat. The restaurant is closed on Sunday. *Ristorante Dino* (Map 3; ☎ *055 28 70 88, Via Maso Finiguerra 6–8)* is a

good little trattoria, with pasta up to L12,000 and main courses from L14,000 to L28,000. It is closed on Sunday.

Da il Latini (Map 5; ☎ *055 21 09 16, Via dei Palchetti 4)*, just off Via del Moro, is an attractive trattoria serving pasta from L6000 and main courses from L14,000. They don't take reservations and the place can get packed – queues are not unusual. So many Florentines can't be wrong. It is closed on Monday.

Trattoria dei 13 Gobbi (Map 5; ☎ *055 21 32 04, Via del Porcellana 9r)* sets a somewhat artificially bucolic scene inside but in a tasteful fashion. A full meal will set you back around L25,000. The trattoria is closed on Monday.

Santa Croce & East of the Centre

Snacks, Bars & Cafes A charming and teeny little place for a long cappuccino over the paper or a tasty lunch (try the pumpkin soup – *crema di zucca)* is *Caffellatte* (Map 5; ☎ *055 47 88 78, Via degli Alfani 39r)*. They are into health foods and are open until 1 am. It is closed on Sunday.

At *Il Nilo* (Map 7; Arco di San Piero 9r) you can pick up fat shawarma and felafel sandwiches for up to L6000. It's open until midnight and is closed on Sunday.

Need a pastry at 4 am? A couple of *bakeries* open to sell their wares straight out of the oven. One without a name or street number is at Via del Canto Rivolto (Map 5), just north of Via dei Neri. As you will see they want you to be quiet and get out of there asap. If the neighbours should become vexed by street noise, they may have to stop the practice.

Restaurants For a cheap and tasty set-lunch menu for just L14,500, head for the vaulted *Caffetteria Piansa* (Map 7; ☎ *055 234 23 62, Borgo Pinti 18r)*. You basically point and choose from a limited number of dishes. Get in early, as by 2 pm it's all over. The restaurant doesn't serve dinner and is closed on Sunday.

Osteria de' Benci (Map 5, ☎ *055 234 49 23, Via de' Benci 13r)* is a consistently good bet. They change their menu often and serve up honest slabs of bistecca alla fiorentina. The food is consistently good and prices moderate. It is closed on Sunday.

Another option for a light lunch is *Antico Noè* (Map 7; ☎ 055 234 08 38, Arco di San Piero 6r), a legendary sandwich bar just off Piazza San Pier Maggiore. They have two sections. The sandwich bar is takeaway only, but next door they run a cosy little restaurant where you can enjoy fine cooking to slow jazz and blues tunes. Try the refreshing *farfalle al salmone e pomodori freschi* (butterfly pasta with salmon and fresh tomato). It is closed on Monday.

Not far off, *Danny Rock* (Map 7; ☎ 055 234 03 07, Via Pandolfini 13r) does not sound promising, but inside is an immensely popular place for pizza, pasta and, perhaps best of all their *insalatoni* (huge salads). One of the latter with a drink or two could make a filling and ultra-healthy meal for about L20,000. Be prepared to queue for a bit.

Osteria del Gatto e la Volpe (Map 5; ☎ 055 28 92 64, Via Ghibellina 151r), on the corner of Via de' Giraldi, serves pizzas from L7000 and pasta from L7500. It is closed on Tuesday. The *Sant'Ambrogio Caffè* (Map 7; ☎ 055 24 10 35, Piazza Sant'Ambrogio 7), along Via Pietrapiana, is a bar and restaurant where you can get a sandwich from L3000 or pasta from L7000. It is closed on Sunday.

Heading further north and away from the city centre, *EDI House* (Map 5; ☎ 055 58 88 86, Piazza Savonarola 8r) is a big bright place where locals pile in to feast mainly on pizza, although they have a reasonable choice of other dishes on the menu. It's moderately priced. It is closed on Tuesday.

International Cuisine For something a little different, you should try out *Ruth's* (Map 7; ☎ 055 248 08 88, Via Farini 2a) by the synagogue. They serve tasty kosher Jewish food – it bears a strong resemblance to other Middle Eastern cuisine and makes a good choice for vegetarians. For L16,000 you can have a plate of mixed dips with couscous, felafel, filo pastry pie and potato salad, quite filling in itself. The *fattoush*, a finely chopped and liquidy salad mixed

with pita croutons, is a tad bitter. It is closed on Friday evening and Saturday.

If meat is OK with you, get yourself down to *La Bodeguita* (Map 3; ☎ 055 21 78 82, Via San Gallo 16r). Although the people running it aren't Cuban, they put on tasty versions of *picadillo* (a spicy minced meat with vegetables and rice) and some good chicken dishes. The mojitos are mean. They encourage you to express your appreciation by scribbling on the walls (better than putting graffiti on the monuments, they reason). It is closed on Sunday.

Not far off you can vary the theme slightly and go Mexican at *Café Caracol* (Map 6; ☎ 055 21 14 27, Via Ginori 10r). Happy hour goes from 5.30 to 7 pm, after which you tuck into nachos, fajitas and other Mexican amuse-gueules. As Mexican goes it ain't going to win any prizes, but where else in Florence can you get corn chips and salsa? It is closed on Monday evening.

For takeaway tandoori and other Indian specialities drop by *Ramraj* (Map 6; ☎ 055 24 09 99, Via Ghibellina 61r). You can eat at the bench if you want. The food is OK if unspectacular, but it is quick and modestly priced. It is closed on Monday.

Vegetarian For *scaloppina di seitan* or a *bavette al gorgonzola*, the place to come is *Sedano Allegro* (Map 7, ☎ 055 234 55 05, Borgo della Croce 20r). Dishes are pretty cheap, ranging from L9000 to L12,000. It is open for lunch and dinner and in the warmer months they open up a garden at the rear. It is closed on Monday.

Oltrarno

Cafes The simple Art-Nouveau decor of *Il Caffè* (Map 5; ☎ 055 239 62 41, Piazza Pitti) makes it a charming place for breakfast or an afternoon coffee. Should you want to eat, they serve cheap no-nonsense set meals for up to L18,000. The cafe is closed on Monday.

Snacks & Bars The pizzeria and restaurant *Borgo Antico* (Map 5; ☎ 055 21 04 37, Piazza Santo Spirito 6r) is a great location in summer, when you can sit at an outside table and enjoy the atmosphere in the piazza. If you decide to go for the expensive menu which changes daily you can get some surprisingly good meals. *Cabiria (Map 5; ☎ 055 21 57 32, Piazza Santo Spirito 4r)* is a popular cafe which also has outdoor seating. It is closed on Tuesday.

If you are in need of food of indifferent quality in the wee hours of the morning, about the only choice you have is *Caffè La Torre (Map 7; ☎ 055 68 06 43, Lungarno Benvenuto Cellini 65r)*. See also the listing under Oltrarno in the Entertainment chapter.

Restaurants The gritty working-class San Frediano quarter of the Oltrarno is sufficiently distant from the hurly-burly of the centre to have a quite individual feel. You can dig up a few fairly simple and solid local eateries here. *All'Antico Ristoro di Cambi (Map 5; ☎ 055 21 71 34, Via Sant'Onofrio 1)* is one such place. The food is traditional Tuscan, the bistecca alla fiorentina succulent and the final bill is unlikely to exceed L45,000. The restaurant is closed on Sunday.

If you don't mind eating elbow to elbow with complete (local) strangers, *Al Tranvai (Map 2; ☎ 055 22 51 97, Piazza Tasso 14r)* is a wonderful rustic Tuscan eatery. They serve up a limited range of pastas as primi and specialise in animal innards, including *trippa alla fiorentina* (tripe). Don't worry, if that doesn't attract they have some meat alternatives. It's nothing fancy but is authentic cooking. You can get away with L30,000 for a full meal. It is closed at the weekend.

Osteria del Cinghiale Bianco (Map 6; ☎ 055 21 57 06, Borgo San Jacopo 43), to the right as you cross Ponte Vecchio, specialises in Florentine food. As the name suggests, wild boar is on the menu – the *pappardelle al cinghiale* (a plump kind of pasta in wild boar sauce) is music to your tastebuds on a cold evening. It is closed on Tuesday and Wednesday.

Angiolino (Map 5; ☎ 055 239 89 76, Via di Santo Spirito 36r) is an excellent trattoria where you can eat a meal, including bistecca, for around L40,000. If offal doesn't turn you off, you might like their *rognoncino*, a main

of chopped kidney in a balsamic vinegar marinade. It is closed on Monday.

Trattoria Casalinga (Map 5; ☎ 055 21 86 24, Via de' Michelozzi 9r) is a bustling, popular eating place. The food is great and a filling meal of pasta, meat or vegetables plus wine will cost under L25,000. Don't expect to linger over a meal, as there is usually a queue of people waiting for your table. It is closed on Sunday. *Trattoria I Raddi (Map 5; ☎ 055 21 10 72, Via dell'Ardiglione 47r)*, just near Via de' Serragli, serves traditional Florentine meals and has pasta from L8000 and main courses from L14,000. It is closed on Sunday.

Il Cantinone di Gallo Nero (Map 5; ☎ 055 41 06 69, Via di Santo Spirito 6r) specialises in crostini, starting at L3500. It is something of a Florentine classic for down-to-earth Tuscan cooking, with local dishes accompanied by good Chianti wines. You will pay around L40,000 a head. It is closed on Monday.

I Tarocchi (Map 5; ☎ 055 234 39 12, Via dei Renai 12–14r) is a popular pizzeria/trattoria serving excellent pizzas for around L10,000. The first and second courses each cost about the same, and the former alone are enough to satisfy most people's hunger. The menu changes daily. It is closed on Monday.

Mr Sandman

The *renai* in the street name Via de Renai refers to the burly *renaioli* (sandmen) who, in the second half of the 19th century, found employment by trawling the depths of the Arno for sand. What previously had been a dredging exercise turned into something more profitable with the building boom that came around the 1860s as the city was drastically restructured. Sand (*rena* to the locals) was in big demand as an essential construction ingredient. The Florentine writer Vasco Pratolini later wrote that they sold sand like bread in those busy days. Not that the renaioli lived in luxury. Working from dawn to dusk, your average sandman collected two cubic metres of sand, enough to earn him his daily bread.

❉ ❉ ❉ ❉ ❉ ❉ ❉ ❉ ❉ ❉ ❉ ❉ ❉ ❉

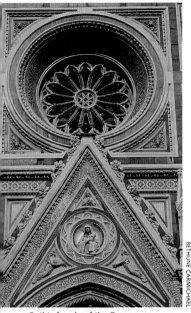

The neo-Gothic facade of the Duomo

Ghiberti's 'Gate of Paradise' at the Baptistry

The Palazzo Vecchio's illuminated Torre d'Arnolfo

The Duomo is full of intricate architectural detail.

BETHUNE CARMICHAEL

DAMIEN SIMONIS

JULIET COOMBE

BETHUNE CARMICHAEL

JOHN HAY

Whether it's ice cream, tripe burgers, mozzarella salads, *panini* or chestnuts you're after, Tuscan cooking is a feast for the eyes as well as the palate.

Osteria Antica Mescita (Map 7; ☎ 055 234 28 36, Via San Niccolò 60r) is a fine little eating hideaway where the kitchen stays open until near after 11 pm. The food is tasty without being spectacular, but throw in a good bottle from their impressive wine collection and the equation is good. You can get away with about L40,000 for a salad, main course, wine and dessert. It is closed on Sunday.

International Cuisine For fine Indian dining at comparatively reasonable prices it is hard to go past *Ashoka* (Map 2; ☎ 055 22 44 46, Via Pisana 86r). Reckon on spending from L40,000 a head. It is closed on Monday.

PLACES TO EAT – MID-RANGE
City Centre
Snacks At *Procacci* (Map 6, ☎ 055 21 16 56, Via de' Tornabuoni 14r) they have for a century been tickling Florentine (and quite a few foreign) palates with their *panini tartufati*. Not so much a nutritional exercise as a ritual, these tasty little numbers can be accompanied by a drop of Tuscan wine or even a cup of tea. The green marble used for the bar and tabletops is the same used in the city's great monuments. Genteel locals sometimes take a bottle to one of the said tables, order some nibblies and generally have a cosy time of it. It's definitely more of a winter scene, when it stays open until about 9 pm (no later than 8 pm in the warmer months). You can also buy wine and foodstuffs, including truffles, to take away (see Food & Drink in the Shopping chapter). It is closed on Sunday and Monday.

Restaurants Ribollita is the house speciality at *Trattoria Coco Lezzone* (Map 6, ☎ 055 28 71 78, Via Parioncino 26r), but they will do you a genuine bistecca alla fiorentina for L60,000 (enough for two in most cases) if you book it ahead. One oddity is that they do not serve coffee in this tiny place tucked away off Via del Purgatorio. The restaurant is closed on Sunday and holidays.

Cantinetta Antinori (Map 6, ☎ 055 29 22 34, Piazza degli Antinori 3) might be the place for you if you suddenly have a moment in which you feel both posh and flush. For about L70,000 a head you can enjoy a reasonable meal accompanied by some fine wines – it is for the latter that most people come here. It's not a bad choice if you have to impress a suit or two. It is closed at the weekend.

If you feel like elegant dining along the river (no views though), try *Ristorante Città di Firenze* (Map 6; ☎ 055 21 77 06, Lungarno Corsini 4). The fare is traditional Tuscan food and the building was for a while home to Louis Bonaparte, king of Holland in the heyday of his nepotistic benefactor Napoleon. The dining room is graced by enormous paintings and wine barrels. Expect to pay around L70,000 a head. Perhaps a nobler tenant than Louis Bonaparte in the same building is the Consorzio Vino Chianti – these guys (hopefully) keep a watch on the quality of Italy's most internationally known wines. It is closed on Monday.

International Cuisine A reasonable representative of the Japanese genre can be found at *Eito* (Map 6, ☎ 055 21 09 40, Via dei Neri 72r). Wednesday is 'sushi' day, when you are offered the choice of two set menus, one with 12 pieces of sushi and six of sashimi (L50,000) and one the other way around (L35,000). Both come with miso soup. Otherwise they have quite a broad selection of dishes, which can be washed down with Kirin or Sapporo beer. The restaurant is closed on Monday.

East of Stazione di SM Novella
An excellent fish restaurant is *Ristorante Lobs* (Map 3; ☎ 055 21 24 78, Via Faenza 75). For L60,000 you can enjoy a seafood menu including oysters and Norwegian salmon and Soave wine from the country's north-east. Otherwise, mains cost around L32,000. Round off with *sorbetto al vodka*. Another plus about this joint is that cooking stops about 12.30 am – a rare thing in a town where few restaurants serve after 11 pm.

PLACES TO EAT

Next door at the ***Trattoria Antichi Cancelli*** *(Map 3;* ☎ *055 21 89 27, Via Faenza 73r)* they specialise in grilled meats. Or you could have a go with *cervello fritto* (fried brains) or even Florentine tripe (not a personal favourite). A full meal with wine and dessert will arrive roughly at the L50,000 mark. It is closed on Monday.

Stazione di SM Novella to Ognissanti
Traditional Tuscan cooking is offered at ***Sostanza*** *(Map 5;* ☎ *055 21 26 91, Via del Porcellana 25r)*. It's one of the best spots in town for bistecca alla fiorentina. Mains start at L18,000. It is closed at the weekend.

Oltrarno
Hidden away in a back street, ***Trattoria Cavolo Nero*** *(Map 5;* ☎ *055 29 47 44, Via Ardiglione 22)* will set you back up to L60,000 a head – try the *carpaccio di Angus con rucola e grana* (carpaccio of Angus steak with rocket and grana cheese). It is closed on Sunday.

L'Erta Canina Club *(Map 2;* ☎ *055 24 22 50, Via all'Erta Canina 6r)* is a strange little place with the look of a misplaced clubhouse. The low-lit atmosphere is tranquil and the food is good. Try the *filetto di manzo lardellato di Brunello*, a beef fillet prepared in Brunello wine. They sometimes organise a little music (of questionable taste) and the place is not bad for a late evening drinkie. After your meal you could take a stroll along this back lane through vineyards guarded by retiring villas. You feel like you're already deep in Chianti country. This piece of real estate must come with an amazing price tag. It is closed on Tuesday.

Ristorante Beccofino *(Map 5,* ☎ *055 29 00 76, Piazza degli Scarlatti)* is a recent addition to the Florentine culinary scene, and a rare breed in this town. The grub is pricey and the surroundings nouvelle chic – no traditional bucolics in here thank you (and check out the stainless steel, floor-lighted loos!). You can sip at the bar and then try a vaguely adventurous style of cooking. Pasta dishes in particular represent a departure from tradition – try the *gnocchetti* with sweet onions. The wine list is impressive. This is a good opportunity to try some lesser known but fine blends – the so-called Super Tuscans that thumb their noses at the DOC establishment. Expect to pay around L70,000 a head. It is closed on Sunday.

International Cuisine Technically operating as a club, ***Momoyama*** *(Map 5;* ☎ *055 29 18 40, Borgo San Frediano 10r)* touts itself as a sushi bar offering 'inventive food'. When you come the first time you fill out a form and possibly show some form of ID to become a member. It is an original dining experience for Florence, with its bare minimalist ochre-coloured decor and tables spread over floors reaching well into the back. As you enter you will see a Japanese chef preparing some of the dishes right in front of you. It's not particularly cheap (reckon on a minimum of L70,000 a head) but quite a change from the Italian stuff (if you have actually managed to get sick of that yet). It is closed on Monday.

Outside Florence
One of the city's better known restaurants is ***La Capponcina*** *(☎ 055 69 70 37, Via San Romano 17r, Settignano)*, which is up in the hills overlooking Florence from the northeast. The kitchen is known in particular for its *tagliata di manzole*, succulent beef fillets sliced up and served on a bed of lettuce. Sitting in the garden is a true pleasure in summer, where you are sure of being several degrees cooler than in town. Count on paying about L70,000 a head for a full meal. You can get bus No 10 from the train station, or Piazza San Marco. This service is replaced from 9 pm by the No 67. The restaurant is a few steps off the central Piazza San Tommaseo, where the bus terminates. It is closed on Monday.

Not dissimilar in terms of price, atmosphere and clientele is the ***Trattoria Cave di Maiano*** *(☎ 055 5 91 33, Via Cave di Maiano 16, Fiesole)*. Getting here without a car is a little tricky as the restaurant is actually in Maiano, a *frazione* (division) of Fiesole, and off the bus routes. You could try getting a taxi from central Fiesole. The restaurant is closed at Monday lunchtime.

In both cases you should book ahead.

PLACES TO EAT – TOP END
City Centre
Cafes One of the city's finest cafes is *Gilli* (Map 6; ☎ 055 21 38 96, *Piazza della Repubblica*), and it's reasonably cheap if you stand at the bar: a coffee at the bar is L1500, but at a table outside it is L5000. It is closed on Tuesday.

Rivoire (Map 6; ☎ 055 21 44 12, *Piazza della Signoria*) is one of Florence's classic old cafes. True, it is inevitably somewhat touristy because of its position, but if only once this is the place to sip on a cup of sticky *cioccolata* after overdosing on art in the Uffizi. It is closed on Monday.

Santa Croce & East of the Centre
The restaurants mentioned in this section can be found on Map 7.

Ristorante Cibrèo (☎ 055 234 11 00, *Via de' Macci 118r*) and its twin osteria, *Cibrèo Caffè* across the road at Via A del Verrocchio 7r, combine to form a fine restaurant – the atmosphere is of a slightly dated elegance, with lots of wood panelling and frosted glass. At the osteria you can eat well for around L40,000, while the restaurant is a much more refined and expensive outing. You can book for the latter but the former is first in, first served. They are closed on Sunday and Monday.

One of the city's finest restaurants, *Enoteca Pinchiorri* (☎ 055 24 27 77, *Via Ghibellina 87*) is noted for its nouvelle cuisine Italian-style. A meal will cost L180,000 a head. It is closed on Sunday and Monday. For those in search of elegant dining and equipped with elastic purses – but not quite *that* elastic – head a bit further down the street to *Ristorante alle Murate* (☎ 055 24 06 18, *Via Ghibellina 64*). A full meal here will set you back about L80,000 a head. It is closed on Monday.

GELATERIE
People queue outside *Gelateria Vivoli* (Map 5; ☎ 055 29 23 34, *Via dell'Isola delle Stinche*), near Via Ghibellina, to delight in the gelati widely considered to be the city's best. It is closed on Monday. *Perchè No?* (Map 6; ☎ 055 239 89 69, *Via dei Tavolini 19r*), off Via del Calzaiuoli, is excellent. It is closed on Tuesday.

La Bottega del Gelato (Map 2; ☎ 055 47 67 76, *Via del Ponte Rosso 57r*) is just off Piazza della Libertà and does a particularly enticing range of fruit-flavoured gelati. It is closed on Sunday.

If you happen to be in the area, drop in to *Baroncini* (Map 2; ☎ 055 48 91 85, *Via Celso 3r*). It is one of the best-known gelaterie in town. They use fresh fruit in the fruit-flavoured options and also do great yogurt and *sorbetto al limone*. It is closed on Wednesday.

SELF-CATERING
You can save money by getting your own groceries and throwing your own sandwiches and the like together. A handy central supermarket is *Standa* (Map 7; *Via Pietrapiana 42*).

Entertainment

Several publications list the theatrical and musical events and festivals held in the city and surrounding areas. The free bimonthly *Florence Today*, the monthly Firenze Information and Firenze Avvenimenti, a monthly brochure distributed by the council, are all available (haphazardly) at the tourist offices. The APT (Azienda di Promozione Tursitica) publishes an annual booklet listing the year's events, as well as monthly information sheets.

Firenze Spettacolo, the city's definititive entertainment publication, is available weekly for L3000 at newsstands. Posters at the tourist offices, the university and in Piazza della Repubblica advertise current concerts and other events.

A handy centralised ticket outlet is Box Office (Map 3; ☎ 055 21 08 04) at Via Luigi Alamanni 39. It opens from 3.30 to 7.30 pm on Monday and from 10 am to 7 pm Tuesday to Saturday. A Web ticket service, Ticket One (www.ticketone.it) allows you to book tickets for theatre, football and other events on the Internet. It also provides a list of outlets around town where you can pick up tickets in person.

PUBS & BARS

Overall, Florence's nightlife is limited. This should perhaps not be all that surprising since, at the end of the day, we are talking about a provincial town. Long-termers find themselves hanging out in the same places, but there is enough variety to hold visitors' interest for a while.

The APT's *Firenze per i Giovani (Florence for Young People)* brochure provides a list a mile long of bars and clubs. For a good overview of the latest events and 'in' spots in the club and live music scene, try to get hold of the local free booklet *Zero55*. You can pick it up in some of the bigger pubs and bars.

Many bars and pubs tend to shut by around 1 am, but there are enough exceptions to this rule to keep you going to 3 am and sometimes later still. It is a little difficult to classify all places strictly as either bars, live music venues or discos/clubs, so the following subdivision is a little arbitrary.

Around Piazza di SM Novella

Foreigners hang about at *The Chequers Pub (Map 3; ☎ 055 28 75 88, Via della Scala 7–9r)*, one of a growing gaggle of UK/Irish-style pubs in Florence.

City Centre & Towards Santa Croce

The rather cramped *Kikuya Pub (Map 5; ☎ 055 234 48 79)*, Via de' Benci 43r has a long happy hour from 7 to 10 pm, when the unusually generous cocktails can cost as little as L5000. You can also hear live music here occasionally.

Robin Hood's Tavern (Map 5; ☎ 055 24 45 79, Via dell'Oriuolo 58r) is yet another of the Irish contingent. They have 'ladies' night' on Thursdays. Just walking past these places makes you think you have time-warped out of Italy.

If you feel like pub-crawling, you could shimmy along to the *Lion's Fountain (Map 7; ☎ 055 234 44 12, Borgo degli Albizi 34r)*. It opens until 2 am on Friday and 2.30 am on Saturday.

Blob (Map 6; ☎ 055 21 12 09, Via Vinegia 21r) is tucked away in the shadow of Palazzo Vecchio. A tiny place with a bar, some cramped upstairs lounge seating and a rather mixed music selection, it can be a cosy nook to hang out until 3.30 am. They will ask you to take out a membership card *(tessera)* for L15,000 (and you may not be able to get and use it until the following day) – hang on to it for future visits.

A cool place to hang out in style is *Café Mambo (Map 7; ☎ 055 247 89 94, Via Giuseppe Verdi 47r)*. It's a hip little bar with a Latin theme where you can sidle up for some saucy salsa lessons if you're of a mind to do so. It is closed on Sunday.

Sant'Ambrogio Caffè (Map 7; ☎ 055 24 10 35, Piazza Sant'Ambrogio 7r), as well as being a place to get snacks, is especially dedicated to the sipping of cocktails. They cost L10,000 a hit. The cafe is closed on Sunday. See also Restaurants under Santa Croce & East of the Centre in the earlier Places to Eat chapter.

Another stop on the cocktail circuit, *Rex Caffè (Map 7; ☎ 055 248 03 31, Via Fiesolana 25r)* is a hip place to sip your favourite mixed concoction, or maybe two in happy hour (from 5 to 9.30 pm). Occasionally you'll strike live music and when it's vinyl the taste is eclectic. You get a mixed crowd in here, from arty types through to students and even a sprinkling of beautiful people. Whether it's a Martini at the bar or a quiet beer sitting at one of the metallic tables, this is one of the better watering holes in town.

The William (Map 7; ☎ 055 246 98 00, Via Magliabechi 7r) is a barn of a place along Irish pub lines, but it has found quite a following among young Florentines in search of a pint of ale.

A fun and buzzy place to hang out until 2 am is *Salamanca (Map 7; ☎ 055 234 54 52, Via Ghibellina 40r)*. The tapas have a vaguely Italian flavour about them but otherwise the place manages to exude an almost convincing pseudo-Spanish atmosphere with plenty of hearty flamenco rock and South American sounds to keep punters returning to the bar for more – it's a favourite with Latin Americans living in Florence. Sangria and Latin American cocktails predominate. It's closed on Tuesday.

Oltrarno

A cool corner bar nicely placed off the main tourist trail is *Il Rifrullo, (Map 7; ☎ 055 234 26 21, Via San Niccolò 55r)*. The bar snacks are generous and the evening cocktails good. You can sit by the bar or wind your way to the garden on warm summer nights.

If Il Rifrullo seems a little too snooty for your tastes, you could mosey around to the nearby *Zoe (Map 5; ☎ 055 24 31 11, Via dei Renai 13r)*, which heaves as its squadrons of punters end up spilling out on to the street. Don't even think about trying to park around here late of an evening. Although the bar attracts a mixed crowd, the majority tend to be aged around 25 or younger. It's closed on Sunday.

Summer Frolics

While some clubs and bars close for a month or more in summer, all sorts of places spring to life to keep Florentines occupied through the hot months. In terms of nightlife, several options are worth looking out for.

The centuries-old former convent and women's prison **Le Murate** *(Map 7; ☎ 0338-5060253, Via dell'Agnolo)* becomes the scene of nightly organised fun known as Vie di Fuga (Escape Routes) from June to September. Music, films projected on a huge screen, and other events are staged each night, though many locals use it as a place to kick on to after other bars have closed. Most nights it stays open until around 3 am.

Just off Piazza della Libertà, the rather odd-looking collection of buildings and performance spaces known as **Parterre** *(Map 2)* comes to life as a kind of all-in-one entertainment scene. Nightly performances of music of all types, theatre (for adults and kids) and so on are the order of the evening. Scattered about are a pizzeria, a gelateria, bars and shops.

Teatro dell'Acqua *(Map 2; ☎ 055 234 34 60, Lungarno Pecori Giraldi)* opens up for fun and music in the summer months. It attracts a mixed crowd and you can also get a bite to eat at the restaurant and pizzeria. You have to pay L5000 for a membership card *(tessera)* the first time you go – just remember to take it along if you decide to come back another time.

As the weather heats up the **Cascine** *(Map 2)* becomes a focal point for live music in Florence. Local and foreign acts appear throughout the warm months on the stage of the park's Anfiteatro.

Cabiria (Map 5; ☎ 055 21 57 32, *Piazza Santo Spirito 4r*) is a popular cafe by day that converts into a busy music bar by night. In summer the buzz extends on to Piazza Santo Spirito, which becomes a stage for an outdoor bar and regular free concerts. The drinking comes to a halt around 2 am on the square and in Cabiria. The cafe is closed on Tuesday.

Just a piazza away, *La Dolce Vita* (Map 5; ☎ 055 28 45 95, *Piazza del Carmine 6r*) attracts a rather more self-consciously select crowd of self-appointed beautiful types. During the week it's a fairly tame affair, with the clientele looking carefully dressy over a cocktail that lasts until closing time around 1 am. Things get busier from Thursday night on, when the same chic punters hang out in rowdier fashion until about 3 am.

One of the weirder places to get a late-night cocktail (and an indifferent pizza if you have the munchies) is *Montecarla* (Map 5; ☎ 055 234 02 59, *Via de' Bardi 2*). The place has changed hands a few times but all have remained faithful to the baroque kitsch aesthetic that inspired the place's originator – a prostitute of some fame in years gone by (hence the feminine version of the bar's name). It's all leopard skins, gaudy cushions, plush drapes and moody corners – very warm and cosy on a winter's evening, although it kind of belts you in the eye when you walk in for the first time. Mixed drinks cost around L12,000 and the place is generally open until at least 3 am. It's closed on Wednesday. They operate a 'membership' policy. You should be able to get away with filling out a card as a pro forma operation.

For all kinds of music from jazz to Latin rhythms, try *Caffè La Torre* (Map 7; ☎ 055 68 06 43, *Lungarno Benvenuto Cellini 65r*). This is a great place to just hang out drinking until the wee hours. The tipples are reasonable (around L10,000 for decent mixed drinks) and this is one of the only places in Florence where you can get a bite to eat well after midnight – that is, even at 4 am! Back to the UK-style pub theme for a moment, a rather pleasant one with a beer garden and largely local punters, if only because it's a bridge too far for most inter-lopers, is *James Joyce* (Map 2, ☎ 055 658 08 56, *Lungarno Benvenuto Cellini 1r*). Beamish is the main drop on tap. It's open until 1 am.

Right at the opposite end of the Oltrarno and a quite pleasant low-key example of the species is *The Gate Pub* (Map 5; ☎ 055 29 51 81, *Borgo San Frediano 102r*).

LIVE MUSIC

In some cases you may be asked to pay for membership – this is effectively like paying a one-off cover charge. If you are staying in Florence for any length of time give a local address so that you receive your card – generally valid for a year.

Often people just blag their way into a place. 'Yes, I'm a member but I left my membership card at home,' must be one of the most oft-used lines in Florence. In some places the request is a formality anyway and if you can't produce a card you will be asked to fill out a new one, or some kind of replacement form. Establishments do this to keep their noses clean with the law and maintain their status as 'clubs', which brings tax breaks.

In addition to the places in this section, some of those listed under Discos/Clubs later in the chapter also present live music on occasion. Check out *Firenze Spettacolo* or *Zero55* to see what's happening where.

City Centre & Towards Santa Croce

The *Jazz Club* (Map 4; ☎ 055 247 97 00, *Via Nuova de' Caccini 3*) is one of Florence's top jazz venues. The atmosphere is low-lit and the music to be enjoyed without necessarily killing the conversation – a good mix. At the weekend you should book a table if you are going in a group. You pay L10,000 to get in (which is for a year's membership). After that expect to pay around L12,000 a drink (a bottle of unspectacular Chianti will cost L35,000).

Another place where you can catch a little jazz, blues or whatever else they happen to come up with is *Bebop* (Map 3; ☎ 055

239 65 44, Via dei Servi 76r). You head downstairs to a mellow environment and averagely priced drinks. Basically the music consists of light covers but can be quite pleasant, and the place doesn't seem to get too crowded. Many nights the music is free, although if they are convinced they have a class act on you may pay as much as L20,000 (including a drink). They close by about 2 am.

Oltrarno

Pinocchio Club (Map 2; ☎ 055 68 33 88, Via Donato Giannotti 13) often has jazz on Friday and Saturday. Call ahead to make sure something is on. It's just south of Piazza Gavinana in the area of the same name south-east of the centre and across the Arno. Take bus No 23 from the Duomo to Piazza Gavinana. From Stazione di Santa Maria Novella take Nos 31, 32, 33 and 71 (night bus).

M'areseis (Map 5; ☎ 055 234 39 21, Via de' Bardi 4–6r) seems to flow in and out of favour, but can be a happening place later in the week. Live acts of all types perform on Wednesday and Thursday, while on Friday and Saturdays the club is put in the hands of DJs. Hang out by the red car opposite the bar or sweat it out where the bands play in the barely lit room to the right of the entrance. You have to pay L10,000 membership the first time around.

Other Areas

Some of the bigger venues are outside the town centre. *Tenax (Map 1; ☎ 055 30 81 60, Via Pratese 46)* is one of the city's more popular clubs and is well out to the north-west of town. It is one of Florence's biggest venues for Italian and international acts. Bus Nos 29 and 30 from Stazione di Santa Maria Novella will get you there, but you'll be looking at a taxi to get home.

Another venue for bands is *Auditorium Flog (Map 2; ☎ 055 49 04 37, Via M Mercati 24b)* in the Rifredi area, also north of the centre but a little closer than Tenax. It's not as big (in any sense) as Tenax but has a reasonable stage and dance area. Bus Nos 8 and 14 go from the train station.

Depending on who is playing at these venues, admission costs from nothing to L20,000. Then the drinks will cost you on top of that – around L10,000 for a mixer. Doors generally open at 10 pm.

DISCOS/CLUBS

Beware of places claiming that entrance is free. Very often late-night bars and clubs operate a rather strange system whereby you pay to leave rather than to enter. This may take several forms and often you get a chit on buying a first drink. You present the chit on your way out.

Around Piazza di SM Novella

Space Electronic (Map 3; ☎ 055 29 30 82, Via Palazzuolo 37) gets a mostly foreign crowd. It's rather tacky but for the record we include it.

City Centre & Towards Santa Croce

The *Maramao Club (Map 7; ☎ 055 24 43 41, Via de' Macci 79r)* has all the appearance of a bar but it stays open well past 2 am and the DJs keep the music suitably deafening so that you can at least imagine you're in a club. A fairly small, narrow affair with a minuscule dance area on what could be described as the poop deck at the back, it can get packed beyond comfort at the weekend. Admission with one drink costs L20,000. Drinks cost L10,000 thereafter. This is one of those places where you are given a card on entry that is then exchanged for a different one on purchase of a drink – you need this to get back out. It's closed on Monday and Tuesday.

A popular dance bar, with live music and DJs, is *Pongo (Map 7; ☎ 055 234 78 80, Via Giuseppe Verdi 59r)*. At its best, some have reported an atmosphere not unlike that in an acceptable London club. Given the limits of Florence nightlife, this is not a bad place to try, but don't leave it until the last half hour (they close at 4 am) as the music and thinning crowd of punters can be a disappointment. Admission costs L10,000 (which covers the cost of a compulsory drink). The bar is closed on Monday and Tuesday.

ENTERTAINMENT

euro currency converter L10,000 = €5.16

Andromeda (Map 6; ☎ 055 29 20 02, Via dei Cimatori 13) is one of those places we mention because it exists. The formula is young foreigners and local lads on the make. Let's say it enjoys a less than flattering reputation among Florentines. *Yab (Map 6; ☎ 055 21 08 84, Via de' Sassetti)* is in the heart of town near the main post office. It's supposedly an 'in' place with the locals but is really a little sad, with a reputation as more of a meat market than a serious dance venue. It is closed on Sunday and from late May to September.

Oltrarno

Somewhat hidden from the main tourist streams, *Jaragua (Map 2; ☎ 055 234 65 43, Via dell'Erta Canina 24a)* is a cool Latin place where you can admire some pretty slick movers or join in if you think you have rhythm. Sip on a Banana Mama, Jaragua or Culo Bello ('Nice Ass').

The Cascine

The city's two main clubs are here. They are quite fun, without exactly being the last word in European nightlife. In both you will be given a card on entry. You use this to get drinks (and food if you want). It is swiped on your way out, which is when you pay. You will be obliged to pay for at least one drink whether you have one or not – this is effectively your admission charge. A word of warning about the Cascine – it is a haunt for prostitutes, pimps and other interesting fauna. A taxi is probably not a bad idea when you head home.

Central Park (Map 2; ☎ 055 35 35 05, Via Fosso Macinante 2) is one of the city's most popular clubs. What music you hear will depend partly on the night, although as you wander from one dance area to another you can expect a general range from Latin and pop through to house. In summer you can also opt to dance inside or under the stars. You will be obliged to buy at least one drink at around L15,000. The place generally stays open until 6 am and is closed on Monday.

Nearby *Meccanò (Map 2; ☎ 055 331 33 71, Viale degli Olmi)* is right up there in popularity with Central Park. Three dance spaces offer house, funk and mainstream commercial music to appeal to a fairly broad range of tastes. Occasionally they put on special theme nights. The main dance floor is dominated by a pair of go-go dancers – presumably their mission is get people moving their booty. From here you can meander your way through the other dance floors. When business is humming, they open the upstairs floor too. Admission usually costs L15,000 to L20,000 and the club is open until 5 am. It is closed on Sunday, Monday and Wednesday.

Other Areas

Both *Tenax* and *Auditorium Flog* (see Other Areas under Live Music earlier in the chapter) usually serve as discos after the bands have finished or when none have been on.

Lidò (Map 2; ☎ 055 234 27 26, Lungarno Pecori Giraldi) is often thought of as a dance club but tends to put on a lot of jazz and soul music. Sometimes it's live, sometimes it's vinyl. The place can be a little cramped and attracts a fairly young crowd. Things generally kick off at 10 pm and admission is free. It's closed on Monday.

A short stroll further east along the Arno, *Escopazza Garden (Map 2; ☎ 055 67 69 12, Lungarno Colombo)* is a popular disco-bar with Florence's best-dressed set. Don't bother arriving before 11 pm unless you want to eat. It only begins to take off as a drinking and dance space after midnight. They sometimes offer live music. The bar is closed on Monday.

Kajà (Map 1; ☎ 055 896 18 98, Via Pistoiese 185) doubles as a pizzeria and 'maxi-disco', which means you can line your stomach before getting down to the business of dancing. Local opinion on it is divided, so given the difficulty of its location it is probably most interesting visiting the venue as an anthropological exercise. During the week admission is generally free, but at the weekend you may pay up to L25,000 to get in, depending on the occasion. It's closed on Monday. This place is out a little west of the A1 motorway in the

ENTERTAINMENT

San Donnino area. Although ATAF bus No 35 will get you close, it will take an eternity and still leave you walking quite a way. The only sensible option is a taxi there and back.

GAY & LESBIAN VENUES

Florence ain't exactly memorable for gay nightlife, but there are a few places you can head to, some genuinely gay and others 'gay-friendly'.

Bars

A relaxed little place to hang out and get acquainted with the remainder of the scene is *Piccolo Café (Map 7; ☎ 055 24 17 04, Borgo Santa Croce 23r)*. You should probably make this your first stop if you are a gay male. Try to pick up a copy of *Il Giglio Fuchsia (The Pink Lily)*, a locally produced gay guide to Tuscany. There are usually some lying around the place. The bar is open until 1 am.

Crisco (Map 7; ☎ 055 248 05 80, Via Sant'Egidio 43r) is a strictly men-only club open until 4 am during the week and 6 am on Friday and Saturday. It's closed on Tuesday.

Discos/Clubs

Florence has only two serious gay clubs where you can dance through the wee hours and then some. *Tabasco (Map 6; ☎ 055 21 30 00, Piazza di Santa Cecilia 3r)* boasts a disco, cocktail bar and dark room. Wednesday is leather night. It stays open until 4 am. On Tuesday, Friday and Saturday there is a disco and the place thumps until 6 am.

The alternative is *Flamingo Bar & Tabasco Disco (Map 7; ☎ 055 24 33 56, Via Pandolfini 26r)*. Italy's first gay bar, it's open until 4 am for gay men only. There's a dark room and video room. Thursday to Saturday it stays open until 5 am, with a disco for gay men and women. It's closed on Monday.

Both places are free to get in, but you are obliged to have at least one drink (at L12,000).

CLASSICAL MUSIC & OPERA

Concerts, opera and dance are performed at various times of the year at the *Teatro Com-*

unale (Map 2; ☎ 055 21 11 58, Corso Italia 16), on the northern bank of the Arno. In May and June the theatre hosts Maggio Musicale Fiorentina, an international concert festival. Contact the theatre's box office.

There are also seasons of drama, opera, concerts and dance at the *Teatro Verdi (Map 7; ☎ 055 21 23 20, Via Ghibellina 101)* from January to April and October to December. The Amici della Musica (☎ 055 60 84 20) organise concerts from January to April and October to December at the *Teatro della Pergola (Map 4; ☎ 055 247 96 51, Via della Pergola 18)*. Several other venues have theatre seasons, including the Teatro della Pergola during the winter.

CINEMAS

You have a few choices of venue for seeing movies in the original language *(versione originale)*. The *Odeon Cinehall (Map 6; ☎ 055 21 40 68, Piazza Strozzi)* screens such movies every Monday evening. For films in English most evenings except Monday, try *Cinema Astro (Map 5; Piazza di San Simone)*. *Astra Cinehall (Map 6; ☎ 055 29 47 70, Via de' Cerretani 54r)* screens films in English from Monday to Wednesday. Finally, *Cinema Goldoni (Map 5; ☎ 055 22 24 37, Via de' Serragli)* presents subtitled movies on Wednesday nights.

From June to September you can enjoy outdoor cinema at *Chiardiluna (Map 2; ☎ 055 233 70 42, Via Monte Uliveto 1)*. Screens are also set up in other places around town, for instance at the *Palazzo dei Congressi*, or Palaconcressi *(Map 3; ☎ 055 260 26 09, Viale Filippo Strozzi)* and *Terrazza Palasport (Map 2; ☎ 055 67 88 41, Viale Paoli)*. Yet another, *Arena 2*, operates at the horse racetrack (Ippodromo Visarno, also known as Ippodromo delle Cascine; Map 2). You enter from Piazzale delle Cascine. *Cinema Poggetto (Map 2, ☎ 055 48 12 85, Via Michele Mercati 24b)*. Programmes for all the summer season outdoor cinemas are available at the tourist office.

THEATRE & DANCE

One of the council's smarter ideas some years back was to convert the Leopolda

ENTERTAINMENT

train station (near the Cascine) into a performance space – in fact several spaces. Theatre, most of it of an avant-garde nature, is frequently the star, although occasionally concerts are put on too at the *Ex-Stazione* *Leopolda* *(Map 2; Viale Fratelli Rosselli 5)*. For programmes and tickets it is easiest to go to Box Office (see the beginning of this chapter) or any of the tourist offices in Florence.

Florentine Flourish

AC Fiorentina, Florence's top football side and Tuscany's only representative in the premier league (Serie A), came to life on 26 August 1926. The team was the result of a fusion between two local clubs, Palestra Libertas and Club Sportivo Firenze. In those earlier years the team's home ground was in Via Bellini, but in 1931 they moved to the Stadio Franchi, still in use today.

That same year Fiorentina entered Serie A and finished the season a creditable fourth. They had already discovered a fashion that would in following years come to dominate the game all over Europe – the purchase of star foreigners. That Fiorentina made it to fourth spot on the table was in no small measure due to the Uruguayan Pedro Petrone's 25 goals!

Things began to go downhill for Fiorentina in the following years and in 1938 the club was demoted to Serie B.

They were back in the top league after the war but since then they have managed to win only two shields – in 1955–56 and 1968–69. On the other hand, they have taken the Coppa Italia (Italy Cup) five times. They might have taken it for a sixth had they not been beaten by Parma in 1999.

In fact, the tail end of the 1998–99 season was a bitter disappointment for the boys from the Arno. They spent much of the season at the top of the table, but as if in a classic foot race, they peaked too soon and were overtaken in the dying rounds of the season by AC Milan and Lazio.

JANE SMITH

AC Fiorentina has been playing its football at the Stadio Franchi since 1936.

These two powered ahead neck and neck to the end of the season. AC Milan took the honours.

Argentine Gabriel Omar Batistuta is Fiorentina's top player nowadays, something of an idol and known as the *rey del gol* (goal king). By the end of the 1998–99 season he had booted well over a hundred Serie A goals in his Italian career. As the 1999–2000 season got under way 'Batigol' looked set to become the all-time record-breaking goal scorer in Serie A football.

The side and its fans seem utterly enthralled by the affable, long-haired 'bomber', as the local press refers to him ecstatically. In 1999 Fiorentina declared 30 September Batistuta Day, with a photo exhibit in the Fortezza da Basso and other festivities. They even launched a Web site with chat lines and guest book dedicated to the champ.

The side's coach is the equally colourful Giovanni Trapattoni, while the president is the cinema impresario Vittorio Cecchi Gori. Quite a line-up.

At the time of writing, the side had gotten off to a disappointing start, with the only true ray of sunshine coming in an upset European Cup victory over Arsenal at Wembley in October 1999.

SPECTATOR SPORT
Football (Soccer)

Your average Florentine is as passionate about football as the next Italian, but their side, AC Fiorentina, has never been quite one of the creme de la creme of the Italian premier league. For a little more history, see the boxed text 'Florentine Flourish'.

If you want to see a match, tickets, which start at L35,000 and can easily rise beyond L200,000, are available at the Stadio Comunale Artemio Franchi in the Campo di Marte (Map 2; ☎ 055 58 78 58) or at the Chiosco degli Sportivi ticket outlet (Map 6; ☎ 055 29 23 63; while you're at it you can have a flutter on the Totocalcio, or football pools) on Via Anselmi, just off Piazza della Repubblica. It is open from 9 am to 1 pm and 3 to 7 pm Tuesday to Thursday; from 9 am to 7 pm on Friday; from 9 am to 1 pm and 3 to 8 pm on Saturday; and from 9.30 am to noon on Sunday.

You can also book them through the Box Office ticket outlet or Ticket One.

Shopping

Let's dispel one illusion from the beginning. Shopping in Florence, no matter how low the lira (or euro), can rarely be qualified as cheap. Italians from other parts of the country can be heard sighing, with much shaking of heads, as they exclaim: '*Dio*, it's even more expensive than in...(insert town name of choice, but leaving out Venice)'.

Much depends on where you are coming from. You may find lots of goodies here that are hard to come by back home. If you have arrived from New York, on the other hand, you may equally discover that the same stuff is on sale in the Big Apple for less. Travellers from other parts of Europe (such as London) may, in spite of the high prices, still find shopping in Florence cheaper than at home. London is, after all, hideously expensive.

It can be fun to hunt around the markets for things like leather, but bear in mind that, with a couple of exceptions, most locals would not be seen dead in them. The merchandise is strictly for the passing tourist trade, although this doesn't mean you cannot find the odd appealing item. Always bargain.

Florence is a rather conservative town, so although the clothes, quality leather goods, ceramics and so on are often fine, they are rarely outrageously off-the-wall or bursting with rebellious originality. Classic styles and looks predominate.

Many products, such as handcrafted stationery, foodstuffs and wine, and certain other crafts, you won't encounter at home, so plenty of potential gift ideas or classy souvenir opportunities present themselves.

Remember that many shops do not open for the Monday morning session (which means they can be closed till 4 pm or even later).

ART GALLERIES

Florence is graced with a fair sprinkling of private galleries, but many deal in a staid diet of 'typical Tuscan' scenes and the like.

There is no particular concentration of them, but if this is your thing you'll bump into them sooner or later.

Galleria Tornabuoni
(Map 6; ☎ 055 28 47 20)
Via de' Tornabuoni 74r. A little more interesting, without completely abandoning mainstream tastes, is this place in the heart of the chic shopping quarter. You can stumble across some quite curious contemporary stuff here.

Biagiotti
(Map 6; ☎ 055 29 42 65)
Via delle Belle Donne 39r. For truly adventurous exhibitions, this place, tucked away in a street named after the one-time trade in perlyhawking that went on here, is worth checking out. What's on may not always be your cup of tea, but you won't know until you pop by.

Galleria Mentana
(Map 6; ☎ 055 21 19 85)
Piazza Mentana 2r. There's sometimes an interesting list of new artists exhibiting in here.

ART PRINTS & POSTERS

Aqua Fortis
(Map 6; ☎ 055 29 21 64)
Borgo San Jacopo 80r. You can find some exquisite old prints, of Florence and elsewhere, in this charming little shop. The prices are not so charmingly little.

BOOKS

After Dark
(Map 3; ☎ 055 29 42 03)
Via de' Ginori 47r. Although rather small, this interesting bookshop offers a mixed collection of new and second-hand books – mostly in English, a few in Italian. You can find some gay literature here too.

BM Bookshop
(Map 5; ☎ 055 29 45 75)
Borgo Ognissanti 4r. This bookshop claims to have the broadest range of books in English in town and it may be true. You can find a fair spread of books on Florence and Tuscany, as well as speciality books on art and fiction.

EPT
(Map 6; ☎ 055 29 45 51)
Via della Condotta 42r. In the centre of town this shop has a fair range of travel books and

maps and so on, with tons of stuff on Florence and Tuscany.

Feltrinelli International
(Map 6; ☎ 055 29 21 96)
Via Cavour 12r. Opposite the APT, it has a good selection of books in English, French, German, Spanish, Portuguese and Russian.

Internazionale Seeber
(Map 6; ☎ 055 21 56 97)
Via de' Tornabuoni 70r. Here you will find a fine selection of art books, as well as a reasonable offering of other books in several languages. The section on Florence and Tuscany is also impressive, though most of the material is in Italian only. It ranges from obscure treatises on Florentine society to the letters of Lorenzo the Magnificent.

Librairie Française
(Map 5; ☎ 055 21 26 59)
Piazza Ognissanti 1r. Located in the same building as the French consulate, this is the best place in town for French texts.

Libreria delle Donne
(Map 7; ☎ 055 24 03 84)
Via Fiesolana 2b. This is Florence's main women's bookshop. Most of the literature is in Italian, but you may find the listings on the notice board useful.

Libreria Il Viaggio
(Map 5; ☎ 055 24 04 89)
Borgo degli Albizi 41r. A good range of books useful to the traveller in Tuscany and beyond can be found here. The shop has a reasonable range of maps too.

L'Ippogrifo
(Map 6; ☎ 055 29 08 05)
Via della Vigna Nuova 5r. Rare books and manuscripts are bought and sold here.

The Paperback Exchange
(Map 4; ☎ 055 247 81 54)
Via Fiesolana 31r. This is the place to track down bargains in English. The store has a vast selection of new and second-hand books in English, including classics, contemporary literature, reference and best sellers, as well as travel guides. It is closed on Sunday.

Touring Club Italiano
(Map 2; ☎ 055 46 10 74)
Viale Spartaco Lavagnini 6r. For the best selection of maps and travel books (including Lonely Planet) on Italy and abroad, check this place out.

CERAMICS

Florence itself is not particularly known for its ceramics, but in the nearby town of Montelupo, west along the Arno, they have been pottering about since the Middle Ages.

If you don't have the chance to head over there to take a look around, plenty of stores in Florence satisfy the mostly foreign passing trade. Of course, the prices tend to be higher here than places more traditionally associated with the craft.

Il Principe
(Map 6; ☎ 055 29 49 79)
Via de' Guicciardini 110r. Here they have quite a good range of brightly enamelled items, from vases and plates to small trinkets.

Luca della Robbia
(Map 6; ☎ 055 28 35 32)
Via Proconsolo 19r. Since the end of the 19th century this shop has been turning out hand-made reproductions of 'robbiane', although they also offer a simpler range of ceramics.

Le Lampade
(Map 3; no phone)
Via Palazzuolo 70r. In this hangar of a workshop they turn out all sorts of stuff, from ashtrays to the most unlikely ornate urns that average humans can barely lift. They also do a lot of work in wood. An encouraging aspect of this place is that they seem to cater to a local market. After all, this is not exactly a star shopping street.

Arte Creta
(Map 6; ☎ 055 28 43 41)
Via del Proconsolo 63r. Elisabetta Di Costanzo turns out some original stuff, breaking with tradition in her use of predominantly green floral scenes on the majority of the objects for sale. They make a refreshing change from the usual stuff.

Marinelli
(Map 7; ☎ 055 234 45 49)
Via Giuseppe Verdi 31r. Since the 1960s a name in the Florentine ceramics business, this permanent display also demonstrates a clearly personal approach to the art that stands out from more traditional ceramics. 'Don't be afraid of white spaces' might be the motto behind these creations. The designs range from portraits to landscapes. Buyers should have their bank accounts well-charged.

CIGARETTES

Dying for a smoke and the shops are closed? There are a couple of dispensers scattered about town. The one on the corner of Borgo de' Greci and Piazza di Santa Croce (Map 7) also dispenses papers, lighters and filters.

CLOTHING & FASHION

Some of the great names in fashion started off in Florence, among them Gucci and Ferragamo. They and other biggies are all represented in Florence, mostly along Via de' Tornabuoni and Via della Vigna Nuova. Another major shopping street is Via Roma, where among other things you will find some good shoe stores (see Shoes later in the chapter).

The serious shopper, however, will find a greater range and probably better prices in Milan, the real fashion capital of the country. Those who don't have the time or inclination to include Milan in their trip should watch out for the sales. The winter sales start shortly after New Year and can go on into February. The summer sales start in July, with stores trying to entice Florentines to part with one last wad of dosh before they flood out of the city on holiday in August. Some shops prolong their sales to the end of August.

One other money-saving tip. Gucci and Prada each have massive wholesale stores in the Tuscan countryside. The savings, especially compared with, for example, London and Paris prices, can be considerable. Some Japanese tour companies organise trips that have these stores as their prime objective!

Family Feud

By the time Guccio Gucci founded a modest saddlery store in Florence in 1905, he had fallen out with his father, a straw-hat maker.

Guccio had five sons whom he brought into the slowly growing business, but he must have been one difficult individual. Having broken with his father, he set about encouraging rivalry between his sons, whom he also pushed to snitch on one another. For their misdeeds he would dish out violent hidings. Charming.

Having thus created the ideal harmonious family, he could hardly have been surprised by the thunderous rifts that would come later.

Aldo got the ball rolling in 1938, when he followed the family tradition and thumbed his nose at father, marching off to establish the first Gucci store in Rome. Aldo invented the company's double G logo and, in the wake of Guccio's death in 1953, expanded operations across Europe and eventually into the USA.

Aldo's son Paolo persuaded him and his brothers to broaden business by selling Gucci goods through outlets other than their own. By the early 1980s, the Gucci label had spread to products as diverse as coffee mugs and perfumes. Profits were booming, but Aldo and Rodolfo in particular resented what they saw as a cheapening of their products and name.

Boardroom spats became so venomous that Paolo tipped US authorities off about Aldo's tax evasion schemes, a step that ultimately landed the ageing head of the family empire in jail. Paolo got the sack, set up his own business (which failed) and in 1994 filed for bankruptcy. He died a year later.

Meanwhile the star of Rodolfo's son, Maurizio, was rising. He had defied his father (surprise surprise) in 1972 by marrying Patrizia, a laundry woman's daughter that Rodolfo described with consummate tact as a 'gold-digger'. In 1983, Maurizio inherited half the Gucci empire when Rodolfo died. He dumped Aldo from the board and bought out Paolo's brother Giorgio. Two years later he left his wife. In 1993 he sold Gucci to Investcorp, a Bahrain-based company.

Patrizia was less than euphoric. To her way of thinking, her divorce settlement of US$1 million had been 'little more than a plate of lentils' and she feared her two daughters might miss out altogether. That she wouldn't have minded seeing Maurizio dead was common knowledge. Wishful thinking became reality when Maurizio was gunned down in 1995. In 1998 Patrizia, who by then was known as the Black Widow, was found guilty of hiring the killer who sent her former husband to Jesus. With that, it would seem that the Gucci family, who would have done any feuding medieval Florentine clan proud, has consumed itself.

The Gucci outlet (☎ 055 865 77 75) is at Via Aretino 63 (the SS67 highway) at the northern edge of Leccio, about 30–40 minutes south-east of Florence on the road to Arezzo. It is open from 9 am to 7 pm Monday to Saturday.

The Prada outlet (☎ 055 919 05 80), which has the elegance of a high street store with a cafe and taxis waiting, is just outside the village of Levanella, about another 30 minutes' drive down the same road towards Arezzo. It opens from 9.30 am to 12.30 pm and 1.30 to 6 pm Monday to Friday (2.30 to 6 pm on Saturday) and in the afternoon only on Sunday. The quickest way from Florence by car is to take the A1 motorway, leave at the Valdarno exit and follow the signs for Montevarchi.

Gucci
(Map 6; ☎ 055 26 40 11)
Via de' Tornabuoni 73r. One of the most successful families in Florentine-born fashion. Of course the soap opera family saga has put a lot of spice into the name (see the boxed text 'Family Feud') but the fashion-conscious take little notice and keep on buying. The Japanese especially can be seen lining up to pay homage.

Ferragamo
(Map 6; ☎ 055 29 21 23)
Via de' Tornabuoni 16r. Another grand Florentine name (see the boxed text 'Ferragamo') the one-time shoe specialists now turn out a range of clothes and accessories for the serious clothing aficionado.

House of Florence
(Map 6; ☎ 055 28 81 62)
Via de' Tornabuoni 6. This is the place where you can spend around L120,000 for a leather belt or silk tie. Conservative handmade clothes and accessories for the well-lined. In fact you are warned of this as you reach the heart of the shop by a little sign reminding you that one never forgets quality but soon forgets the price paid for it. That might be open to debate.

Neuber
(Map 6; ☎ 055 21 57 63)
Via de' Tornabuoni 17. Here is another Mecca of Florentine class for men and women who want to cut an elegant swathe through life.

Loretta Caponi
(Map 6; ☎ 055 21 36 68)
Piazza Antinori 4r. If nothing is too good for your infant or small child, particularly girls, this store sells exquisite small persons' clothing (and a few things for big people too), some of it finely embroidered. Your three-year-old may not fully appreciate it, but will be dressed to impress.

Luisa
(Map 6; ☎ 055 21 78 26)
Via Roma 19–21r. For quality men's and women's clothing, this place is a regular stop on the Florentines' shopping circuit.

Raspini
(Map 6; ☎ 055 21 30 77)
Via Roma 25–29r. A classic Florentine purveyor of fine footwear, they also sell an enticing range of quality fashion for guys and gals.

Stockhouse Il Giglio
(Map 3; ☎ 055 21 75 96)
Borgo Ognissanti 86r. Cheap is a relative term in Florence, but you can pick up some interesting men's and women's fashion items here and occasionally turn up some genuine bargains. Name labels can come in at a considerable discount.

Stockhouse One Price
(Map 5; ☎ 055 28 46 74)
Borgo Ognissanti 74r. Although more densely stocked (in a smaller space) this place is along similar lines to Stockhouse Il Giglio.

Aside from these, all the well-known names pop up. To get you started, look out for the following (because they are packed into such a dense and small area, they do not appear on the map) on Via de' Tornabuoni: Louis Vuitton (No 26r); Damiani (No 30r); Trussardi (No 34r); Cartier (No 40r); Beltrami (No 48r); Yves St Laurent (No 31r); Gianfranco Lotti (No 57r); Bulgari (No 61r); Prada (No 67r) and Max Mara (No 89r). On Via della Vigna Nuova you can find: Furla (No 28r; for bags and accessories); Versace (No 38r); La Coste (No 33r); Valentino (No 47r) and Armani (No 52r). If they can't keep you occupied, there are still other stores on these and surrounding streets.

CRAFTS

Bartolucci
(Map 6; ☎ 055 21 17 73)
Via della Condotta 12r (www.bartolucci.com). The Bartolucci clan use pinewood to create a remarkable range of toys, models and trinkets that may appeal as much to adults as to kids. They have a second branch (☎ 055 239 85 96) at Borgo dei Greci 11a/r.

Ferragamo

Born in 1898 outside Naples, Salvatore Ferragamo made his first pair of shoes for his sister's first communion at the age of nine. They must have been good, because four years later he was already in charge of a shoe shop with six workers.

Ferragamo was hoping for bigger things and he moved to the USA in 1914. After a brief stint in Boston with his brothers, he headed across to Hollywood, where he started designing shoes and boots for the film industry – everything from Egyptian sandals to cowboy boots. From there it was a short step to making footwear for the stars when they were off the screen, and he began to build up an elite clientele, from Mary Pickford to John Barrymore.

When he returned to Italy in the early 1930s, Ferragamo set up a 'factory' in Via Mannelli in Florence with 60 employees all making certain parts of the shoes by hand. Ferragamo designed and created the shoes in Florence and sold them in the USA. That all went fine until the Great Depression hit and brought bankruptcy in 1933. By the time he had business up and running again, his clientele had become largely local. He was still creating new designs, including the cork wedge, which he patented in 1936.

In 1938, Ferragamo bought the Palazzo Spini-Feroni on Via de' Tornabuoni, where he had already moved his shop. The war years were difficult and Ferragamo did not resume exporting beyond Italy until 1947. By the 1950s, he had 700 employees producing 350 pairs of shoes a day entirely by hand. The glitterati, Italian and foreign, were again flocking to his store. Everyone from Audrey Hepburn to Sophia Loren was wearing Ferragamo's designs.

Salvatore died in 1960 and his wife, Wanda, took over. Under her and Fiamma, the eldest of their six children, the Ferragamo label was attached to a growing range of women's fashion accessories. Fiamma in particular was responsible for the expansion of production. She abandoned the policy of producing the shoes by hand. By the time Fiamma died in 1998, the company had a turnover of more than US$500 million.

La Bottega di Leonardo
(Map 6; ☎ 055 21 75 05)
Via de' Guicciardini 45r. This compact little store sells various odds and ends aimed at the passing tourist trade, but the kids might be interested in the Leokits – wooden models of some of Leonardo da Vinci's wacky inventions.

Zona
(Map 5; ☎ 055 230 22 72)
Via di Santo Spirito 11. Here you can find all sorts of handcrafted gewgaws. Lots of pleasing candles, South American textiles, stylish toys for the kids and more.

Cafissi
(Map 6; ☎ 055 29 21 64)
Borgo San Jacopo 80r. From tables to ducks, hand-turned items in wood are the curiosity here. It might be an expensive way to furnish your place, but a little browsing can't hurt. And who knows, you might just be tempted by one of the little wooden ducks.

Messico e Nuvole
(Map 7; ☎ 055 24 26 77)
Borgo degli Albizi 54r. Handcrafts from the American Indians and Mexico are the speciality

here, although the prices might induce you to wait until you do a trip to Mexico or the States.

DEPARTMENT STORES

Italian department stores are not as widespread or mega-galactic in size as some of their counterparts in the UK, USA or France. They can be useful places to look for reasonable quality clothing and cosmetics at more accessible prices. You won't find too many of the big names though.

La Rinascente
(Map 6; ☎ 055 239 85 44)
Piazza della Repubblica 1. The prince of Italian department stores, the Florence branch is rather modest but worth a look around.

COIN
(Map 6; ☎ 055 28 05 31)
Via de' Calzaiuoli 56r. A slightly downmarket version of La Rinascente, this is the place for practical shopping that most visitors probably won't need to do while in Florence.

ocal businesses present a lively display to tempt you away from Florence's more renowned
ttractions – and a further opportunity to empty your purse of some *lire*.

From cheese to pottery, religious artefacts to wine, and leather shoes to leather belts, Florence offers plenty of souvenirs to remind you of your stay.

Standa
(Map 7; ☎ 055 234 78 56)
Via Pietrapiana 42/44. This is the place to do your grocery shopping.

FOOD & DRINK

After eating and drinking your way through Florence, you may want to take some tasty reminders home with you. You can find a lot of local products in many simple *alimentari* (delicatessens). Remember also that the *enoteche* (wine shops) and *osterie* (snack bars) where you may have eaten often also sell bottles of wine. They can advise on the relative merits of their products.

Procacci
(Map 6; ☎ 055 21 16 56)
Via de' Tornabuoni 64r. You can come here to nibble and sip (see Snacks under Places to Eat – Mid-Range in the Places to Eat chapter) or buy stuff to take away, from fine Tuscan wines to home-made honey and jams. But the star is the truffle. You can obtain white truffles here in season or content yourself with a *panino tartufato*.

Lanzo Caffè
(Map 6; ☎ 055 29 08 34)
Via dei Neri 69r. This is not a bad store for an interesting mix of attractively packaged foodstuffs, such as *panforte* (a type of nougat) and products like honey from various parts of the region, along with a reasonable selection of wines from Tuscany and beyond.

Pegna
(Map 6; ☎ 055 28 27 01)
Via dello Studio 8. An interesting selection of Tuscan wines and foods, such as bottled *ribollita* (vegetable stew), are on sale, alongside products from other parts of Italy. It's a little pricey, so don't go buying your De Cecco pasta (which you can get in any decent supermarket) here.

Magazzino Toscano
(Map 6; ☎ 055 28 47 24)
Via dei Magazzini 2–4r. A great open space is dedicated to the sale of a wide selection of Tuscan products, from wines to sweets. You can also find books (some in English) on aspects of Tuscan cuisine, along with an array of kitchenware. The wine selection actually includes some good drops from beyond Tuscany.

La Galleria del Chianti
(Map 6; ☎ 055 29 14 40)
Via del Corso 41r. In spite of the name, the shop has on its shelves a selection of fine wines from around Tuscany, as well as top quality drops (such as Poli Grappa from Bassano del Grappa in Il Veneto) from other parts of the country.

Enoteca Romano Gambi
(Map 6; ☎ 055 29 26 46)
Borgo SS Apostoli 21-23r. This is another quality foodstuffs outlet. The shop claims to sell the 'best Tuscan biscuits' among a broad selection of other products ranging from wine and olive oil to chocolate. The prices are not exactly rock bottom, but the place is at least worth a browse.

GOLD & JEWELLERY

Back in 1563, Grand Duke Ferdinando I decided enough was enough. The butchers and greengrocers who for centuries had sold meat and vegies to the good citizens of Florence at their stalls along the Ponte Vecchio had to go. Not for central Florence the stench and rotting mess of dead flesh, but the glamour of all that glisters. The gold merchants haven't budged since.

Gherardi
(Map 6; ☎ 055 28 72 11)
Ponte Vecchio 8r. This is one of the name jewellers on the bridge where the prices on large clumps of gold adornment will make even the sturdiest credit card tremble. Cheaper items such as simple pendants might suit your shopping budget marginally better.

Vettori
(Map 6; ☎ 055 28 20 30)
Ponte Vecchio 37r. Another name location where you can have pieces handcrafted to suit your particular requirements.

Bijoux Cascio
(Map 6; ☎ 055 238 28 51)
Via Por Santa Maria 1r. A little easier on your fraying purse strings, these jewellers are also well-known in Florence for the beauty and finesse of their handmade pieces.

LEATHER

Florence has made something of a reputation for itself as a producer of fine leather goods. It has also long attracted foreigners looking for leather bargains. It is possible to find jackets, shoes, bags, wallets and just about anything else made of this material, and the quality ranges from exquisite to execrable.

In the latter category falls a lot of the cheap stuff on display in the street markets of Il Mercato Nuovo and San Lorenzo. People flock to them in search of a great buy, but you should beware of shoddy workmanship and materials. Always bargain hard – no matter what the stallholders tell you, there are no fixed prices on these goods. If you can't get the price you want on an item first time, look around some more.

Via de' Gondi and, more particularly, Borgo de' Greci are lined with leather shops of every possible description.

Getting away from the markets, some shops you might like to at least have a look around include:

Scuola del Cuoio
(Map 7; ☎ 055 24 45 33)
Piazza di Santa Croce 16. This is not a bad place to snoop around. If you get lucky you may see apprentices beavering away at some hide. Otherwise it is not a bad place to get some measure of quality-price ratios. Access is through the Basilica di Santa Croce.

Desmo
(Map 6; ☎ 055 29 23 95)
Piazza Rucellai 10. For those with fuller wallets, and perhaps with a desire to replace them with new ones, this is a good address for leather accessories and a range of clothes as well.

Il Bisonte
(Map 6; ☎ 055 21 19 76)
Via del Parione 31r. Here they concentrate on accessories, ranging from elegant bags in natural leather through to distinguished desktop items, leather-bound notebooks, briefcases and the like.

Bojola
(Map 6; ☎ 055 21 11 55)
Via de' Rondinelli 25r. For more than 150 years they have been turning out high-quality items here for the discerning lover of animal hides. From classic belts and wallets (which start at around L70,000) through to classy travel bags, this is one of Florence's top stops in the search for fine gifts.

MARKETS

The daily markets at San Lorenzo and Il Mercato Nuovo (also known as Mercato del Porcellino, or Piglet's Market) are the most visible in town, and the curious but uncommitted shopper can enjoy a rather tacky browse at either. Next to the predictable stocks of cheap (and sometimes nasty) leather gear are phalanxes of tourist tat and other far-from-useful paraphernalia. To get the feel for a real Florentine market, you need to look elsewhere.

Mercato delle Cascine
(Map 2)
Le Cascine, Viale Abramo Lincoln. Open on Tuesday only until around midday, this is Florence's only all-in-one market. Sufficiently far from the city centre to put most tourists off, it specialises in off-the-back-of-a-truck clothes and fabrics, along with other household products and a modest produce section. It's interesting to see Florentines in search of bargains here.

Mercato dei Pulci
(Map 7)
Piazza dei Ciompi. This flea market is where the townsfolk gather to poke about amid the mountains of junk and bric-a-brac that every self-respecting household should be able to cough up sooner or later. From antique furniture to ancient comic books, all sorts of junk turns up here. It's fun for a browse and occasionally you'll find genuinely interesting little items. It's in action daily except Sunday.

Mercato Centrale
(Map 3)
Piazza del Mercato Centrale. The main daily-produce market is under cover in the 19th-century market hall. Outside are all the leather and tat stalls of San Lorenzo. You can shop here Monday to Friday.

Mercato di Sant'Ambrogio
(Map 7)
Piazza Ghiberti. Buzzier and without the tourist tat element, this produce market is the best place to do your daily hunting for fresh products, from fruit and veg through to all sorts of local cheeses, sausages and other goodies. It operates daily except Sunday.

Mercato di Santo Spirito
(Map 5)
Piazza Santo Spirito. A cheerful little market with all sorts of odds and ends is held on this square most mornings.

Mercato dei Liberi Artigiani
(Map 6)
Loggia del Grano. Probably most easily described with the unfortunate phrase of 'hippy market', you can trot along here for floppy clothes, far-out head gear and a sometimes interesting range of mainly silver jewellery. It operates most days.

MISCELLANEOUS

Filistrucchi

(Map 7; ☎ 055 234 49 01)

Via Giuseppe Verdi 9. Need a wig or other theatrical devices? This has been *the* place to come for masks and the like since the early 18th century.

MUSIC

Ricordi Mediastore

(Map 6; ☎ 055 21 41 04)

Via de' Brunelleschi 8r. This nationwide chain store is Italy's vague equivalent of Virgin. They stock a solid range of CDs and tapes, Italian and international. You can also get sheet music.

KAOS

(Map 3; ☎ 055 28 26 43)

Via della Scala 65r. For all you hip young things, the best stock in the latest club sounds, along with some very old vinyl, can be picked up at this record store.

MUSICAL INSTRUMENTS

Ceccherini & Co

(Map 6; ☎ 055 21 00 31). Via de' Ginori 31r. This is a good address for those in search of instruments, including guitars.

PAPER & STATIONERY

Delicately and finely decorated paper is something of a speciality in Florence. You will find many shops selling sometimes exquisite letter paper, cards and the like, along with notebooks and other accessories covered in this kind of paper.

Festina Lente Edizioni

(Map 6; ☎ 055 29 26 12)

Via della Condotta 18r. For unusual stationery, postcards and so on, including exercise books with silk-print covers, this could be an interesting stop.

Nicoletta Manneschi

(Map 6; ☎ 055 21 34 36)

Via de' Castellani 16r. Nicoletta does all sorts of weird and wonderful things with papier mache, rice paper and similar things. Some of the items are a little trashy, but the book covers have a rough, original feel to them. Most of the more fanciful items would probably not survive the trip home anyway.

Pineider

(Map 6; ☎ 055 28 46 55)

Piazza della Signoria 13r. These purveyors of paper and related products have been in business since 1774 (they have another branch at Via de' Tornabuoni 76r). If you want to make a gift of stationery, this is the city's class act.

PERFUME

Officina Profumo Farmaceutica di Santa Maria Novella

(Map 3; ☎ 055 21 62 76)

Via della Scala 16. You can get all manner of scents at this centuries-old apothecary. See the following Pharmacy section.

Experimenta

(Map 6; ☎ 055 21 03 94)

Via dello Studio 25r. Want to have a chocolate or coffee wash? Get your tasty smelling bath foam, and other less unusual perfume products here.

PHARMACY

The ancient pharmacy of the Officina Profumo Farmaceutica di Santa Maria Novella (Map 3; ☎ 055 21 62 76) on Via della Scala 16 was set up by Dominican monks in the 13th century and opened to the public in the 17th century. When Napoleon confiscated church property early in the 19th century, the business went into private hands, in which it has continued to prosper. All sorts of traditional and herbal medicines and potions made to recipes handed down by the monks through to the present owners are made to treat everything from sore feet to bad breath. Need any witch hazel (*amamelide*) or St John's Wort (*iperico*)? Extract of heliotrope? This is the place for you. From the entrance you pass through a long hall to the 'pharmacy', a magnificent room with a high vaulted and frescoed ceiling. Here you buy mainly essences and perfumes. Pass on to the *erboristeria* (natural medicine) shop, which backs on to the cloister of the Basilica di Santa Maria Novella, for your herbal remedies. A sign of the times is that the Officina has opened branches in, among others, Rome, Milan, Venice, Bologna, Lucca, London and Paris.

PHOTOGRAPHY

You can lay your hands on film or have rolls developed in a plethora of places all over the centre of town.

Carnicelli
(Map 6; ☎ 055 21 43 52)
Piazza Duomo 4r. For more serious photography needs you could try this place. They also provide the standard services.

Bongi
(Map 6; ☎ 055 239 88 11)
Via Por Santa Maria 84-86r. This is a good store for photographic equipment, repairs and so on.

SHOES

Francesco da Firenze
(Map 5; ☎ 055 21 24 28)
Via di Santo Spirito 62r. If only every shoemaker made shoes this way. Hand-stitched leather is the key to this tiny family business. Expect to pay a fair amount for your footwear, but the investment will pay off. You can have shoes and sandals made to specification.

B&C
(Map 2; ☎ 055 22 23 63)
Via Romana 144. The shop doesn't really look like much, but you can get hold of some good quality women's footwear from a limited range at modest prices.

Casadei
(Map 6; ☎ 055 28 72 40)
Via de' Tornabuoni 33r. This is an interesting one for the ladies. You can go to town with the plastic on classically stylish knee-high boots or let your imagination fly a little on all sorts of shoes in a surprising (for this fairly conservative town) range of primary colours and angular design.

Fratelli Rossetti
(Map 6; ☎ 055 21 66 56)
Piazza della Repubblica 43–45. For one of the last words in classic elegant shoes, you should have a browse here.

Sergio Rossi
(Map 6; ☎ 055 29 48 73)
Via Roma 15. If you like your footwear (women only here) a little more adventurous, this could be the place for you.

SOUVENIRS

Florence does its level best to provide its guests with tacky reminders of their stay. From bad-taste T-shirts through to straw hats, David statuettes to cheap leather goods, you'll surely find what the dark and kitsch side of your nature deeply and secretly desires. Il Mercato Nuovo and the San Lorenzo market are reasonable hunting grounds, as are many of the stores in the heart of town.

TOYS

Dreoni
(Map 6; ☎ 055 21 66 11)
Via Cavour 33r. Florence's leading toy store ain't exactly Manhattan's FAO Schwarz, but it's full of fun stuff for kids and models that seem to attract just as many adults (well, blokes).

Città del Sole
(Map 5; ☎ 055 21 93 45)
Borgo Ognissanti 33-37r. Need a cute yo-yo? This shop is stacked with brightly coloured playthings for the discerning small anklebiter.

The Disney Store
(Map 6; ☎ 055 29 16 33)
Via del Calzaiuoli 69r. Probably shouldn't be mentioning this highly un-Italian shop, but kids seem to love it. If you need to mollify the little darlings, perhaps this is one method of bribery that will work.

WATCHES

Want a Rolex? Since the mid-19th century Orologeria Svizzera G Panerai & Figli (Map 6; ☎ 055 21 57 95), Piazza San Giovanni 16, has been the Florence rep for the best Swiss watchmakers. This is the top of the line, though it would probably be cheaper to go to Switzerland for your timepiece – fancy forking out up to L6,000,000 for one of those aforementioned Rolexes?

Excursions

Tuscany is jammed with striking cities, captivating villages and dreamy countryside and much of it is fairly easily reached, if perhaps not so quickly digested, in day trips from Florence. In a book dedicated to Florence alone it is impossible to do much more than deal glancing blows to the array of options. For a more complete survey of the splendours of this region, get hold of Lonely Planet's *Tuscany*.

ACCOMMODATION

This chapter is designed for the day-tripper, so no accommodation information has been provided. If you plan to do overnight trips, approach each town's APT (Azienda di Promozione Tursitica) or Pro Loco (local tourist info outlet) for accommodation lists.

An increasingly popular type of accommodation is *agriturismo*. What began as a modest means of extra income for people running farmhouses and the like in the countryside has become big business. Staying in an agriturismo generally guarantees modest prices and often charming accommodation on family property.

GETTING AROUND

General information on transport around Tuscany is given in the Getting There & Away chapter. Some specifics are given for each destination in this chapter.

To get around the countryside and small villages outside Florence, your own transport is ideal. Buses connect most places, but are often infrequent. It can be a frustrating way to get around if you end up somewhere that doesn't ring your bell and you have to wait ages to get out again.

Cycling is definitely an option but your thighs, calves, knees and butt need to be trim, taught and terrific as areas like the Chianti are distressingly hilly. It's surprising how all that beautiful scenery can come to appear diabolical in the eyes of the sweat-bathed, cramp-plagued cyclist. In any case you will need a good bike with lots of gears!

AROUND FLORENCE
Fiesole

Founded at the latest in the 5th century BC, Fiesole had a five-century head start on Florence. The main northern Etruscan settlement, Fiesole was in many respects a far more pleasant site for a town than the sweaty malarial river valley in which Roman Florentia was founded. As the stoic Romans set about building their town, the Etruscans sat back and probably regarded them with considerable ambivalence.

Then as now, the view over the Roman city is a draw card. Add the verdant olive groves and pretty valleys and you can understand why the likes of Boccaccio, Marcel Proust, Gertrude Stein and Frank Lloyd Wright (it's unlikely they have anything else in common!) have resided here.

The APT (☎ 055 59 87 20), Piazza Mino da Fiesole 36, has information on the town, walks and other activities.

Things to See & Do Opposite the tourist office in Piazza Mino da Fiesole is the **Duomo**. Much of its medieval splendour was lovingly erased by 19th-century renovation. Behind it is the **Museo Bandini**, featuring an impressive collection of early Tuscan Renaissance works.

Opposite the entrance to the museum on Via Portigiana, the **Zona Archeologica** features a 1st-century BC Roman theatre that is used from June to August for the Estate Fiesolana, a series of concerts and performances. Also in the complex are a small Etruscan temple, Roman baths and a small archaeological museum.

Both museums open from 9 am to 7 pm (to 5 pm in winter) daily except the first Tuesday of each month. The L10,000 ticket gives entry to both.

Getting There & Away ATAF bus No 7 from the main train station, Stazione di Santa Maria Novella, in Florence connects with Piazza Mino da Fiesole.

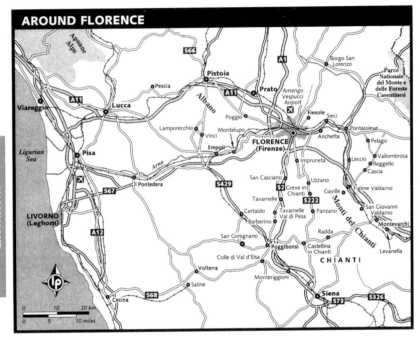

AROUND FLORENCE

Medici Villas

The Medicis built several opulent villas in the countryside around Florence as their wealth and prosperity grew during the 15th and 16th centuries. Most of the villas are now enclosed by the city's suburbs and industrial sprawl, and are easily reached by taking ATAF buses from the main train station. Ask at the APT in Florence about bus numbers and opening times.

The **Villa Medicea La Petraia**, about 3.5km north of the city, is one of the finest. Commissioned by Cardinal Ferdinando de' Medici in 1576, this former castle was converted by Buontalenti and features a magnificent garden. It's on Via della Petraia and opens from 9 am daily except on the second and third Monday of the month. Closing times vary from 4.30 pm in the winter months to 7.30 pm from June to August. Admission costs L4000.

Further north of the city, the **Villa Medicea di Castello** was the summer home of Lorenzo il Magnifico. You can visit the park only. Admission details are the same as for the Villa Medicea La Petraia.

The **Villa Careggi** (☎ 055 427 97 55), Viale Pieraccini 17, is open from 8 am to 6 pm daily except Sunday (groups must book ahead). Entry to the villa, where Lorenzo il Magnifico breathed his last in 1492, is free but access is limited as it is used as administrative offices for the local hospital.

Another Medici getaway was the **Villa di Poggio a Caiano**, about 15km from Florence on the road to Pistoia. Set in magnificent sprawling gardens, the interior of the villa is sumptuously decorated in frescoes and furnished much as it was early in the 20th century as a royal residence of the Savoys. You can wander in the grounds for free. Visits inside (L4000) are permitted every hour from 9.30 am to 6.30 pm (to 5.30 pm from mid-September to May). The easiest way to get there without your own transport is with the COPIT bus service running between Florence and Pistoia – there is a bus stop right outside the villa.

NORTH OF FLORENCE
The Mugello

The area north-east of Florence leading up to Firenzuola, near the border with Emilia-Romagna, is known as the Mugello. The Medicis came from around here and some of their castles and villas are open to the public. One of Tuscany's premier wine areas straggles along the Sieve river valley.

For information on the Medici properties, walking, cycling, wine tours and other activities, contact the APT in Florence or the Associazione Turismo Ambiente (☎ 055 845 87 93), Piazza Dante 29, Borgo San Lorenzo. SITA has regular buses to Borgo San Lorenzo, and less frequent ones fan out to other parts of the Mugello.

EAST OF FLORENCE
Vallombrosa and Around

An interesting little excursion, most easily done with your own transport, has as its prime objective the cool forest of Vallombrosa and the *abbazia* (abbey) of the same name. Although you can get to many of the following spots by bus, doing things this way would turn the excursion into a project of several days!

Exiting Florence eastwards along the SS67 (follow the blue signs for Arezzo), you first strike a **Commonwealth war cemetery**, half a kilometre short of Anchetta. It is sobering to stop here and think of the soldiers who died in and around Florence in 1944. You follow the road to **Sieci**, whose Romanesque church is accompanied by a graceful, slender bell tower. A detour north (signposted) would take you up to the **Castello del Trebbio**, a typical 12th-century fortified rural outpost, at one time owned by the Pazzi family, that now operates as an agriturismo. You can go horse riding here and/or stock up on wine.

Back on the SS67, you next pass through **Pontassieve**, a busy little town picturesquely set astride the gushing Sieve river. Shortly afterwards take the SS70 for

Pelago, perched high on a ledge overlooking farming valleys. From here it's another 12km to Vallombrosa. As you wind higher, the forest thickens with the fir trees planted over the centuries by the Vallombrosan monks and the air freshens noticeably (it's a great little escape from the heat of Florence in the summer).

The abbey is almost 1000m above sea level. Back in the 11th century, San Giovanni Gualberto formed this branch of the Benedictine order in the midst of what no doubt was a still more impressive forest. The monks set themselves the task of wiping out simony and corruption in the Church in Florence and eventually the abbey came to play a key role in the city's politics. The monks were booted out by Napoleon and only since the 1950s have they returned to reclaim the monastery. You can wander into the grounds at any time. The church is open from 9 am to noon and 3 to 6 pm.

The surrounding area is great for picnics and walks, including one up to **Monte Secchieta** (1449m). At the abbey and in **Saltino**, 2km farther down the road, you will find a few restaurants and places to stay. From here we follow the road south to **Reggello** and **Cascia** (which has a small Romanesque church) and finally on to **Figline Valdarno**. The centre of this town, once known as Florence's granary, has a couple of interesting buildings, including the 14th-century Palazzo Pretorio, once the seat of local power. Much of the city wall and its towers still stand.

Another detour here would see you heading 6km south-west to **Gaville** (you could catch the local Maddii bus) to see the 11th-century Romanesque Pieve di San Romolo, set in olive groves.

Back in Figline Valdarno, you can follow the SS67 back up to Florence.

WEST OF FLORENCE

This section could conceivably be accomplished as a one-day circuit, but you would need to start early and not waste too much time in any one place, especially if you are relying on public transport.

Prato

postcode 59100 • pop 171,100

This textile town, 17km north-west of Florence, was founded by the Ligurians, taken by the Etruscans and finally absorbed into the Roman federation. By the 11th century Prato was an important centre for wool production. Today, although capital of a recently created separate province, it is close to being absorbed by Florence's suburban sprawl.

Information Prato's APT tourist office (☎ 0547 2 41 12), Via B Cairoli 48–52, is open from 9 am to 1 pm and 4 to 7 pm (2.30 to 6 pm in winter) Monday to Saturday.

Things to See & Do The **Museo Civico**, with its small but impressive collection of largely Tuscan paintings, is housed in the imposing medieval Palazzo Pretorio on Piazza del Comune. Among the artists are Filippo Lippi and Vasari. The museum is open from 10 am to 7 pm daily except Tuesday (mornings only on Sunday). Admission costs L10,000.

Along Via Mazzoni from Piazza del Comune is Piazza del Duomo and the 12th-century **Cattedrale di Santo Stefano**. The rather simple Pisan-Romanesque facade features a lunette by Andrea della Robbia, but the most extraordinary element is the **Pulpito della Sacra Cintola** jutting over the piazza on the right-hand side of the main entrance. The pulpit was expressly added on so that the *sacra cintola* (sacred girdle) could be displayed to the people five times a year (Easter, 1 May, 15 August, 8 September and 25 December). It is believed the girdle (or belt) was given to St Thomas by the Virgin Mary, and brought to the city from Jerusalem after the Second Crusade.

Places to Eat A pleasant spot for a meal is ***Ristorante Lo Scoglio*** (*☎ 0547 2 27 60, Via Verdi 40*), where you'll pay around L40,000 a head. It's closed on Monday.

Getting There & Away CAP and Lazzi buses operate regular services to Florence and Pistoia from in front of the train station,

which is on Piazza della Stazione. Prato is on the Florence–Bologna and Florence–Lucca train lines.

Pistoia

postcode 51100 • pop 90,200

Lying at the foot of the Apennines and 30 minutes west of Florence by train (barely an energetic spit from Prato), Pistoia has grown beyond its well-preserved medieval ramparts and is today a world centre for the manufacture of trains. In the 16th century the city's metalworkers created the pistol, named after the city.

The APT tourist office (☎ 0573 2 16 22), Piazza del Duomo, is open from 9 am to 1 pm and 3 to 6 pm daily.

Piazza del Duomo The **Cattedrale di San Zeno's** Pisan-Romanesque facade boasts a lunette by Andrea della Robbia. Inside, in the Cappella di San Jacopo, is the remarkable silver Dossale di San Jacopo (Altarpiece of St James). It was begun in the 13th century, with artisans adding to it over the ensuing two centuries until Brunelleschi contributed the final touch, the two half-figures on the left side.

The venerable building between the Duomo and Via Roma is the **Antico Palazzo dei Vescovi**. There are guided tours four times a day through the wealth of artefacts dating as far back as Etruscan times.

Across Via Roma is the **Battistero** (Baptistry). Elegantly banded in green and white marble, it was started in 1337 to a design by Andrea Pisano.

Dominating the eastern flank of Piazza del Duomo, the Gothic Palazzo del Comune houses the **Museo Civico**, with works by various Tuscan artists from the 13th to 19th centuries. The museum is open from 10 am to 6 pm Tuesday to Saturday, and 9 am to 12.30 pm on Sunday and holidays. Admission costs L6000 (free on Saturday afternoon).

The portico of the nearby **Ospedale del Ceppo** will stop even the more monument-weary in their tracks, for the terracotta frieze by Giovanni della Robbia is quite unique.

Places to Eat If you are looking for something a little special but still affordable, try your luck at *Lo Storno* (☎ *0573 2 61 93, Via del Lastrone 8*), a 600-year-old *osteria*. You are unlikely to spend more than L50,000 a head for a full meal. *Trattoria Vecchia Toscana al Vicoletto* (☎ *0573 2 92 30, Via Panciatichi 4*) is good but slightly more expensive, with pasta from L10,000. Both places are closed on Sunday.

Getting There & Away From Florence the easiest option is the train. Otherwise COPIT buses also travel there. In Pistoia, Florence-bound buses leave from Piazza Treviso.

Vinci

A small country road (the SP13) leads south out of Pistoia towards Empoli. After a long series of winding curves through the Monte Albano hills (a beautiful drive) and 1.5km short of Vinci you come across a sign pointing left (east) to the Casa di Leonardo in a place called **Anchiano**. Here it is believed Leonardo da Vinci was born the bastard child of a Florentine solicitor, Piero. Whether or not it is the real thing, you can poke your nose around inside from 9.30 am to 7 pm (to 6 pm in winter) for free.

Back down on the SP13, you are just short of Vinci itself. The town is dominated by the **Castello dei Guidi**, named after the feudal family that lorded it over this town and the surrounding area until Florence took control in the 13th century. Inside the castle nowadays is the **Museo Leonardiano**. This contains an intriguing set of more than 50 models based on Leonardo's far-sighted designs. The hours are the same as for his house and admission costs L7000. Down below the castle is the **Museo Ideale Leonardo da Vinci**, a private competitor to the above museum and a little on the silly side. It opens from 9 am to 1 pm and 3 to 7 pm daily. Admission costs L5000 and is not really worth it.

COPIT buses run regularly between Empoli and Vinci. To get to/from Pistoia you need to change at Crocifisso for the Pistoia–Lamporecchio bus. The drive from Pistoia is lovely, as indeed is the ride be-

tween the Villa di Poggio a Caiano (see Medici Villas under Around Florence earlier in the chapter) and Vinci via the wine centre of **Carmignano**.

Empoli

From Vinci you can head south to Empoli, a busy provincial centre of 43,000 on the Arno. It's a fairly nondescript sort of a place, though the small centre is pleasant enough. The Romanesque white and green marble facade (reminiscent of what you have seen at the Baptistry in Florence) of the **Collegiata di Sant'Andrea** in Piazza Uberti is testimony that the medieval settlement that emerged from a place called Emporium have been of some importance. Subject to the Guidi lords, in the 12th century the city was allowed to raise defensive walls. In 1182 it chose to join Florence to escape the feudal yoke.

On the western edge of town rises the somewhat worn profile of the 12th-century **Chiesa di Santa Maria a Ripa**. The original town, documented in the 8th century, lay here.

Montelupo

Hop on a train on the Pisa–Florence line to head back to Florence. If you have the time and the inclination, you could get out at Montelupo, a market town on the confluence of the Arno and Pesa. The town has been a celebrated centre of Tuscan ceramics production since medieval times and there is no shortage of shops here to browse or bequeath money to.

Before you do buy anything, you might want to inspect the **Museo Archeologico e della Ceramica**, opposite the tourist office at Via Baccio da Montelupo 43. It houses examples of pottery from prehistoric times to the 18th century. The museum, housed in the 14th-century Palazzo del Podestà, opens from 9 am to noon and 2.30 to 7 pm Tuesday to Sunday. Admission costs L5000.

Across the Pesa stream, the Medici villa known as the **Ambrogiana** and built for Ferdinando I is now a mental hospital.

To get to Florence (or to head west towards Pisa) the easiest bet is the train.

EXCURSIONS

THE CHIANTI REGION

For centuries the medieval comunes of Florence and Siena quarrelled nastily over just how much of the hills and valleys that lie between them belonged to each. The final division split the area into Il Chianti Fiorentino and Il Chianti Senese. When you explore this area, known as 'Il Chianti', you begin to understand what the fuss was about. This rich wine country, with one of the best-known labels in the world, is an enticing region.

Florence and Siena buried the hatchet long ago (although you might find this hard to believe if you talk to the Florentines and Sienese about one another), leaving the Chianti open to a new invasion. They don't call it Chiantishire for nothing. In some of the small-town tourist offices they just assume everyone who wanders in speaks English!

Of the wines, Chianti Classico is the best-known generic label, sold under the Gallo Nero (Black Cockerel) symbol.

You can get around by bus, but your own wheels make exploration a mighty bit easier. Alternatively, you could stride out or put your legs into circular motion.

Budget accommodation is not the area's strong point and you'll need to book well ahead.

JANE SMITH

Quaffing Chianti wine is an excellent way of washing down a hearty Tuscan meal.

Il Chianti Fiorentino

About 20km south of Florence on the Strada Chiantigiana that links Florence with Siena is **Greve in Chianti**, the first good base for exploring the area. You can get there easily from Florence on a SITA bus. The unusual triangular square, Piazza Matteotti, is the old centre. The tourist office (☎ 055 854 52 43) is at Via L Cini 1, 500m east of the piazza.

Montefioralle is an ancient castle-village, only 2km west of Greve. It's worth the uphill walk, particularly to see its church of Santo Stefano, which contains precious medieval paintings.

If you are heading down from Florence under your own steam, you might want to call in at the **Castello di Verrazzano** along the way. It's about 1.5km west of the Strada Chiantigiana, just before Greti. The word castle, as often in this area, is a little hyperbolic – these places tended to be fortified manors. This one is well known for its wine. You can drop by to taste and buy, or to take sustenance at the restaurant on the terrace, from where you have fine views across the valleys. Ring ahead (☎ 055 85 42 43) to confirm the restaurant is open. Another castle, **Uzzano**, lies a little further south. Follow the signs east of the Strada Chiantigiana.

About 5km west of Greve, in a magnificent setting of olive groves and vineyards, is the massive, turreted **Badia di Passignano**, an abbey founded in 1049 by Benedictine monks of the Vallombrosan order.

Travelling south of Greve along the Chiantigiana you will pass the medieval village of Panzano; after about 1km, turn off for the Chiesa di San Leolino at **Pieve di Panzano**. Built in the 10th century, it was rebuilt in Romanesque style in the 13th century. You can then continue south into Il Chianti Senese (see later in this chapter).

Another route south from Florence could start from the Certosa in Galluzzo (see Certosa di Galluzzo under South of the Old City in the Things to See & Do chapter). You could take the *superstrada* (expressway) that connects Florence with Siena or the more tortuous and windy road that runs roughly parallel to the superstrada. Follow the latter to Tavernuzze, where you could make a detour for **Impruneta**, about 8km to the south-east. Impruneta is famed for its production of terracotta – from roof tiles to more imaginative garden decorations. The centre of town is Piazza Buondelmonti. Not the most fascinating of Chianti towns by any stretch, Impruneta has been around since the 8th century. Its importance historically was due above all to the supposedly miraculous image of the Madonna dell'Impruneta in the Basilica di Santa Maria, which looks onto the piazza.

Back at Tavernuzze, you head south past the US war cemetery to **San Casciano in Val di Pesa**. An important wine centre, the town came under Florentine control in the 13th century and was later equipped with a defensive wall, parts of which remain intact. The town centre itself is not overly interesting, however, so you could just drink in the views and then hit the road again. Just before Bargino, take the side road east for Montefiridolfi. It's one of those charming little detours that takes you winding up onto a high ridge through vineyards and olive groves. Along the way you pass the **Castello di Bibbione**, a ponderous stone manor house. Another 1.5km brings you to a big Etruscan tomb. You can keep going until you hit a crossroads. From there turn west for **Tavarnelle Val di Pesa**, from where you can reach the charming medieval *borgo* (ancient town) of **Barberino Val d'Elsa**, worth a stop for a brief stroll along the main street.

Heading directly south from Barberino would take you to Poggibonsi, from where you can make bus connections for San Gimignano and Volterra (see the relevant sections later in this chapter). Some of the spots indicated above can be reached by bus (especially with SITA buses) from Florence, but you need to have saintly patience to make onward connections.

Certaldo

About 15km west of Barberino lies this pretty hilltop town, well worth the effort of a detour, although this move takes you out of Chianti territory.

The upper town (Certaldo Alto) is particularly captivating in the warm glow of the dying day's sun. The upper town has Etruscan origins, while the lower town in the valley sprang up in the 13th century – by which time both had been absorbed into the Florentine republic.

The **Boccaccio family residence**, where Giovanni Boccaccio died and was buried in 1375, was in the upper town. You can visit the largely reconstructed version of his house (it was severely damaged in WWII) from 10 am to 12.30 pm and 2.30 to 6 pm daily (admission free) along Via Boccaccio (the upper town's main drag). The library inside contains several precious copies of Boccaccio's *Decameron*. A couple of doors up, the Chiesa di SS Jacopo e Filippo houses a cenotaph to the writer. The whole walled borgo of the upper town is commanded by the stout figure of the **Palazzo Pretorio**, the seat of power whose 14th-century facade is richly decorated with family coats of arms. You can wander inside from 10 am to 1 pm and 2.30 to 7.30 pm daily for L5000. Frescoed halls lead off the charming Renaissance courtyard.

Il Chianti Senese

Castellina in Chianti is one of the best-organised towns for tourists, with lots of hotels and restaurants. Its tourist office (☎ 0577 74 02 01) is at the central Piazza del Comune 1 and open from 10 am to 1 pm and 3.30 to 7.30 pm daily (morning only on Sunday).

You might prefer to head east to **Radda in Chianti**, which has retained much of its charm despite the tourist influx. It is also handy for many of Chianti's most beautiful spots. The staff at the information office (☎ 0577 73 84 94, ✉ proradda@chiantinet.it) at Piazza Ferrucci 1 are helpful. They can help with info on walking, wineries and the like. The office has a Web site at www.chianti net.it.

A captivating walled medieval stronghold is **Monteriggioni**, just off the SS2 about 12km short of Siena. The walls date back to the 13th century and, although some of the towers still stand only because of later surgical intervention, the place transports you to another age.

EXCURSIONS

Getting Around

SITA buses connect Florence and Siena, passing through Castellina and Radda, as well as other small towns.

SIENA

postcode 53100 • pop 59,200

'Doing Siena' in a day is a hazardous undertaking, but a visitor to Florence with a little spare time can become superficially acquainted with the Arno city's southern rival. The more time spent here, the better.

Little has changed from medieval times and the compact city centre bristles with architectural jewels such as the Palazzo Pubblico in Il Campo, Siena's main square, and the Duomo. The volume of art housed in its churches and museums is giddying.

History

According to legend Siena was founded by the son of Remus, and the symbol of the wolf feeding the twins Romulus and Remus is as ubiquitous in Siena as in Rome. Probably of Etruscan origin, a real town only really emerged when, in the 1st century BC, the Romans established a military colony called Sena Julia.

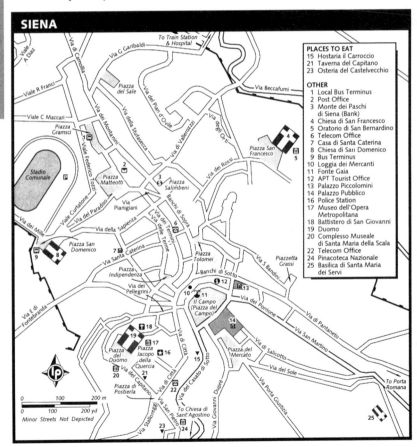

SIENA

PLACES TO EAT
15 Hostaria il Carroccio
21 Taverna del Capitano
23 Osteria del Castelvecchio

OTHER
1 Local Bus Terminus
2 Post Office
3 Monte dei Paschi di Siena (Bank)
4 Chiesa di San Francesco
5 Oratorio di San Bernardino
6 Telecom Office
7 Casa di Santa Caterina
8 Chiesa di San Domenico
9 Bus Terminus
10 Loggia dei Mercanti
11 Fonte Gaia
12 APT Tourist Office
13 Palazzo Piccolomini
14 Palazzo Pubblico
16 Police Station
17 Museo dell'Opera Metropolitana
18 Battistero di San Giovanni
19 Duomo
20 Complesso Museale di Santa Maria della Scala
22 Telecom Office
24 Pinacoteca Nazionale
25 Basilica di Santa Maria dei Servi

In the 12th century Siena's wealth, size and power grew with its involvement in commerce, banking and trade. Rivalry with Florence also increased and in 1260 Ghibelline Siena defeated Florence at the Battle of Montaperti. The Florentines later turned the tables and Siena was obliged to join the Tuscan Guelph League.

During this period Siena prospered under the rule of the Consiglio dei Nove (Council of Nine), a group dominated by the middle class. Many of the fine buildings in the Sienese Gothic style, which give the city its striking appearance, were constructed under the council's direction, including the cathedral and Palazzo Pubblico. The Sienese school of painting had its beginnings at this time with Guido da Siena and peaked in the early 14th century with the work of artists like Duccio di Buoninsegna, Simone Martini, and Pietro and Ambrogio Lorenzetti.

Plague in 1348 and foreign rule signalled decline, but the real blow came when Holy Roman Emperor Charles V conquered Siena in 1555 and handed it over to Florence's Cosimo de' Medici. He barred the inhabitants from operating banks and thus curtailed Siena's power for good. The Sienese have never forgotten the horrors of the military campaign or the humiliation of submission to Florence.

Siena was home to St Catherine, one of Italy's most famous saints. But saints don't make money. Siena today relies for its prosperity on tourism and the success of its Monte dei Paschi di Siena bank, founded in 1472.

Orientation

Streets and lanes swirl around Il Campo, the sloping central piazza and stage of Il Palio, the chaotic bareback horse race held twice a year. The city centre is compact, if a little confusing at times.

By bus you will arrive at Piazza San Domenico, which affords a panoramic view of the city. Walk east along Via della Sapienza and turn right into Banchi di Sopra to reach Il Campo. From the train station you will need to catch a local bus to Piazza Matteotti.

Tickets Please

If you plan to visit every last monument in sight, you should consider a seven-day cumulative ticket, or *biglietto unico*. Between 16 March and 31 October it costs L32,000 and gives you access to the Museo Civico, Complesso Museale di Santa Maria della Scala, Museo d'Arte Contemporanea, Museo dell'Opera Metropolitana, Libreria Piccolomini, Battistero di San Giovanni, Chiesa di Sant'Agostino and the Oratorio di San Bernardino. For the rest of the year it costs L7000 less as the last two of these monuments are shut.

Drivers note that streets within the walls are blocked to normal traffic – even if you are staying at a hotel in the centre of town you will be required to leave your car in a car park after dropping off your bags.

Information

The APT tourist office (☎ 0577 28 05 51, fax 0577 27 06 76) is at Piazza del Campo 56 and in summer is open from 8.30 am to 7.30 pm Monday to Saturday and from 9 am to 2 pm on Sunday. For the rest of the year, the hours are 8.30 am to 1 pm and 3.30 to 6.30 pm Monday to Friday (to noon on Saturday).

Il Campo

This magnificent, shell-shaped and cafe-lined square has been the city's civic centre since it was laid out by the Consiglio dei Nove in the mid-14th century. The square's paving is divided into nine sectors, representing the council members. In the upper part of the square is the 15th-century **Fonte Gaia** (Gay Fountain). The fountain's panels are reproductions – the originals, by Jacopo della Quercia, are in the Palazzo Pubblico.

Palazzo Pubblico At the lowest point of the piazza, this impressive building is also known as the Palazzo Comunale (town hall). Its graceful bell tower, the **Torre del Mangia**, is 102m high and dates from 1297. Inside is

EXCURSIONS

the **Museo Civico,** based on a series of rooms with frescoes by artists of the Sienese school. Of particular note is Simone Martini's famous *Maestà* in the Sala del Mappamondo. You can climb to the top of the tower.

The opening hours for the Palazzo Pubblico and the museum vary throughout the year: it opens from 10 am to 11 pm Monday to Saturday and from 9 am to 1.30 pm on Sunday in July and August. At other times of the year it closes as early as 4 pm. Admission costs L8000, or L4000 for students.

Duomo

Begun in 1196 and largely completed by 1215, the Duomo is one of Italy's great Gothic churches. Giovanni Pisano began the magnificent facade of white, green and red polychrome marble that was completed towards the end of the 14th century.

The Duomo's interior is rich with artworks. The most precious feature is the inlaid-marble floor, decorated with 56 panels depicting historical and biblical subjects.

Through a door from the north aisle is the **Libreria Piccolomini,** which Pope Pius III (pope in 1503) built to house the books of his uncle, Enea Silvio Piccolomini, who was Pope Pius II. The walls of the small hall are covered by an impressive series of frescoes by Bernardino Pinturicchio. In the centre of the hall is a group of statues known as the *Tre Grazie (Three Graces),* a 3rd-century AD Roman copy of an earlier Hellenistic work. The Libreria Piccolomini is open from 9 am to 7.30 pm from mid-March to the end of October; it's open from 10 am to 1 pm and 2.30 to 5 pm for the rest of the year. Admission costs L2000.

Museo dell'Opera Metropolitana

The great artworks in this museum formerly adorned the Duomo. Its main draw card is Duccio di Buoninsegna's striking early-14th-century *Maestà,* painted on both sides as a screen for the Duomo's high altar. The museum is open from 9 am to 7.30 pm daily from 16 March to 31 September, until 6 pm in October, and for the rest of the year until 1.30 pm. Admission costs L6000.

Battistero di San Giovanni

Behind the Duomo and down a flight of stairs is the Battistero di San Giovanni (Baptistry of St John). The marble font by Jacopo della Quercia is decorated with bronze panels depicting the life of St John the Baptist by artists including Lorenzo Ghiberti and Donatello. The baptistry has the same opening hours as the Museo dell'Opera Metropolitana, except that it also opens from 2.30 to 5 pm during the winter months. Admission costs L3000.

Complesso Museale di Santa Maria della Scala

Located on the south-western side of Piazza del Duomo, this former pilgrims hospital boasts frescoes by Domenico di Bartolo in the main ward and an impressive collection of Roman and Etruscan artefacts. The complex is open from 10 am to 6.30 pm in summer, with reduced hours during the rest of the year. Admission costs L8000.

Pinacoteca Nazionale

Located in the 15th-century Palazzo Buonsignori, a short walk south of the Duomo at Via San Pietro 29, this gallery houses masterpieces by Sienese artists. Look for Duccio di Buoninsegna's *Madonna dei Francescani,* the *Madonna col Bambino* by Simone Martini and a series of Madonnas by Ambrogio Lorenzetti. The gallery is open from 9 am to 7 pm Tuesday to Saturday, from 8 am to 1 pm on Sunday and from 8.30 am to 1.30 pm on Monday. Admission costs L8000.

Chiesa di San Domenico

Work on this imposing Gothic church began in the early 13th century, but it has been much altered over the centuries. St Catherine of Siena took her vows in its Cappella delle Volte. In the **Cappella di Santa Caterina** the saint's head is contained in a tabernacle on the altar.

The **Casa di Santa Caterina,** where St Catherine was born, is on Costa di Sant'Antonio, off Via della Sapienza. The rooms are decorated with frescoes and paintings by Sienese artists, including Sodoma. It is open from 9 am to 12.30 pm and 2.30 to 6 pm daily. Admission is free.

Other Churches & Palaces

Also worth investigating when they are open (from mid-March to the end of October) are the **Oratorio di San Bernardino**, part of the Chiesa di San Francesco complex (entrance L4000 if you don't have the *biglietto unico* – see the 'Tickets Please' boxed text earlier in the chapter), and the **Chiesa di Sant'Agostino** (L3000), Prato di Sant'Agostino. The former houses a modest museum of religious artworks.

From the Loggia dei Mercanti north of Il Campo, take Banchi di Sotto eastwards to the **Palazzo Piccolomini**, the city's finest Renaissance palace. It houses the city's archives and a small museum open from 9 am to 1 pm Monday to Saturday. Admission is free. Farther east are the 13th-century **Basilica di Santa Maria dei Servi**, with a fresco by Pietro Lorenzetti, and the 14th-century **Porta Romana**.

Places to Eat

Hostaria il Carroccio (☎ 0577 4 11 65, Via Casato di Sotto 32), off Il Campo, has excellent pasta for around L10,000. Try the *pici*, a kind of thick spaghetti, followed by the *friselle di pollo ai zucchini* (bite-sized juicy chicken bits with a courgette side). It's closed on Wednesday.

Taverna del Capitano (☎ 0577 28 80 94, Via del Capitano 8) is a good spot for local food. A full meal will probably cost about L35,000. More expensive but highly regarded is the nearby *Osteria del Castelvecchio* (☎ 0577 4 95 86, Via Castelvecchio 65). Both of these are closed on Tuesday.

Getting There & Away

Siena is not on a major train line, so the best option from Florence is the bus. Regular buses leave from Piazza San Domenico for Florence, San Gimignano (change at Poggibonsi) and Volterra (change at Colle Val d'Elsa). By car take the SS2, a fast superstrada connecting Florence and Siena, or the SS222 (la Chiantigiana) through the Chianti hills.

Il Palio

This spectacular event, held twice yearly on 2 July and 16 August in honour of the Virgin Mary, dates back to the Middle Ages and features a series of colourful pageants, a wild horse race around Il Campo and much eating, drinking and celebrating in the streets.

Ten of Siena's 17 town districts, or *contrade*, compete for the coveted *palio*, a silk banner. Each of the contrade has its own traditions, symbol and colours, and its own church and palio museum. The centuries-old local rivalries make the festival very much an event for the Sienese, though the horse race and pageantry continue to attract larger crowds of tourists.

On festival days Il Campo becomes a racetrack, with a ring of packed dirt around its perimeter serving as the course. From about 5 pm representatives of each *contrada* parade in historical costume, bearing their individual banners.

The race is run at 7.45 pm in July and 7 pm in August. For not much more than one exhilarating minute, the 10 horses and their bareback riders tear three times around Il Campo with a speed and violence that makes your hair stand on end.

Even if a horse loses its rider it is still eligible to win and since many riders fall each year, it is the horses who in the end who are the focus of the event. There is only one rule: riders are not to interfere with the reins of other horses. The national TV network, RAI, have to meet incredible demands made by the Sienese in order to obtain the TV rights for the event.

Book well in advance if you want to stay in Siena at this time and join the crowds in the centre of Il Campo at least four hours before the start, or even earlier if you want a place on the barrier lining the track. If you can't find a good vantage point, don't despair – the race is televised live and then repeated throughout the evening on TV.

If you happen to be in town in the few days immediately preceding the race, you may get to see the jockeys and horses trying out in Il Campo – almost as good as the real thing.

EXCURSIONS

SAN GIMIGNANO
postcode 53037 • pop 7100

The 13 towers of this walled town look like some medieval Manhattan. The towers were symbols of the power and wealth of the city's families and once numbered 72. In 1348, the plague decimated the population and weakened the power of its nobles, leading to the town's submission to Florence five years later.

Information
The Associazione Pro Loco (☎ 0577 94 00 08) is at Piazza del Duomo 1. It is open from 9 am to 1 pm and 3 to 7 pm daily (to 6 pm in winter).

Things to See & Do
Buy the L18,000 ticket, which allows admission into most of San Gimignano's museums, from the ticket office of any of the city's sights.

Piazza della Cisterna is lined with houses and towers dating from the 13th and 14th centuries. In the adjoining Piazza del Duomo stands the Romanesque cathedral (known as the **Collegiata**). The frescoes inside are noteworthy and in the **Cappella di Santa Fina** are beautiful ones by Domenico Ghirlandaio. The cathedral and chapel are open from 9.30 am to 12.30 pm and 3 to 5.30 pm daily.

The **Palazzo del Popolo**, left of the Duomo, still operates as the town hall. From the internal courtyard, climb the stairs to the **Museo Civico**, which features paintings from the Sienese and Florentine schools of the 12th to 15th centuries. Climb the palazzo's **Torre Grossa** for the views.

The palace, tower and museum are open from 9.30 am to 7.30 pm daily in summer, with shorter hours during the rest of the year.

Places to Eat
Trattoria La Mangiatoia (☎ *0577 94 15 28, Via Mainardi 5*) is one of the city's better restaurants, with pasta costing from about L9000. It's closed on Tuesday.

A relative newcomer offering fine food at moderate prices is *Osteria al Carcere* (☎ *0577 94 19 05, Via Castello 5*). It has an original menu, including half a dozen soups at L11,000. It's closed on Wednesday.

Getting There & Around
From Florence and Siena you can reach San Gimignano by bus (change at Poggibonsi). There's also a bus to Volterra. Bus timetables are posted on a pillar to the left as you face the Pro Loco office.

VOLTERRA
postcode 56048 • pop 13,400

When the Etruscan trade settlement of Velathri passed to the Romans, they renamed it Volaterrae. A long period of conflict with Florence started in the 12th century and ended when the Medici took possession of the city in the 15th century.

Perched high on a rocky plateau, the town's well-preserved medieval ramparts give Volterra a forbidding air. The city has a long tradition of producing alabaster.

The tourist office (☎ 0588 8 61 50) is at Piazza dei Priori 20. A L12,000 ticket buys you admission to all the main sights.

Things to See & Do
Piazza dei Priori is surrounded by austere medieval mansions. The 13th-century **Palazzo dei Priori** is the oldest seat of local government in Tuscany. The **Palazzo Pretorio**, also from the 13th century, is dominated by the Torre del Porcellino (Piglet's Tower), so named because of the wild boar sculpted on its upper section. Behind the Palazzo dei Priori, along Via Turazza, is the **Duomo**, built in the 12th and 13th centuries. The **Baptistry** features a font by Andrea Sansovino.

East of the square on Via Minzoni, the **Museo Etrusco Guarnacci** contains Etruscan artefacts unearthed locally, including a collection of some 600 funerary urns. The best exhibits are on the 2nd and 3rd floors. The museum opens from 9 am to 7 pm daily (until 2 pm from November to mid-March).

Places to Eat
The *Trattoria del Sacco Fiorentino* (☎ *0588 8 85 37, Piazza XX Settembre*) is a little eatery serving up fine food with a happy selection of local wines. It's closed on Friday.

hianti grapes on the vine in Montefioralle

BETHUNE CARMICHAEL

scape the tourist hordes in the Tuscan countryside

Chianti wine is one of Italy's finest drops.

Fiesole's 1st-century-BC Roman theatre

ome from the fields: traditional Tuscan farming

Tuscany is prime olive-growing country.

The jumbled rooftops of medieval Siena

Detail of the 12th-century cathedral in Prato

The wedding cake facade of San Michele, Lucca

The Leaning Tower of Pisa does its thing.

Getting There & Away
Buses from Piazza Martiri della Libertà connect the town with Siena, Florence and San Gimignano. For Siena and Florence you need to change at Colle Val d'Elsa.

LUCCA
postcode 55100 • pop 87,000
Founded by the Ligurians, Lucca became a Roman colony in 180 BC and a free comune during the 12th century. In 1314 it fell under the control of Pisa, but under the leadership of local adventurer Castruccio Castracani degli Anterminelli the city regained its independence, which it maintained until 1799.

Information
The tourist office (☎ 0583 41 96 89) is in Piazzale Verdi, on the western edge of the walled city. It is open from 9 am to 6 pm daily in summer (to 3 pm in winter, when it also closes on Sunday and holidays).

Things to See & Do
Lucca's Romanesque **Duomo**, on Piazza San Martino, dates from the 11th century. The exquisite facade, in the Lucca-Pisan style, was designed to accommodate the pre-existing bell tower.

In the centre of the old town, the **Chiesa di San Michele in Foro** is another dazzling Romanesque church, which was started in the 11th century. The wedding-cake facade is topped by a figure of the Archangel Michael slaying a dragon.

Lucca's busiest street, **Via Fillungo**, threads its way through the medieval heart of the old city and is lined with fascinating, centuries-old buildings. The **Torre delle Ore** (city clock tower) is about halfway along. Just to the east, the houses of **Piazza Anfiteatro** look onto what was the Roman-era amphitheatre.

Places to Eat
One of the best compromises in town is *Trattoria Da Giulio in Pelleria (☎ 0583 5 59 48, Via delle Conce 45)*. A somewhat impersonal barn of a place, it serves up high-quality food at very affordable prices.

It's closed on Sunday and Monday. *Ristorante Buca Sant'Antonio (☎ 0583 5 58 81, Via della Cervia 3)* is a rather classier affair where you'll need about L50,000 a head for a full meal. It's closed on Sunday evening and Monday.

Getting There & Away
Lazzi (☎ 0583 58 48 77) operates buses to Florence, Pisa and Rome. They leave from Piazzale Verdi. Lucca is on the Florence–Viareggio train line. By car, the A11 passes to the south of the city.

PISA
postcode 56100 • pop 98,000
Known today above all for an architectural project gone terribly wrong, the Leaning Tower of Pisa was Rome's main naval base during the Punic Wars and long an important port. The discovery of about a dozen Roman vessels during work on a suburban train station in 1999 was the archaeological sensation of the decade.

The city's so-called Golden Days began late in the 9th century when it became an independent maritime republic and a rival of Genoa and Venice. The good times rolled on into the 12th and 13th centuries. The majority of the city's finest buildings date from this period. Florence took Pisa in 1406 and the Medicis re-established its university. Galileo Galilei, Pisa's favourite son, taught here.

Information
The APT tourist office (☎ 050 56 04 64) is housed in a little cube of a building just outside the city walls. It opens from 8 am to 8 pm Monday to Saturday (9.30 am to noon and 3 to 5.30 pm in the low season).

Things to See & Do
The Pisans can justly claim that the **Campo dei Miracoli** is one of the most beautiful squares in the world. Set among its immaculate lawns is one of the world's greatest concentrations of Romanesque splendour – the Duomo, the Baptistry (Battistero) and the Leaning Tower (Torre Pendente).

EXCURSIONS

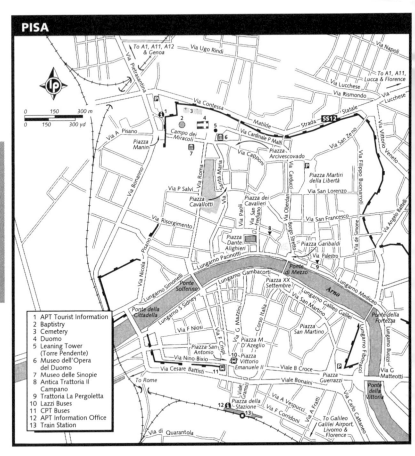

PISA

1 APT Tourist Information
2 Baptistry
3 Cemetery
4 Duomo
5 Leaning Tower
  (Torre Pendente)
6 Museo dell'Opera
  del Duomo
7 Museo delle Sinopie
8 Antica Trattoria Il
  Campano
9 Trattoria La Pergoletta
10 Lazzi Buses
11 CPT Buses
12 APT Information Office
13 Train Station

A staggered pricing system operates for tickets to one or more of the monuments in and around the square. L10,000 gets you entry to two monuments, L15,000 to four – the two museums, the Battistero and the Cemetery (Cimitero). The Duomo itself is not included and costs an extra L2000.

The majesty of Pisa's **Duomo** made it a model for Romanesque churches throughout Tuscany. Begun in 1064, it is covered inside and out with the alternating bands of (now somewhat faded) dark green and cream marble that were to become characteristic of the Pisan-Romanesque style.

The **Leaning Tower** is one of the world's great cockups. The Duomo's bell tower *(campanile)*, built on shaky ground, was in trouble from the start. The tower has been closed since 1990 while engineers try to work out how to stop its lean turning into a topple.

The unusual, round **Baptistry** took centuries to complete. The acoustics beneath the dome are remarkable. It is open from 8 am to 9 pm (9 am to 5 pm in winter).

Located behind the white wall to the north of the Duomo, the **Cemetery** is said to contain soil shipped from Calvary during the Crusades. It's open from 8 am to 8 pm daily (9 am to 5 pm in winter).

The **Museo delle Sinopie** houses reddish-brown sketches drawn onto walls as the basis for frescoes, discovered in the cemetery after WWII. The *sinopie* have been restored and provide a fascinating insight into the process of creating a fresco (if frescoes fascinate you, that is). The museum is open from 8 am to 8 pm daily (9 am to 1 pm and 3 to 5 pm in winter).

The **Museo dell'Opera del Duomo** in Piazza Arcivescovado, near the Leaning Tower, features many artworks from the tower, Duomo and Baptistry. It is open daily from 9 am to 1 pm and 3 to 7.30 pm (5.30 pm in winter).

Take time to wander through the engaging streets of the old city centre, often neglected by high-speed tourists.

Places to Eat

The *Antica Trattoria il Campano* (☎ *050 58 05 85, Vicolo Santa Margherita*), in an old tower near Piazza Sant'Ombono, is full of atmosphere; a full meal is likely to set you back L40,000. It's closed on Wednesday.

A wonderful sprawling place is *Trattoria La Pergoletta* (☎ *050 54 24 58, Via delle Belle Torri 40*), tucked away out of sight just north of the river. Expect to pay about L40,000 a head. It's closed on Monday.

Getting There & Away

The easiest way to get to and from Florence is by train. By car take the A11 (tollway).

Language

Although some Italians have studied English in school, English speakers are generally hard to find. In a place as popular with tourists of every possible persuasion as Florence, you'll find that staff at many hotels, pensioni and restaurants speak at least a little English. However, any attempt on your part to get to grips with Italian will endear you to the locals. Given the almost unending influx of non-Italian speaking foreigners in the city, it comes as a pleasant diversion for locals to hear out-of-towners making the effort.

Italian is a Romance language related to French, Spanish, Portuguese and Romanian, all descended from Latin. All these tongues belong to a wider collection known as the Indo-European group of languages, of which English is one. Indeed, as English and Italian share common roots in Latin, you'll recognise many Italian words.

Florence is the birthplace of modern literary Italian. It was here in the 13th and 14th centuries that some of the greatest literature in the Italian tradition was penned – above all by the likes of Dante, Petrarch and Boccaccio.

They wrote chiefly in the Florentine dialect, which for centuries after was considered by many the yardstick of 'good' standard Italian. The Italian of today is something of a composite. What you hear on the radio and TV, in educated discourse and indeed in the everyday language of many people is the result of centuries of cross-fertilisation between the dialects, greatly accelerated in the postwar decades by the modern media.

Dialects die hard, however, and from Venice in the north-east to Sicily in the south, a veritable compendium of dialects remains in greater or lesser use. Even where dialect use has declined, standard Italian is still invariably coloured by the local accent. In reality, the difference between many of Italy's dialects is so great that they could well be classed as separate languages – no less so than other Romance languages such as Spanish and Portuguese.

Florentines may argue that their dialect *is* the national language, and it's true it formed the basis of 'standard' Italian (due mainly to the status of Florence as Italy's major political, economic and cultural power base in the centuries leading up to unification in 1861). However, even those with a reasonable grounding in Italian may find many Florentines surprisingly hard to understand, at least at first. No one can deny the peculiarity of the local accent. Here and in other parts of Tuscany you're bound to hear the hard 'c' pronounced as a heavily aspirated 'h'. *Voglio una Coca Cola con cannuccia* (I want a Coca Cola with a straw) in Florence sounds more like *Voglio una Hoha Hola hon hannuccia*!

If you have more than the most fundamental grasp of the language, you need to be aware that many Italians still expect to be addressed in the third person formal (*lei* instead of *tu*). Also, it's not considered polite to use the greeting *ciao* when addressing strangers unless they use it first; it's better to say *buongiorno* (or *buona sera*, as the case may be) and *arrivederci* (or the more polite form, *arrivederla*). We have used the formal address for most of the phrases in this guide. Use of the informal address is indicated by 'inf' in brackets. Italian also has both masculine and feminine forms (usually ending in 'o' and 'a' respectively). Where both forms are given in this guide, they are separated by a slash, the masculine form first.

If you'd like a more comprehensive guide to the language, get a copy of Lonely Planet's *Italian phrasebook*.

Pronunciation

Setting aside the vagaries of Florentine pronunciation and dialect, Italian is not so difficult to pronounce once you learn a few easy rules. Although some of the more clipped vowels, and stress on double letters, require careful practice for English speakers, it's easy enough to make yourself understood.

Vowels

Vowels are generally more clipped than in English:

a   as in 'art', *caro* (dear); sometimes short, *amico/a* (friend)
e   as in 'tell', *mettere* (to put)
i   as in 'inn', *inizio* (start)
o   as in 'dot', *donna* (woman); as in 'port', *dormire* (to sleep)
u   as the 'oo' in 'book', *puro* (pure)

Consonants

The pronunciation of many Italian consonants is similar to that of their English counterparts. Pronunciation of some consonants depends on certain rules:

c   as 'k' before 'a', 'o' and 'u'; as the 'ch' in 'choose' before 'e' and 'i'
ch as the 'k' in 'kit'
g   as the 'g' in 'get' before 'a', 'o', 'u' and 'h'; as the 'j' in 'jet' before 'e' and 'i'
gli as the 'lli' in 'million'
gn as the 'ny' in 'canyon'
h   always silent
r   a rolled 'rr' sound
sc as the 'sh' in 'sheep' before 'e' and 'i'; as 'sk' before 'a', 'o', 'u' and 'h'
z   as the 'ts' in 'lights', except at the beginning of a word, when it's as the 'ds' in 'suds'

Note that when **ci**, **gi** and **sci** are followed by **a**, **o** or **u**, the 'i' is not pronounced unless the accent falls on the 'i'. Thus the name 'Giovanni' is pronounced 'joh-*vahn*-nee'.

Word Stress

A double consonants is pronounced as a longer, more forceful sound than a single consonant.

Stress generally falls on the second-last syllable, as in *spa-**ghet**-ti*. When a word has an accent, the stress falls on that syllable, as in *cit-**tà***, 'city'.

Greetings & Civilities

Hello.	*Buongiorno.*
	Ciao. (inf)
Goodbye.	*Arrivederci.*
	Ciao. (inf)
Yes.	*Sì.*
No.	*No.*
Please.	*Per favore/Per piacere.*
Thank you.	*Grazie.*
That's fine/ You're welcome.	*Prego.*
Excuse me.	*Mi scusi.*
Sorry (forgive me).	*Mi scusi/Mi perdoni.*
What's your name?	*Come si chiama?*
	Come ti chiami? (inf)
My name is ...	*Mi chiamo ...*
Where are you from?	*Di dov'è?*
	Di dove sei? (inf)
I'm from ...	*Sono di ...*
Just a minute.	*Un momento.*

Language Difficulties

I understand.	*Capisco.*
I don't understand.	*Non capisco.*
Do you speak English?	*Parla inglese?*
	Parli inglese? (inf)
Does anyone here speak English?	*C'è qualcuno che parla inglese?*
How do you say ... in Italian?	*Come si dice ... in italiano?*
What does ... mean?	*Che vuole dire ...?*
Please write it down.	*Può scriverlo, per favore?*
Can you show me (on the map)?	*Può mostrarmelo (sulla carta/pianta)?*

Getting Around

What time does ... leave/arrive?	*A che ora parte/ arriva ...?*
the (city) bus	*l'autobus*
the (intercity) bus	*il pullman/corriere*
the train	*il treno*

I'd like a ... ticket.	*Vorrei un biglietto ...*
one-way	*di solo andata*
return	*di andata e ritorno*
1st-class	*prima classe*
2nd-class	*seconda classe*

I want to go to ...	*Voglio andare a ...*
The train has been cancelled/delayed.	*Il treno è soppresso/ in ritardo.*

the first	*il primo*
the last	*l'ultimo*
platform number	*binario numero*
ticket office	*biglietteria*
timetable	*orario*
train station	*stazione*

I'd like to rent ...	*Vorrei noleggiare ...*
a bicycle	*una bicicletta*
a car	*una macchina*
a motorcycle	*una motocicletta*

Directions

Where is ...?	*Dov'è ...?*
Go straight ahead.	*Si va sempre diritto.*
	Vai sempre diritto. (inf)
Turn left.	*Giri a sinistra.*
Turn right.	*Giri a destra.*
at the next corner	*al prossimo angolo*
at the traffic lights	*al semaforo*
behind	*dietro*
in front of	*davanti*
far	*lontano*
near	*vicino*
opposite	*di fronte a*

Around Town

I'm looking for ...	*Cerco ...*
a bank	*un banco*
the church	*la chiesa*
the city centre	*il centro (città)*
the ... embassy	*l'ambasciata di ...*
my hotel	*il mio albergo*
the market	*il mercato*
the museum	*il museo*
the post office	*la posta*
a public toilet	*un gabinetto/ bagno pubblico*
the telephone centre	*il centro telefonico*
the tourist office	*l'ufficio di turismo/ d'informazione*

I want to change ...	*Voglio cambiare ...*
money	*del denaro*
travellers cheques	*degli assegni per viaggiatori*

bridge	*il ponte*
cathedral	*il duomo/la cattedrale*

Signs

INGRESSO/ ENTRATA	ENTRANCE
USCITA	EXIT
INFORMAZIONE	INFORMATION
APERTO/CHIUSO	OPEN/CLOSED
PROIBITO/ VIETATO	PROHIBITED
POLIZIA/ CARABINIERI	POLICE
QUESTURA	POLICE STATION
CAMERE LIBERE	ROOMS AVAILABLE
COMPLETO	FULL/NO VACANCIES
GABINETTI/BAGNI	TOILETS
UOMINI	MEN
DONNE	WOMEN

church	*la chiesa*
main square	*la piazza principale*
ruins	*le rovine*
tower	*la torre*

Accommodation

I'm looking for ...	*Cerco ...*
a guesthouse	*una pensione*
a hotel	*un albergo*
a youth hostel	*un ostello per la gioventù*

Where is a cheap hotel?	*Dov'è un albergo che costa poco?*
What is the address?	*Cos'è l'indirizzo?*
Could you write the address, please?	*Può scrivere l'indirizzo, per favore?*
Do you have any rooms available?	*Ha camere libere/C'è una camera libera?*

I'd like ...	*Vorrei ...*
a bed	*un letto*
a single room	*una camera singola*
a double room	*una camera matrimoniale*
a room with two beds	*una camera doppia*
a room with a bathroom	*una camera con bagno*

to share a dorm	*un letto in dormitorio*
How much is it ...?	*Quanto costa ...?*
per night	*per la notte*
per person	*per ciascuno*
May I see it?	*Posso vederla?*
Where is the bathroom?	*Dov'è il bagno?*
I'm/We're leaving today.	*Parto/Partiamo oggi.*

Shopping

I'd like to buy ...	*Vorrei comprare ...*
How much is it?	*Quanto costa?*
I (don't) like it.	*(Non) Mi piace.*
May I look at it?	*Posso dare un'occhiata?*
I'm just looking.	*Sto solo guardando.*
It's cheap.	*Non è caro/a.*
It's too expensive.	*È troppo caro/a.*
I'll take it.	*Lo/La compro.*
Do you accept ...?	*Accettate ...?*
credit cards	*carte di credito*
travellers cheques	*assegni per viaggiatori*
more	*più*
less	*meno*
smaller	*più piccolo/a*
bigger	*più grande*

Time, Date & Numbers

What time is it?	*Che ora è/ore sono?*
It's (8 o'clock).	*Sono (le otto).*
in the morning	*di mattina*
in the afternoon	*di pomeriggio*
in the evening	*di sera*
today	*oggi*
tomorrow	*domani*
yesterday	*ieri*
Monday	*lunedì*
Tuesday	*martedì*
Wednesday	*mercoledì*
Thursday	*giovedì*
Friday	*venerdì*
Saturday	*sabato*
Sunday	*domenica*

January	*gennaio*
February	*febbraio*
March	*marzo*
April	*aprile*
May	*maggio*
June	*giugno*
July	*luglio*
August	*agosto*
September	*settembre*
October	*ottobre*
November	*novembre*
December	*dicembre*

0	*zero*
1	*uno*
2	*due*
3	*tre*
4	*quattro*
5	*cinque*
6	*sei*
7	*sette*
8	*otto*
9	*nove*
10	*dieci*
11	*undici*
12	*dodici*
13	*tredici*
14	*quattordici*
15	*quindici*
16	*sedici*
17	*diciassette*
18	*diciotto*
19	*diciannove*
20	*venti*
21	*ventuno*
22	*ventidue*
30	*trenta*
40	*quaranta*
50	*cinquanta*
60	*sessanta*
70	*settanta*
80	*ottanta*
90	*novanta*
100	*cento*
1000	*mille*
2000	*due mila*
one million	*un milione*

Emergencies

Help!	Aiuto!
Call ...!	Chiami ...!
	Chiama ...! (inf)
a doctor	un dottore/
	un medico
the police	la polizia
There's been an accident!	C'è stato un incidente!
I'm lost.	Mi sono perso/a.
Go away!	Lasciami in pace!
	Vai via! (inf)

Health

I'm ill.	Mi sento male.
It hurts here.	Mi fa male qui.
I'm ...	Sono ...
asthmatic	asmatico/a
diabetic	diabetico/a
epileptic	epilettico/a
I'm allergic ...	Sono allergico/a ...
to antibiotics	agli antibiotici
to penicillin	alla penicillina
antiseptic	antisettico
aspirin	aspirina
condoms	preservativi
contraceptive	anticoncezionale
diarrhoea	diarrea
medicine	medicina
sunblock cream	crema/latte solare (per protezione)
tampons	tamponi

FOOD
Basics

breakfast	prima colazione
lunch	pranzo
dinner	cena
restaurant	ristorante
grocery store	alimentari
I'd like the set menu.	Vorrei il menu turistico.

Is service included in the bill?	È compreso il servizio?
I'm a vegetarian.	Sono vegetariano/a.
What is this?	(Che) cos'è?

Menu
Useful Words

affumicato	smoked
al dente	firm (as all good pasta should be)
alla brace	cooked over hot coals
alla griglia	grilled
arrosto	roasted
ben cotto	well-done (cooked)
bollito	boiled
cameriere/a	waiter/waitress
coltello	knife
conto	bill/cheque
cotto	cooked
crudo	raw
cucchiaino	teaspoon
cucchiaio	spoon
forchetta	fork
fritto	fried
menù	menu
piatto	plate
ristorante	restaurant

Staples

aceto	vinegar
burro	butter
formaggio	cheese
limone	lemon
marmellata	jam
miele	honey
olio	oil
olive	olives
pane	bread
pane integrale	wholemeal bread
panna	cream
pepe	pepper
peperoncino	chilli
polenta	cooked cornmeal
riso	rice
risotto	rice cooked with wine and stock
sale	salt
uovo/uova	egg/eggs
zucchero	sugar

Meat & Fish

acciughe	anchovies
agnello	lamb
aragosta	lobster
bistecca	steak
calamari	squid
coniglio	rabbit
cotoletta	cutlet or thin cut of meat, usually crumbed and fried
cozze	mussels
dentice	dentex (type of fish)
fegato	liver
gamberi	prawns
granchio	crab
manzo	beef
merluzzo	cod
ostriche	oysters
pesce spada	swordfish
pollo	chicken
polpo	octopus
salsiccia	sausage
sarde	sardines
sgombro	mackerel
sogliola	sole
tacchino	turkey
tonno	tuna
trippa	tripe
vitello	veal
vongole	clams

Vegetables

asparagi	asparagus
carciofi	artichokes
carote	carrots
cavolo/verza	cabbage
cicoria	chicory
cipolla	onion
fagiolini	string beans
melanzane	aubergine
patate	potatoes
peperoni	peppers
piselli	peas
spinaci	spinach

Fruit

arance	oranges
banane	bananas
ciliegie	cherries
fragole	strawberries
mele	apples
pere	pears
pesche	peaches
uva	grapes

Soups & Antipasti

brodo – broth

carpaccio – very fine slices of raw meat

insalata caprese – sliced tomatoes with mozzarella and basil

insalata di mare – seafood, generally crustaceans

minestrina in brodo – pasta in broth

minestrone – vegetable soup

olive ascolane – stuffed, deep-fried olives

prosciutto e melone – cured ham with melon

ripieni – stuffed, oven-baked vegetables

stracciatella – egg in broth

Pasta Sauces

alla matriciana al ragù – tomato and bacon meat sauce (bolognese)

arrabbiata – tomato and chilli

carbonara – egg, bacon and black pepper

napoletana – tomato and basil

panna – cream, prosciutto and sometimes peas

pesto – basil, garlic and oil, often with pine nuts

vongole – clams, garlic, oil and sometimes tomato

Pizzas

All pizzas listed have a tomato (and sometimes mozzarella) base.

capricciosa – olives, prosciutto, mushrooms and artichokes

frutti di mare – seafood

funghi – mushrooms

margherita – oregano

napoletana – anchovies

pugliese -- tomato, mozzarella and onions

quattro formaggi – with four types of cheese

quattro stagioni – like a capricciosa, but sometimes with egg

verdura – mixed vegetables; usually courgette/zucchini and aubergine/eggplant, sometimes carrot and spinach

Glossary

ACI – Automobile Club Italiano, the Italian automobile club
aereo – aeroplane
affittacamere – rooms for rent (cheaper than a *pensione*, and not part of the classification system)
affresco – fresco; the painting method in which watercolour paint is applied to wet plaster
agriturismo – tourist accommodation on farms
AIG – Associazione Italiana Alberghi per la Gioventù, Italy's youth hostel association
albergo – hotel (up to five stars)
alimentari – grocery shop or delicatessen
alto – high
ambasciata – embassy
ambulanza – ambulance
anfiteatro – amphitheatre
Annunciazione – Annunciation
appartamento – apartment, flat
apse – (English) domed or arched area at the altar end of a church
APT – Azienda di Promozione Turistica, the provincial tourist office
arco – arch
arte – guild
assicurato/a – insured
atrium – (Latin) forecourt of a Roman house or a Christian basilica
autobus – bus
autostazione – bus station/terminal
autostop – hitchhiking
autostrada – freeway, motorway

bagno – bathroom; also toilet
balìa – emergency committee (historical)
bancomat – Automatic Teller Machine
basilica – in ancient Rome, a building used for public administration, with a rectangular hall flanked by aisles and an *apse* at the end; later, a Christian church built in the same style
battistero – baptistry
benzina – petrol
bicicletta – bicycle

biglietto – ticket
binario – (train) platform
borgo – ancient town or village, sometimes used to mean equivalent of *via*
brioche – pastry
busta – envelope

camera – room
camera doppia – double room with twin beds
camera matrimoniale – double room with a double bed
camera singola – single room
campanile – bell tower
campeggio – camping site
cappella – chapel
carabinieri – police under the jurisdiction of the Ministry of Defence (see *polizia*)
carta telefonica – phonecard (also *scheda telefonica*)
carta d'identità – ID card
cartoleria – stationary shop
cartolina (postale) – postcard
casa – house
casa dello studente – accommodation for students available on campus during holidays
castello – castle
cattedrale – cathedral
cena – evening meal
cenacolo – refectory
centro – centre
centro storico – old town (literally, historical centre)
chiesa – church
chiostro – cloister; covered walkway, usually enclosed by columns, around a quadrangle
cin cin – cheers (a drinking toast)
Cinquecento – 16th century
CIT – Compagnia Italiana di Turismo, the Italian national tourist/travel agency
codice fiscale – tax number
colazione – breakfast
colonna – column
comune – equivalent to a municipality or

county; town or city council; historically, a commune (self-governing town or city)
contado – district
contorno – side dish
contrada – town district
coperto – cover charge
corso – main street, avenue
cortile – courtyard
Crocifissione – Crucifixion
CTS – Centro Turistico Studentesco e Giovanile, the student/youth travel agency
cupola – dome

deposito bagagli – left luggage
digestivo – after-dinner liqueur
distributore di benzina – petrol pump (see *stazione di servizio*)
duomo – cathedral

enoteca – wine shop, nowadays often a basic restaurant with a fine range of wines to taste
espresso – express mail; express train; short black coffee

farmacia (di turno) – pharmacy (open late)
fermo posta – poste restante
ferrovia – train station
festa – festival
fiume – river
fontana – fountain
foro – forum
francobollo – postage stamp
fresco – (English) see *affresco*
FS – Ferrovie dello Stato, the Italian state railway

gabinetto – toilet, WC
gelato – ice cream
gonfaloniere – standard-bearer
grotta – cave
guardia di finanza – fiscal police

intonaco – whitewash

largo – (small) square
lavanderia – laundrette
lavasecco – dry-cleaning
lettera – letter

locanda – inn, small hotel
loggia – covered area on the side of a building; porch

Madonna col Bambino – Madonna with Baby Jesus (often the subject of paintings, drawings and sculptures)
Maestà – depiction of the Trinity, Christ or Mary enthroned (often the subject of paintings, drawings and sculptures)
mare – sea
menù del giorno – menu of the day
mercato – market
mescita di vini – wine outlet
monte – mountain, mount
motorino – moped
municipio – town hall
museo – museum

Novecento – 20th century

oggetti smarriti – lost property
ospedale – hospital
ostello – hostel
ostello per la gioventù – youth hostel
osteria – snack bar/cheap restaurant

pacchetto – package, parcel
pala – altarpiece
palazzo – palace or mansion; a large building of any type, including an apartment block
panino – bread roll with filling
parco – park
parlamento – people's plebiscite (historical)
pasticceria – shop selling cakes, pastries and biscuits
pedaggio – toll
pensione – small hotel, often with board
permesso di soggiorno – residence permit
piazza – square
piazzale – (large) open square
pietà – (literally, pity or compassion) sculpture, drawing or painting of the dead Christ supported (usually) by the Madonna
pietre dure – semiprecious 'hard stone', often cut, used to decorate many Florentine buildings

pietra forte – dun-coloured 'strong stone' characteristic of the exterior of many Florentine buildings
pietra serena – grey 'tranquil stone' used to great effect by Brunelleschi and others in the interiors of Renaissance churches, alternated with intonaco, or whitewash, surfaces
podestà – external martial
polizia – police
polyptych – altarpiece consisting of more than three panels (see *triptych*)
ponte – bridge
porta – gate
portico – portico; covered walkway, usually attached to the outside of buildings
pranzo – lunch
priori – governors (historical)
pronto soccorso – first aid, casualty ward

Quattrocento – 15th century
questura – police station

raccolta – collection
raccomandata – registered mail
ribollita – vegetable stew
riva – river bank
rocca – fortress

sagra – festival (generally monothematic and dedicated to food product)
sagrestia – sacristy
sala – room
salumeria – delicatessen
santuario – sanctuary
Seicento – 17th century
servizio – service charge
signoria – government (historical)

sindaco – mayor
stazione – station
stazione di servizio – service/petrol station
strada – street, road
superstrada – expressway; highway with divided lanes

teatro – theatre
telegramma – telegram
tessera – membership card
tondo – circular painting
torre – tower
torrente – stream
trattoria – cheap restaurant
treno – train
Trinità – Trinity
triptych – painting or carving on three panels, hinged so that the outer panels fold over the middle one, often used as an altarpiece (see *polyptych*)
trompe l'oeil – painting or other illustration designed to 'deceive the eye', creating the impression that the image is real

ufficio postale – post office
ufficio stranieri – (police) foreigners bureau
Ultima Cena – The Last Supper (often the subject of paintings, drawings and sculptures)

via – street, road
via aerea – air mail
villa – town house or country house; also the park surrounding the house
vinai – wine bar or shop

FREE Lonely Planet Newsletters

We love hearing from you and think you'd like to hear from us.

Planet Talk

Our FREE quarterly printed newsletter is full of tips from travellers and anecdotes from Lonely Planet guidebook authors. Every issue is packed with up-to-date travel news and advice, and includes:

- a postcard from Lonely Planet co-founder Tony Wheeler
- a swag of mail from travellers
- a look at life on the road through the eyes of a Lonely Planet author
- topical health advice
- prizes for the best travel yarn
- news about forthcoming Lonely Planet events
- a complete list of Lonely Planet books and other titles

To join our mailing list, residents of the UK, Europe and Africa can email us at go@lonelyplanet.co.uk; residents of North and South America can email us at info@lonelyplanet.com; the rest of the world can email us at talk2us@lonelyplanet.com.au, or contact any Lonely Planet office.

Comet

Our FREE monthly email newsletter brings you all the latest travel news, features, interviews, competitions, destination ideas, travellers' tips & tales, Q&As, raging debates and related links. Find out what's new on the Lonely Planet Web site and which books are about to hit the shelves.

Subscribe from your desktop: www.lonelyplanet.com/comet

LONELY PLANET

Guides by Region

Lonely Planet is known worldwide for publishing practical, reliable and no-nonsense travel information in our guides and on our Web site. The Lonely Planet list covers just about every accessible part of the world. Currently there are thirteen series: travel guides, shoestring guides, walking guides, city guides, phrasebooks, audio packs, city maps, travel atlases, diving and snorkeling guides, restaurant guides, first-time travel guides, healthy travel and travel literature.

AFRICA Africa – the South ● Africa on a shoestring ● Arabic (Egyptian) phrasebook ● Arabic (Moroccan) phrasebook ● Cairo ● Cape Town ● Cape Town city map● Central Africa ● East Africa ● Egypt ● Egypt travel atlas ● Ethiopian (Amharic) phrasebook ● The Gambia & Senegal ● Healthy Travel Africa ● Kenya ● Kenya travel atlas ● Malawi, Mozambique & Zambia ● Morocco ● North Africa ● South Africa, Lesotho & Swaziland ● South Africa, Lesotho & Swaziland travel atlas ● Swahili phrasebook ● Tanzania, Zanzibar & Pemba ● Trekking in East Africa ● Tunisia ● West Africa ● Zimbabwe, Botswana & Namibia ● Zimbabwe, Botswana & Namibia travel atlas
Travel Literature: The Rainbird: A Central African Journey ● Songs to an African Sunset: A Zimbabwean Story ● Mali Blues: Traveling to an African Beat

AUSTRALIA & THE PACIFIC Auckland ● Australia ● Australian phrasebook ● Bushwalking in Australia ● Bushwalking in Papua New Guinea ● Fiji ● Fijian phrasebook ● Islands of Australia's Great Barrier Reef ● Melbourne ● Melbourne city map ● Micronesia ● New Caledonia ● New South Wales & the ACT ● New Zealand ● Northern Territory ● Outback Australia ● Out To Eat – Melbourne ● Papua New Guinea ● Papua New Guinea (Pidgin) phrasebook ● Queensland ● Rarotonga & the Cook Islands ● Samoa ● Solomon Islands ● South Australia ● South Pacific Languages phrasebook ● Sydney ● Sydney city map ● Tahiti & French Polynesia ● Tasmania ● Tonga ● Tramping in New Zealand ● Vanuatu ● Victoria ● Western Australia
Travel Literature: Islands in the Clouds ● Kiwi Tracks ● Sean & David's Long Drive

CENTRAL AMERICA & THE CARIBBEAN Bahamas, Turks & Caicos ● Bermuda ● Central America on a shoestring ● Costa Rica ● Cuba ● Dominican Republic & Haiti ● Eastern Caribbean ● Guatemala, Belize & Yucatán: La Ruta Maya ● Jamaica ● Mexico ● Mexico City ● Panama ● Puerto Rico
Travel Literature: Green Dreams: Travels in Central America

EUROPE Amsterdam ● Amsterdam city map ● Andalucía ● Austria ● Baltic States phrasebook ● Barcelona ● Berlin ● Berlin city map ● Britain ● British phrasebook ● Brussels, Bruges & Antwerp ● Budapest city map ● Canary Islands ● Central Europe ● Central Europe phrasebook ● Corsica ● Croatia ● Czech & Slovak Republics ● Denmark ● Dublin ● Eastern Europe ● Eastern Europe phrasebook ● Edinburgh ● Estonia, Latvia & Lithuania ● Europe ● Finland ● France ● French phrasebook ● Germany ● German phrasebook ● Greece ● Greek phrasebook ● Hungary ● Iceland, Greenland & the Faroe Islands ● Ireland ● Italian phrasebook ● Italy ● Lisbon ● London ● London city map ● Mediterranean Europe ● Mediterranean Europe phrasebook ● Norway ● Paris ● Paris city map ● Poland ● Portugal ● Portugal travel atlas ● Prague ● Prague city map ● Provence & the Côte d'Azur ● Romania & Moldova ● Rome ● Russia, Ukraine & Belarus ● Russian phrasebook ● Scandinavian & Baltic Europe ● Scandinavian Europe phrasebook ● Scotland ● Slovenia ● Spain ● Spanish phrasebook ● St Petersburg ● Switzerland ● Trekking in Spain ● Ukrainian phrasebook ● Vienna ● Walking in Britain ● Walking in Ireland ● Walking in Italy ● Walking in Switzerland ● Western Europe ● Western Europe phrasebook
Travel Literature: The Olive Grove: Travels in Greece

INDIAN SUBCONTINENT Bangladesh ● Bengali phrasebook ● Bhutan ● Delhi ● Goa ● Hindi/Urdu phrasebook ● India ● India & Bangladesh travel atlas ● Indian Himalaya ● Karakoram Highway ● Kerala ● Mumbai ● Nepal ● Nepali phrasebook ● Pakistan ● Rajasthan ● Read This First: Asia & India ● South India ● Sri Lanka ● Sri Lanka phrasebook ● Trekking in the Indian Himalaya ● Trekking in the Karakoram & Hindukush ● Trekking in the Nepal Himalaya
Travel Literature: In Rajasthan ● Shopping for Buddhas

LONELY PLANET

Mail Order

Lonely Planet products are distributed worldwide. They are also available by mail order from Lonely Planet, so if you have difficulty finding a title please write to us. North and South American residents should write to 150 Linden St, Oakland, CA 94607, USA; European and African residents should write to 10a Spring Place, London NW5 3BH, UK; and residents of other countries to PO Box 617, Hawthorn, Victoria 3122, Australia.

ISLANDS OF THE INDIAN OCEAN Madagascar & Comoros ● Maldives ● Mauritius, Réunion & Seychelles

MIDDLE EAST & CENTRAL ASIA Arab Gulf States ● Central Asia ● Central Asia phrasebook ● Hebrew phrasebook ● Iran ● Israel & the Palestinian Territories ● Israel & the Palestinian Territories travel atlas ● Istanbul ● Istanbul to Cairo ● Jerusalem ● Jordan & Syria ● Jordan, Syria & Lebanon travel atlas ● Lebanon ● Middle East on a shoestring ● Syria ● Turkey ● Turkish phrasebook ● Turkey travel atlas ● Yemen
Travel Literature: The Gates of Damascus ● Kingdom of the Film Stars: Journey into Jordan

NORTH AMERICA Alaska ● Backpacking in Alaska ● Baja California ● California & Nevada ● Canada ● Chicago ● Chicago city map ● Deep South ● Florida ● Hawaii ● Honolulu ● Las Vegas ● Los Angeles ● Miami ● New England ● New Orleans ● New York City ● New York city map ● New York, New Jersey & Pennsylvania ● Pacific Northwest USA ● Puerto Rico ● Rocky Mountain States ● San Francisco ● San Francisco city map ● Seattle ● Southwest USA ● Texas ● USA ● USA phrasebook ● Vancouver ● Washington, DC & the Capital Region ● Washington DC city map
Travel Literature: Drive Thru America

NORTH-EAST ASIA Beijing ● Cantonese phrasebook ● China ● Hong Kong ● Hong Kong city map ● Hong Kong, Macau & Guangzhou ● Japan ● Japanese phrasebook ● Japanese audio pack ● Korea ● Korean phrasebook ● Kyoto ● Mandarin phrasebook ● Mongolia ● Mongolian phrasebook ● North-East Asia on a shoestring ● Seoul ● South-West China ● Taiwan ● Tibet ● Tibetan phrasebook ● Tokyo
Travel Literature: Lost Japan

SOUTH AMERICA Argentina, Uruguay & Paraguay ● Bolivia ● Brazil ● Brazilian phrasebook ● Buenos Aires ● Chile & Easter Island ● Chile & Easter Island travel atlas ● Colombia ● Ecuador & the Galapagos Islands ● Latin American Spanish phrasebook ● Peru ● Quechua phrasebook ● Rio de Janeiro ● Rio de Janeiro city map ● South America on a shoestring ● Trekking in the Patagonian Andes ● Venezuela
Travel Literature: Full Circle: A South American Journey

SOUTH-EAST ASIA Bali & Lombok ● Bangkok ● Bangkok city map ● Burmese phrasebook ● Cambodia ● Hanoi ● Healthy Travel Asia & India ● Hill Tribes phrasebook ● Ho Chi Minh City ● Indonesia ● Indonesia's Eastern Islands ● Indonesian phrasebook ● Indonesian audio pack ● Jakarta ● Java ● Laos ● Lao phrasebook ● Laos travel atlas ● Malay phrasebook ● Malaysia, Singapore & Brunei ● Myanmar (Burma) ● Philippines ● Pilipino (Tagalog) phrasebook ● Singapore ● South-East Asia on a shoestring ● South-East Asia phrasebook ● Thailand ● Thailand's Islands & Beaches ● Thailand travel atlas ● Thai phrasebook ● Thai audio pack ● Vietnam ● Vietnamese phrasebook ● Vietnam travel atlas

ALSO AVAILABLE: Antarctica ● The Arctic ● Brief Encounters: Stories of Love, Sex & Travel ● Chasing Rickshaws ● Lonely Planet Unpacked ● Not the Only Planet: Travel Stories from Science Fiction ● Sacred India ● Travel with Children ● Traveller's Tales

Index

Text

Bold indicates maps.

Bold indicates maps.

Boxed Text

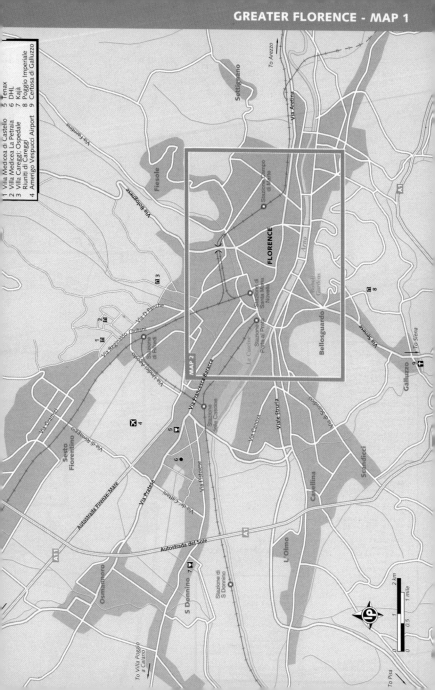

1 Villa Medicea di Castello
2 Villa Medicea La Petraia
3 Villa Careggi; Ospedale
  Riuniti di Careggi
4 Amerigo Vespucci Airport

5 Tenax
6 DHL
7 Kalà
8 Poggio Imperiale
9 Certosa di Galluzzo

To Arezzo

Settignano

Via Aretina

Via Faentina

Fiesole

Via Bolognese

Stazione Campo
di Marte

FLORENCE

Arno

Boboli
Gardens

MAP 2

Stazione di
Santa Maria
Novella

Stazione di
Porta al Prato

Bellosguardo

Via Senese

To Siena

Via D. Panche

Stazione di
Rifredi

Via Reginaldo Giuliani

Via Umberto Agnolo

Le Cascine

Via G. Garibaldi

Galluzzo

Via di Scandicci

Via Gramsci

Sesto
Fiorentino

Via di Rinnegro

Via Francesca Baracca

Stazione
delle Cascine

Via Cimina

Viale Etruria

Scandicci

Via Ottavini

Via de' Cattani

Via Pistoiese

Via Prateria

Casellina

Autostrada Firenze-Mare

L'Olmo

Autostrada del Sole

Osmannoro

S Donnino

Stazione di
S Donnino

To Villa Poggio
a Caiano

To Pisa

2 km

1 mile

0.5

0   1

MAP 2 - CENTRAL FLORENCE

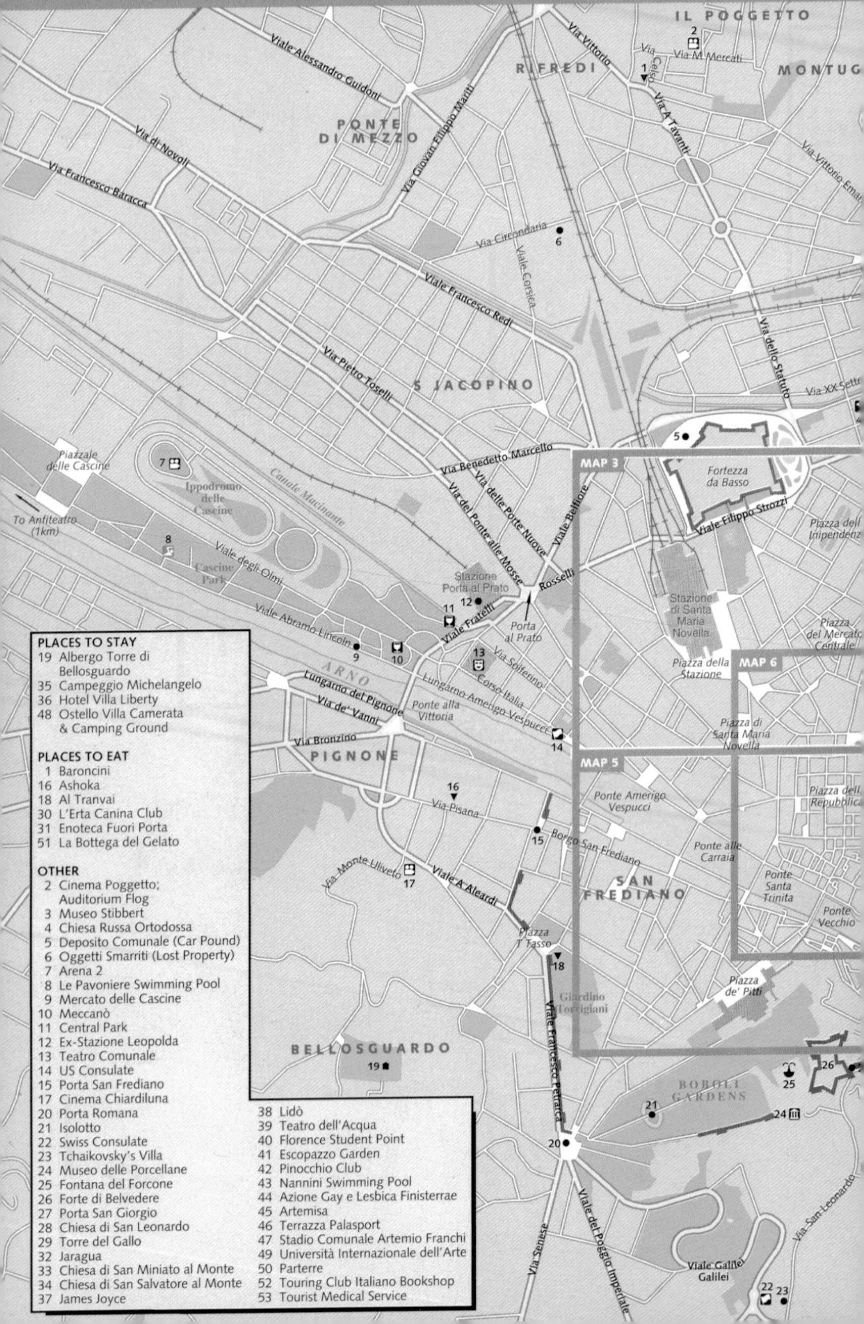

PLACES TO STAY
19 Albergo Torre di Bellosguardo
35 Campeggio Michelangelo
36 Hotel Villa Liberty
48 Ostello Villa Camerata & Camping Ground

PLACES TO EAT
1 Baroncini
16 Ashoka
18 Al Tranvai
30 L'Erta Canina Club
31 Enoteca Fuori Porta
51 La Bottega del Gelato

OTHER
2 Cinema Poggetto; Auditorium Flog
3 Museo Stibbert
4 Chiesa Russa Ortodossa
5 Deposito Comunale (Car Pound)
6 Oggetti Smarriti (Lost Property)
7 Arena 2
8 Le Pavoniere Swimming Pool
9 Mercato delle Cascine
10 Meccanò
11 Central Park
12 Ex-Stazione Leopolda
13 Teatro Comunale
14 US Consulate
15 Porta San Frediano
17 Cinema Chiardiluna
20 Porta Romana
21 Isolotto
22 Swiss Consulate
23 Tchaikovsky's Villa
24 Museo delle Porcellane
25 Fontana del Forcone
26 Forte di Belvedere
27 Porta San Giorgio
28 Chiesa di San Leonardo
29 Torre del Gallo
32 Jaragua
33 Chiesa di San Miniato al Monte
34 Chiesa di San Salvatore al Monte
37 James Joyce
38 Lidò
39 Teatro dell'Acqua
40 Florence Student Point
41 Escopazzo Garden
42 Pinocchio Club
43 Nannini Swimming Pool
44 Azione Gay e Lesbica Finisterrae
45 Artemisa
46 Terrazza Palasport
47 Stadio Comunale Artemio Franchi
49 Università Internazionale dell'Arte
50 Parterre
52 Touring Club Italiano Bookshop
53 Tourist Medical Service

0   250   500 m
0   250   500 yd

Via Bolognese

Vittorio Emanuele II
Via Faentina
49
48
Viale Alessandro Volta
Via San Domenico
Viale Augusto Righi
Via Ciseri
51
50
Viale Don G. Minzoni
Viale Alessandro Volta
Via A. Baldesi
Via G. Marconi
Lorenzo il Magnifico
52
Piazza della Libertà
Viale Spartaco Lavagnini
Viale dei Mille

MAP 4

Piazza Savonarola
Viale Giacomo Matteotti
47
CAMPO DI MARTE
Giardino dei Semplici
Piazza San Marco
Giardino della Gherardesca
46
Viale Pasquale Paoli
Via Giuseppe La Farina
Stazione Campo di Marte
Via Madrielli
Via Luigi l'Attico
Via Gabriele d'Annunzio
Piazza M. D'Azeglio
Viale Antonio Gramsci
Via del Mazzetta
45
Via Andrea del Sarto

MAP 7

40
Viale Edmondo de Amicis
44
Via Vincenzo Giberti
MADONNONE
Piazza di Santa Croce
Via Cimabue
Via Aretina
Ponte alle Grazie
Via Amalfi
Lungarno Pecori Giraldi
BELLARIVA
43
N NICCOLÒ
39
38
Lungarno del Tempio
Via Piagentina
Via Campofiore
Lungarno Cristoforo Colombo
Lungarno Aldo Moro
Ponte San Niccolò
41
ARNO
Ponte G Da Verrazzano
Piazza Giuseppe Poggi
37
Lungarno Francesco Ferrucci
Via di Villamagna
31
30
32
Piazzale Michelangelo
35
36
42
Via Coluccio Salutati
34
Viale Michelangelo
Viale dell'Erta Canina
33
Viale Galileo Galilei
Via Donato Giannotti
29

MAP 3

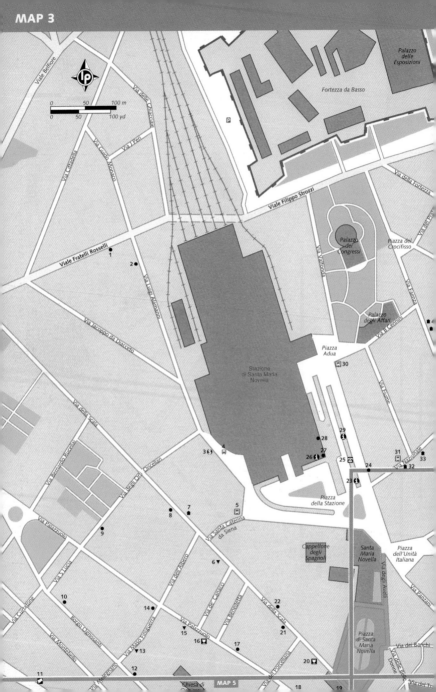

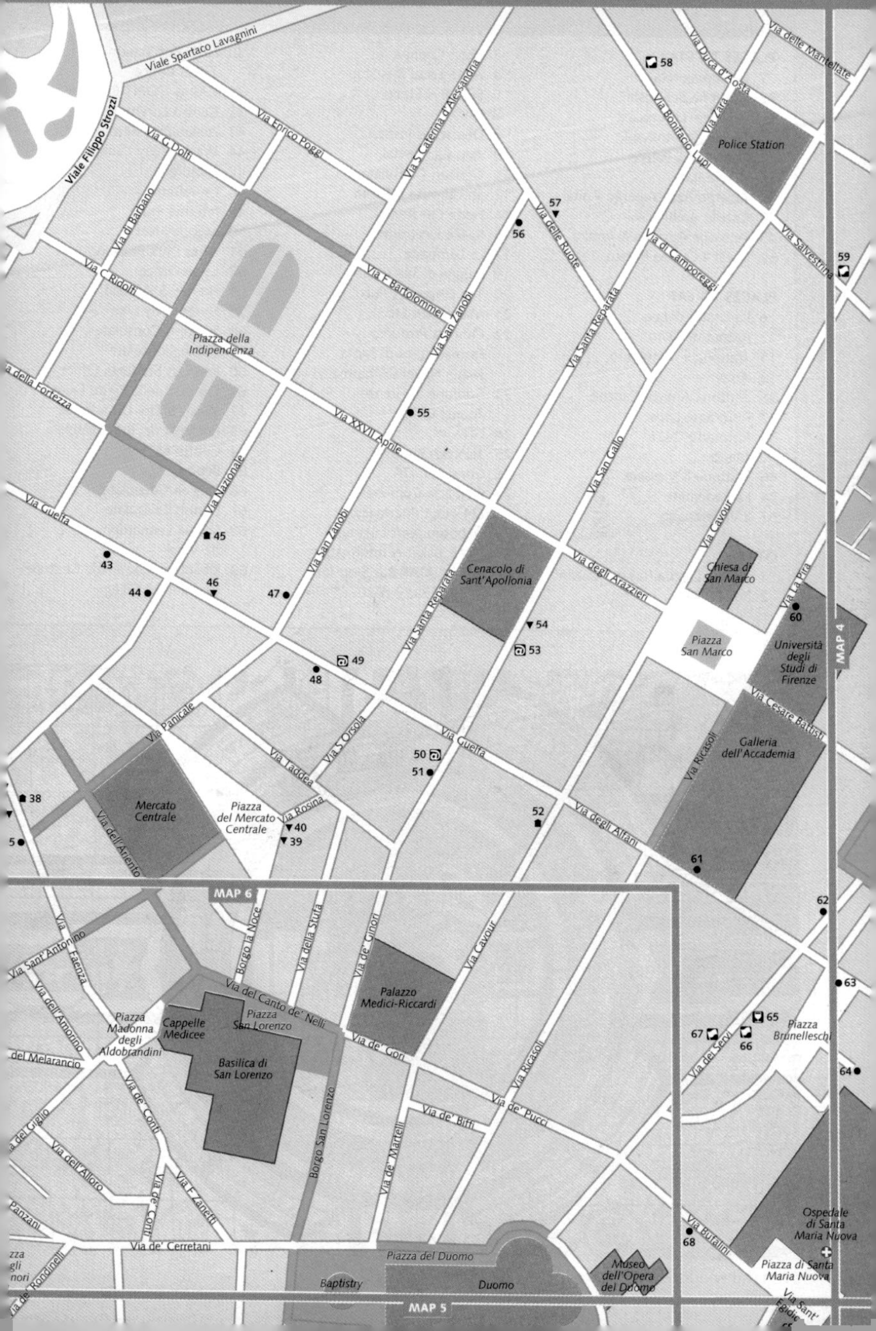

MAP 3

Viale Spartaco Lavagnini

Viale Filippo Strozzi

Via G. Dotti

Via Enrico Poggi

Via C. Ridolfi

Via de' Fattucci

Via della Fortezza

Via S. Caterina d'Alessandria

Via Duca d'Aosta

Via delle Mantellate

🖼 58

Via Bonifacio

Via Fibbia

Police Station

Via Silvestrina

Via F. Bartolommei

Via San Zanobi

Via Saluta Reparata

Via delle Ruote

57 ▼

● 56

59 🖼

Piazza della Indipendenza

Via XXVII Aprile

● 55

Via San Gallo

Via Cavour

Via Guelfa

Via Nazionale

Via San Zanobi

Via Santa Reparata

Via degli Arazzieri

Chiesa di San Marco

▼ 45

● 43

● 44

46 ▼

47 ●

Cenacolo di Sant'Apollonia

▼ 54

🖼 53

Piazza San Marco

Via della Pergola

60 ●

Università degli Studi di Firenze

48 ●

🖼 49

Via Cesare Battisti

Via Panicale

Via Faenza

Via S. Orsola

Via Guelfa

Via degli Alfani

Galleria dell'Accademia

50 🖼

51 ●

Via Ricasoli

Via dell'Ariento

▼ 38

● 5

Mercato Centrale

Piazza del Mercato Centrale

Via Rosina

▼ 40

▼ 39

52 ■

61 ●

62 ●

MAP 6

Via Sant'Antonino

Faenza

Via del Canto de' Nelli

Borgo La Noce

Via della Stufa

Via de' Ginori

Via Cavour

63 ●

Via del Giglio

Via dell'Amorino

del Melarancio

Piazza Madonna degli Aldobrandini

Cappelle Medicee

Piazza San Lorenzo

Palazzo Medici-Riccardi

Via de' Gori

65 🖼

66

67 🖼

Piazza Brunelleschi

64 ●

Basilica di San Lorenzo

Borgo San Lorenzo

Via de' Martelli

Via de' Pucci

Via de' Conti

Via de' Biffi

Via Panzani

Via dell'Alloro

Via de' Cerretani

Piazza degli Agnolnori

Via de' Rondinelli

Via de' Cerretani

Piazza del Duomo

Baptistry

Duomo

Museo dell'Opera del Duomo

68 ●

Via Bufalini

Ospedale di Santa Maria Nuova

Piazza di Santa Maria Nuova

Via Sant'Egidio

MAP 5

MAP 4

MAP 3

PLACES TO STAY
7 La Romagnola
32 Pensione Bellavista;
   Pensione Le Cascine
33 Ostello Spirito Santo
34 Machiavelli Palace
38 Nuova Italia
41 Albergo Azzi; Albergo Anna
42 Ostello Archi Rossi
45 Pensione Ausonia & Rimini
52 Hotel Il Guelfo Bianco

PLACES TO EAT
6 La Grotta di Leo
13 Ristorante Dino
15 Trattoria il Contadino
18 Amon
36 Trattoria Antichi Cancelli
37 Ristorante Lobs
39 Ristorante ZàZà
40 Mario
46 Trattoria Il Messere
54 La Bodeguita
57 Il Vegetariano

OTHER
1 Centro Lingua Italiana Calvino
2 Box Office

3 Exact Change
4 ATAF Local Bus Stop
5 SITA Bus Station
8 KAOS
9 Deutsches Institut
10 Avis Car Rental
11 German Consulate
12 Stockhouse Il Giglio
14 Hertz Car Rental
16 Space Electronic
17 Le Lampade
19 Loggia di San Paolo
20 The Chequers Pub
21 Mail Boxes Etc
22 Officina Profumo
   Farmaceutica di Santa
   Maria Novella (Pharmacy)
23 Comune di Firenze
   Tourist Office
24 CIT
25 Telecom Booths
26 Consorzio ITA
27 Farmacia Comunale
   (24-Hour Pharmacy)
28 Deposito (Left Luggage)
29 ATAF Ticket & Information
   Office; ATAF Bus Stop for
   Nos 7, 13, 62 & 70

30 Lazzi Bus Station &
   Ticket Office
31 CAP & COPIT Bus Station
35 Centro Lorenzo de' Medici
43 Alinari Bike Rentals
44 Wash & Dry Laundrette
47 Motorent
48 Laundrette
49 Internet Train
50 Mondial Net
51 After Dark Bookshop
53 CyberOffice
55 Firenze & Abroad
56 Florence By Bike
58 Swedish Consulate
59 Dutch Consulate
60 Erasmus Students Office
61 Opificio delle Pietre Dure
62 Wash & Dry Laundrette
63 Rotonda del Brunelleschi
64 Centro MTS
65 Bebop
66 Belgian Consulate
67 Danish Consulate
68 Scuola Leonardo
   da Vinci
69 Biblioteca Comunale Centrale;
   Giardini dei Ciliegi

BETHUNE CARMICHAEL

Even the windows are works of art in Florence.

MAP 4

PLACES TO STAY
3 Pensione Losanna;
  Pensione Donatello
4 Hotel Regency
5 Hotel Le Due Fontane
12 Hotel Monna Lisa

PLACES TO EAT
1 EDI House
7 Caffellatte

OTHER
2 Norwegian Consulate
6 Wash & Dry
8 Onda Blu Laundrette
9 WWW.Village
10 The Paperback
   Exchange Bookshop
11 Jazz Club

MAP 7

MAP 5

MAP 3

Chiesa di
Ognissanti

Piazza
d'Ognissanti

Ospedale di
San Giovanni
di Dio

Ponte
Amerigo
Vespucci

Via Sant'
Onofrio

A R N O

Piazza C
Goldoni

Palazzo dei
Rucellai

Piazza San
Pancrazio

Palazzo
Corsini

Chiesa
della Santa
Trinità

Piazza
del Tiratoio

Piazza
di Cestello

Chiesa di
San Frediano
in Cestello

Ponte alla
Carraia

SAN FREDIANO

Piazza
N Sauro

Piazza degli
Scarlatti

Ponte
Santa Trinità

Palazzo
Guicciardini

Piazza
del Carmine

Borgo della Stella

SANTO
SPIRITO

Piazza de'
Frescobaldi

Palazzo
Frescobaldi

Borgo San Jacopo

Basilica di
Santa
Maria del
Carmine

Basilica di
Santo Spirito

Piazza
Santo
Spirito

Mercato
di Santo
Spirito

Piazza
San Felice

Piazza
del Pitti

Giardino
Torrigiani

Palazzo
Pitti

Museo
Zoologico
La Specola

BOB
GARD

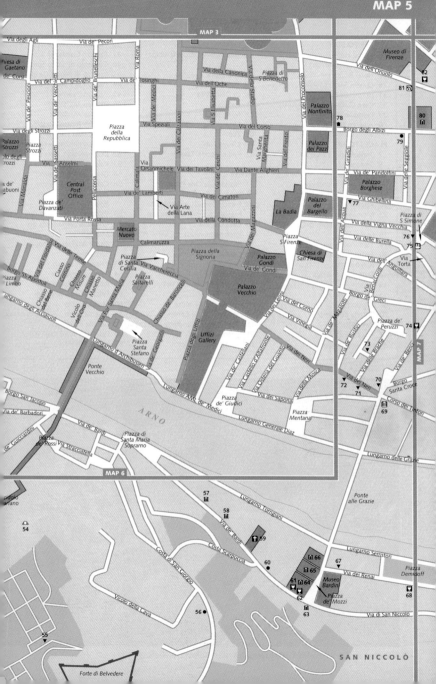

MAP 5

MAP 3

Via degli Agli
Via de' Pecori
Via degli Strozzi
Chiesa di Gaetano de' Corsi
Via del Campidoglio
Via de' Pescioni
Via de' Vecchietti
Via Roma
Via de' Brunelleschi
Via de' Tosinghi
Via della Canonica
Piazza di S Benedetto
Via dell'Oche
Via de' Medici
Via S Elisabetta
Museo di Firenze
Via dell'Oriuolo
82
81
Via Speziali
Via del Corso
Via Santa Margherita
Palazzo Nonfinito
78
Borgo degli Albizi
80
Piazza della Repubblica
Via de' Calzaiuoli
Via de' Cerchi
Via del Presto
Via Sant'Egidio
Palazzo dei Pazzi
79
Palazzo Strozzi
Piazza Strozzi
olo degli rozzi
Via de' Sassetti
Via degli Strozzi
Via de' Anselmi
Via Orsanmichele
Via dei Tavolini
Via Dante Alighieri
Palazzo Borghese
Via Ghibellina
Via de' Pandolfini
Via de' Giraldi
Via della Vigna Vecchia
Piazza di S Simone
77
Via Monalda
Via de' Labuoni
Central Post Office
Via de' Lamberti
Via Arte della Lana
Via de' Cimatori
La Badia
Palazzo del Bargello
76
75
Via Pellicceria
Via Porta Rossa
Via della Condotta
Piazza S Firenze
Via delle Burella
Via dell'Anguillara
Via Torta
Mercato Nuovo
Calimaruzza
Piazza della Signoria
Palazzo Gondi
Chiesa di San Firenze
Piazza de' Peruzzi
74
Piazza di Santa Cecilia
Via Vacchereccia
Via de' Baroncelli
Via de' Gondi
Palazzo Vecchio
Via de' Leoni
Via del Corno
Borgo de' Greci
Borgo dei Albizi
Piazza Saltarelli
Classo Cornino
Chiasso Manetto
Piazza di Limbo
Borgo SS Apostoli
Chiasso delle Misure
Via Bui Santa Maria
Via de' Cerchi
Chiasso de' Baroncelli
Piazza Santa Stefano
Uffizi Gallery
Via dei Castellani
Via de' Neri
Via de' Rustici
Via de' Bentaccordi
73
72
71
70
Via dell'Acqua
Via de' Magazzini
Via de' Magalotti
Vicolo dell'Oro
Lungarno degli Acciaiuoli
Lungarno d'Archibusieri
Ponte Vecchio
Via dei Girolami
Via de' Saponai
Via della Mosca
Via dei Leoni
Via del Corno
Piazza de' Peruzzi
69
Borgo Santa Croce
Corso dei Tintori
Borgo San Jacopo
Via de' Barbadori
A R N O
Piazza de' Giudici
Piazza Mentana
Lungarno Generale Diaz
Via de' Guicciardini
Via de' Bardi
Piazza de' Rossi
Via Stracciatella
Piazza di Santa Maria Soprarno
Lungarno delle Grazie
MAP 6
Ponte alle Grazie
Lungarno Torrigiani
57
ordoio ariano
54
58
Via de' Bardi
Lungarno Serriston
59
Costa di San Giorgio
Costa Scarpuccia
60
66
67
Via dei Renai
Piazza Demidoff
65
Museo Bardini
68
61
64
Vicolo della Cava
62
63
Piazza de' Mozzi
56
Via di San Niccolò
55
Forte di Belvedere
SAN NICCOLÒ

MAP 5

JULIET COOMBE

The next Botticelli? A street artist recreates masterpieces in chalk.

MAP 6

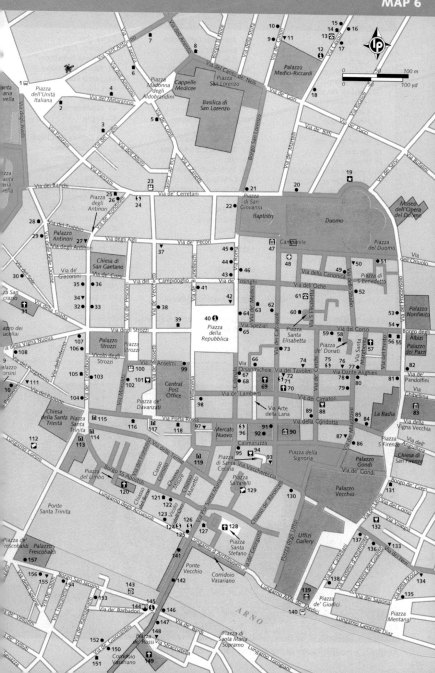

0   50   100 m
0   50   100 yd

MAP 6

PLACES TO STAY
2 Grand Hotel Baglioni
3 Giotto
4 Albergo Majestic
5 Hotel Bellettini
6 Pensione Accademia
7 Hotel Globus
8 Giada
14 Hotel Le Casci
25 Hotel Abaco
28 Pensione Ferretti
39 Pendini
55 Brunori
56 Pensione Maria Luisa de'
   Medici; Centro Linguistico
   Sperimentale
58 Albergo Firenze
60 Hotel Brunelleschi;
   Torre della Pagliazza
63 Maxim
105 Albergo Scoti
116 Hotel Porta Rossa
118 Pensione TeTi & Prestige
121 Hotel Alessandra
127 Aily Home
131 Bernini Palace
151 Pensione la Scaletta

PLACES TO EAT
11 Café Caracol
27 Cantinetta Antinori
34 Procacci
37 Ristorante Self-Service
   Leonardo
42 Gilli
50 Hostaria il Caminetto
54 Trattoria Le Mossacce
72 Gelateria Perchè No?
74 Ristorante Paoli
76 Trattoria del Pennello
87 Vini e Vecchi Sapori
93 Rivoire
97 Trattoria Pasquini
111 Trattoria Coco Lezzone
133 Eito
134 Trattoria da Benvenuto
148 Le Volpi e l'Uva
155 Osteria del Cinghiale Bianco

PUBS & BARS
88 Andromeda
94 Tabasco
101 Yab
132 Blob

SHOPPING
9 Ceccherini & Co
15 Dreoni
18 Feltrinelli International
   Bookshop
22 Orologeria Svizzera G Panerai
   & Figli
26 Bojola
29 Biagiotti
32 Neuber
35 Loretta Caponi
36 Galleria Tornabuoni
41 Ricordi Mediastore
43 Sergio Rossi
44 Luisa
45 Raspini
49 Experimenta
52 Pegna
53 Arte Creta
59 La Galleria del Chianti
62 The Disney Store
64 Fratelli Rossetti
65 La Rinascente
73 COIN
81 Luca della Robbia
84 Bartolucci
85 Festina Lente Edizioni
86 Magazzino Toscano
89 EPT Bookshop
95 Bongi
103 House of Florence
104 Casadei
106 Gucci
107 L'Ippogrifo
109 Desmo
110 Il Bisonte
122 Enoteca Romano Gambi
125 Bijoux Cascio
136 Lanzo Caffè
137 Mercato dei Liberi Artigiani;
   Loggia del Grano

JULIET COOMBE

Amannati's marble figures dance gleefully around the base of the *Neptune Fountain*.

MAP 6

The stony residents of the Boboli Gardens lend it a unique and magical charm.

JULIET COOMBE

MAP 7

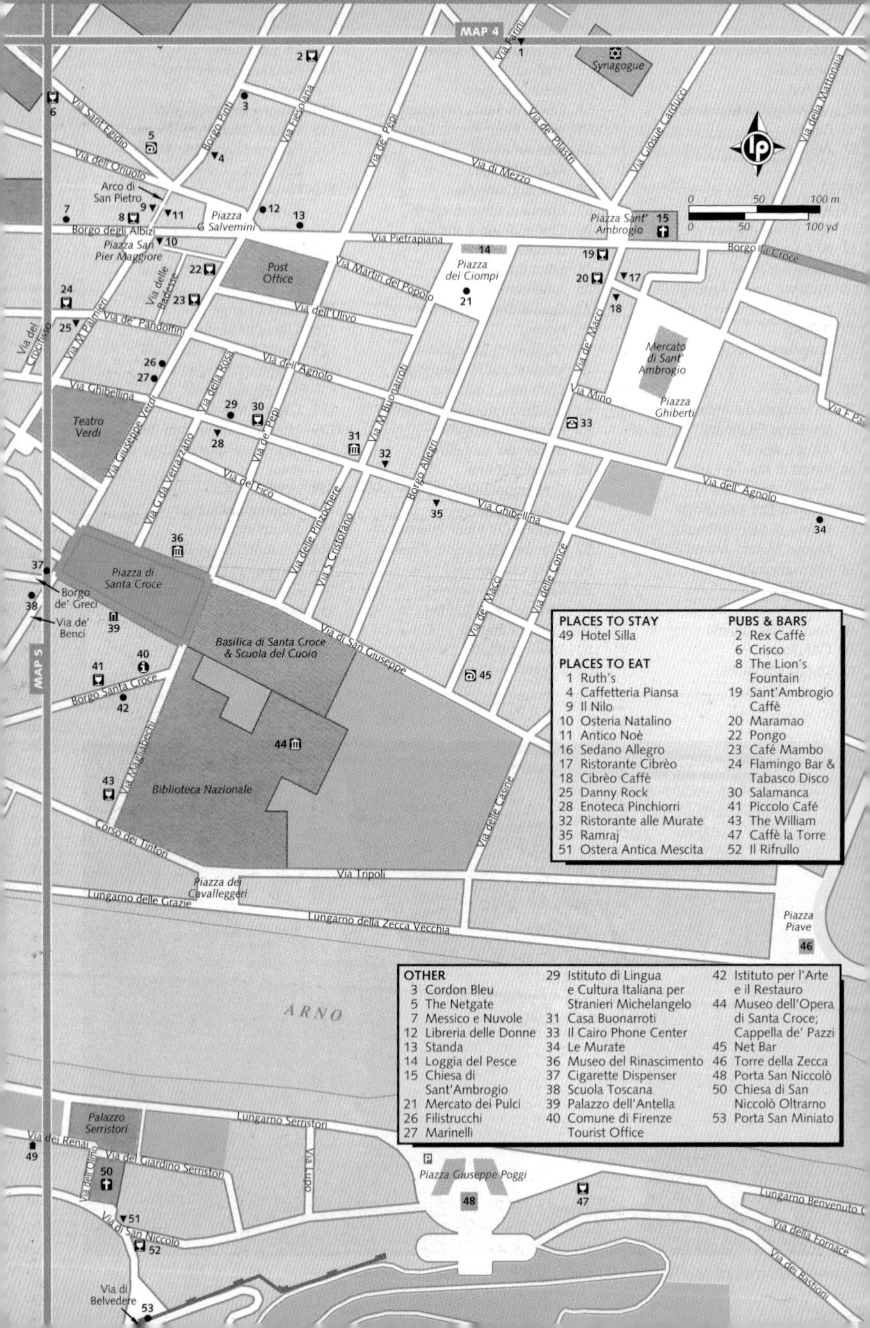

MAP 4
MAP 5
Synagogue
Via Farini
Via de' Pilastri
Via Giosuè Carducci
Via della Mattonaia
Via di Mezzo
Via de' Pepi
Via Fiesolana
Borgo Pinti
Via Sant'Egidio
Via dell'Oriuolo
Arco di San Pietro
Piazza G Salvemini
Borgo degli Albizi
Piazza San Pier Maggiore
Via delle Badesse
Post Office
Via Pietrapiana
Piazza dei Ciompi
Via Martiri del Popolo
Via dell'Ulivo
Piazza Sant' Ambrogio
Borgo la Croce
Via de' Macci
Mercato di Sant' Ambrogio
Piazza Ghiberti
Via Mino
Via F Pa
Via de' Pandolfini
Via M Palmieri
Via del Crocifisso
Via dell'Agnolo
Via della Rosa
Via M Buonarroti
Via Ghibellina
Teatro Verdi
Via Giuseppe Verdi
Via G da Verrazzano
Via del Fico
Via delle Pinzochere
Via S Cristofano
Borgo Allegri
Via dell' Agnolo
Via Ghibellina
Via delle Conce
Piazza di Santa Croce
Borgo de' Greci
Via de' Benci
Basilica di Santa Croce & Scuola del Cuoio
Via di San Giuseppe
Borgo Santa Croce
Via Magliabechi
Biblioteca Nazionale
Via delle Casine
Corso dei Tintori
Via Tripoli
Piazza dei Cavalleggeri
Lungarno delle Grazie
Lungarno della Zecca Vecchia
Piazza Piave
ARNO
Palazzo Serristori
Lungarno Serristori
Via dei Renai
Via del Giardino Serristori
Via dell'Olmo
Via Lupo
Piazza Giuseppe Poggi
Lungarno Benvenuto Cellini
Via della Fornace
Via dei Bastioni
Via di San Niccolò
Via di Belvedere
0 50 100 m
0 50 100 yd
PLACES TO STAY
49 Hotel Silla
PLACES TO EAT
1 Ruth's
4 Caffetteria Piansa
9 Il Nilo
10 Osteria Natalino
11 Antico Noè
16 Sedano Allegro
17 Ristorante Cibrèo
18 Cibrèo Caffè
25 Danny Rock
28 Enoteca Pinchiorri
32 Ristorante alle Murate
35 Ramraj
51 Ostera Antica Mescita
PUBS & BARS
2 Rex Caffè
6 Crisco
8 The Lion's Fountain
19 Sant'Ambrogio Caffè
20 Maramao
22 Pongo
23 Café Mambo
24 Flamingo Bar & Tabasco Disco
30 Salamanca
41 Piccolo Café
43 The William
47 Caffè la Torre
52 Il Rifrullo
OTHER
3 Cordon Bleu
5 The Netgate
7 Messico e Nuvole
12 Libreria delle Donne
13 Standa
14 Loggia del Pesce
15 Chiesa di Sant'Ambrogio
21 Mercato dei Pulci
26 Filistrucchi
27 Marinelli
29 Istituto di Lingua e Cultura Italiana per Stranieri Michelangelo
31 Casa Buonarroti
33 Il Cairo Phone Center
34 Le Murate
36 Museo del Rinascimento
37 Cigarette Dispenser
38 Scuola Toscana
39 Palazzo dell'Antella
40 Comune di Firenze Tourist Office
42 Istituto per l'Arte e il Restauro
44 Museo dell'Opera di Santa Croce; Cappella de' Pazzi
45 Net Bar
46 Torre della Zecca
48 Porta San Niccolò
50 Chiesa di San Niccolò Oltrarno
53 Porta San Miniato

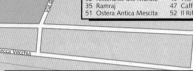

NEIL SETCHFIELD

JULIET COOMBE

JULIET COOMBE

JULIET COOMBE

JULIET COOMBE

From the ancient to the modern, the classic to the crass, the streets of Florence are a visual assault on the senses.

MAP LEGEND

BOUNDARIES

.... Provincial

HYDROGRAPHY

.... Coastline
.... River, Creek
.... Lake
.... Canal

ROUTES & TRANSPORT

.... Freeway
.... Primary Road
.... Secondary Road
.... Tertiary Road
.... Unsealed Road
.... City Freeway
.... City Highway

.... City Road
.... City Street, Lane
.... Pedestrian Mall
.... Tunnel
.... Train Route & Station
.... Tramway
.... Cable Car or Chairlift

AREA FEATURES

.... Park, Gardens
.... Cemetery
.... Market

.... Forest
.... Beach
.... Rocks

.... Building
.... Hotel
.... Urban Area

MAP SYMBOLS

FLORENCE ..... Provincial Capital
Pistoia .... City
Pescia .... Town
Uzzano .... Village

.... Point of Interest

.... Place to Stay
.... Camp Site
.... Caravan Park
.... Hut or Chalet

.... Place to Eat
.... Pub or Bar

.... Airport
.... Ancient or City Wall
.... Bank
.... Bus Station, Bus Stop
.... Cave or Cavern
.... Church, Cathedral
.... Cinema
.... Embassy or Consulate
.... Fountain
.... Hospital or Clinic
.... Information
.... Internet Cafe
.... Monument
.... Mountain

.... Mountain Range
.... Museum
.... National Park
.... Parking Area
.... Police Station
.... Post Office
.... Ruins
.... Shopping Centre
.... Stately Home
.... Synagogue
.... Telephone
.... Theatre
.... Toilet
.... Transport

Note: not all symbols displayed above appear in this book

LONELY PLANET OFFICES

Australia
PO Box 617, Hawthorn, Victoria 3122
☎ 03 9819 1877 fax 03 9819 6459
email: talk2us@lonelyplanet.com.au

USA
150 Linden St, Oakland, CA 94607
☎ 510 893 8555 TOLL FREE: 800 275 8555
fax 510 893 8572
email: info@lonelyplanet.com

UK
10a Spring Place, London NW5 3BH
☎ 020 7428 4800 fax 020 7428 4828
email: go@lonelyplanet.co.uk

France
1 rue du Dahomey, 75011 Paris
☎ 01 55 25 33 00 fax 01 55 25 33 01
email: bip@lonelyplanet.fr
www.lonelyplanet.fr

World Wide Web: www.lonelyplanet.com *or* AOL keyword: lp
Lonely Planet Images: lpi@lonelyplanet.com.au

onely Planet's eKno

heap calls, easy messaging and email

'hen you're out of sight, not out of mind.

ou need eKno

you're on the move and your family wants to reach you with an important essage . . . Or you're crossing a border and want to make a booking for a otel in the next town . . . Or you want to arrange a rendezvous with some-ne you met biking in Vietnam . . . Or you want to leave a message for a iend living in London . . .

o get eKno

Kno is a global communications service for travellers. eKno gives you heap long distance calls plus eKno voice and email message services. eKno :ts your friends and relatives leave you easily retrieved eKno messages – no iatter where you are – and gives you an easy way to keep in eKno contact vith other travellers. eKno is easy to use and doesn't cost the earth.

'ou tap into eKno with your private number. This number, plus a PIN, gives ou access to your eKno message bank and a world of cheap international Kno calls.

Lonely Planet's eKno

Join Now
Tear out an eKno card, contact us online, or with a toll free call – and you're eKoff.

Join Online
The easiest way to join is online at
www.ekno.lonelyplanet.com
for all the info on eKno.
It is the best place for the most up to date information and any current joining offers.

Join by phone
To join from:

Australia	1 800 674 100
US	1 800 707 0031
Canada	1 800 294 3676
UK	0800 376 1704
New Zealand	0800 11 44 84
Germany	0 800 000 7138
International	+1 213 927 0101

Once you've joined, to use eKno always dial the access number for the country you're in.

Access Numbers

Australia	1 800 11 44 78
US	1 800 706 1333
Canada	1 800 808 5773
UK	0 800 376 1705
New Zealand	0 800 11 44 78
Germany	0 800 000 7139
International	+1 213 927 0100

New countries are being added all the time. To join from another country and for further information, visit the eKno website at *www.ekno.lonelyplanet.com*.
If the country you are in is not listed here or on the website, you can dial the international numbers listed above to join or access the service.

Toll free calls are provided where possible.

Details correct as at 5 May 1999

Where Did eKno Come From?

eKno – it's Lonely Planet for one number. *Ek* means one from Karachi to Kathmandu, from Delhi to Dhaka, and *no* is short for number.

We travel. Actually we travel quite a bit. And although we've used a heap of phonecards, we could never find one that really hit the spot. So we decided to make one. We joined with eKorp.com, an innovative communications company, to bring you a phonecard with the lot – budget calls from a stack of countries, voice messages you can pick up all over the world and even reply to, a way to keep in touch with other travellers and your own web mail address – and all from one number.

With eKno, you can ring home and home can ring you.

Now there are even more reasons to stay in touch.

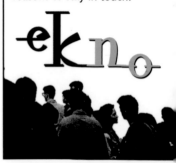

Ref code: LPBON069